THE EPISTLE TO THE
EPHESIANS

ITS AUTHORSHIP, ORIGIN AND PURPOSE

BY

C. LESLIE MITTON

Wipf and Stock Publishers
EUGENE, OREGON

Wipf and Stock Publishers
150 West Broadway
Eugene, Oregon 97401

The Epistle to the Ephesians
Its Auhorship, Origin and Purpose
By Mitton, C. Leslie

ISBN: 1-59244-041-X
Publication Date: September, 2002
Previously published by Oxford at the Clarendon Press, 1951.

PREFACE

In the study of the New Testament the centre of interest is no longer the critical investigation of problems connected with the authorship, date, provenance, and destination of the various books. In recent years our attention has been focused rather on their subject-matter. This is all to the good, for there was a regrettable tendency to mistake information about these critical questions for knowledge of the New Testament itself. What is, however, undoubtedly of first importance is the message of the New Testament, and its clear and memorable expression. Accurate answers to the questions why, when, where, and by whom these truths were uttered, though desirable, are of secondary importance.

The fact, however, that we have been able to relegate merely critical problems to the circumference of our interest should not lead us to imagine that all these problems have been solved, or that their solution can be completely ignored as a matter of no concern whatever. Some problems still remain, and sometimes they raise their heads and with importunity demand attention. The lack of a convincing solution to them becomes a persistent and galling irritant, and for one's own peace of mind an answer must be sought.

So it was in my case with the Epistle to the Ephesians. The more I read of other people's views, and tried to reconcile their divergence and incompatibility, the more perplexing did the problems surrounding it become. Since the weighing of all the arguments as presented by others failed to point to any clear solution, it became necessary to try to find some new factors in the situation which would tilt the scale to one side or the other. This book is the outcome of that investigation. Apart from the omission of two somewhat lengthy essays, it is in the same form as a thesis which was accepted by the Faculty of Theology in the University of London for the Degree of Doctor of Philosophy. These essays dealt with H. J. Holtzmann's Theory of the Relationship between Colossians and Ephesians, and with E. J. Goodspeed's Theory of the Formation of the Pauline Corpus. It was thought advisable, however, to omit these from the present publication.

It was not until the book was in the printer's hands that I was able to gain access to a copy of Ernst Percy's recent book, *Die Probleme der Kolosser- und Epheserbriefe*, published at Lund in 1946. This is an important examination of the problems connected with these two epistles, and the author deals most carefully and in great detail with every aspect of their mutual relationship. He is able to decide confidently in favour of the Pauline authorship of Colossians, and only a little less confidently for the Pauline authorship of Ephesians, though with great frankness he enumerates certain features which cannot adequately be reconciled with that conclusion. He does not, however, deal at length with the relationship between Ephesians and the other Pauline epistles, which we have found to be of crucial significance. The book is nevertheless a very weighty contribution to the literature of the subject, and its weight goes into the scale on the side of Pauline authorship.

I owe a very special debt of gratitude to Rev. Dr. Vincent Taylor, not only for constant and valuable advice during all the stages of preparing this book, but also for his untiring encouragement over a period of twenty years, during which he has never failed to provide the intellectual stimulus necessary to enable me to maintain habits of study amid the busy life of a circuit minister in the Methodist Church.

I would like also to acknowledge most kindly help and counsel received from the Rev. Dr. W. F. Howard and Prof. R. H. Lightfoot, and to thank most warmly the Rev. Cyril Wainwright, B.A., B.D., for most valuable work in correcting the proofs, and my son, Ian, for help in preparing the indexes.

I have appreciated very greatly the patience and understanding of the staff of the Clarendon Press, and their readiness to meet the author's wishes, especially in the preparation of the very complicated Appendixes.

My thanks are due also to my wife and family for the patient and good-humoured hospitality which they have always shown to this intruder into the life of the home, which has only too often proved itself a rival claimant to time which rightly belonged to them.

C. L. M.

SHERWOOD, NOTTINGHAM

May 1951

CONTENTS

PART IV
THE DATE OF EPHESIANS

APPENDIXES

BIBLIOGRAPHY

The abbreviations are not listed separately in alphabetical order, because they are used only in conjunction with the author's name

Abbott, T. K.	(ICC)	*International Critical Commentary on Ephesians and Colossians.*
Abbott-Smith, G.	(MNT)	*Manual Greek Lexicon of the New Testament.*
Alington, C. A.	(NTRG)	*The New Testament: a Reader's Guide.*
Bacon, B. W.	(INT)	*Introduction to the New Testament.*
Beare, F. W.	(IP)	*First Epistle of Peter.*
Bennett, W. H.	(GE)	*The General Epistles.*
Carrington, P.	(PCC)	*The Primitive Christian Catechism.*
Charles, R. H.	(ICC)	*International Critical Commentary on Revelation.*
Charteris, A. H.	(C)	*Canonicity.*
Chase, F. H.	(HDB)	*Hastings's Dictionary of the Bible.*
Clogg, F. B.	(INT)	*Introduction to the New Testament.*
Cook, S.	(IB)	*An Introduction to the Bible.*
Dibelius, M.	(KEP)	*An die Kolosser, Epheser. An Philemon.*
„	(FA)	*A Fresh Approach to the New Testament and Early Christian Literature.*
Dodd, C. H.	(*Ab. Com.*)	*Abingdon Bible Commentary.*
„	(JE)	*Moffatt Commentary on the Johannine Epistles.*
„	(MCR)	*Moffatt Commentary on Romans.*
„	(MP)	*The Mind of Paul.*
Duncan, G. S.	(PEM)	*St. Paul's Ephesian Ministry.*
Findlay, G. G.	(EE)	*Epistle to the Ephesians, Expositor's Bible.*
Glasson, T. F.	(SA)	*Second Advent.*
Goodspeed, E. J.	(CP)	*Christianity Goes to Press.*
„	(ECL)	*History of Early Christian Literature.*
„	(FNT)	*The Formation of the New Testament.*
„	(INT)	*Introduction to the New Testament.*
„	(ME)	*The Meaning of Ephesians.*
„	(NC)	*New Chapters in New Testament Study.*
Graham, E.	(NCHS)	*New Commentary on Holy Scripture*, S.P.C.K.
Grieve, A. J.	(SPC)	*Supplement to Peake's Commentary.*
Hanson, S.	(UCNT)	*The Unity of the Church in the New Testament: Colossians and Ephesians.*
Harnack, A.	(BAP)	*Die Briefsammlung des Apostels Paulus.*
„	(ONT)	*Origin of the New Testament.*
Harrison, P. N.	(PPE)	*The Problem of the Pastoral Epistles.*
„	(PTE)	*Polycarp's Two Epistles to the Philippians.*
Holtzmann, H. J.	(ENT)	*Einleitung in das Neue Testament.*
„	(*Kritik*)	*Kritik der Epheser- und Kolosserbriefe.*
Hort, F. J. A.	(IP)	*1 Peter.*
„	(PRE)	*Prolegomena to St. Paul's Epistles to the Romans and Ephesians.*

Howard, W. F.	(FG)	*The Fourth Gospel in Recent Criticism and Interpretation.*
,,	(CJ)	*Christianity according to St. John.*
James, M. R.	(ANT)	*Apocrypha to the New Testament.*
Jülicher, A.	(EB)	*Encyclopedia Biblica.*
,,	(INT)	*Introduction to the New Testament.*
Kenyon, F. G.	(RD)	*Recent Developments in the Textual Criticism of the Greek Bible.*
Kilpatrick, G. D.	(OM)	*Origins of the Gospel according to St. Matthew.*
Knox, J.	(MNT)	*Marcion and the New Testament.*
,,	(PLP)	*Philemon among the Letters of Paul.*
Knox, W. L.	(PCG)	*St. Paul and the Church of the Gentiles.*
Lake, K.	(EEP)	*The Early Epistles of St. Paul.*
Lock, W.	(HDB)	*Hastings's Dictionary of the Bible.*
McNeile, A. H.	(INT)	*Introduction to the New Testament.*
Manson, T. W.	(CB)	*Companion to the Bible.*
Michael, J. H.	(MCP)	*Moffatt Commentary on Philippians.*
Michaelis, W.	(DP)	*Die Datierung des Philipperbriefes.*
Moffatt, J.	(ILNT)	*Introduction to the Literature of the New Testament.*
Nock, A. D.	(SP)	*St. Paul.*
Oxford Committee	(NTAP)	*The New Testament in the Apostolic Fathers.*
Paley, W.	(HP)	*Horae Paulinae.*
Peake, A. S.	(CINT)	*Critical Introduction to the New Testament.*
,,	(PC)	*Peake's Commentary on the Bible.*
Robinson, J. A.	(SPEE)	*St. Paul's Epistle to the Ephesians.*
Sanday and Headlam	(ER)	*International Critical Commentary on Romans.*
Scott, C. A. A.	(CAP)	*Christianity according to St. Paul.*
,,	(FP)	*Footnotes to St. Paul.*
,,	(RG)	*Romanism and the Gospel.*
Scott, E. F.	(LNT)	*Literature of the New Testament.*
,,	(MCC)	*Moffatt Commentary on Colossians, Philemon, and Ephesians.*
Selwyn, E. G.	(IP)	*First Epistle of Peter.*
Simcox, W. H.	(WNT)	*Writers of the New Testament.*
Streeter, B. H.	(FG)	*The Four Gospels.*
,,	(PC)	*The Primitive Church.*
Taylor, V.	(BTG)	*Behind the Third Gospel.*
Von Soden, H.	(HECL)	*History of Early Christian Literature.*
Westcott and Hort	(WH)	*The N.T. in the Original Greek.*
Zahn, Th.	(INT)	*Introduction to the New Testament.*

PART I

THE FINDINGS OF THE PAST

INTRODUCTION

In the Authorized Version of the Bible, out of the twenty-seven books which constitute the New Testament, fourteen are ascribed to Paul and called epistles. The scholars who were entrusted with the preparation of the Revised Version were well aware that it was no longer possible to regard the 'Epistle to the Hebrews' as the work of Paul, but, since their terms of reference did not permit any modification of the titles of the various books, the same designation of 'Hebrews' as a Pauline epistle appears in the Revised Version as in the Authorized. Modern scholarship, however, is agreed in dissociating 'Hebrews' from the name of Paul. In so doing it has reaffirmed the attitude of the early Church, which for a long time declined to regard this 'epistle' as Pauline, while acknowledging its high standing among the Christian writings.

More recently three others of these fourteen 'epistles', the three usually grouped together and known as the 'Pastoral Epistles', have not only come under suspicion as regards their claimed Pauline authorship but, in their present form, have, by the common consent of the great majority of scholars, been denied the right to be known as genuine Pauline letters. The doubts and misgivings of earlier scholars have been carefully followed up and fully stated by P. N. Harrison in his book on *The Problem of the Pastoral Epistles*, and his conclusions have won general acceptance. As a result these three 'epistles' are now regarded as preserving a few small fragments of Paul's genuine correspondence, but the general framework into which these are incorporated and the great bulk of the actual contents are the work of a compiler who edited and enlarged the genuine fragments which he had before him. He wrote in the name of Paul, because part of what he produced was Paul's writing, and in the remainder he was seeking to commend to a subsequent generation what he honestly believed Paul's message to them would have been.

Out of the fourteen 'epistles', therefore, only ten are still, with any degree of confidence, accepted as the direct product of the mind of Paul. Among these ten, however, it must be admitted that there are some which cannot be accepted as genuine with complete assurance. Dibelius in 1936 summarized very fairly the general conclusions of modern critical investigation concerning these ten epistles. He wrote: 'Six are regarded almost universally as genuine' (FA, p. 150). These six are Romans, 1 and 2 Corinthians, Galatians, Philippians, and 1 Thessalonians. The other four, Ephesians, Colossians, Philemon, and 2 Thessalonians, he describes as 'subject to dispute'. Dibelius himself decides in favour of the Pauline authorship of the last three, and in this verdict too he is representative of the majority of modern scholars. Concerning Ephesians, however, he inclines rather to the rejection of the Pauline authorship.

It may, then, fairly be said that of the four letters 'subject to dispute' the one most insecure in its claim to be genuinely Pauline is Ephesians. In fact, among the outstanding problems connected with these remaining ten epistles, which are commonly called 'Pauline', Ephesians presents us with one of the most perplexing issues. E. J. Goodspeed, who has himself made important contributions to the study of Ephesians, writes: 'Among the books of the New Testament, none is more in need of clarification than the letter to the Ephesians.' It is with the hope of achieving some measure of clarification of this problem that this book is written.

The great majority of British scholars have continued to maintain the traditional authorship of Ephesians, but in most cases only with some considerable hesitation and misgiving. It is not that they feel that Pauline authorship is indubitable and any other alternative completely impossible. Rather they adopt it, after weighing the conflicting evidence, as the more likely of two possible alternatives. They hold that it is easier to account for the non-Pauline characteristics in the epistle under the supposition of Pauline authorship than to explain the abounding Pauline characteristics on the supposition of a non-Pauline authorship.

To the general conservative trend of British scholarship there is, however, one outstanding exception, and that is J. Moffatt. In his *Introduction to the Literature of the New Testament* he rejects decisively the traditional ascription of authorship to Paul, so decisively in fact that he does not even group Ephesians with the Pauline literature but deals with it under the heading of 'Homilies and Pastorals' in association with 1 Peter, Hebrews, and James. There he considers in great detail the question of authorship and presents a strong case for the rejection of Pauline authorship. There are those, as for instance E. J. Goodspeed, who regard Moffatt's statement of the case as conclusive and unanswerable, but the majority of British scholars have declined to be persuaded by Moffatt's arguments. A very different state of affairs is, however, to be found among American and continental scholars, a majority of whom would probably be found to accept Moffatt's conclusions on this issue.

It is not possible, therefore, by assessing the relative authority of supporters and opposers to get any clear guide to the correct verdict. It still remains 'not proven', and the student is puzzled that such contrary conclusions are reached by equally qualified and, apparently, disinterested scholars.

Moreover, the difficulty of reaching a final decision is emphasized by the acknowledgement of protagonists on each side of the strength of the case of their opponents. Dibelius, for instance, writes: 'Among the letters of the New Testament to which authenticity is denied, Ephesians is the one closest to those which are acknowledged as genuine' (FA, p. 185). Jülicher, who declines to abandon belief in Pauline authorship, nevertheless concedes that 'many separate points in the epistle would certainly become more intelligible on the assumption that it was written by a disciple of the apostle'. And E. F. Scott, who in his later books is a strong upholder of Pauline authorship, and claims that 'the weight of the evidence is decidedly in favour of Paul's authorship', nevertheless admits that 'the question of the authenticity of Ephesians must be regarded as an open one' (LNT, p. 180).

It is to this still open question that we are seeking to find a convincing answer.

I

DEPARTURES FROM TRADITION

We have seen that the traditional view of the authorship of Ephesians, while discarded by many scholars, is still upheld by the majority of British scholars. There are, however, other parts of the traditional view which even conservative scholars have been compelled to abandon.

This traditional view not only ascribed the epistle to Paul but assumed also that it was a letter, in the same sense in which the other Pauline writings are letters; that it was addressed to the Christian community in Ephesus; and that it was written from Rome during Paul's last imprisonment there, shortly before his death. Of these three further elements in the traditional view, the first two have been generally abandoned, and the third is left open to question, even by those who maintain the Pauline authorship of the epistle.

Actually 'Ephesians' is not really a letter at all. It is an address or pamphlet arranged as a letter. The letter form is superficial. It is almost as though the author felt he must conform to some accepted convention. The writer moreover reveals hardly any acquaintance with those to whom he writes. He might be addressing complete strangers. It is, therefore, inconceivable that if Paul is the writer, those to whom he writes should be the Christians at Ephesus with whom he had spent a memorable ministry of two years, and to whom he was greatly attached. If we retain our belief in Pauline authorship, we are compelled to forgo that part of the traditional view which regards the Church at Ephesus as the recipients.

Not only do the contents of 'Ephesians' lead us to this conclusion, but also certain manuscripts of the New Testament of very early date and outstanding authority, which have become available to students only in comparatively recent years, reveal the fact that in their text of the 'epistle' there is no mention of Ephesus as the destination. The words ἐν Ἐφέσῳ are omitted in the opening sentence of the 'epistle'; or else they have been introduced into the text only by some later reviser; or else a later reviser, working from a reliable manuscript, has deleted the words from the less reliable text on which he is working. The two fourth-century manuscripts, Vaticanus and Sinaiticus, agree in the omission of ἐν Ἐφέσῳ; the corrector of 67, 'whose corrections are evidently taken from another quite different MS of great excellence, now lost' (Hort, PRE, p. 75), deletes the words as constituting an intrusion into the correct text; and among the most recently discovered papyri of very early date, probably about A.D. 200, what E. J. Goodspeed calls the 'Ann Arbor–Chester Beatty' papyri (NTI, p. 233) also omit these words. Moreover, it is clear from the writings of several of the great Christian writers of the first few centuries that the same two words were missing from the text of the New Testament which they used.

Advocates of the Pauline authorship, therefore, usually now regard the 'epistle' as a kind of circular letter, addressed to several churches, of which Ephesus was probably one, or else as a general letter to Gentile Christians, to which the name of Ephesus came to be attached for some reason which cannot now be ascertained.

For a long time Rome was accepted as the provenance of all four of the so-called 'Captivity Epistles', Ephesians, Colossians, Philemon, and Philippians. It cannot be said that this has been disproved, but much strong evidence has been produced to make it exceedingly likely that Paul was for a time imprisoned at Ephesus, even though there is no record of it in Acts, and if so, it may well have been during that imprisonment that some or all of these four letters were written. The fullest recent treatment of this issue is to be found in G. S. Duncan's book on *St. Paul's Ephesian Ministry*.

In this book the writer shows that the arguments used to support a Roman origin for the Imprisonment Epistles are not unanswerable and produces many other arguments in favour of an Ephesian origin. His arguments do not apply equally strongly to each one of these four epistles, but a reasonable case has been presented for conceding an Ephesian origin for Colossians, and Ephesians, if Pauline, almost certainly shared the same place of origin as Colossians. It is, however, very noticeable to the careful reader of this book that the evidence which the author of the book is able to derive from 'Ephesians' is entirely negligible. The other three all furnish strong arguments in favour of an Ephesian origin, but 'Ephesians' seems to stand proudly aloof. It gives support neither to an Ephesian nor to a Roman origin. It is coldly impartial. This is only one instance of the persistently stubborn refusal of 'Ephesians' to be fitted convincingly into any known Pauline context.

Since, however, our first aim must be to reach a decision on the question of authorship, none of these uncertainties about destination or provenance need concern us at this stage of our inquiry. If a verdict is reached against Pauline authorship, they cease to present any real problem. If the verdict is for Pauline authorship, they will need further explanation. They have been briefly mentioned here to show that the whole context of Ephesians is beset with perplexities. It is not just the question of authorship which awaits a conclusive answer, but such other questions as 'When?', 'Whence?', 'Whither?', 'Why?' also remain unanswered. Certainly no final answer to them has been given on the basis of Pauline authorship. If on these points the traditional view has proved itself unsatisfactory, it is at any rate possible that, in the matter of authorship also, the traditional view is open to question.

II

THE CASE AGAINST PAULINE AUTHORSHIP

BEFORE we seek to discover any new approach which may throw light on the question of authorship it will be well to summarize briefly the main arguments which have already been used for and against Pauline authorship. At a later stage some of these arguments will have to be reconsidered in more detail. Our purpose now is not so much to assess their value and reach a conclusion as to give a concise review of the discussion at its present stage. There will be no attempt to be exhaustive. All that is intended is to indicate the main lines on which the argument has so far proceeded. Nor shall we attempt to make the review in chronological order, since in such a presentation the relative weight of the arguments on each side could not easily be assessed by the reader.

It will make for clarity if we divide the arguments into five groups, and under each group list firstly the arguments against Pauline authorship and then the arguments in favour of it, so that their comparative value can be gauged. It is necessary to deal first with the arguments 'against' because it is there that the burden of proof lies. Pauline authorship can rightly be assumed until it is disproved, and, in the main, the arguments in favour of Pauline authorship consist in successfully countering the arguments against it.

The grouping of the arguments under five headings is in some degree arbitrary and it is only done for the sake of convenience. Certainly no rigid line can be drawn between the various groups, and the names suggested for them are only approximate titles. But it is hoped that the convenience in comparing the two sets of arguments will justify the method.

The five groups under which the arguments will be arranged are:

1. Linguistic arguments.
2. Stylistic arguments.
3. Literary arguments.
4. Historical arguments.
5. Doctrinal arguments.

Group 1 will overlap with both 2 and 5. Group 3 will include some arguments that do not belong very clearly to any group in particular. In Group 5 will be listed arguments that deal with differences of thought and outlook, even though they are not actually of a doctrinal nature.

Our first step therefore will be the enumeration of the main arguments which have been used to question and disallow the epistle's claim to Pauline authorship. Among more recent authors the protagonists on this side are J. Moffatt, M. Dibelius, and E. J. Goodspeed. The views of these three will frequently be quoted, but excerpts will also be given from the writings of those who maintain Pauline authorship (such as Hort, Abbott, McNeile, Peake, and Dodd) to show that the difficulties in accepting it are keenly felt even by those who do not feel justified in rejecting it.

1. *Linguistic Arguments*

Many of the words and phrases in Ephesians have an un-Pauline ring about them. They have no parallels in the other Pauline epistles. Some, indeed, are not only negatively un-Pauline, in that they do not belong to the recognized Pauline vocabulary, but they are claimed as positively non-Pauline, in that they replace some other word or phrase which is regularly used in the definitely Pauline epistles.

(*a*) About ninety words in Ephesians are not elsewhere used in the Pauline epistles. Many of these cannot be claimed as significant, but some of them can.

(*b*) For instance, in Ephesians ὁ διάβολος is used twice (iv. 27 and vi. 11). Not only does this word not appear elsewhere in Paul's writings, but in his writings the same meaning is conveyed by some other word, usually σατανᾶς.

(*c*) The phrase ἐν τοῖς ἐπουρανίοις, which occurs five times in Ephesians, as though it were a favourite phrase with the author, has no parallel in the other Pauline epistles.

(*d*) ὁ ἠγαπημένος is not used elsewhere by Paul as a title for Christ, although by the end of the first century it was coming into common use in this sense. Dibelius quotes instances of it from 1 Clement, Barnabas, Hermas, and Ignatius (KEP, p. 48).

(*e*) Moffatt also speaks of 'the unique employment of prepositions like ἐν (115 times) and κατὰ' (ILNT, p. 387). These two prepositions are used in Ephesians far in excess of the Pauline average.

(*f*) Moffatt also mentions as 'un-Pauline touches' such phrases as ἴστε γινώσκοντες (v. 5), 'the Father of Glory' (i. 17), 'before the foundation of the world' (i. 4 = John xvii. 24), (ILNT, p. 387).

(g) Moffatt further points to 'an unparalleled number of genitival formations (95 in all, out of 155 verses)'. He does not specify exactly what he means by a 'genitival formation', but he quotes as illustrations such strange compounds as ἁφὴ τῆς ἐπιχορηγίας (iv. 16) and ἐπιθυμία τῆς ἀπάτης (iv. 22).

Moffatt believes that these linguistic peculiarities are sufficient to cast serious doubt on the claim to Pauline authorship, but not to determine the issue beyond further question. His verdict is: 'The linguistic data may be allowed to leave the problem of authorship fairly open' (ILNT, p. 387). E. J. Goodspeed, however, believes that they have a more decisive bearing on the issue. He claims (INT, p. 234) that 'the novel element in the vocabulary . . . is mostly akin to works like Luke–Acts, 1 Clement, 1 Peter, and Hebrews, written towards the close of the first century'. It is therefore not only the fact that some of the elements in the language of Ephesians are un-Pauline, but also the fact of their marked kinship with Christian literature of post-Pauline date that leads Goodspeed to interpret their significance as pointing to a date later than Paul's lifetime.

2. *Stylistic Arguments*

Even more remarkable than the linguistic differences between Ephesians and the other Pauline epistles is the difference in style. It is, however, more difficult to give specific illustrations of this, although all students of this epistle have noted it.[1] Even those who have retained their belief in Pauline authorship treat it as a serious difficulty, needing special explanation. Others have seen in it strong evidence of the non-Pauline origin of the epistle.

Sanday and Headlam, in their commentary on Romans (ER, p. lv), find occasion to compare the style of Romans with that of Ephesians: 'In the matter of style . . . Ephesians stands at the furthest possible remove from Romans.' They describe the 'energy and vivacity' of Romans, the 'rush of words', the 'rapid, terse, incisive language', and continue: 'We shut up the epistle to the Romans, and we open that to the Ephesians; how great is the contrast! We cannot speak here of vivacity, hardly of energy. . . . In its place we have a slowly moving, onwards advancing mass, like a glacier working its way inch by inch down the valley.' They try to

[1] Even as early a writer as Erasmus felt this difficulty. He wrote of Ephesians: 'Certe stilus tantum dissonat a caeteris Pauli epistolis ut alterius videri possit nisi pectus atque indoles Paulinae mentis hanc prorsus illi vindicaret.'

give some impression of this difference by a numerical connotation. Working from the Revisers' Greek Testament, they point out that on the average there is, in Romans, a punctuation mark in every 1·4 lines; in Ephesians, however, there is one only to every 3 lines. More notable still is the fact that in Romans there is a question-mark for each 6·5 lines, but in Ephesians only one in 270 lines.

Hort, too (PRE, pp. 152–3), acknowledges the difference in style in Ephesians, with its 'unusually long sentences', and allows that 'it would not be easy to find exact parallels elsewhere in Paul's epistles'. He recognizes that 'the vehement moods of the earlier contexts have subsided' and been replaced by a 'lofty calm'. He does not approve Von Soden's explanation of this difference, but he quotes it to illustrate the kind of difference in style which he himself is wishing to describe: 'The author of Ephesians betrays a wholly different temperament as a writer from Paul, a phlegmatic instead of a choleric temperament.' Hort admits this difference, which Von Soden seeks to explain on the basis of two different temperaments at work, but he himself prefers to find the explanation in a change within Paul's own mind as a result of the 'mellowing effect of years' and the 'sense of dangers surmounted'.

Jülicher also (INT, pp. 142–3) speaks of the 'unwonted stiffness of the style', 'the cumbrous chains of sentences, full of participles and relative pronouns', 'the numerous lengthy passages each consisting in reality of a single sentence (i. 3–14; i. 15–23; ii. 1–10; iii. 1–19)', and 'the obvious overcrowding and diffuseness of style'.

None of these writers, however, abandons Pauline authorship on account of these differences, remarkable though they are. Nor does C. H. Dodd, though he seems to find this difference in style the most difficult feature to account for. After meeting the other difficulties with a measure of confidence he confesses: 'The difficulty of the un-Pauline style still remains.' Similarly A. S. Peake (INT, p. 55), while continuing to maintain Pauline authorship, concedes that 'the weightiest objection is the un-Pauline character of the style'.

Of those who reject Pauline authorship, Dibelius emphasizes the weight of this argument from style, but it is not for him the deciding factor. In fact he writes that the stylistic peculiarities by themselves hardly suffice to demonstrate the spurious character of the epistle, though he feels the difficulty of the accumulation of synonymous expressions, the profusion of genitive constructions (so difficult to translate), and the elongated sentences, sometimes lacking proper logical and grammatical sequence.[1]

[1] Dibelius (KEP, p. 64): 'Wenn man sich einmal von der Unechtheit des Eph

Moffatt, however, finds in this peculiarity of style the most decisive indication of non-Pauline origin. We saw earlier that, in his judgement, the linguistic data 'leave the problem of authorship fairly open'. Then he continues: 'But the idiosyncrasies of the style are by no means so easily explained' (ILNT, p. 387). A little later (p. 388) he writes that 'the cumulative impression' made by the separate items of difficulty in the thought and expression 'is that of a writer who occupies a later standpoint of his own'. And then he adds: 'This is more than corroborated by the style.' He too notes the lengthy sentences 'at once elaborate and irregular', and 'the relatival and participial constructions whose logical bearing it is frequently almost impossible to determine'. He finally characterizes the difference thus: 'In Paul's letters there is always something of the cascade; in Ephesians we have a slow bright stream which brims its high banks' (p. 389).

In short, we are uncomfortably aware in Ephesians of a somewhat artificial eloquence, which Paul elsewhere seemed deliberately to avoid (cf. 1 Cor. i. 17; ii. 4, 13).

One peculiarity of this rather self-conscious elevation of tone deserves a little further amplification. It is what we called earlier, in a phrase from Dibelius, 'the accumulation of synonymous expressions'. It is one aspect of the diffuseness which so many have noted as a characteristic of the style of Ephesians. Moffatt calls it the use of 'redundant, epexegetic formations', and gives as examples *βουλὴ τοῦ θελήματος, κράτος τῆς ἰσχύος* (ILNT, p. 387). Jülicher too notes that 'instances of the coupling of two synonymous nouns by means of a genitive or a preposition are remarkably numerous'. The examples he chooses are: *τὸ μεσότοιχον τοῦ φραγμοῦ* (ii. 14); *ὁ νόμος τῶν ἐντολῶν ἐν δόγμασιν* (ii. 15); *εἰς μέτρον ἡλικίας τοῦ πληρώματος τοῦ Χριστοῦ* (iv. 13). All these are felt to be more wordy than Paul's direct and unaffected style.

Such variations of style as have been indicated are, it is claimed, more readily explicable as due to a different author than as the mark of a different phase within the experience of the same author.

überzeugt hat, treten natürlich noch alle stilistischen Eigentümlichkeiten des Textes in ein besonderes Licht, obwohl sie für sich allein kaum zum Beweis der Unechtheit ausreichen. In Frage kommt vor allem die Häufung synonymer Ausdrücke . . . und die Fülle der (uns meist schwer übersetzbaren) Genetivkonstruktionen. Aber auch die weit ausgesponnenen Perioden anakoluthischer oder nicht anakoluthischer Art geben zu denken.'

3. *Literary Arguments*

(*a*) Even a superficial comparison of Ephesians and Colossians reveals a large measure of similarity between the two, and a more careful study leads to the discovery that this similarity is both exceedingly close and curiously intricate. Moffatt describes this as the 'most obvious feature of Ephesians', and as 'almost decisive upon the larger question of the period and authorship of Ephesians'. He recognizes that the relationship may be explicable under the assumption of Pauline authorship, but after a comparative analysis of the two writings he is convinced that what is found in Ephesians 'may be fairly regarded as a set of variations played by a master hand on one or two themes suggested by Colossians', and that the master hand is not Paul's own but 'sub-Pauline' (ILNT, p. 375). Against those who protest that so original a creation as Ephesians could not be the work of an imitator enlarging on another's writing, Moffatt instances the Synoptic Gospels, in which earlier sources have been skilfully blended and enlarged. His final verdict is that Ephesians is 'a catholicised version of Colossians written in Paul's name to Gentile Christendom' (p. 393).

Dibelius attaches even more importance to this particular argument and its bearing upon the question of authorship. He claims that the relationship between Ephesians and Colossians is the issue which settles the question,[1] and more recently, in his *Fresh Approach to the New Testament*, he enlarges on the claim: 'What speaks decisively for the spuriousness of Ephesians . . . is its linguistic dependence upon Colossians, coupled with a completely different construction of thought' (p. 170). In KEP, p. 64, he enumerates several cases where the phraseology of Colossians is reproduced in Ephesians, but with a different connotation. For instance, the words *κεφαλή, σῶμα, μυστήριον* are borrowed by Ephesians from Colossians, but in Ephesians are used with a different significance. This would be most difficult to account for if Paul was the author of both, but readily understandable if an imitator was responsible for Ephesians.

Dibelius appears to be fully justified in his opinion that this relationship between the two epistles is a crucial issue for anyone who is seeking a decision on the question of authorship. It will not, however, be pursued further at this stage, for it must be carefully investigated in later chapters.

[1] 'Das Verhältnis von Eph zu Col bietet den Punkt dar, von dem aus die Echtheitsfrage zu entscheiden ist' (Dibelius, KEP, p. 63).

(*b*) *The relationship of Ephesians to other New Testament writings.* Many writers have noticed the similarities between Ephesians and 1 Peter. Moffatt not only names many theological conceptions which are shared by the two epistles, but he prints in parallel columns many verses from them which have considerable verbal correspondence (ILNT, pp. 381–3). Jülicher even makes mention of a suggestion that the same author may have composed both epistles. The majority of scholars seem to feel that the closeness of some of the correspondences almost proves some kind of literary dependence between the two, but there is no general agreement as to which is the borrower. If it could be shown conclusively that Ephesians used 1 Peter, that would be nearly unanswerable proof of non-Pauline authorship. If, however, it is 1 Peter which is the borrower, the question of authorship is not affected. Moffatt, however, feels that the evidence points to the priority of 1 Peter. He writes: 'The probabilities on the whole point to an acquaintance on the part of the "auctor ad Ephesios" with the simpler 1 Peter' (p. 382). So he regards the relationship as pointing to a sub-Pauline date for Ephesians.

Moffatt also draws many parallels between Ephesians and the Lukan writings. The similarity, however, to the Johannine writings has made a more widespread impression. Jülicher sees in Ephesians 'a development of Pauline doctrine in the direction of Johannine theology', and Lock even ventures the surprising opinion: 'It would be a tenable view that the writer of Ephesians was the author of the Fourth Gospel, writing in the name of St. Paul' (DB, i. 717).

There are also affinities with Hebrews, not, it is true, such as to suggest any literary dependence, but nevertheless indicative of 'a common atmosphere of religious feeling and phraseology' (Moffatt, ILNT, p. 385).

Even if these parallels fall short of proving any literary dependence between Ephesians and these other New Testament books, it is at any rate beyond doubt that Ephesians has a much closer link with these books than any other Pauline letter has. This in itself places Ephesians in a category of its own among the Pauline epistles, and may legitimately be used as an argument against the traditional ascription of authorship.

(*c*) Another characteristic of Ephesians, which isolates it among the Pauline epistles, is the extremely superficial nature of its letter-form.

We have already noticed that in the earliest and most reliable texts there is no name of the Church to which it was sent. Dibelius complains that there are 'no concrete situations of a particular church to recognise'. Jülicher also comments on 'the lack of definite features in its teaching', and adds that 'in fact Ephesians almost gives one the impression of a printed sermon'. This is what Moffatt means when he declares it to be a homily rather than a letter. As such it is unique among the Pauline writings.

Supporters of Pauline authorship meet these difficulties by claiming that Ephesians was a circular letter, intended for many churches; and so in the opening verse there was a blank space into which different place-names could be introduced. Moffatt, however, is not satisfied with this improvised expedient. He writes: 'The circular hypothesis is not free from difficulties. Primitive Christian epistles designed for a wide circle of churches were composed otherwise (cf. 1 Cor. i. 1–2, Gal. i. 1); the notion of copies with blanks for the local address is not true to ancient methods of epistolography; besides we should expect traces of several readings, and at best the retension of ἐν' (ILNT, p. 392). Dibelius declines to regard these difficulties as a 'strict proof of un-genuineness' but concedes that they constitute 'a problem, perhaps insoluble' (KEP, p. 63).

(*d*) Ephesians contains several personal references to Paul as the author. This in itself is not unusual in a Pauline letter. Both Galatians and 2 Corinthians contain long passages of autobiographical interest, and other letters have instances where Paul introduces his name, as though invoking the full authority of his reputation and calling, to give weight to a solemn pronouncement or to reinforce an urgent plea. But the personal references in Ephesians are felt to be of another order. It is claimed that they do not sound like Paul's own genuine words about himself; that they do not ring true.

These references appear in what is really a lengthy parenthesis, iii. 1–13. The particular phrases to which exception has been taken are:

(i) iii. 2. The writer speaks of Paul's special commission to carry the Gospel to the Gentiles, and of this commission he very curiously adds: 'If so be that you have heard of the dispensation of that grace of God, which was given me to you-ward.' Even allowing for the possibility that some group other than the Christians at Ephesus are the people addressed, and also that 'if so be that' may be rendered 'for surely', it still remains a real difficulty why Paul should use such a sentence in writing to any group of Christians to whom he should wish to send this epistle.

(ii) iii. 4: 'Whereby, when ye read, ye can perceive my understanding in the mystery of Christ.'

Under provocation and unscrupulous defamation, Paul could be goaded into vigorous self-defence, 'to glory a little', as he describes it, though in so doing he knew that he was speaking 'as one beside himself' (2 Cor. xi. 16, 23). But here this commendation of his own spiritual insight is quite unprovoked and even a little complacent. It does not accord well with what we know of Paul from other sources.

The short phrase 'when ye read' has caused even greater difficulty. The usual way of defending it is to make it refer to the preceding verses in Ephesians. The improbability of this interpretation, however, drove Hort to make the still more improbable suggestion that it is the prophetic books of the Old Testament which are meant. Moffatt is sure that it must refer to Colossians, and this interpretation would not necessarily exclude Pauline authorship of Ephesians, though it could hardly be fitted in with the thought of Ephesians as a circular letter since it assumes that its readers have already read what he had written to the Colossians. It would necessitate the assumption that Ephesians is the letter referred to in Col. iv. 16. But if it is this Laodicean letter, why is it so impersonal? Paul's relationship with Laodicea was much the same as that with Colossae, and his letter to the Colossians is not impersonal. Goodspeed claims that this mention of 'reading' proves that, when Ephesians was written, the rest of Paul's letters were already available in their collected form, and it is the reading of these published letters which will prove Paul's 'understanding in the mystery of Christ'.

(iii) iii. 8: 'I am less than the least of all saints.' We know that there were moments in Paul's experience when he was overwhelmed with the sense of his unworthiness to be an apostle of Christ's Gospel. The recollection of his ruthless, brutal persecution of the first Christians wrings from him the cry of deep humiliation: 'I am not meet to be called an apostle' (1 Cor. xv. 9). It breaks from him out of the anguish of his heart. But here in Ephesians there is no note of deep distress and agonized shame. It sounds calmly deliberate, even self-conscious and a little theatrical. E. J. Goodspeed does not overstate the position when he writes of this sentence: 'It gives scholars who maintain that Paul wrote it great embarrassment' (INT, p. 231).

4. *Historical Arguments*

(*a*) The external evidence is wholly on the side of those who maintain Pauline authorship. Among all the early writers of the

Christian Church there is never the slightest hint that questions it. Moreover, the epistle seems to be known and quoted as Paul's as early as any of the other Pauline epistles. One of the most difficult tasks for those who reject the tradition of Pauline authorship is to find a satisfactory explanation of this acknowledged fact.

(*b*) The internal evidence is much less unanimous. Certain elements in the epistle are said to reflect a condition of life in the Christian Church not only later than the other letters but later than any period which can be brought within the limits of Paul's own lifetime.

For instance, there is the attitude to the place of the Gentiles in the Church. In his other letters Paul is their champion, vigorously demanding for them full equality within the Church with the Jews. So far as we know from Paul's other epistles and from other sources, this Gentile controversy could not be regarded as settled during Paul's lifetime. But in Ephesians it has been settled. Hort, in his defence of Pauline authorship, feels he has to take account of this remarkable change, for he writes: 'Here in the epistle to the Ephesians the assured position of the Gentile Christians is simply taken for granted.' That is, in Ephesians the controversy is over. No longer is the full status of the Gentile within the Church questioned. It is no longer a debated issue demanding vehement partisanship, as in the early days, but it is a closed question to which an acknowledged solution has been found. Our historical judgement as to the date when this can be claimed to have become the accepted position will greatly affect our attitude to the question of authorship.

There are similar issues, involving historical judgement, as for instance references to circumcision, to the Church, to the status of 'apostles and prophets', the Second Advent, the insistent plea for unity within the Universal Church. Since, however, these involve doctrinal points as well as historical, it will be more convenient to consider them in the next section.

5. *Doctrinal Arguments*

These arguments seek to show that in several particulars Ephesians not only differs in point of view from Paul's other letters but differs in such a degree as to be inconsistent with what we know of Paul from other reliable sources.

This type of argument is exceedingly vulnerable and should be used only with the utmost caution, because rigid consistency is not the mark of virile minds as they confront new and changing situations. Within the space of a few years there can sometimes be remarkable changes in the outlook of a man, which are nevertheless quite understandable developments. We shall argue later that theological differences of the kind indicated in this section, which can be shown to exist between Colossians and Ephesians, do take on immense significance. When, however, the differences are between writings separated from each other by an interval of years, as for instance between Ephesians and Thessalonians, or even Romans, great caution must be exercised.

Yet even when full allowance has been made for changes due to development within a growing mind, one has to admit that these doctrinal arguments cannot be summarily dismissed. McNeile, for instance, supports strongly the Pauline authorship of Ephesians, but he acknowledges that this group of arguments is the weightiest of all: 'This is the only criterion to which serious importance can be attached, and upon it those who deny the genuineness of the epistle lay chief weight' (INT, p. 159). McNeile is not right in saying that those who reject Pauline authorship do so mainly on these grounds. Moffatt, as we saw, believes that doctrinal and linguistic arguments leave the issue 'fairly open' and sees the deciding factor in the style. Dibelius, on the other hand, attaches crucial importance only to the arguments based on the relationship between Colossians and Ephesians. But the fact that McNeile accords to these doctrinal arguments priority in importance over the others shows that they do at any rate carry a measure of conviction.

In estimating the significance of these doctrinal differences one should take account of them *all*, and allow them to make a cumulative impression. It gives an untrue presentation of their significance to isolate each in turn, produce the arguments that seem to nullify it, and then eliminate it entirely from further discussion before proceeding to the next point. In dealing with points hostile to Pauline authorship this method of 'divide and conquer' has been used with misleading effect. Each possible enemy is attacked and accounted for individually. No concentration of units is permitted. A fair assessment, however, of their significance will take into account the sum total as well as each individual item in the total. It is true that no single point is of such consequence as to be convincing in itself, but if the whole sequence of single points is viewed together, it cannot fail to impress one as most remarkable that so many un-Pauline elements occur together within so small a compass.

The following are the main arguments which have been used to claim doctrinal inconsistency between Ephesians and the other

Pauline epistles. The first three are related to the Church and the next five are concerned with Christology. The remainder are separate items which do not fall into any special grouping.

(*a*) *The Universal Church*

The manner in which this author writes of the Church is felt to be strangely different from Paul's. The Church has not only come to fill a much larger place in his thought, but it is always 'the Church', in the sense of the Universal Church, of which he speaks. As Abbott puts it: 'The writer never speaks of local churches, but only of the (one) Church' (ICC, p. xix). This by itself has been taken to indicate a period later than Paul's lifetime, when 'the several local churches were drawing together in resistance to a common danger, and binding themselves together by a single organisation' (Abbott, ICC, p. xix). It is, however, not only the consistent references to the Church as one world-wide whole which are remarkable, but other modes of speaking about the Church also seem to be developments in thought which would more naturally be associated with a post-Pauline era. E. J. Goodspeed notes these particulars as follows: 'The writer of Ephesians is far more of an ecclesiastic than Paul. He finds in the Church a great spiritual fellowship, built upon apostles and prophets (ii. 20–2), the medium of God's revelation (iii. 10), and the avenue of man's praise (iii. 21). It is the Bride of Christ (v. 25–32)' (INT, p. 236). It is argued that Paul would not have been likely to ascribe these functions to the Church. Certainly they are far in advance of what he wrote elsewhere.

(*b*) *The Plea for Unity*

Not only is the Church invariably spoken of in its universal aspect, but there is an emphatic insistence on the need for unity within this world-wide community. In Paul's other letters we find frequent pleas for harmony within the individual churches, but in Ephesians the call for concord is something different and new. It is a plea for harmony and unity amongst all the units which make up the whole Church (iv. 3–6). Abbott acknowledges that 'it is indeed remarkable that in Ephesians the thought of the unity of the Church is so dominant that Christ's work is represented as having immediate reference to it rather than to individuals (cf. v. 25–7, 29, 32 with Gal. ii. 20)' (ICC, p. xix). Goodspeed makes much of this 'remarkable' emphasis, and claims that it presupposes a time when the sects were already beginning to appear, and this did not happen till after Paul's death (INT, p. 233).

(c) '*Apostles and Prophets*'

Moreover, within the sphere of the Church, an unusual degree of authority is ascribed to 'the apostles and prophets', which is reminiscent of the campaign for the proper recognition of duly authorized leaders which took place in the generation after Paul.

In ii. 20 the 'apostles and prophets' are described as the foundation of the Church, of which Jesus Christ is the chief cornerstone. This is somewhat strikingly at variance with Paul's vigorous declaration in 1 Cor. iii. 11: 'Other foundation can no man lay than that which is laid, which is Jesus Christ.' Even if we feel that no real importance can be attached to what may be little more than a change of metaphor in ascribing to Christ a place of crucial importance in the Church, nevertheless the unexpected elevation of 'apostles and prophets' to so exclusively important a status does not harmonize readily with what we know of Paul's mode of thought.

In iii. 5 the two offices appear in combination again. God's secret purpose, so long undisclosed, has now at last been revealed, and the revelation has been made to 'his holy apostles and prophets in the Spirit'. Once again we see that a status of extreme importance is accorded to them. More than that, there is the peculiarity of the epithet 'holy'. It is true that Paul commonly uses the adjective *ἅγιοι* as a noun to signify all who have accepted the sign of baptism and are thereby marked off as 'believers'. But this significance is not found when *ἅγιος* is used adjectivally; nor indeed, if it were, would it be an appropriate epithet for 'apostles and prophets', who obviously would be members of the Christian community. In this phrase, 'holy' is an adjective expressive of an attitude of extreme deference to those so described. Hort, though he finds an explanation for Paul's use of the epithet in this connexion, admits the very real difficulty it raises: 'It is said that this epithet would naturally be used only by a writer of the next or a later generation, to whom the apostles were venerated figures of the past. Doubtless this would be a natural origin for the epithet' (PRE, p. 145). Goodspeed, however, sees in it a piece of evidence that Ephesians belongs to the Christian literature of the last two or three decades of the first century: 'The expression "holy apostles" recalls Luke i. 70, Rev. xxi. 14, Rev. xviii. 20. The grouping of holy apostles is hardly the way in which Paul as we know him through his letters would have expressed himself. In fact it points to an attitude more like that of Matthew, Luke and Revelation' (INT, p. 232).

Jülicher, whose judgements are marked with clear-minded

discernment, wise caution, and scrupulous fairness, is also fully aware of the difficulties for Pauline authorship in these two passages. He writes: 'The greatest difficulties are presented by individual passages. . . . ii. 20 and iii. 5 present such difficulties' (INT, p. 144).

(d) Christ and God

The Christology of Ephesians also has certain distinguishing features as compared with the other Pauline epistles. Hort admits this: 'It is undeniably true that in Ephesians Christ is spoken of as the agent in certain Divine acts in which the earlier epistles and that to the Colossians speak of God or the Father as agent' (PRE, p. 136). He gives the following instances:

(i) In Eph. ii. 16 Christ is the one who achieves reconciliation. In Col. i. 20 and ii. 13–14 it is God who is active in reconciliation, working through Christ.

(ii) In Eph. iv. 11 it is Christ who appoints apostles, prophets, evangelists, and others to their position in the Church, whereas in 1 Cor. xii. 28 it is God Himself who exercises that function.

(e) The Death of Christ

In Ephesians the Death of Christ no longer holds the central position. Certainly it is not ignored. There are references to His Blood, His Cross, and His Sacrifice of Himself. But it is one interest among others, and has become secondary to the Exaltation of Christ. Dibelius remarks that in Ephesians the Death of Christ has receded, and His Exaltation has come to the fore.[1] Abbott also allows the validity of this argument: 'It is . . . very remarkable that the whole circle of thought which in Paul has its centre in the death of Christ, here falls into the background' (ICC, p. xix). In the section i. 15–ii. 10, where reference is twice made to the Resurrection, and where the whole theme is the work of redemption, the Death is not mentioned.

(f) The Jew–Gentile Controversy

Ephesians alone sees the settlement of the Jew–Gentile issue as a fulfilment of the work of Christ. In the section on Historical Arguments we noticed that in Ephesians all strife and misunderstanding between Jews and Gentiles is at an end, and this is claimed as evidence of a post-Pauline date. Certainly that misunderstanding

[1] 'Die Gedankenwelt des Eph bietet gewiss manches Eigentümliche; . . . des Zurücktreten des Todes Christi und das Hervortreten seiner Erhöhung, i. 20 ff. ii. 5 ff.' (Dibelius, KEP, p. 63).

loomed large in Paul's thinking. It was a constant stumbling-block in the early days of the Christian mission, though it was not wholly barren of good fruit in that it compelled such Christian leaders as Paul to clear-minded thinking on the implications of their new faith. As a result Paul had much to say on the Jew–Gentile controversy, but deeply as he longed for harmonious co-operation between both parties, he did not represent this co-operation as a primary object of Christ's work on earth. Abbott puts it in this way: 'St. Paul never represents it as the object, or even an object of Christ's work to bring into one Jews and Gentiles' (ICC, p. xix). To illustrate the frequent references in Ephesians to this issue he quotes ii. 13–18, ii. 19–22, iii. 5 ff., iv. 7–16.

(g) *The Second Coming*

It is a well-known fact that the early years of Paul's missionary work were spent in constant expectation of the Second Coming of Christ and the end of this present world order. This anticipation and his desire to correct misinterpretations of it constitute the principal theme of two of his letters, and all the letters reflect the prominent place this belief had in his mind. Even when it is not explicitly present, its implications are felt, as when he seeks to frame rules about the advisability of marriage among Christians, in answer to a question raised by the Corinthian Church. Even the letter to the Philippians, which has generally been regarded as the last of Paul's epistles, has at least five direct references to this expected Second Coming. Nor are these five references crowded into one specially relevant section. They are evenly distributed throughout the letter, each of the four chapters containing at least one of the references. So they may be said to reflect the general background of Paul's thought at that time.

It is true that in Colossians this note is greatly reduced in frequency. Only once does it emerge (at iii. 4), but as one reads one is aware of a familiar pressing urgency in Colossians as in the other letters. It seems as though, for the writer, the time is not long.

In Ephesians, however, it is different. There is no suggestion of a Second Coming; even the note of urgency is missing. Moreover, so far from any sudden end of the world being shortly expected, the writer seems to anticipate a long period of development for the Christian community. In iii. 21 he writes: 'Unto God be the glory in the church and in Christ Jesus *unto all generations* for ever and ever.' Hort states the position with extreme caution: 'The immediate imminence of the Coming of the Lord has faded out of view; the anticipation of it now seems to include a sense of its possible remoteness.' McNeile is more forthright: 'In Ephesians the writer looks forward to . . . a consummation to be reached in the far future by the spiritual growth of the church, . . . the Body of Christ must be built up "till we all attain unto the unity of the faith" (iv. 13), . . . and this leaves room for the "ages to come" (ii. 7)' (INT, pp. 159 f.).

(*h*) *The Descent into Hades*

Another element in Christology which is peculiar to Ephesians among the Pauline epistles is the 'Descent into Hades', which, it is generally believed, is referred to in iv. 9–10. Goodspeed feels strongly the incongruity of this passage. His comment on it is as follows:

'It is an extraordinary thing to have to fit into the Pauline phraseology, and is generally passed over in silence by those who seek to reconstruct Paul's thought. The instinct that leads them to do this is right, for it is almost impossible to suppose such a view had any place in Paul's thought. In fact he virtually excludes it by what he says in Rom. x. 6–7. The Descent into Hades is the natural sequel to Luke's doctrine of the Ascension, reflected in Eph. iv. 9. To suppose Paul, who has no ascension doctrine, should yet have the sequel to it in the "Descensus ad Inferos", is putting the cart before the horse' (INT, p. 234).

(*i*) *Marriage*

In Ephesians marriage is given high honour. It is quoted as a symbol of the relationship between Christ and His Church. It is treated as an ideal human institution (v. 22–33). This is oddly in contrast with Paul's attitude to marriage in the earlier letters. There, at best, it appears as a permitted expedient, a concession to the violence of human passions, something certainly much to be preferred to fornication, but nevertheless a sign of weakness in a Christian. The mature Christian will not need to avail himself of this concession (1 Cor. vii).

Certainly it may be argued that Paul's reluctance to countenance marriage is not so much due to any belief in the inherent wickedness of the marriage relationship as to his conviction that the Second Coming of Christ is imminent, certainly so near as to make the begetting of children an irrelevance, and the cares attendant on married life a distraction from piety, without any compensating justification. His arguments are urged 'by reason of this preenst distress'.

If the different attitudes towards the Second Coming can be

reconciled as representing an earlier and a later stage in Paul's own experience, so probably can this change of attitude toward marriage. But many feel that the change is so great as to point to a different author rather than to a later phase in the life of the same author.

(j) Children

Goodspeed also sees in the added interest in the upbringing of children evidence of a post-Pauline date. He writes: 'The injunction in vi. 4 to bring their children up with Christian training and instruction is out of keeping with Paul's attitude; all he had to say to parents in Colossians (written supposedly at the same time as Ephesians, if by Paul) was: "Do not irritate your children" Col. iii. 21' (INT, p. 235).

The discipline of children would, of course, take on new importance as the expectation of an early end to all things diminished.

(*k*) Two words which play a big part in Ephesians, μυστήριον and οἰκονομία, carry in Ephesians, it is argued, a significance not found elsewhere in the Pauline literature. Particularly, it is claimed, the very unusual significance of μυστήριον in v. 32 is indicative of a later date than Paul's lifetime.

This argument will carry more weight if it can clearly be shown that the meaning of these two words in Ephesians is distinguishable from the meaning they carry in Colossians. If, however, between the later use in Ephesians and the earlier uses there stands an interval of several years, a change in the significance of a word need not be regarded as unusual.

(l) Circumcision

It is also said that the attitude of Ephesians to circumcision is different from that found in Paul's other letters. Hort feels himself obliged to counter this argument, and in so doing conveniently states it thus (with reference, particularly to Eph. ii. 11): 'The epistle to the Ephesians speaks of circumcision not simply as obsolete but as in itself contemptible, in a way that St. Paul's writings never do.'

The care Hort takes to meet the argument shows that it is at any rate worthy of a considered reply.

A further word of warning must be uttered against any careless use of this argument based on doctrinal differences. We should expect changes and modifications in both the style and thought of a vigorous and adaptable character. If, of course, the change represents a large measure of incongruity, or appears to be utterly opposed, not merely to one former utterance, but to the whole way of thinking elsewhere evident, then it may be regarded as significant. Or even if minor changes appear in great numbers, one may feel compelled to doubt whether a period of development can be accepted as an adequate explanation. If, however, two letters are represented as written at the same time (as Colossians and Ephesians appear to be), differences of thought between them become charged with extreme importance. But a few differences which have none of these special characteristics cannot be held to be important. Each reader must decide for himself whether these twelve differences listed above constitute significant or insignificant variations from the normal Pauline scheme of thought.

The foregoing five groups of arguments make no pretence of being exhaustive, but they represent the main objections which have been raised against the traditional assumption that Paul was the author of Ephesians. Moffatt's summary of the conclusions to which these arguments impel him will serve to represent the position of those who find them convincing:

'To sum up. The cumulative force of the arguments already noted is in favour of a Paulinist, imbued with his master's spirit, who composed this homily in his name as Luke composed the Pauline speeches in Acts (either from a sense of what Paul would have said under the circumstances or from some basis in tradition). From the writing of such speeches to the composition of an epistolary homily on the basis of an epistle like Colossians it was an easy step. The writer designed his work to be read (iii. 4) by the church as a manifesto of Paul's mind upon the situation; it was a pamphlet or tract for the times, insisting on the irenical needs of the church (like Acts) and on the duty of transcending the older schisms which had embittered the two sections of Christendom' (ILNT, p. 388).

III

THE CASE FOR PAULINE AUTHORSHIP

PALEY, in his *Horae Paulinae*, published in 1790, writes of Ephesians: 'It does not appear to have ever been disputed that the epistle before us was written by St. Paul.' It is, therefore, only in comparatively recent years that any doubt has been felt about the Pauline authorship. The epistle claims to be by Paul, and until the nineteenth century no one challenged the claim. On this issue, therefore, the burden of proof lies with those who seek to maintain a contrary opinion. For this reason it will be found that the main arguments of those who support Pauline authorship consist in successfully rebutting the arguments of those who would reject it.

In the last chapter we mentioned the names of Hort, Abbott, McNeile, Peake, and Dodd as representative of those scholars who believe the traditional ascription of authorship to be correct. In this chapter we shall indicate in outline the arguments they use to counter those already given on the other side.

First, however, we must utter a warning. Just as those who are inclined to reject Pauline authorship are in danger of seeing too much significance in variations of style and thought, and of failing to make adequate allowance for what Peake calls 'the versatility of Paul's genius' (PC, p. 815), as though Paul were a dull model of stunted consistency, so we find that those who maintain Pauline authorship sometimes seek support for their position in arguments which should be used only with extreme caution, or perhaps not used at all. Such unreliable arguments are the following four:

1. A recent writer on Paul's epistles introduces into his discussion of the authorship of Ephesians this sentence: 'Whether or no this is a genuine letter from Paul or a mere imitation affects its value considerably.' This is a perfectly legitimate expression of opinion, though many would strongly dissent from it. As a factor, however, in a disinterested search for an honest answer to a legitimate inquiry it is utterly out of place. As a plea for the retention of Pauline authorship it is unworthy. Quite possibly the fear of losing something of value has made scholars cautious in abandoning time-honoured assumptions, and rightly so; but to whisper that fear into the ears of others, and to use it, not only to advise caution but to influence them against their own considered judgement, is utterly

unjustifiable. The question of the authorship of Ephesians has been acutely raised by others, and the only honourable way of meeting the question is fearlessly to seek an honest answer without allowing possible consequences to sway us with considerations of gain or loss. In fact, all honest inquiry must pursue its way with the conviction that to know the truth will in the end be for our good, however unsettling its immediate effect may be upon our treasured presuppositions.

This is not the place to discuss at length what difference the abandonment of Pauline authorship would make to the value of Ephesians, but a strong case could be made for the claim that the gains would fully offset the losses. Certainly the Epistle to the Hebrews has not lost any of its value because it is no longer regarded as Pauline. In fact its segregation from the Pauline Corpus not only gives us a clearer picture of the specifically Pauline interpretation of the Christian Gospel but provides us with one further witness to the truth of the central facts of our faith. It is at any rate possible that a similar gain, rather than loss, would follow if Ephesians had to be removed from the collection of Pauline writings.

Or again it may be argued that the value of any particular writing depends not on the author who wrote it but on the intrinsic truth which it contains; that Paul's writings are so valuable to us, not because they are by the great missionary apostle, but because they unfold precious truths; that it is not the greatness of the epistles which is dependent on the greatness of their writer, but the greatness of the writer which is proved by the greatness of his writings.

However that may be, considerations of possible gain or loss are all a menace to honest inquiry. Fear of consequences is indeed a poor ally in the search for truth, and the appeal to such fear should be allowed no place in our discussion.

2. A second line of argument, not unlike the first one, which needs to be guarded against, is the attempt to prejudice a reader against the rejection of Pauline authorship by describing what would be left, in the event of such a rejection, by some word which suggests worthlessness. In the quotation already referred to it is styled 'a mere imitation'. Sometimes the words 'forgery', 'counterfeit', 'fake' have been used. If it can be shown that Pauline authorship cannot be retained, all that has happened is that we can no longer regard Paul as the author, and words should not be used which suggest that more than this has happened. Such words cloak the issue with a mist of misrepresentation. Even to say that the letter is therefore 'not

genuine' may, for some readers, mean something far more damning than to say accurately that it is not a 'genuinely Pauline epistle'.

Care must be taken therefore lest these colourful but unfair descriptions of the alternative to Pauline authorship affect our judgement. We must not shrink from what is true merely because someone has called it by a derogatory name.

3. A third argument which is greatly overworked claims that Paul must have been the author because no one else could possibly have produced a work of such excellence. C. A. Alington, for instance, writes: 'The opponents of the Pauline authorship have to face a far more serious difficulty in calling into existence an otherwise unknown writer who could produce' such a work (NTRG, p. 204). In a similar strain, E. F. Scott writes of Ephesians: 'If not by Paul, it must have been written by some one equal to him in genius and religious insight. Can we believe that in the Church of Paul's day there was an unknown teacher of this supreme excellence?' (LNT, p. 180). Scott here overstates the greatness of this hypothetical 'unknown teacher'. Great as is the intrinsic worth of Ephesians, it is not true to say that the man who wrote it (if other than Paul), and who obviously owed a great debt to Paul's teaching, was necessarily the 'equal in genius and religious insight' of the man who not only wrote Romans, 1 and 2 Corinthians, Galatians, and Philippians, but also accomplished all that is told of Paul in Acts. But apart from this overstatement, have we any right to deny that any man capable of writing such an epistle was to be found in the first century of Christians other than Paul himself? Our knowledge of the early Church is not sufficient to justify so sweeping a disqualification. Certainly we should be warned against too easy an acceptance of it by the recollection that precisely this argument was used by those who insisted that Paul must have written 'Hebrews'. 'With the example of Hebrews before us', writes B. W. Bacon, 'it will not do to say that the age from 75 to 100 A.D. . . . was incapable of producing so splendid a reproduction of Pauline thought' (INT, pp. 116–17).

4. A fourth argument needing a word of caution is so daring and ingenious as to be almost startling. It is a *tour de force* indeed, which nevertheless has commended itself to some upholders of Pauline authorship. This argument takes the elements in Ephesians which are most glaringly unlike Paul, and triumphantly declares that their very unlikeness proves that they cannot be the work of an imitator,

because an imitator would most scrupulously have avoided anything so manifestly un-Pauline. Therefore they must have come from Paul's own hand. So not only the Pauline, but also the un-Pauline elements, all go to prove that Paul wrote the letter. C. A. Alington acknowledges that Ephesians has a 'pronounced difference of style from any other Pauline epistle', and 'an unusual number' of new words and phrases, but he will not allow that these constitute any objection to Pauline authorship. Rather they are clear evidence confirming it. He writes: 'The obvious answer to this objection is that any brilliant writer—and the author of this letter has real literary genius—who wished, as he shows in i. 1 and iii. 1, to pass his composition off as a genuine work of St. Paul, would surely have avoided what would (from an imitator's point of view) be such elementary blunders' (NTRG, p. 203). So even the un-Pauline characteristics are claimed as unmistakable evidence of their Pauline origin. Abbott especially seems to find satisfaction in this rather violent exposition of un-Pauline characteristics. He uses it three times within two pages of his commentary (ICC, pp. xvi–xvii). In connexion with the phrase ὁ Θεὸς τοῦ κυρίου ἡμῶν Ἰησοῦ Χριστοῦ (i. 3 and i. 17) he writes: 'It is certainly an unexpected expression, but it is one which no later imitator, holding such lofty views of Christ as here expressed, would have ventured on without Pauline precedent.' He uses a similar plea to neutralize any question arising from ἐμοὶ τῷ ἐλαχιστοτέρῳ πάντων ἁγίων (iii. 8). Then he returns to his argument and reinforces it thus: 'From this point of view, not only ἅπαξ λεγόμενα, but still more the use of new expressions for Pauline ideas, instead of offering an argument against the Pauline authorship become arguments against forgery.'

In a similar way B. Weiss overcomes the difficulty of accounting satisfactorily for Eph. vi. 21–2, which is almost identically a verbatim reproduction of Col. iv. 7–8. The passage with its deliberate duplication presents difficulties for those who interpret Ephesians as a genuine Pauline epistle. Because of this and other similar difficulties in the epistle, Weiss argues that therefore it must be genuine, because no imitator would introduce a passage which would so clearly invite suspicion (*Manual of Introduction to the New Testament*, vol. i, p. 348).

With such good friends an imitator need never fear detection. Any slip or inconsistency, any instance of his own personality peeping through into his work is only further proof that his work is genuine, because no imitator would be foolish enough to make such a slip or to include in his work any kind of discrepancy.

Such an argument is surely a somewhat desperate expedient. It may even be asked whether those who resort to it do not thereby reveal a consciousness of some weakness in the position they seek to maintain.

With these preliminary warnings against arguments which do not deserve the importance often attached to them, we will proceed to review the arguments presented in the preceding chapter against Pauline authorship in order to see how they have been answered. Also the more positive arguments for Pauline authorship which have been brought into the debate will be summarized.

The solid basis for these supporting arguments is the undeniable fact that from earliest days Ephesians was unquestionably accepted as Pauline. None of the doubts and hesitations which beset Hebrews and the Pastoral Epistles affected Ephesians. Moreover, unlike Hebrews, it specifically claims to be written by Paul, and unlike the Pastoral Epistles, it was never at any time separated from the rest of the Pauline Corpus. This attitude of unhesitating acceptance prevailed until the nineteenth century, so free was the epistle from anything that was patently un-Pauline. On these grounds it is confidently claimed that the outlook and phrasing of the epistle must be fundamentally Pauline, and such differences as may exist entirely superficial and certainly not such as to require the supposition of a different author to explain them. It is far easier, the claim continues, to explain the apparently un-Pauline characteristics while retaining Pauline authorship than to explain the many remarkably Pauline characteristics while rejecting Pauline authorship.

1. *Linguistic Arguments*

(*a*) Although there are more than ninety words in Ephesians not elsewhere used in the Pauline epistles, the tables in P. N. Harrison's book on *The Problem of the Pastoral Epistles* show that this is not an unusual number in proportion to the length of the epistle. Several of the undoubtedly genuine epistles have an even higher percentage of words which are not found in the other Pauline writings.

(*b*) Though elsewhere Paul uses *Σατανᾶς* rather than *διάβολος*, this is not of any significance. Both words are used, apparently interchangeably, in Acts and the Fourth Gospel. 'The difference is only that between the Hebrew and the Greek forms, and is analogous to that between *Κηφᾶς* and *Πέτρος*, of which the former is used twice and the latter four times in the Epistle to the Galatians' (Abbott, ICC, p. xvi).

(*c*) The phrase ἐν τοῖς ἐπουρανίοις, repeated five times in Ephesians, has certainly no exact parallel in the other Pauline epistles, but the adjective ἐπουράνιος occurs in 1 Cor. xv. 40, 48, 49 and Phil. ii. 10.

(*d*) Armitage Robinson acknowledges that ὁ ἠγαπημένος is unique here in Paul's writings as a title for Christ, and yet was commonly used as such by the end of the first century. This, however, he does not regard as evidence of a post-Pauline date, but rather as proving that the term was a common one in general use, which might quite easily have appeared in any of Paul's epistles.

The other peculiarities mentioned in (*e*), (*f*), and (*g*) on pp. 20, 21, and 22 are not regarded as sufficiently important to require any further explanation, apart from the claim that the same man writing at a different time, in different circumstances, and dealing with a different theme might quite naturally use them.

Goodspeed, we noted, emphasized not the numerical significance of these linguistic peculiarities, but their kinship with writings of a later date than Paul. Dodd acknowledges this 'fresh vocabulary', which 'tends to be of a certain marked type', but is of the opinion, nevertheless, that it 'may perhaps be accounted for by the subject-matter and the new lines of thought' (*Ab. Com.*, p. 1223).

Besides these answers to criticisms there are some more positive arguments which have been put forward. McNeile claims that there are 'at least 25 thoroughly Pauline words and expressions in Ephesians (found in Romans, 1 and 2 Corinthians, Galatians and Philippians) which do not occur in Colossians' (INT, p. 155).

Abbott points out that the thoroughly Pauline combination of particles, ἄρα οὖν, occurs once in Ephesians, though it is not used in the New Testament apart from the Pauline epistles; and διὸ, a favourite of Paul, occurs in Ephesians five times, though not once in Colossians.

Jülicher (INT, p. 143) demonstrates that 'much that is specifically Pauline can be found in Ephesians, such as the metaphorical use of οἰκοδομή (ii. 21, iv. 12, 16, 29), περισσεύειν (i. 8) used transitively, the words, καταντᾶν, ἀρραβών, ἀπολύτρωσις, ἀνακεφαλαιοῦσθαι and so on', and 'we are continually being reminded of Pauline ideas and modes of expression'.

Paley also, in *Horae Paulinae*, though he claims that at the time he writes no one has questioned the Pauline authorship of Ephesians, makes some useful points. He shows (p. 109) that it is a characteristic of Pauline style that the word πλοῦτος is used 'metaphorically as an augmentative of the idea to which it happens to be subjoined', e.g. 'the riches of his glory', 'of his goodness', 'of his wisdom'. This same use is found in Ephesians at i. 7, ii. 4, ii. 7, iii. 8, iii. 16, whereas no similar use is found in the rest of the New Testament, with the possible exception of Jas. ii. 5.

Paley also notes (p. 109) 'another singularity' of Paul's style, which 'may be deemed a badge of authenticity'. It is 'a species of digression which may be properly denominated "going off at a word" '. He names as instances:

2 Cor. ii. 14 at the word 'savour',
2 Cor. iii. 1 at the word 'epistle',
2 Cor. iii. 12 at the word 'veil'.

Instances of this peculiarity are noted in Ephesians at iv. 8–11 (at the word 'ascended') and v. 12–15 (at the word 'light').

2. *Stylistic Arguments*

Defenders of Pauline authorship make no attempt to minimize the acknowledged difference of style found in Ephesians. They are able, however, to suggest several considerations to account for it.

There is, first of all, the complete absence from Ephesians of any controversial note, which is unique in the Pauline writings. It is claimed that Paul, having dealt vigorously with certain dangerous errors in his letter to the Colossians, now deliberately turns his back on anything that savours of dispute, and quietly and calmly gives considered and dignified utterance to certain great truths which have impressed themselves upon his thoughts.

McNeile sees the whole epistle as something closely akin to a 'poem in prose' (INT, p. 155), and as such requiring a quite different technique from the cut and thrust of running debate, or the clearly enunciated instructions of a teacher.

Peake also argues that 'we must allow for the influence of enforced inactivity', due to a prolonged imprisonment (CINT, p. 56).

Many writers emphasize that the whole of the first half of the epistle is in the form of a prayer, and the language of prayer can sometimes take on a wholly different tone from that of ordinary conversation or of a spoken address.

F. B. Clogg summarizes these arguments thus: 'The first three chapters are almost a prayer: Paul is not here the spiritual father eager to correct his converts, nor is he a fiery combatant replying to attacks—he is contemplating the mystery of God's purpose for the world, and his style befits his high mood of contemplation' (INT, p. 96).

E. F. Scott, after facing the differences in style frankly, gives this as his verdict: 'It is difficult to believe that an imitator could have produced a work so like the writings of Paul and yet so splendid and original' (MCC, p. 119).

Moreover, different though the style may be in some respects from other Pauline writings, it is not so different as one would anticipate, if the author were not Paul.

3. *Literary Arguments*

(*a*) *The relationship to Colossians.* The very close interdependence between these two epistles is admitted without question. Whereas, however, as we have seen, there are those who see in it evidence of an imitator's work, the supporters of Pauline authorship claim that the manner of the interdependence is such as to favour their point of view. They argue that what is found in Ephesians is exactly what one would expect if Paul wrote it immediately after Colossians while its theme and phraseology were still fresh in his mind.

Paley seems to have been the first to point out that though much of Colossians is reproduced in Ephesians, Ephesians is very far from being a slavish duplication of Colossians. He writes: 'An impostor might transcribe into a forgery entire sentences and phrases, yet the dislocation of words, the partial recollection of phrases and sentences, the intermixture of new terms and new ideas with terms and ideas before used . . . would not have occurred to the invention of a forger; nor if they had occurred, would they have been so readily executed. This studied variation was a refinement in forgery which I believe did not exist' (HP, p. 101).

Other writers have followed this lead, claiming that an imitator would have kept much closer to his model, and that this flexible use of Colossians suggests that it is the product of the same mind at work, dealing with a similar, though not identical theme, and writing while the earlier work is still clearly remembered. This explanation does justice, according to C. H. Dodd, to what he calls 'the freedom and power of Ephesians, combined with such close similarity to Colossians' (*Ab. Com.*, p. 1225).

Peake (INT, p. 51), and others too, follow a lead taken from the work of H. J. Holtzmann, who argued that in some particulars Ephesians seemed to be the original and Colossians the copy, though in other instances it was clearly Ephesians which was secondary. Holtzmann did not interpret this as evidence of Pauline authorship, but the supporters of Pauline authorship seize on this point of Holtzmann's to claim that if two interdependent works both show evidence of originality, and each at some points also seems to borrow from the other, the most natural explanation is that the same mind has produced them both. (This point is elaborated further on pages 72–4.)

Other writers cannot understand why, if the writer is an imitator, he should pick out Colossians for such extensive borrowing, and in comparison shows so little interest in the other Pauline letters. Abbott, for instance, asks why an imitator should choose to follow Colossians and yet ignore the other Pauline epistles; and Jülicher too declares himself unable to imagine any purpose that would prompt an imitator to produce a work so closely built upon Colossians 'when he himself did not lack independent ideas and was also acquainted with other Pauline epistles' (INT, pp. 146–7).

Many writers, therefore, claim that the close relationship between these two letters is best interpreted as evidence of the authenticity of Ephesians rather than the reverse. E. F. Scott may be taken as representing their point of view: 'We get the impression that in pondering his answer to the Colossian heretics, Paul had arrived at certain great conceptions, which he now wished to develop for their own sake. So he decided that while the theme of Colossians was still fresh in his mind, he would write another letter in which he would leave all controversial issues aside and set forth fully, in their positive significance, the ideas which possessed him' (LNT, p. 181).

Some of these arguments will themselves be examined and criticized in the later investigation into the relationship between these two letters, but for the moment it is sufficient to state those arguments which have carried conviction for others.

(*b*) One of two explanations is usually given to account for the similarities which are found to exist between Ephesians on the one hand, and such writings as 1 Peter, Hebrews, Luke–Acts, and the Johannine literature on the other. Either it is that the writers of these works had the opportunity of acquaintance, indirectly if not directly, with Ephesians; or else both they and Ephesians are in a measure dependent on and so reflect a common background of formalized teaching and belief.

If it is felt to be unlikely that the Apostle Peter knew this particular epistle, even though he may have known Romans, it is argued that he may well have had opportunity of close contacts with Paul during his Roman imprisonment, and so the ideas which were uppermost in Paul's mind at that time would be familiar to Peter, and would not unnaturally influence his thoughts when he wrote 1 Peter. If, of course, 1 Peter is not claimed as the work of the apostle, its dependence upon Ephesians ceases to be a problem, though normally those who insist on the Pauline authorship of Ephesians maintain also the Petrine authorship of 1 Peter.

(*c*) It is an admitted peculiarity of Ephesians that the epistle lacks any personal note and is devoid of a specific destination. The explanation which is put forward as sufficient to account for these unusual omissions is that the letter was written as a circular letter, containing a general message, not to one particular church but to all Christians in a certain area. It would be carried to each of the churches in this area at the same time that Tychicus took the letter to Colossae and the personal note to Philemon. On this assumption, it is said, these omissions would be completely accounted for.

Many people identify Ephesians with the letter described in Col. iv. 16 as 'the epistle *from* Laodicea', and see in that rather peculiar description of what is clearly a letter from Paul further evidence that the letter was in the nature of a circular, which, in its round of the churches, would be brought to Colossae from Laodicea.

This explanation may account for the omission of the place-name in our earliest copies of the letter, and also for Marcion's practice of referring to Ephesians as Paul's letter to the Laodiceans.

(*d*) The personal references in chapter iii, to which some have taken exception, are accepted as quite appropriate to Paul. His reference to himself as 'less than the least of all the saints' is not felt to be substantially different from his admission in 1 Cor. xv. 9 that he is 'the least of the apostles'. The unquestioning acceptance of these words about himself for so many centuries is a strong argument against those who now assert that they sound most unlike Paul.

4. *Historical Arguments*

(*a*) *External evidence.* The chief strength of the argument which seeks to retain Pauline authorship lies here. This epistle seems to have been known among the early writers of the Christian Church as early as any of the others, and always it is known as Paul's. No doubt as to his authorship of it is even remotely suggested. B. W. Bacon writes: 'Ephesians is surpassed by scarcely any other New Testament writing besides 1 Corinthians in explicit attestation from the earliest times' (INT, p. 116). And Charteris in *Canonicity* writes:

'The testimony of the early church is unanimous in favour of the Pauline origin of the epistle. The only doubt has been as to its destination' (p. 237).

Marcion (*c.* A.D. 150) certainly included it, in his canon of the New Testament, among the Pauline epistles. The fact that he speaks of it as the letter to the Laodiceans (and not Ephesians) does not introduce any element of doubt about authorship, for it is quite certain that the letter in question is the one we know as Ephesians. The quotations from it cited by Tertullian in his denunciation of Marcion make this quite clear.

There is also general agreement that Polycarp knew the epistle. It is true that his use of it does not conclusively prove that he accepted it as Paul's, but there can be little doubt that he did. The date of Polycarp's letter to Philippi is not certain. Usually it has been taken as approximately contemporaneous with Ignatius's letters, but P. N. Harrison has made a case for regarding the letter as in fact two letters, one written to commend Ignatius's letters, and the other, which shows an intimate acquaintance with Paul's letters, perhaps as late as A.D. 140.

It is less certain but still reasonably sure that Ignatius (*c.* A.D. 110) was familiar with this epistle. There are those who question whether the similarities can be interpreted as evidence of Ignatius's actual acquaintance with the epistle itself, but most scholars feel justified in accepting this point of view. Once again we cannot claim complete certainty that he knew it to be by Paul, but there is certainly no sign of anything to the contrary.

There may even be earlier attestation than this, for it is possible, perhaps even probable, that Clement of Rome (*c.* A.D. 96) shows some traces of acquaintance with it. Certainly the Committee of the Oxford Society of Historical Theology who prepared *The New Testament in the Apostolic Fathers* do not give this a high degree of probability. They admit similarities between the two epistles, but are inclined to accept the common use of liturgical forms as the explanation of them rather than a direct literary dependence. Moffatt, however, and other scholars with him, interprets the evidence as much more favourable to the claim that Ephesians was known to Clement (ILNT, p. 384).

A more detailed examination of the external evidence is contained in Chapter XV.

(*b*) The critics of Pauline authorship point out that in Ephesians the issue of equality between Jews and Gentiles within the Church has been finally settled, and they see in this an indication of a post-Pauline date. Anderson Scott, however, not only denies this assumption, but carries the attack into his opponents' lines by claiming that this very point of emphasis in Ephesians almost compels one to accept Pauline authorship. He quotes from Eph. ii. 12 the statement that the Gentiles who are being addressed had been 'aliens from the commonwealth of Israel', but now they are 'partakers of the same inheritance, members of the same body, sharers in the same body' with the Jews (iii. 6). Of these passages he asks challengingly: 'Is it the least likely that anyone would address Gentiles in these terms after A.D. 70, at a time when Jerusalem was in ruins, when God's promises to Israel appeared to have utterly failed—would anyone when addressing people, many of whom would be proud of Provincial Citizenship, and some possibly proud of Imperial Citizenship, felicitate them on their new status in terms of citizenship of a race which was under political eclipse?' He presses home his counter-attack: 'Is it likely that before A.D. 70 this would be done by anyone else than Paul with his keen perception of the inestimable privileges enjoyed by Israel (see Rom. ix. 4–5)?' (FP, p. 173).

If this argument is valid, then the very passages cited as difficulties, irreconcilable with Pauline authorship, become even greater difficulties for those who argue for a date for Ephesians after A.D. 70.

5. *Doctrinal Arguments*

There are certain differences in doctrine between Ephesians and the other Pauline epistles, and no attempt is made to pretend that they do not exist. It is, however, claimed that such differences as do occur can be adequately explained as developments within Paul's own mind; that they do not involve any real inconsistency; that in fact very often 'the germ' from which these later ideas have developed 'is found in St. Paul's other writings' (Abbott, ICC, p. xx).

Both Dodd (*Ab.Com.*, p. 1224) and Peake (PC, p. 815) emphatically claim that Paul's mental equipment was such as to compel us to expect such changes rather than to be surprised by them. Hort's words may be quoted as representative of this commonly expressed opinion:

'A mind like his, in constant living contact with truth, needing and receiving fresh enlightenment from day to day, for dealing with the new and changing needs of the Churches, must assuredly have known growth. New experience must have brought new light, giving comparatively clear vision of truths hitherto imperfectly grasped or even overlooked altogether, and often changing the relative importance of truths already familiar. . . . It would therefore be unreasonable to take the presence of new doctrinal ideas . . . as evidence of different authorship, unless there be real want of harmony between the later and the earlier teaching, and unless the later way of thinking and speaking cannot be easily conceived as a natural outgrowth of the earlier in the case of a single man, and that such a man as we know St. Paul to have been' (PRE, p. 123).

In order to confirm this claim examples are quoted of writers who within a period of years have given evidence of remarkable change in their outlook. One such example, which has been more than once quoted, is that of G. B. Shaw. His drama *St. Joan* reveals a sympathetic appreciation of religious experience which his earlier works gave us little ground for anticipating.

One consequence of this line of argument seems to be that Ephesians, if it is indeed a Pauline epistle, must be regarded as the last which he wrote, in spite of the fact that this place of honour has usually been accorded to Philippians. If Ephesians is to be fitted into the Pauline literature, it must be regarded as the climax of Paul's teaching. 'Its thought is the crown of Paulinism' (Dodd, *Ab. Com.*, p. 1224).

Besides this general answer to all points of theological difference noted in Ephesians, some of the points raised in the previous chapter have been answered more specifically.

(*a*) *The Universal Church.* The conception of the Universal Church in Ephesians, as distinct from individual and local churches, is said to be an altogether natural development of 'germs' of thought already found in Paul's other letters.

C. A. Alington, for instance, writes: 'The universality of the Church had always been central in Paul's thought. We have seen him fiercely defending it in Galatians, and expounding to the Romans its relation to the existence of a chosen people' (NTRG, p. 204).

Abbott points to the following passages as instances of this idea in 'germ' form: 1 Cor. xv. 9; Gal. i. 13; Phil. iii. 6, where Paul speaks of himself as persecuting the 'Church of God'; and 1 Cor. xii. 28, where he uses the word 'church' with, apparently, more than local significance. In Col. i. 18, 24 the word has clearly a universal application (ICC, p. xix). Peake also fully agrees: 'We have no ground for the assumption that the conception of the Catholic Church must have been later than Paul, indeed it is quite in line with his thought and action' (CINT, p. 56).

Abbott also denies the relevance of the argument that this emphasis on the Universal Church presupposes a time when the sects were beginning to appear and the individual churches were being compelled to draw nearer to one another in self-defence. He points out that in Ephesians this Universal Church 'is not represented as made up of individual churches, but of individual men; nor is there any mention of external unity or common organisation' (ICC, p. xix).

(*b*) The insistent plea in Ephesians for unity within the Church need not be taken as evidence of a post-Pauline date. Peake quotes examples of the same insistence in Paul's other letters. He instances Paul's 'attempt to keep the churches together, expressed in the collection for the saints at Jerusalem', and 'his feeling that local idiosyncrasies must be curbed by the general practice of the Church (1 Cor. xiv. 33, 36)' (INT, p. 56).

Armitage Robinson, also, sees in this plea for unity a perfectly natural development from some of Paul's earlier utterances. He speaks of 'the doctrine of the unity of mankind in Christ, and of the purpose of God for the world through the Church' as 'that doctrine into which he had been advancing year by year under the discipline of his unique circumstances' (SPEE, p. 10). The appeal for unity is, therefore, nothing more than the earnest prayer that his dearest hope for the Church may be realized.

(*c*) '*Apostles and Prophets*'. In defence of these words it is pointed out that the combination is thoroughly Pauline, and the high authority ascribed to these offices not unexpected. For, in the catalogue of those who have been equipped with special gifts for the service of the Church, in 1 Cor. xii. 28, 'apostles and prophets' head the list.

The epithet 'holy', as applied to them, has been felt to be awkward, and some have tried to overcome the difficulty by suggesting that it is really a gloss which has crept into the text (so Jülicher), while others propose a modification of the customary punctuation, introducing a comma after ἁγίοις, so that ἀποστόλοις καὶ προφήταις are then read in apposition (Abbott, ICC, p. 82). Abbott, however, sees no problem in the word. He writes: 'So far as the difficulty is in the writer's application of the term ἁγίοις, it appears to be due very much to the importation into ἁγίοις of the modern notion of holiness' (ICC, p. xvi). 'But ἅγιος is used of anything which is set apart for a sacred purpose' (ICC, p. 82).

(*d*) *Christ and God.* Ephesians names Christ as the agent of certain activities which Paul is accustomed to ascribe to God. Hence it has been claimed that in Ephesians there is a higher Christology than in Paul's writings. But Peake shows that in Paul's other letters there is a similar failure to maintain a clear distinction between the functions ascribed to God and to Christ (INT, p. 56): 'Thus in Romans all things are through God, in 1 Cor. viii. 6 all are through Christ.'

Abbott also points out that the differences in Ephesians are not always in the direction of exalting Christ. In Col. iii. 13 it is Christ who forgives, while in Eph. iv. 32 it is God in Christ.

(*g*) *The Second Coming.* Ephesians, as we saw, includes no expectation of an early return of Christ such as we find in other Pauline letters. Instead there seems to be anticipated a long period of earthly history for the Church, 'a series of *αἰῶνες ἐπερχόμενοι* '.

Peake counters this argument against Pauline authorship by the unusual suggestion that 'the ages to come may very well be considered as following the Parousia rather than preceding it'. But the more usual explanation is to interpret this postponement of the expected date of the Parousia as evidence of a change in Paul's own thought. Hort observes: 'Nothing was more natural than that a change like this should come over Paul's mind, when year after year passed away, and still there was no sign of the Lord's coming, and when the spread of the faith through the Roman Empire, and the result which it was producing, would give force to all such ways of thinking as are represented by the image of the leaven leavening the lump' (PRE, p. 142).

T. F. Glasson in his study of *The Second Advent* similarly interprets the significance of this change in Ephesians. In describing the development of this doctrine in Paul's thought he writes: 'The final stage is found in Ephesians. . . . Ephesians is the climax and coping stone of his thought. . . . Its wealth of thought seems to demand a Paul for its author' (p. 207).

In the last chapter, under the heading of 'Doctrinal Arguments', several other particular items were named as casting doubt on Pauline authorship which will not be individually answered at this point. They are those which were enumerated as (*e*), (*f*), (*h*), (*j*), (*k*), and (*l*). It is enough to say that the defenders of Pauline authorship find them unconvincing, claiming that the supposed differences there indicated can all be adequately accounted for as the result of development within Paul's own mind, as he confronts new problems and grasps more clearly certain aspects of the unfolding Christian Faith.

In conclusion, we quote two passages from defenders of the Pauline authorship of Ephesians in which they summarize their verdicts after the various arguments have been fully weighed. The first is from E. F. Scott:

> 'Against all these arguments . . . we must set not only the supreme excellence of the epistle but the inimitably Pauline stamp on all its thinking. It may be confidently said that there is nothing in Ephesians which Paul might not have written. Some ideas are more highly developed in this than in the other epistles, but they are always Paul's ideas, and it is difficult to see how anyone but himself could have so drawn out their deeper implications. In like manner it may be asserted that while the style is peculiar, it has no characteristic which is not at least suggested in Paul's other writings' (MCC, p. 121).

The second is from McNeile, and occurs after his consideration of the doctrinal differences:

> 'These facts will appeal differently to different minds. To some they will seem to be real differences in points of view, which could have been reached only by a "sub-Pauline" writer approximating to the Johannine position, a Paulinist with a style of his own and the beginnings of a later vocabulary. But while any conclusion must be reached with hesitation, they hardly appear to the present writer strong enough to constitute a proof that the author was other than the author of Colossians, expressing, without controversy, his maturest thoughts on the greatest of all themes' (INT, p. 162).

IV

OPEN VERDICTS

THE two preceding chapters have given a summarized statement of the arguments which have been used for and against the Pauline authorship of Ephesians, and who can say with confidence that those on the one side clearly outweigh those on the other? The scales are poised very near the balance, and the open-minded student finds himself imagining that they are tilting now to one side, now to the other, till, in sheer self-defence against endless vicissitude, he takes himself firmly in hand, compels himself to give the benefit of the doubt to one of the two sides, and henceforward treats the question, so far as it concerns him personally, as settled. It is the discomfort of inconclusiveness which drives him to a clear-cut decision rather than the pressure of inescapable evidence.

It is clear that Peake has felt this disconcerting uncertainty before finally reaching his conclusion in favour of Pauline authorship. 'It is true', he admits, 'that a measure of doubt hangs over the epistle, but . . . the case for spuriousness has not been made out, and till that is done it is safer to accept its genuineness' (CINT, p. 57). We have already seen that E. F. Scott admits that 'the question of authenticity . . . must be regarded as an open one' (LNT, p. 180). Dodd and McNeile also, though giving their judgement hesitatingly in favour of Pauline authorship, seem to suggest that the verdict which really commends itself to them is that of *non liquet*. But that is an unsatisfactory conclusion to have to reach, in fact it is no conclusion at all, and indecision is a galling state of mind, so that on the evidence so far available it is probably the wisest course to accept the traditional point of view. It is only as some fresh evidence can be brought forward that we may hope to find the equal balance tilting definitely to one side, and so permitting a confident decision.

For those who wish to pursue the question farther, the position adopted by Jülicher is particularly interesting and significant. After giving the most careful and clear-minded consideration to all the relevant facts of the case, he found himself unable to reach a definite conclusion either way, and insisted on maintaining an open mind on the issue, because he felt that the evidence did not point clearly to any one verdict. He summarizes his position thus: 'Many separate points in the epistle would certainly become more intelligible on the assumption that it was written by a disciple of the Apostle—though even then he must have come into extraordinarily close contact with his master—but not so the epistle as a whole. Although then Ephesians may not belong to our unquestioned Pauline heritage, it would be equally impossible to deny the Apostle's authorship with any confidence' (INT, p. 147). Elsewhere he gives as his opinion that 'perhaps the question ought to be left open, as not yet ripe for settlement' (EB, vol. i, p. 865). It may well point the way to further useful inquiry if we can find what were the weak points in the arguments of one side or the other by reason of which that side failed to carry Jülicher's judgement. If further light can be thrown on these points, there may appear a way of advance to some definite conclusion.

Jülicher fully conceded the force of the argument against Pauline authorship. His judgement is: 'On the whole the hypothesis that a Pauline Christian, intimately familiar with the Pauline epistles, especially with Colossians, writing about A.D. 90, has in Ephesians sought to put in a plea for the true catholicism in the meaning of Paul, and in his name, is free from any serious difficulty' (EB, vol. i, p. 865). Elsewhere he also wrote: 'Of course the whole tone of the epistle would be quite comprehensible on the supposition that a Pauline Christian of about the year A.D. 90 was its author' (INT, p. 144).

In view of this favourable appreciation of the case against Pauline authorship it will be particularly illuminating to inquire what were the considerations which nevertheless withheld him from being fully persuaded to accept a position which he can describe not only as 'quite comprehensible' but also as 'free from any serious difficulty'. It is probable that these considerations represent the most crucial issues, and if some further light can be thrown on them, that may well be the means of providing some new evidence which will lead us from an open verdict to a more positive conclusion.

This is how Jülicher himself describes the 'restraining factors' which prevented him from definitely discarding the traditional ascription of authorship: 'It is impossible to see what purpose he' (a later writer in Paul's name) 'could have served, or why he made such a particularly thorough use of Colossians, when he himself did not lack independent ideas and was also acquainted with other Pauline epistles' (INT, pp. 146–7). Elsewhere he protests that no 'clear hypothesis of the circumstances under which a Paulus redivivus might have composed the epistle to the Ephesians has ever been provided' (quoted by Goodspeed in ME, p. 15).

B. W. Bacon similarly feels the weight of these 'restraining factors', and expresses his hesitation thus: 'But to find a motive sufficient to induce a teacher of such fervid genius to condescend to such slavish toil' (i.e. the imitation of Colossians), 'even if to that age less dishonest than to ours, when without any such false pretence his doctrine would be scarcely less acceptable and incomparably more unfettered, there is a task indeed.'

We may summarize therefore the 'restraining factors' which withheld Jülicher from abandoning Pauline authorship, in spite of his acknowledgement of the force and reasonableness of the arguments against it, as follows:

1. No set of circumstances has yet been suggested into which the production of Ephesians by a disciple of Paul after his death can convincingly be placed.
2. No sufficient motive has been proposed to account for the production of such a letter in the name of Paul, yet written by a disciple of Paul.
3. We have already noted the curious relationship of Ephesians to Colossians—its very close dependence on Colossians, and yet, in comparison, its neglect of other Pauline epistles; its strangely pliable use of phrases borrowed from Colossians, and the absence of considerable verbatim borrowings. This relationship is very hard to explain on the assumption that Ephesians is an imitative work based on Colossians by some non-Pauline author.
4. No adequate explanation is forthcoming of the recognition from earliest times of Ephesians as a Pauline epistle, and of its undisputed place in the Pauline Corpus, except on the assumption of Pauline authorship.

It is the special contribution which E. J. Goodspeed has made to this inquiry that he has put forward positive suggestions to meet each one of these four difficulties. He has reconstructed a situation, in the generation following the death of Paul, in which Ephesians might well have been written. He has suggested a motive for its production and a probable explanation of its peculiar relationship to Colossians, and also of its secure place in the Pauline Corpus from the earliest times.

Little mention has so far been made of the name of E. J. Goodspeed. This is not because his contribution to this discussion is less notable than that of others but because it belongs to very recent years, and it is much less well known in this country than it deserves to be. Moreover, his suggestions come as new factors into the condition of apparent stalemate which the inquiry seemed to have reached before he let new light in upon the subject. For these reasons a chapter will be given to recording in outline the positive suggestions which he has to make regarding the circumstances and motives which led to the writing and publication of Ephesians.

V

THE CONTRIBUTION OF E. J. GOODSPEED

WHATEVER E. J. Goodspeed has written is marked by a stimulating freshness of touch, and his contribution to the study of Ephesians is no exception. His own solution to the problem of this epistle, outlined in several of his books and worked out fully in *The Meaning of Ephesians*, is presented with persuasiveness and enthusiasm. Some of the details are perhaps little more than ingenious guesses, but several of its main features do correspond to certain facts in the situation. The theory as a whole is an invigorating challenge to thought and a pointer to new possibilities. A careful consideration of it, though it may not lead to an unqualified endorsement of its claims, will certainly bring to our notice features of the problem which deserve our closest attention.

Goodspeed does not elaborate the purely negative arguments against Pauline authorship. In his *Introduction to the New Testament* (pp. 231 ff.) he gives a useful summary of them, but he regards the case already presented by Moffatt as unanswerable, and does not claim to add anything substantial to it. His chief aim is rather to supply what earlier critics of Pauline authorship failed to provide—a positive suggestion of what may have been the situation in which just such a writing as Ephesians could have been produced at a post-Pauline date. This is a commendable aim, for it was the failure of earlier writers to envisage such a situation which left Jülicher still unwilling to abandon Pauline authorship, though acutely aware of the strength of the arguments against it.

Goodspeed's contribution therefore really begins where Moffatt's arguments end. His theory is primarily addressed to those who have been convinced by the arguments against Pauline authorship, or at any rate impressed by their strength. To those, however, who are not already persuaded by them, and feel no necessity of looking for some alternative to Pauline authorship, this theory has little to offer. Indeed it may appear little more than 'a tissue of improbabilities'. To those, however, who have felt keenly the difficulties of accepting Pauline authorship, or who are puzzled by the even balance between the arguments for and against, and find themselves inclining now to one side and now to the other, Goodspeed has suggestions to make which may throw light on an obscure situation and are at least worthy of careful scrutiny.

His approach to the problem is markedly original. It is true that others have glanced in the same direction and wondered if a solution might lie there. But it has only been a passing glance. Johannes Weiss, for instance, tentatively raised the question whether perhaps the author of Ephesians might not have been the same man who first collected the Pauline letters. But he did not pursue the inquiry. Jülicher, too, recognized that in many ways the most appropriate explanation of the purpose of Ephesians was that it was written to introduce a collection of Pauline letters (INT, pp. 127–8).

These stray and hesitating hints Goodspeed has vigorously followed up and, using them as his starting-point, has constructed a theory which claims to describe for what purpose and in what circumstances Ephesians came to be written. This theory, he believes, not only accords with all the known facts about the epistle, but also 'illumines' the epistle, both as a whole and particularly in those passages which hitherto have appeared most obscure.

His reconstruction of the circumstances which led to the composition of Ephesians, in the first generation after Paul, is briefly as follows.

Paul's letters had been written to individual churches to meet specific and pressing needs. As the years passed they were for the most part neglected, if not forgotten. The Gospel according to Matthew and Luke–Acts, though not written till twenty years after the death of Paul, show no trace of their influence. In particular, it is almost incredible that Acts should contain not even the least suggestion of Paul's letter-writing activities if his epistles were as well known in A.D. 80 as we often assume they were.

Some of these letters, however, were valued sufficiently by those who first received and read them to be placed in the strong-box of the church and given safe keeping, though they were not used, and perhaps even their very existence was overlooked. Indeed in the churches as a whole even Paul's name gradually dropped out of familiar use in the twenty-five years that followed his death. In some local churches, however, he was remembered, and perhaps, in one or two instances, his letter to the church was not only treasured but read and studied, if not by the church as a whole, at any rate by individual members of it who had special reason to reverence his memory. This was so in the case of the letter to the Colossians.

Closely connected with the church at Colossae was a man of deep spiritual insight who was also devotedly attached to Paul. He was acquainted with Paul's letter to the church, and had read and re-

read it until he knew it almost by heart. He was probably also familiar with the little personal letter which we know as 'Philemon', and which was originally carried to its destination by the same messenger who delivered 'Colossians'. His attachment to this relic of his master was, however, just a personal loyalty with no public significance, and apparently he was unaware of the existence of other letters to other churches.

Then came a momentous event. The Acts of the Apostles was published, probably about A.D. 85, and in its moving story Christian people could for the first time read a connected account of the missionary activities of Paul. He who had been to this new generation just an honoured name from the past now stood forth clearly as an exceedingly great man, in fact the pre-eminent hero in the rapid expansion of the Christian Church. Moreover, those who had known of him only through his association with one centre of Christian work now caught a glimpse of the extent and scope of his restless energy. What he had done in one area known to the reader he was now seen to have done in other areas widely separated from one another. There too was the record of many towns where he had done work of special importance. These biographical chapters awakened in the minds of the second generation of Christians a new sense of the magnitude of Paul's work for the Church, and a fresh and vivid interest in him. In one reader's mind it raised the hope that perhaps some of these other churches, as well as Colossae, had received letters from Paul, and perhaps also kept them. He would at any rate make inquiries. The list of churches worth approaching was there ready for him in Acts.

The inquiry was richly fruitful. Six different churches proved to have, in their box of treasures, letters from Paul: Rome, Corinth, Galatia, Colossae, Philippi, and Thessalonica.

In support of this suggestion that Acts exercised a determining influence on one who already knew Paul's letters to the Colossians and to Philemon by setting him in pursuit of other Pauline letters, Goodspeed points to the fact that, apart from these two, all the other letters which came to find a place in the Pauline Corpus could have been successfully traced from the information contained in Acts, whereas Acts would have given no clue to the discovery of these two.

At last, having completed his search, this eager collector has in his possession copies of these long-neglected Pauline letters. No man ever before has seen and read more than one or two of them at most. He is the first to read them all. He reads them over and over again, and his heart and mind thrill at what he finds. He recognizes that before him is a priceless treasure for all Christian people. It is true that the individual letters often dealt with past issues of no more than local importance, but Paul's treatment of them gave expression to permanent ethical and spiritual truths. Each individual letter contained only a few broken lights of the splendid gospel of the Lord Christ, yet when they all stood together they made a most satisfying whole. There was hardly a single aspect of the Faith which was not illumined by them, and hardly a single problem of his own day for which there was not some appropriate word of guidance. There was in them an astonishingly up-to-date relevance and remarkable unity and completeness. Of course they must be made available to other Christians. How could this best be done? Should he publish them just as they were, and leave them to make their own cumulative impression on the readers, without any added explanation or introduction? Would there be a danger in that case that certain readers might miss some of the permanent value in them because of the transient circumstances with which they dealt? Would it not be wise, and in the interests of the greater usefulness of this most precious collection, if he prepared an introduction for it, which would lift the essential Pauline message above merely topical issues of other days, and restate it as an expression of eternal truth, with an emphasis upon those aspects of it which had special relevance to the pressing needs and problems of this later generation? Yes, he must prepare such an introduction. And that is how the Epistle to the Ephesians came to be written. It was to stand first among the collected letters of Paul, so that strangers to Paul's teaching might in the very first epistle get a general grasp of the whole significance of his thought, before the actual letters were reached.

The last thing this collector and compiler wishes is to obtrude his own personality. He merely wants to present Paul most effectively and acceptably to his own contemporaries. So far as possible it must be Paul himself who speaks in this introduction, and in Paul's own words and phrases. But these words must be no longer tied to the contingent and the transitory. They must be understood in their universal significance. So the writer deliberately submits his own mind to the mind of Paul, that it may become the vehicle of Paul's own thought, finding expression, where possible, in the words which Paul has already used in the letters just collected. Because Colossians has been for so long familiar to him in its every phrase and thought, it dominates what he writes. But memorable phrases and doctrines from other letters also claim their place.

What he writes, he writes in Paul's name. It is his pious aim to let Paul speak through him, to let the words of Paul be regrouped and moulded in his mind into an adequate summary of Paul's thought. To have introduced his own name would have been a gross impertinence. What he constructs is deliberately derived from Paul's letters, and so quite properly it goes forth in Paul's name.

Such is the reconstructed situation out of which Goodspeed claims that Ephesians emerged.

He makes much of the argument that Ephesians is composed largely of materials derived, not only from Colossians, but from the other Pauline letters as well, and believes that he can fully demonstrate its truth. He emphasizes his claim in these words: 'Ephesians is a mosaic of Pauline materials; it is almost a Pauline anthology; it is altogether built up of Pauline materials; . . . it reads like a commentary on the Pauline epistles' (ME, p. 8). He uses two illuminating analogies to illustrate the relationship between Ephesians, the introductory epistle, and the main corpus of the Pauline epistles: 'It is like an overture to an opera, foreshadowing the successive melodies that are to follow. The materials of which it is composed are drawn from the letters' (ME, pp. 20–1). 'The enthusiastic summary of Pauline thought (in Ephesians) may be compared to the prologue of the Gospel of John in its relation to what followed it. The principal Pauline doctrines are rapidly sketched, with no supporting argument, but as though already established and needing only to be touched upon' (ME, p. 23).

It is not an integral part of this solution of the problem that the collector of the letters, who is also the author of Ephesians, should have a name, or be identified with any known figure in the early Church. But Goodspeed is willing to hazard a guess. In his earlier books it is named as only a remote possibility, but his later books put it forward with increasing confidence. The name he suggests is that of Onesimus, the slave on whose behalf Paul wrote to Philemon and Archippus. Certainly Onesimus would have reason to treasure the letters to Colossians and Philemon, since they played so important a part at the most critical period in his life. He would feel himself under a great debt of obligation to Paul, and would be glad to be able to repay some part of it. Moreover, the very presence of the letter to Philemon in the Pauline Corpus seems to require some special explanation. It is a curiously personal letter to be given so public a status. If, however, Onesimus was the collector and publisher of the Corpus, that special explanation is ready at hand. If it is asked whether a runaway slave would be capable of producing a piece of writing like Ephesians, the answer is twofold. Firstly, some slaves were kept by their masters primarily because of their literary ability. Their usefulness to their owners lay entirely in this sphere. Secondly, there is some probability that Onesimus was at any rate capable enough to become bishop of Ephesus, for it was an Ephesian bishop of that name to whom Ignatius addressed a letter and to whom he referred in terms of great respect. Provided the runaway slave was a young man of about twenty and the bishop an old man of seventy, there is nothing inherently impossible in the identification of the two. Goodspeed does not claim that this identification is more than a guess. He writes: 'This is all in the realm of conjecture, it is true, but it has no small degree of probability' (CP, p. 58).

Such, in brief, is Goodspeed's theory, and full credit must be given to him for an original and fascinating contribution to the solution of our problem. He offers a possible answer to the doubts which made Jülicher, for instance, hesitate to accept a non-Pauline origin for the epistle. It will be remembered that it was his inability to formulate adequate answers to four pertinent questions which kept him from explicitly abandoning Pauline authorship (see pp. 41–3). Goodspeed's theory suggests answers to these questions:

1. It reconstructs a situation in which such an epistle as Ephesians may have been written in the post-Pauline era.
2. It suggests a sufficient motive for its composition.
3. It accounts for its curious relationship with Colossians.
4. It explains why the epistle, though not by Paul, should nevertheless, from earliest times, have had its place in the Pauline Corpus.

Moreover, it meets the complaint of Bacon and others that the use of Paul's name by a later writer is something less than honest, by proposing a legitimate reason for its use, and absolving us from any need to brand the writer as an unscrupulous forger.

Among American scholars this theory appears to have had a good reception. John Knox not only accepts it in all its main features but provides corroborating evidence for it in his studies of Philemon and Marcion. He differs from Goodspeed only in denying the suggestion that Acts led to the formation of the Pauline Corpus. This is because he prefers to date Acts in the middle of the second century. F. W. Beare, in his recent commentary on 1 Peter, also approves the theory and speaks of its general acceptance in America. He writes: 'Most scholars now regard Ephesians as a work of the second Christian generation, and the studies of Prof. E. J. Goodspeed would appear to have established this conclusion beyond serious dispute.'

English scholars have been much more cautious. Very few have commented upon it, either favourably or unfavourably. No one has yet taken in hand to submit it to a searching criticism. This may be due, in part at any rate, to the fact that the majority of them have decided in favour of Pauline authorship, and so the theory appears as a fanciful hypothesis created to meet a purely imaginary need which in fact does not exist. There are, however, one or two who have broken the silence and given guarded approval to its main features. A. J. Grieve, for instance, after describing it in outline, adds: 'Some such solution is far from improbable' (SPC, p. 35). Similarly, S. Cook writes of Ephesians: 'It reads as a theological tract, perhaps a circular letter, as an introduction to Paul's letters, or probably as a later condensation of his teaching' (IB, p. 75). W. L. Knox is still more explicit in his approval: 'The best explanation (of Ephesians) seems to be that it is intended as an introduction to the genuine Pauline letters; it is possible that the writer is their first collector.' He adds in a footnote: 'The solution put forward above is that of Goodspeed. . . . His general view of the author's intention and the occasion of the writing appears to offer a convincing solution both of the authorship of the epistle and of its great value and importance as a statement of Paulinism' (PCG, p. 184).

We may assume therefore that the theory need not be dismissed out of hand. But though it may be a possible solution to the puzzling problems which beset this epistle, that does not mean that it can, without further careful investigation, be accepted as even a probable one, still less a proved one. We must inquire, for instance: Is the proposed solution itself free from serious objections, even apart from its rejection of Pauline authorship? If it meets some difficulties, does it not also create others? Even if we do not take too seriously the highly speculative nature of one or two of its less essential features, is it not true that some of its main assumptions are built on very fragile foundations? Only when these questions have been satisfactorily answered can the theory be classed as probable rather than merely possible.

There are some points in this suggested solution which, while interesting and thought-provoking, are not strictly integral to the theory. They could be dispensed with and yet its main framework remain unaffected. For instance, the association of the first collection of the Pauline Corpus with the publication of Acts is not an indispensable item, nor is the guess that it was Onesimus who was both the collector of the letters and the composer of Ephesians. Indeed it is questionable whether both of these items together could be claimed as true. For if Onesimus was the collector, his friendship with Paul would almost certainly have provided him with some knowledge of the wide scope of Paul's associations with the other Christian churches throughout the Roman Empire. It is doubtful whether he would have needed the information that Acts provides in order to intitiate an inquiry into the possible existence of Pauline letters other than those already known to him.

On the other hand, it might be urged that the publication of Acts nevertheless proved the occasion of the collection of the Pauline letters, not so much, as Goodspeed argues, by providing new information to a would-be collector, but rather by stirring up such a widespread ferment of interest in Paul that a great demand for further knowledge of him arose in the Church, and so provided an ideal moment for assembling and publishing those letters of his which still survived, whereas previously there had been no demand for Pauline relics.

Goodspeed himself attaches very great importance to that part of the theory which attributes the appearance of Paul's letters to a single act of publication, after a whole generation of neglect, during which the individual letters had disappeared from the consciousness of the Church. Indeed he regards this sudden emergence of the complete Corpus as a crucial event, perhaps the most crucial event in the formation of the New Testament. He calls it 'the roof-tree of the New Testament Literature', 'the watershed, the great divide, of the New Testament continent' (NC, p. 72). He himself therefore would not lightly discard it. He defends it vigorously against the more cautious and more widely accepted theory of Harnack, who assumed, though he did not claim to prove, that each letter in the first place became increasingly known in the area to which it had been sent; then to these individual letters others were added from neighbouring areas, until many small groups, varying in content, existed in different centres; then at last in some church, no longer identifiable, the whole collection, as we know it today, reached completion, and in time came to be shared and accepted by all other churches. Goodspeed's theory can, however, be modified so as not to be wholly inconsistent with Harnack's assumption of a gradual development of the Pauline Corpus. Such modification would require us to assume that though Ephesians was written in the presence of the complete Corpus, its purpose was not to introduce it as an entirely new thing for the benefit of the whole Church, but rather to commend it in its completed form to Christian communities who had hitherto known only Colossians and Philemon. That may mean that Ephesians was added as an introduction, when the other letters at last reached Asia Minor and were completed by the addition of the two already known there, and its primary aim was to serve the need of the Christians in the neighbourhood of Ephesus.

Goodspeed's theory of the origin of the Corpus need not therefore be regarded as an indispensable item in his theory of the origin of Ephesians. We should not, however, assume too quickly that it is not the true account. He himself has presented a strong case in support of it. The mere fact that it is novel and contrary to previous assumptions does not entitle us to reject it until adequate grounds can be given for such a course.

Before, however, it could be accepted, several questions would require an answer: Is it true that Paul's letters were so generally neglected, in the generation after Paul's death, as this theory presupposes? If so, did they all return to the knowledge of the Church together and at the same time, in such a way as to suggest an act of publication? Or did they just 'trickle' into circulation, one by one, as most writers on the subject have assumed? If there was one act of publication, then there must have been one original order in which the epistles appeared. Can we find traces of that original order? Is there any evidence that Ephesians ever stood at its head, as we should expect, if its original purpose was to serve as an introduction to the whole Corpus?

We have seen that certain features of the theory may be regarded as non-essential. They may be discarded without destroying the main structure. What then are the indispensable items in it, the disproving of any one of which would invalidate the whole? They appear to be three, and it may well prove that in these three lie the keys of the situation. At any rate, it is probable that through the investigation of them there lies the way of further progress towards a finally satisfying solution. These three items are:

1. That the relationship of Ephesians and Colossians is best explained on the assumption that Ephesians is the work of one, other than Paul, who had for some reason come to know Colossians so intimately as almost to know it by heart.
2. That the indisputable Pauline elements in Ephesians are in fact direct borrowings from the genuine epistles by a later

writer, who is aiming at producing a generalized summary of Pauline teaching such as might have been issued as an introduction to the collected letters.

3. That these explanations and the assumption that Ephesians was written in these circumstances about A.D. 90 'illumine' the whole epistle and particularly throw light on those points which, on the basis of Pauline authorship, have been most perplexing.

If any one of these items can be disproved, the whole structure falls in ruins. But however this particular theory is affected, it is probable that further light will be thrown on the problem as a whole by the elucidation of these three issues. So we proceed to ask:

(*a*) What is the precise relationship of Ephesians to Colossians? What can we learn of the author of Ephesians from this relationship?

(*b*) What is the actual extent and character of the Pauline elements in Ephesians? Are they best explained as due to identity of authorship with the other epistles? Or are they the result of deliberate borrowing from the genuine epistles by a later imitator of Paul?

(*c*) Do the ascertainable facts support, or even allow, a date for the epistle as late as A.D. 90? And if so, does the acceptance of such a date in fact 'illumine' the whole epistle, and especially the more obscure points in it?

PART II

THE RELATIONSHIP OF EPHESIANS AND COLOSSIANS

VI. THE INTERDEPENDENCE OF EPHESIANS AND COLOSSIANS

Among the Pauline epistles, no other two have such close resemblance to each other as Colossians and Ephesians. There is unmistakably a large measure of interdependence between them. This interdependence must now be examined in order to determine whether it yields any clue to the authorship of Ephesians; whether the relationship proves (or suggests) that the same author wrote both epistles, or whether it may be claimed as evidence that the author of Ephesians was some other than the author of Colossians.

It is not unanimously agreed that Paul should be regarded as the author of Colossians. Some notable scholars have declined to recognize it as a genuine Pauline writing, but the tendency in recent years has been towards its acceptance. In 1909 A. S. Peake wrote: 'We may feel some confidence that the authenticity of Colossians will come to be accepted in the near future by general consent' (CINT, p. 52). This confidence has not been misplaced, and the years since 1909 have seen a growing consensus of opinion towards the recognition of Colossians as a genuine Pauline letter. The difficulties have not been entirely removed. There are notable differences, both in thought and vocabulary, between Colossians and the other eight Pauline epistles, and the crucial question to be decided was whether these could be regarded as possible developments in the thought and expression of the same man over a period of years and in face of novel problems or whether they indicated that a different mind was at work. There seems to be no insuperable difficulty in regarding these differences as the result of the development and adaptation within the mind of Paul, but the deciding factor for many scholars has been the close relationship that appears to exist between Colossians and Philemon. Of Philemon, C. H. Dodd writes that it 'carries its authentication on its face', and 'to reject it is a mere eccentricity of criticism' (*Ab. Com.*, p. 1223). He continues: 'But its acceptance has a bearing on the more difficult question of the authenticity of Colossians.' It is the strong link that binds Colossians to Philemon, coupled with the undoubted authenticity of Philemon, which has proved the deciding factor in the general acceptance of Colossians as Pauline (cf. J. Knox, 'Philemon and the Authenticity of Colossians', *Jour. of Religion*, xviii, pp. 144 ff., 1938).

In this consideration of the relationship between Colossians and Ephesians it will therefore be assumed that Paul was the author of Colossians. If, however, any further evidence were to be produced in favour of the non-Pauline origin of Colossians, which led to the recognition of Colossians as a non-Pauline writing, this would also involve the abandonment of the Pauline authorship of Ephesians, which in any case is open to doubt, even when Colossians is ascribed to Paul. It would lose the chief of its somewhat precarious supports if Colossians could not confidently be accepted as Paul's.

This consequence would follow because it is usually believed that Ephesians reveals dependence on Colossians. In the mutual interdependence, of which we have already spoken, priority has been almost universally accorded to Colossians, so that such borrowing as has taken place is attributed to Ephesians. We shall assume here that this is a true assessment of the relationship, and in this chapter shall take it for granted. Since, however, this explanation has been questioned, it will be necessary at a later stage in the argument to examine the evidence. We believe, however, that the evidence confirms the assumption that Colossians should be regarded as the earlier writing, and that the close similarities between it and Ephesians are to be explained as the result of the author of Ephesians availing himself of what had already been written in Colossians.

The Extent of the Interdependence

The large measure of interdependence between these two epistles has been widely recognized. Some writers have tried to indicate for the benefit of readers the extent of this interdependence. Abbott (ICC, p. xxiii) quotes from De Wette a list of fifty-four verses in Ephesians side by side with the corresponding verses from Colossians, on which they seem to be dependent. Moffatt (ILNT, pp. 375–81) gives an even fuller statement, and in parallel columns prints in full the verses both in Ephesians and in Colossians which have close correspondence to one another. Both these lists, however, though considerable, fail to represent adequately the extent of the interdependence, and need to be supplemented.

In Appendix I, at the end of this book (pp. 279 ff.), there is provided a full text of Ephesians, with parallel passages in Colossians recorded in full opposite the verses where there appears to be interdependence. Where the correspondence is so close as to represent a verbatim similarity the corresponding words are undermarked with a thick line (————); where the correspondence is less exact, but still recognizable, the words are undermarked with a less thick line (————). Other words, where the similarity is less distinct, are marked by a thick dotted line (------------). For calculation purposes, however, this third group is ignored, and only those marked with *continuous* lines are counted.

The total number of words in Ephesians is 2,411. Of this total, 387 are undermarked with thick lines, and a further 251 with less thick lines. Together they make up 26·5 per cent. of the whole, so it can be said that more than a quarter of the words in Ephesians are borrowed from Colossians. This is a very remarkable degree of interdependence.

Colossians is a shorter epistle, and so the result of these calculations, when based on Colossians, is even more impressive. The total number of words in this epistle is 1,570. Of this total, 408 appear undermarked with thick lines and 126 with less thick lines. Together the words marked make up 34 per cent. of the whole, so that more than a third of the words in Colossians reappear in Ephesians.

No other two epistles of Paul even approach so great a measure of similarity to one another.

The Character of the Interdependence

The character of this interdependence between Ephesians and Colossians is unusual. The similarities are far too close and numerous to be explained merely by pleading that both epistles are by the same author, who is quite at liberty to express similar thoughts in similar phrases on different occasions. There is no similar degree of correspondence between any other two of Paul's letters. There must have been a deliberate intention, either by Paul himself or by some other writer, to reproduce much of what had already been written in Colossians. On the other hand, the borrowing is exceedingly free. There is nothing rigid or mechanical about it. It is not at all the kind of borrowing that can be associated with a writer who has a document open in front of him as he writes and laboriously incorporates sections from it into his own work. It suggests rather that the author of Ephesians was thoroughly familiar with Colossians, so that his mind could move easily along the lines of developing argument in that epistle, and also could readily associate together similar phrases from different parts of the epistle. It is doubtful if the author of Ephesians knew Colossians completely by heart; if he had, the number and extent of exact similarities would have been greater; but he must have known it with a degree of intimacy only a little less than that.

It is surprising, in view of the large measure of interdependence between the two epistles, to find an almost complete absence of any long passage appearing in exactly the same form in each epistle. With so high a rate of correspondence one would expect whole sentences to be reproduced in precise imitation. But this is not so.

With one notable exception, the greatest number of consecutive words in Ephesians which correspond exactly with consecutive words in Colossians, is no more than seven, and even this limited extent of correspondence does not occur in more than three instances. Of these, the first (Eph. i. 1–2 = Col. i. 1–2) is of little significance because it is the opening greeting of the epistle, and is similar not only to the opening greeting in Colossians but also to that in other Pauline epistles. The other two instances are found in Eph. iii. 2 (= Col. i. 25) and Eph. iii. 9 (= Col. i. 26). An exact correspondence of five consecutive words is also found in Eph. i. 7 (= Col. i. 14) and Eph. iv. 16 (= Col. ii. 19).

These five parallels represent the largest measure of exact correspondence between the two epistles. In all other cases modifications are introduced which render the correspondence something less than exact. Words are inserted or omitted, or else varied in their order. Though the percentage of interdependence, therefore, is so high, and though similarities in some cases persist over a sequence of several verses, the almost entire lack of identical repetition suggests that these similarities are not of the kind we should anticipate if they were the result of one author copying another document open in front of him.

It should be noted that the underlining used in pp. 59–66 is different from the method adopted in Appendix I, to which reference is made on p. 57. In the Appendix the lines indicate different degrees of correspondence between words in separate columns. In pp. 59–66 they are used merely to enable the eye to pick out easily certain peculiarities which are referred to in the text.

In view of this complete absence of sustained and exact correspondences between the two epistles, the one exception, to which reference has already been made, is all the more surprising and remarkable, and is therefore quoted in full:

Eph. vi. 21–2	Col. iv. 7–8
ἵνα δὲ εἰδῆτε καὶ ὑμεῖς τὰ κατ' ἐμέ, τί πράσσω, πάντα γνωρίσει ὑμῖν Τύχικος ὁ ἀγαπητὸς ἀδελφὸς καὶ πιστὸς διάκονος ἐν κυρίῳ, ὃν ἔπεμψα πρὸς ὑμᾶς εἰς αὐτὸ τοῦτο, ἵνα γνῶτε τὰ περὶ ἡμῶν καὶ παρακαλέσῃ τὰς καρδίας ὑμῶν.	τὰ κατ' ἐμὲ πάντα γνωρίσει ὑμῖν Τύχικος ὁ ἀγαπητὸς ἀδελφὸς καὶ πιστὸς διάκονος καὶ σύνδουλος ἐν κυρίῳ, ὃν ἔπεμψα πρὸς ὑμᾶς εἰς αὐτὸ τοῦτο, ἵνα γνῶτε τὰ περὶ ἡμῶν καὶ παρακαλέσῃ τὰς καρδίας ὑμῶν.

In these passages, twenty-nine consecutive words from Colossians are repeated exactly in Ephesians, in the same order and without any addition. The only difference is that the two words *καὶ σύνδουλος* are omitted. This prolonged identity of expression in a passage which one would not naturally regard as important is a matter for inquiry. It almost suggests that the writer at this point, at any rate, referred to his copy, to make sure that he reproduced it exactly; or else that there was good reason for his knowing it so well that he could reproduce not only its substance but its very phraseology. This passage must be given further consideration at a later stage in the discussions.

Apart from this outstanding exception, the correspondence between the epistles is always something less than verbatim reproduction. No other single passage suggests deliberate copying from a document. If therefore copying is not the explanation of the remarkable similarities, we must suggest some other. It will assist us in our search for such an explanation if we can determine more precisely the nature of this interdependence, and the explanation in turn, once it is found, will have its bearing on the question of authorship.

We begin, therefore, by quoting instances of this inexact correspondence between the two epistles and indicating the kind of variations which are introduced.

(*a*) Eph. i. 4	Col. i. 22
ἡμᾶς ἁγίους καὶ ἀμώμους κατενώπιον αὐτοῦ.	ὑμᾶς ἁγίους καὶ ἀμώμους καὶ ἀνεγκλήτους κατενώπιον αὐτοῦ.

Here the words *καὶ ἀνεγκλήτους* occur in Colossians, but are omitted from the corresponding phrase in Ephesians.

(*b*) Eph. i. 7	Col. i. 14
ἐν ᾧ ἔχομεν τὴν ἀπολύτρωσιν διὰ τοῦ αἵματος αὐτοῦ, τὴν ἄφεσιν τῶν παραπτωμάτων.	ἐν ᾧ ἔχομεν τὴν ἀπολύτρωσιν, τὴν ἄφεσιν τῶν ἁμαρτιῶν.

Here Ephesians introduces an extra phrase, διὰ τοῦ αἵματος αὐτοῦ, apparently from Col. i. 20, and changes the ἁμαρτίων of Colossians into the equivalent but different word παραπτωμάτων.

(*c*) Eph. ii. 5	Col. ii. 13
καὶ ὄντας ἡμᾶς νεκροὺς τοῖς παραπτώμασιν συνεζωοποίησεν τῷ Χριστῷ.	καὶ ὑμᾶς νεκροὺς ὄντας τοῖς παραπτώμασιν καὶ τῇ ἀκροβυστίᾳ τῆς σαρκὸς ὑμῶν, συνεζωοποίησεν ὑμᾶς σὺν αὐτῷ.

Here the phrase in Colossians καὶ τῇ ἀκροβυστίᾳ τῆς σαρκὸς ὑμῶν is omitted from the corresponding parallel in Ephesians. The order of the first four words is varied, and in Ephesians a simple dative follows συνεζωοποίησεν, whereas Colossians has σύν with the dative.

(*d*) Eph. iii. 2	Col. i. 25
τὴν οἰκονομίαν τῆς χάριτος τοῦ θεοῦ τῆς δοθείσης μοι εἰς ὑμᾶς.	τὴν οἰκονομίαν τοῦ θεοῦ τὴν δοθεῖσάν μοι εἰς ὑμᾶς.

Here Ephesians introduces the words τῆς χάριτος into the phrase from Colossians, and attaches the descriptive participle δοθείσης to them instead of to οἰκονομίαν.

(*e*) Eph. iv. 2	Col. iii. 12
ταπεινοφροσύνης καὶ πραΰτητος μετὰ μακροθυμίας, ἀνεχόμενοι ἀλλήλων.	ταπεινοφροσύνην, πραΰτητα, μακροθυμίαν, ἀνεχόμενοι ἀλλήλων.

Here the difference lies in the phrasing. Exactly the same meaning is expressed in each case, and the same words are used, but Ephesians introduces καὶ and μετὰ with the genitive to vary the three accusatives of Colossians.

(*f*) Eph. iv. 16	Col. ii. 19
ἡ κεφαλή, Χριστός, ἐξ οὗ πᾶν τὸ σῶμα συναρμολογούμενον καὶ συνβιβαζόμενον διὰ πάσης ἁφῆς τῆς ἐπιχορηγίας.	τὴν κεφαλήν, ἐξ οὗ πᾶν τὸ σῶμα διὰ τῶν ἁφῶν καὶ συνδέσμων ἐπιχορηγούμενον καὶ συνβιβαζόμενον.

In these two passages the meaning is the same, and the same words are largely used, but it is the general sense and not the exact wording which is reproduced. In Ephesians the explanatory *Χριστός* is added, and *συναρμολογούμενον* is introduced, in place of *ἐπιχορηγούμενον*. This omitted word, however, seems to linger in the writer's mind in association with this passage from Colossians, and so he introduces it later, but as a noun, *ἐπιχορηγία*. The plural *ἁφῶν* is replaced by the singular *ἁφῆς*, but with no change of meaning, and *συνδέσμων* is omitted (though the word appears in another connexion at Eph. iv. 3).

(*g*) Eph. iv. 22–4	Col. iii. 8–10
ἀποθέσθαι ὑμᾶς κατὰ τὴν προτέραν ἀναστροφὴν τὸν παλαιὸν ἄνθρωπον τὸν φθειρόμενον κατὰ τὰς ἐπιθυμίας τῆς ἀπάτης, ἀνανεοῦσθαι δὲ τῷ πνεύματι τοῦ νοὸς ὑμῶν καὶ ἐνδύσασθαι τὸν καινὸν ἄνθρωπον τὸν κατὰ θεὸν κτισθέντα.	ἀπόθεσθε καὶ ὑμεῖς τὰ πάντα . . . ἀπεκδυσάμενοι τὸν παλαιὸν ἄνθρωπον σὺν ταῖς πράξεσιν αὐτοῦ, καὶ ἐνδυσάμενοι τὸν νέον τὸν ἀνακαινούμενον εἰς ἐπίγνωσιν κατ' εἰκόνα τοῦ κτίσαντος αὐτόν . . .

These two passages reveal close similarity, and yet the similarity is far from being a rigid imitation. The writer of Ephesians has in mind the remembered contrast between 'putting off the old man' and 'putting on the new man', and also a recollection of the new man as being restored to God's original intention in the creation. Ephesians represents this last thought in a different phrasing from Colossians, but there can be no doubt that there is interdependence between the two. Here, then, we have an instance of a characteristic trait of the relationship between these two epistles, a very close interdependence, and yet the freest development and rearrangement of the borrowed ideas.

(*h*) Eph. iv. 32	Col. iii. 12
γίνεσθε δὲ εἰς ἀλλήλους χρηστοί, εὔσπλαγχνοι, χαριζόμενοι ἑαυτοῖς καθὼς καὶ ὁ θεὸς ἐν Χριστῷ ἐχαρίσατο ὑμῖν.	ἐνδύσασθε οὖν . . . σπλάγχνα οἰκτιρμοῦ, χρηστότητα, ταπεινοφροσύνην, πραΰτητα, μακροθυμίαν, ἀνεχόμενοι ἀλλήλων καὶ χαριζόμενοι ἑαυτοῖς καθὼς καὶ ὁ κύριος ἐχαρίσατο ὑμῖν οὕτως καὶ ὑμεῖς.

The closing phrases in these passages are clearly interdependent. The subject of *ἐχαρίσατο* is, however, phrased differently, and the change from *ὁ κύριος* to *ὁ θεὸς ἐν Χριστῷ* may be deliberate and significant; or it may be that the writer of Ephesians had a general, but not exact, recollection of the sentence from Colossians, and believed himself to be reproducing the substance of it. There is a further similarity between *χρηστοί, εὔσπλαγχνοι* in Ephesians and *σπλάγχνα οἰκτιρμοῦ, χρηστότητα* in Colossians. The association of these two ideas, in Ephesians expressed by adjectives and in Colossians by nouns, is not in itself evidence of dependence, but the fact that in each case the association is linked with the same closing phrase puts the matter beyond doubt. This reproducing of the meaning by using the corresponding adjectives for nouns, and vice versa, is a further characteristic of the relationship between these two epistles.

(*i*) Eph. v. 19–20	Col. iii. 16–17
λαλοῦντες ἑαυτοῖς ψαλμοῖς καὶ ὕμνοις καὶ ᾠδαῖς πνευματικαῖς, ᾄδοντες καὶ ψάλλοντες τῇ καρδίᾳ ὑμῶν τῷ κυρίῳ, εὐχαριστοῦντες πάντοτε ὑπὲρ πάντων ἐν ὀνόματι τοῦ κυρίου ἡμῶν Ἰησοῦ Χριστοῦ τῷ θεῷ καὶ πατρί.	διδάσκοντες καὶ νουθετοῦντες ἑαυτούς, ψαλμοῖς, ὕμνοις, ᾠδαῖς πνευματικαῖς ἐν τῇ χάριτι ᾄδοντες ἐν ταῖς καρδίαις ὑμῶν τῷ θεῷ καὶ πᾶν ὅτι ἐὰν ποιῆτε ἐν λόγῳ ἢ ἐν ἔργῳ, πάντα ἐν ὀνόματι κυρίου Ἰησοῦ, εὐχαριστοῦντες τῷ θεῷ πατρὶ δι' αὐτοῦ.

These two closely parallel passages exhibit the features which we have already seen to mark the use that Ephesians makes of Colossians: for example, omission (as of *ἐν τῇ χάριτι*), addition (as of *καὶ ψάλλοντες*), and modification (singular *τῇ καρδίᾳ* for *ἐν ταῖς καρδίαις*). It should be noted too that the *τῷ θεῷ* of Colossians is replaced in Ephesians by *τῷ κυρίῳ*.

Specially worthy of note is one further very remarkable peculiarity. In Colossians the phrase *ἐν ὀνόματι κυρίου Ἰησοῦ* is linked with 'do': 'Whatsoever ye do, do all in the name of the Lord Jesus.' In Ephesians the phrase is repeated, but in grammar and sense is linked with *εὐχαριστοῦντες*. Now in Colossians the word *εὐχαριστοῦντες* is adjacent to this phrase, but it is a relationship merely of position, without any link in sense or grammar. It is perhaps a very significant fact for our purpose that a relationship of mere contiguity in Colossians should thus be transformed in Ephesians into a relationship of sense.

These nine passages have been cited and examined because they represent the passages in Ephesians which are most closely parallel to passages from Colossians, and illustrate the manner in which Ephesians uses and adapts Colossians. In spite of very close resemblances, exact identity of word-sequences do not occur (apart from the passage about Tychicus). The most protracted verbatim correspondence does not exceed seven words, and on only three occasions exceeds five. Very often there is exceedingly close similarity, but it is always something less than the repetition of identical words: a word or a phrase is omitted; or the order of the words is changed; or words and phrases are replaced by something different, though often roughly equivalent. All this happens in passages where it would have been quite appropriate to repeat the exact words of Colossians.

All this suggests that the dependence of Ephesians on Colossians is not that which one would associate with the work of an imitator, hard at work with a copy of Colossians open in front of him. His acquaintance with Colossians is not dependent on what he reads in a document, but it is a familiarity which has become part of his own mental equipment.

This impression is confirmed by consideration of another group of passages in Ephesians to which we now turn our attention.

The characteristic of this further group of passages from Ephesians is not merely that they have close resemblances to passages in Colossians, but that in a single passage in Ephesians we find, combined, ideas and words borrowed from widely separated parts of Colossians. Instances of these can be seen in the lists in Appendix I, but the passages where they occur and the frequency of their occurrence are more readily detected from Appendix III.

In Appendix III there is found a list of the verses in Ephesians which have parallels in Colossians. The list has been so arranged as to indicate clearly where sequences of verses in Ephesians have a general relationship of similarity with sequences of verses in Colossians. It will be seen that there is a rough correspondence between the following:

(*a*)	Eph. i. 1–23	and	Col. i. 1–27
(*b*)	Eph. i. 20–ii. 22	,,	Col. ii. 7–14*
(*c*)	Eph. ii. 12–16	,,	Col. i. 20–2
(*d*)	Eph. iii. 1–21	,,	Col. i. 23–9
(*e*)	Eph. iv. 2–4	,,	Col. iii. 12–15
(*f*)	Eph. iv. 22–v. 6	,,	Col. iii. 5–12*
(*g*)	Eph. v. 19–vi. 9	,,	Col. iii. 16–iv. 1
(*h*)	Eph. vi. 18–22	,,	Col. iv. 2–8

The two passages from Colossians marked * break the orderly sequence of progression. Also, in Ephesians, (*a*) and (*b*) overlap. In the four verses which are included in both these sections (Eph. i. 20–3), echoes from Col. ii. 7–14 begin to be heard, intermingled with words and phrases from Col. i. Also (*c*) is really a short verse-sequence within the larger sequence of (*b*), but it merits separation because its dependence is largely on Col. i. 20–2 rather than on Col. ii. 7–14.

Actually, however, this neatly listed catalogue of corresponding sections in the two epistles may be very misleading unless the fuller lists in Appendix III are carefully noted. For there it will be seen that there are many verses reproduced in Ephesians from Colossians which do not fit into these sequences at all, and that phrases from widely separated passages in Colossians are brought together into a single verse in Ephesians. This indeed is one of the most important, and significant, characteristics of the interdependence. Moreover, even with the corresponding sequences, the order in which the borrowings from Colossians appear in Ephesians has very little similarity to their order in Colossians. For instance, the order in which the verses in Col. i are reflected in Eph. i is as follows: 1, 2, 22, 14, 20, 9, 27, 16, 20, 12, 5, 3, 4, 9, 10, 12, 27, 16, 18, 19, 24.

These further considerations also confirm the impression that the dependence between these two epistles is not that attributable to the work of a copyist working from a written original in front of him. Rather it suggests the work of one whose mind was saturated with the contents of Colossians as he composes Ephesians, so that echoes from different parts of Colossians become associated in his mind if an idea or a word serve as a link between them.

It will be well to examine one or two instances of this phenomenon, which we will call 'conflation', so that we may be the better equipped to sense the kind of interdependence which exists between these two epistles.

(*a*) Eph. i. 7	Col. i. 14
ἐν ᾧ ἔχομεν τὴν ἀπολύτρωσιν διὰ τοῦ αἵματος αὐτοῦ, τὴν ἄφεσιν τῶν παραπτωμάτων.	ἐν ᾧ ἔχομεν τὴν ἀπολύτρωσιν τὴν ἄφεσιν τῶν ἁμαρτιῶν.
	Col. i. 20
	εἰρηνοποιήσας διὰ τοῦ αἵματος τοῦ σταυροῦ αὐτοῦ.

In Eph. i. 7 it is Col. i. 14 which is being followed, but the word ἀπολύτρωσιν has enough similarity in meaning to εἰρηνοποιήσας in Col. i. 20 to call to the writer's mind the phrase that follows it, and so διὰ τοῦ αἵματος αὐτοῦ is introduced.

(*b*) Eph. i. 15–16	Col. i. 9
διὰ τοῦτο κἀγὼ ἀκούσας τὴν καθ' ὑμᾶς πίστιν ἐν τῷ κυρίῳ Ἰησοῦ καὶ τὴν ἀγάπην τὴν εἰς πάντας τοὺς ἁγίους, οὐ παύομαι εὐχαριστῶν ὑπὲρ ὑμῶν μνείαν ποιούμενος ἐπὶ τῶν προσευχῶν μου.	διὰ τοῦτο καὶ ἡμεῖς, ἀφ' ἧς ἡμέρας ἠκούσαμεν, οὐ παυόμεθα ὑπὲρ ὑμῶν προσευχόμενοι.
	Col. i. 4
	ἀκούσαντες τὴν πίστιν ὑμῶν ἐν Χριστῷ Ἰησοῦ καὶ τὴν ἀγάπην ἣν ἔχετε εἰς πάντας τοὺς ἁγίους.

Here a word-sequence from Col. i. 4 is incorporated into what is substantially a free quotation of Col. i. 9. It seems likely that the word ἀκούω in Col. i. 9 made a mental link, in the mind of the writer of Ephesians, with ἀκούσαντες in Col. i. 4, and led to the incorporation of the phrases that follow it.

(*c*) Eph. ii. 1–5	Col. ii. 13
καὶ ὑμᾶς ὄντας νεκροὺς τοῖς παραπτώμασιν καὶ ἁμαρτίαις ὑμῶν, ἐν αἷς ποτε περιεπατήσατε κατὰ τὸν αἰῶνα τοῦ κόσμου τούτου κατὰ τὸν ἄρχοντα τῆς ἐξουσίας τοῦ ἀέρος, τοῦ πνεύματος τοῦ νῦν ἐνεργοῦντος ἐν τοῖς υἱοῖς τῆς ἀπειθείας· ἐν οἷς καὶ ἡμεῖς πάντες	καὶ ὑμᾶς νεκροὺς ὄντας τοῖς παραπτώμασιν καὶ τῇ ἀκροβυστίᾳ τῆς σαρκὸς ὑμῶν, συνεζωοποίησεν ὑμᾶς σὺν αὐτῷ.

Eph. ii. 1–5 (*cont.*)	Col. iii. 6
ἀνεστράφημέν ποτε ἐν ταῖς ἐπιθυμίαις τῆς σαρκὸς καὶ τῶν διανοιῶν, καὶ ἤμεθα τέκνα φύσει ὀργῆς, ὡς καὶ οἱ λοιποί· ὁ δὲ θεὸς πλούσιος ὢν ἐν ἐλέει διὰ τὴν πολλὴν ἀγάπην αὐτοῦ ἣν ἠγάπησεν ἡμᾶς, καὶ ὄντας ἡμᾶς νεκροὺς τοῖς παραπτώμασιν συνεζωοποίησεν τῷ Χριστῷ.	. . . δι' ἃ ἔρχεται ἡ ὀργὴ τοῦ θεοῦ· ἐν οἷς καὶ ὑμεῖς περιεπατήσατέ ποτε, ὅτε ἐζῆτε ἐν τούτοις.

In this passage from Ephesians the framework is derived from Col. ii. 13. The passage opens with a phrase from it, and concludes with a repetition of the same phrase and also the phrase which ends the verse. Into this framework is introduced much material which is not derived from Colossians and also three phrases from Col. iii. 6. It seems as though the mention of παραπτώμασιν links up in the mind of the writer with the list of evil things mentioned in Col. iii. 5, which in that context are associated with the former life of the Colossian Christians and also with the wrath of God. Both these associations are reflected in Eph. ii. 1–5.

This same treatment of Colossians is evident throughout Ephesians, as the list in Appendix III plainly shows. Further instances may be found and examined in Appendix I at the following contexts:

(*d*) Eph. ii. 11–15: Col. ii. 11–14 and i. 21–2
(*e*) Eph. iii. 4: Col. iv. 3 and i. 26
(*f*) Eph. iii. 17: Col. i. 23 and ii. 7
(*g*) Eph. iv. 16: Col. i. 18, ii. 19, and ii. 2

In these four instances also it will be found that some similarity of thought or wording between the passages from Colossians serves as a link to lead to their combination in Ephesians.

It is a process similar to this which accounts for the somewhat unexpected result of the counting of coincidences between Ephesians and Colossians. In Ephesians it was found that there were 387 words with thick underlining and in Colossians 408. We should not have anticipated that Colossians, the shorter letter, would record the larger number. The explanation of this is seen by consideration of two illustrative contexts:

(i) The words τὰ πάντα ἐν τοῖς οὐρανοῖς καὶ ἐπὶ τῆς γῆς (Col. i. 16) and τὰ πάντα . . . εἴτε τὰ ἐπὶ τῆς γῆς εἴτε τὰ ἐν τοῖς οὐρανοῖς (Col. i. 20) are combined in Eph. i. 10 as τὰ πάντα τὰ ἐπὶ τοῖς οὐρανοῖς καὶ τὰ ἐπὶ τῆς γῆς. So that eighteen words in Colossians which are undermarked with thick lines are represented in Ephesians by eleven.

(ii) The words πάσης ἀρχῆς καὶ ἐξουσίας (Col. ii. 10) and εἴτε κυριότητες εἴτε ἀρχαὶ εἴτε ἐξουσίαι (Col. i. 16) are combined in Eph. i. 21 as πάσης ἀρχῆς καὶ ἐξουσίας . . . καὶ κυριότητος. So that seven words in Colossians with thick underlining are represented in Ephesians by five.

These instances of 'conflation' have been cited to substantiate the claim that the literary relationship between Ephesians and Colossians is based on memory rather than on documents. The character of the interdependence proves that one of the epistles was known almost by heart by the writer of the other, not, however, in a mechanical way, but so intimately and understandingly that word-sequences and meaning-sequences (sometimes in modified words) can be associated together from different parts of Colossians, re-moulded and worked naturally into the new composition so that it reads as an original work.

VII

THE PRIORITY OF COLOSSIANS

IN the previous chapter the extent and character of the interdependence between Colossians and Ephesians were described. Certain conclusions about the author of Ephesians may be drawn from the results of this investigation. Before, however, proceeding to these conclusions we must pause to give some reasons for the assumption, which we have been making, that Colossians is prior to Ephesians, and that therefore such borrowing as has taken place must be attributed to Ephesians. It would have been more logical to try to reach a conclusion on this issue before the last chapter, but the examination of the character of the interdependence itself helps to direct us to a right conclusion.

We believe that Colossians should be regarded as having been written earlier than Ephesians for the following reasons:

1. This has been the almost universally accepted conclusion, so that many studies of the two epistles do not even argue the matter but take it for granted. This in itself is far from being a conclusive argument, but it does mean that the burden of proof lies with those who claim that Ephesians is the earlier writing and that Colossians borrowed from it. Those who have taken up this position have most signally failed to win any general support, and most of them base their arguments on a very debatable hypothesis. Moffatt (ILNT, p. 159) gives the names of twelve scholars who have maintained the priority of Ephesians, but all except one of these twelve are mainly influenced in their decision by the assumption that Ephesians is the letter referred to in Col. iv. 16 as *τὴν ἐκ Λαοδικίας*. This proposed identification is, however, exceedingly uncertain, and even if it were accepted as possible, it need not imply the priority of Ephesians, for the letter described as *τὴν ἐκ Λαοδικίας* may have been one that Paul still intended to write rather than one which he had already written. Mayerhoff appears to be the only one to assert the priority of Ephesians without basing his arguments for this opinion on the identification of Ephesians with the problematical 'letter from Laodicea'. Apart from this solitary voice, and those who feel compelled to believe that Ephesians is referred to in Col. iv. 16 as a letter already written, all others accept the priority of Colossians, however different their other conclusions about these epistles may

be. Not only those who claim that both are Pauline but also those who deny Pauline authorship to either, and those too who claim that Ephesians is a non-Pauline writing based on a letter of Paul to the Colossians, are almost unanimous in asserting the priority of Colossians.

This consensus of opinion would almost justify us in treating the matter as sufficiently agreed, and not needing special demonstration. One or two arguments, however, are added, without being fully elaborated, to indicate the grounds on which this agreement is based.

2. There are doctrinal differences between the two epistles, and the most natural explanation of them is that Ephesians shows development as compared with Colossians, as though it represents some later stage in the same author's thought, or else a different mind modifying, even while it tried to imitate, the thought of Colossians. These disparities will have to be considered in some detail at a later stage. Here only two will be mentioned to illustrate the kind of difference which is meant.

In Ephesians the word 'Church' always means the Universal Church, and it carries a mystical sense, in that it means something more than the aggregate of the individual churches. There is no quite similar use of the word in the other Pauline epistles apart from Colossians, where it occurs twice in this sense. In Colossians, however, the word is also used to mean the individual congregation, which is the meaning of the word in the earlier Pauline epistles. W. F. Lofthouse in an article on 'The Church, Which is His Body' (in *Expository Times*, vol. lvii, No. 6) summarizes Paul's use of the word thus: 'Save for one Epistle, to the Ephesians, and two sentences in the sister epistle, to the Colossians, and once, if it be Pauline, in the Pastorals, he speaks only of individual churches, or of convictions and practices shared in common by them.' In the use of this word 'church', therefore, Ephesians, if we interpret it as Paul's, seems to stand at the peak of a developing phase in his theological thought. Its use of the word is deliberate and purposeful, and is felt to be a conscious appropriation of the novel use of the word, which appeared for the first time in Colossians.

A second instance may be mentioned briefly. The Second Coming of Christ plays a prominent part in the earlier letters of Paul. In Colossians it has receded into the background, but has not been excluded from his thought. If we interpret Col. iii. 4 ('When Christ, who is our life, shall be manifested, then shall ye also be manifested with him in glory') in connexion with Paul's earlier epistles, it is natural to see it as a reference to the Parousia. In Ephesians, however, not only are all thoughts of the Parousia absent, but they are replaced by an expected development of the Church in the life of the world, which reaches far into the future. This too suggests that Ephesians represents a later mode of thought than Colossians.

There are other similar differences in doctrine which are best interpreted as later developments in Ephesians of earlier forms which are found in Colossians. These, however, will require more detailed consideration, and will be examined later.

3. Besides differences in doctrine there are other points at which Ephesians is different from Colossians, where the differences appear to be deliberate improvements on Colossians, improvements, at least, when judged from the point of view of Ephesians. For instance, in Col. iii. 18–21 and iv. 2 there are five brief sentences, each one concisely advising the behaviour proper respectively to wives, husbands, children, parents, and masters of slaves. The passage, however, which gives counsel to slaves (Col. iii. 22–5) is much longer than any one of these. In fact it is as long as all five put together. This is natural enough in a letter which accompanied the note to Philemon, with its special plea for the slave Onesimus. Indeed, the aim of the concluding sentence in the section ('For he that doeth wrong shall receive again for the wrong that he hath done; and there is no respect of persons') seems to be to warn other slaves against taking liberties with a Christian master on the grounds of the special favours being sought for Onesimus. It is a solemn caution to slaves not to presume on the leniency shown to a fellow-slave.

In a general letter, such as Ephesians is, this disproportionate length in the section addressed to slaves would be out of place. So the other five sections are lengthened out by suitable additions, so that in Ephesians the passage about the conduct of slaves is not unduly long in comparison with them. Moreover, a significant change is made. The warning note of severity, appropriate in Col. iii. 25 but out of place in Ephesians, is changed into a sentence of encouragement for the good servant ('whatsoever good thing each one doeth, the same shall he receive again from the Lord' Eph. vi. 8); and the solemn pronouncement, 'there is no respect of persons', is transferred from the section addressed to slaves to the one directed to the masters, and is specifically related to God's attitude in the judgement of men (whereas in Colossians it seems rather to relate to the community of Christians in their treatment of erring fellow-Christians). This is a wise adjustment, for in a general letter such as

Ephesians emphasis on God's impartiality is more relevant to masters than to slaves; for it is masters of high social standing, rather than slaves, who normally need more to be reminded that special favours on grounds of worldly importance are not to be looked for from God but all, rich and poor alike, are treated with complete impartiality.

This twofold adaptation of Col. iii. 25 is best explained as a later modification by the writer of Ephesians. Eph. vi. 8–9 is clearly related to and interdependent with Col. iii. 25. But it would be an extremely hard task to make a case for the originality of the Ephesian passage and for the derivation of Col. iii. 25 from it.

4. We have just considered a sentence in Colossians which has been remodelled and reinterpreted in Ephesians, in the process of changing it from a particular application to local circumstances into an exhortation suitable for general readers. Colossians is addressed to an individual situation. Ephesians is a treatment of similar themes on quite general lines. Colossians adapts its theology and its moral counsel to meet the needs of one particular Christian community at one particular time. In Ephesians much of this theology and moral teaching is used again, but with such modifications as make it suitable for all readers. It expresses truths in a form appropriate to all Christians and all ages.

It may be possible to argue that this general epistle was written first, and that afterwards Paul used it as a ready store from which to draw ammunition for his campaign against the trouble-makers at Colossae. It is, however, a much more probable explanation to say that Paul, or a later disciple of his, takes the main thoughts with which he had brilliantly countered the heretical teachers at Colossae, and works them up into a calm and comprehensive statement of the enduring Christian truths of which they were a particular expression.

5. A consideration of the character of the interdependence between these two epistles points also to the same conclusion. In particular, the phenomenon which we called 'conflation', as a result of which unrelated passages in Colossians are brought together in Ephesians because of some common element in them both, which serves to link them together in the mind of the writer of Ephesians, argues strongly for according an earlier date to Colossians.

Each of these five arguments could be enlarged, but fuller treatment seems unnecessary, since there is no champion who still cares to advocate the priority of Ephesians. Moreover, some of the arguments are given fuller treatment in later chapters. Other arguments in favour of regarding Ephesians as the work of a Paulinist writing after Paul, which will be advanced later, will also have the effect of adding weight to the argument for the priority of Colossians.

Although no outstanding scholar can any longer be found to advocate the complete priority of Ephesians to Colossians, some mention at least must be made here of the proposed solution of the problem of their relationship which H. J. Holtzmann put forward in 1872 in his *Kritik der Epheser- und Kolosserbriefe*, a book which Moffatt describes as 'the standard treatise' on the subject (ILNT, p. 149). His contention is that in their present form neither Colossians nor Ephesians can be regarded as wholly prior to the other, but that each shows some measure of dependence on the other, and each has marks of originality as compared with the other. This complicated relationship he proposes to resolve as follows. Only a small portion of the present epistle to the Colossians is genuinely Pauline; this small Pauline nucleus, the original letter to the Colossians, was used by a later writer as the basis for a greatly enlarged work, which we know as 'Ephesians'; at a later stage either this same author or another expanded the small, original Pauline letter to the Colossians by incorporating extensive borrowings from the non-Pauline 'Ephesians'. As a result, therefore, both primary and secondary characteristics are to be found in both Colossians and Ephesians, and complete priority cannot be accorded to either.[1] Holtzmann went further. He claimed to be able to distinguish the original Pauline elements in Colossians from the later additions, and separate the original, brief letter from the subsequent borrowings from Ephesians.

This theory received a fairly widespread welcome at the time of its first appearance, though very few scholars were prepared to accept it in precisely the form in which Holtzmann had elaborated it. Some sought to simplify it, others to elaborate it still further. With the passing of the years, however, and the opportunity thus provided for further investigation and careful assessment, the theory has appeared less and less acceptable, so that no modern scholar seems at all disposed to champion it. The nearest approach to a word of approval among modern scholars appears in J. Knox's

[1] 'In jedem der beiden Briefe laufen Merkmale des Ursprünglichen und des Secundären nebeneinander her und durcheinander hin, so dass man sich auf eine Hypothese verwiesen sieht, der zufolge gegenseitige Abhängigkeit denkbar erscheint' (H. J. Holtzmann, ENT, p. 265).

book *Christ, the Lord* (p. 102, footnote): 'For myself I feel sure . . . that Paul wrote a letter to the church at Colossae, which corresponds generally with the document we have; but I am strongly inclined to believe that the letter has undergone considerable interpolation. The work of H. J. Holtzmann . . . especially as it touches the authenticity of Colossians has probably been too quickly dismissed.'

Among scholars generally, however, it is felt that Holtzmann has failed to demonstrate the composite character of Colossians, and that his judgements on what is Pauline and what non-Pauline in the epistle are extremely subjective. Also the exceedingly complicated processes which this theory presupposes are regarded as highly improbable.

Von Soden, for instance, deals carefully with Holtzmann's arguments for partitioning Colossians into Pauline and non-Pauline elements, but is not convinced of their validity. At first he was willing to concede that Col. i. 15–20 might be a post-Pauline insertion, but could see no reason for doubting the Pauline origin of all the rest; and some years later he seems to have come to accept the whole letter, without any exception, as genuinely Pauline. As we have already seen, this has been the general tendency in recent years, and today scholars are increasingly inclined to accept Colossians, in substantially its present form, as a genuinely Pauline epistle.

W. Lock criticizes Holtzmann's theory mainly on the ground of the subjectivity of his judgements as to what is Pauline and what non-Pauline in Colossians, and the absence of any objective tests in the formation of them. The judgements themselves are therefore to be regarded as 'very precarious' (HDB, vol. i, p. 717).

Moffatt also objects to this subjectivity, and in addition is critical of the complexity of the theory: 'Such filigree-criticism has failed to win acceptance; the literary criteria are too subjective, and the evidence for bisecting the error attacked in Colossians is not convincing' (ILNT, p. 157).

Jülicher rejects it as 'too complicated to be accepted' (quoted in Abbott, ICC, p. lii), and Peake's verdict is similar: 'The complexity of the hypothesis tells fatally against it' (CINT, p. 52). G. G. Findlay speaks of it as 'this complicated and too ingenious hypothesis', and of Holtzmann's book in which the theory is propounded he says: 'A work more subtle and scientific, more replete with learning, and yet more unconvincing . . . we do not know' (EE, pp. 10–11).

One cannot help feeling that it is chiefly the great name of

Holtzmann which commands respect, and not the theory on its own merits. Had it been promulgated under a less eminent name it would have received far less respectful attention. Moreover, although Holtzmann's theory appears mainly as an inquiry into literary relationships, the basis of it is in part, at any rate, a theological judgement as to what doctrinal teaching may be legitimately regarded as Pauline. Had not this theological judgement led to the rejection of certain elements in Colossians as non-Pauline, his verdict on the literary relationships of Colossians and Ephesians might have been different. Any such theological judgement which has no support from manuscript authority or from literary criticism is indeed an extremely subjective foundation even for a conjecture, and is certainly too insecure to sustain an elaborate theory.

We proceed, therefore, on the assumption that Holtzmann's theory has not won acceptance, that Colossians may be treated as the work of Paul, and that Ephesians may be regarded as a later amplification of Colossians, either by Paul himself or by a later writer using the name of Paul.

VIII

THE BEARING OF THE INTERDEPENDENCE OF EPHESIANS AND COLOSSIANS UPON THE AUTHORSHIP OF EPHESIANS

Our review of the relationship between Colossians and Ephesians, and the character of their interdependence, not only afforded additional grounds for believing in the priority of Colossians, but revealed significant facts about the manner in which Colossians was used by the author of Ephesians.

C. H. Dodd (in *Ab. Com.*, p. 1225) writes of this author, if other than Paul: 'He must be held to have modelled his great work slavishly on Colossians . . . to the extent of imitating its arrangement and borrowing its phrases.' This judgement, however, is not fair to the facts. The manner of the dependence is anything but slavish; it is flexible and supple in adaptation, and displays a large measure of independence as well as dependence. Moreover, the word 'imitate', as applied to the arrangement, does not accurately describe the relationship between the two. In fact, the word 'imitation' is out of place in the comparison. There is borrowing, admittedly, and the following of certain lines of thought, but the borrower uses his borrowings only after he has made them his own, having first thoroughly digested them in his own mind, and, in some cases, reminted the words for his own purpose. As we have already emphasized, there is no trace of evidence to suggest that the writer of Ephesians had his eyes glued to a copy of Colossians, or even made reference to it as he wrote. One may legitimately claim that all that he used of Colossians, with the possible exception of Col. iv. 7–8, was already in his mind, so fully assimilated as to be part of his own mental equipment.

These conclusions limit us to two theories concerning the authorship:

1. The first alternative is that the tradition of the Church is right and that Paul himself was the author.

If, however, Paul was the author, certain facts about the time of writing, in relation to Colossians, must be insisted on. He must have written it immediately after Colossians, and great emphasis should be placed on the word 'immediately'. It means that he wrote Ephesians on the same day, or perhaps the day after, while the actual phrasing he had used in Colossians was still fresh in his mind. Even an interval of a week would have made so large a number of close similarities most unlikely.

Sometimes it happens that a man who can write shorthand uses the time spent in the train on a railway journey to sketch out in shorthand some letters he wishes to write. The motion of the train prevents his writing them there and then as he would wish them to be written, but to have them drafted out will save much time when he comes to write or type them finally at his home or in his office. If he does this that same evening, his memory will give him great assistance in interpreting the shorthand characters where the movement of the train has caused them to be ill-formed and illegible. If, however, he leaves it over for a week or so, he will find that what he intended to write has so far escaped his memory that even the imperfect shorthand character will in places fail to recall to his mind what he wished to say. How much less would he be able to reproduce, without help of notes, depending only on his memory, considerable sections of a letter written many days before.

The references in both letters to Tychicus imply that both were written at the same time. Tychicus is represented as the bearer of both letters, and it is unlikely that Tychicus, already commissioned to deliver Colossians and Philemon, would be kept waiting for more than a day or two at most in order that a third letter might be added to them.

There are, however, as we shall see in the next chapter, certain very real difficulties involved in an assumption that Ephesians was written immediately after Colossians, and in order to avoid these difficulties, and yet do justice to the very close dependence of Ephesians on Colossians, an alternative suggestion has been made. It is this: that Ephesians was not written until some considerable time after Colossians, but that, before writing it, Paul re-read and studied carefully a copy of his letter to the Colossians which he had had made and retained for future use. In this way the reproduction of its phrases and thoughts in Ephesians is explicable, even on the supposition that a considerable interval of time separated the two letters. Moffatt appears to be willing to concede that, if Paul is the author of Ephesians, this alternative suggestion may describe the manner of its link with Colossians (ILNT, p. 375).

There are, however, strong arguments against it. Not only have we no evidence that Paul was accustomed to retain copies of his letters for future reference, but also it hardly seems consistent with what we know of Paul that he should studiously turn up the copy of an old letter in order to find inspiration and ideas, and words too, in which to clothe those ideas.

What, however, is even more conclusive against it is the reference in Ephesians to Tychicus as the bearer of the letter and as Paul's personal emissary. We noted (pp. 58–9) that this reference (Eph. vi. 21–2) is an exact verbatim reproduction of twenty-nine consecutive words from Col. iv. 7–8 (apart from one slight variation). On the basis of Pauline authorship, this extent of identity can hardly be explained in any other way than by assuming that Paul here copies from what he sees written in Colossians. So exact a reproduction could hardly be made from memory alone. If Ephesians was dispatched at the same time as Colossians (though not to the same communities of Christians), and by the same bearer, it would be entirely natural for Paul deliberately to reproduce the mention of Tychicus in identical words. If, however, Ephesians belongs to some wholly different occasion, many months later than the original writing of Colossians, it would be a most unnatural thing for Paul to repeat the whole passage verbatim, even if, by a coincidence, Tychicus did happen to be the bearer of the later letter as well as of the earlier one. If Paul wrote Ephesians as well as Colossians, the only satisfactory explanation of this passage is that the two letters were written at approximately the same time and dispatched together by the same messenger. Until further evidence is forthcoming, therefore, the alternative suggestion that Ephesians was written some considerable time after Colossians, but after a careful review of a retained copy of Colossians, must be rejected as unsatisfactory and improbable.

We assume, therefore, that if Ephesians is Paul's work, it was written so soon after Colossians as to be, for all practical purposes, simultaneous with it.

There is nothing novel about this insistence. Indeed it is generally conceded by those who uphold the traditional ascription of authorship to Paul. C. H. Dodd, for instance, who gives his verdict in favour of the Pauline authorship, though not without hesitation, writes: 'This epistle, if genuine, must have been written practically simultaneously with Colossians' (*Ab. Com.*, p. 1224). McNeile, Lock, and Dibelius all make precisely the same point. E. Graham, too, who believes that 'Ephesians, which is in any case the crown of Pauline writings, is the work of Paul himself', in seeking to do justice to 'the extremely intricate and deep-rooted connexion between the two epistles', affirms that it 'cannot be satisfactorily explained except on the supposition that they were composed at roughly the same time by one writer in whose mind the ideas and phrases characteristic of both epistles were living and adaptable' (NCHS, p. 538). The words 'living' and 'adaptable' well describe the use Ephesians has made of Colossians, but for our present purpose the phrase 'at roughly the same time' is the one we wish to emphasize, because it expresses a truth which has not been given the attention it merits.

E. F. Scott, who in his later books supports the Pauline authorship of Ephesians, gives a good summary of the position when he writes: Paul 'decided, while the theme of Colossians was still fresh in his mind, he would write another letter in which he would leave all controversial issues aside, and set forth more fully, in their positive significance, the ideas which possessed him' (LNT, p. 181). The phrase 'fresh in his mind' represents the truth we are emphasizing, but it is not quite as exact as it might be. For how long does a letter remain 'fresh in one's mind' to the extent that its substance and phrases can be reproduced in the measure and manner that Colossians is reproduced in Ephesians? For a letter is not like a speech, which has been carefully prepared, partly memorized, and perhaps delivered on more than one occasion. Such a speech may linger in the author's mind for a period of weeks. But a letter, written to meet a special emergency, is in quite a different category, and in order for such a letter to be still 'fresh in the mind', so fresh as to enable it to be reproduced as Colossians is reproduced in Ephesians, we believe that the more precise phrases already quoted should be applied to it. The second letter must have been 'composed at roughly the same time' or 'written practically simultaneously'.

The importance of this conclusion will be evident in the next chapter.

2. There is, however, a second alternative. In general terms C. H. Dodd describes it as follows: 'It is therefore often held that the epistle is the work of a disciple of Paul, writing after his death, and using Colossians as the basis of a new work in which he sought to set forth some fresh developments of Paulinism, true, as he believed, to the general spirit of his master, though never explicitly thought out by him' (*Ab. Com.*, p. 1224). Something more explicit, however, needs to be said about such an author's relationship to Colossians. It is true that he uses it 'as a basis' for what he writes, but not, as we have seen, by laboriously and conscientiously reproducing large sections from a copy open before him. The manner in which Colossians is reproduced in Ephesians shows that if the author is such as

Dodd describes, what he knows of Colossians is already assimilated within his mind in such a way that it has become part of his own mental equipment. This means that he must have known the greater part of Colossians almost by heart, and not as a recent acquisition, but something which he had read and re-read till every phrase of it had become part of his own vocabulary and some of the thoughts from it part of his own theological outlook. Only someone with such a long and deep intimacy with Colossians could reproduce it in the remarkable way in which it is reproduced in Ephesians.

These, therefore, are the two possible solutions of the problem of the authorship of Ephesians which remain open to us after our examination of the extent and character of the dependence of Ephesians upon Colossians. On this criterion alone it may well seem that the former alternative is more probable, and that the facts of the relationship are quite amenable to the interpretation that Paul was the author of both epistles, and that he wrote Ephesians within a few hours of completing Colossians. The freedom with which phrases from the earlier letter are rearranged and modified appears to be more readily attributable to Paul than to a later imitator.

There are, however, two items in our investigation so far which appear to present a measure of difficulty for the assumption of Pauline authorship for both epistles. The first of these consists of the phenomenon illustrated on pages 65–6, in paragraphs (*a*), (*b*), and (*c*). We noted how two passages from Colossians are sometimes 'conflated' in one passage in Ephesians, and the link between the two passages, which brings them together in the mind of the writer of Ephesians, is some word or idea common to them both. In (*a*) it was the thought of reconciliation implicit in both *ἀπολύτρωσιν* and *εἰρηνοποίησας* which serves as the connecting link for uniting phrases from Col. i. 14 and 20 in Eph. i. 7. In (*b*), which is the most impressive of the three instances, it is the use of the verb *ἀκούω* (which introduces phrases in Col. i. 9 and 4) which serves to link those phrases together into a single whole in Eph. i. 15–16. It is as though the word *ἀκούω* set in motion two chains of recollection, and led to their combination in Ephesians. In (*c*) it is the word *παραπτώματα* in Col. ii. 13, linking up in the mind of the writer with the list of sins which immediately precedes Col. ii. 6, which leads to the incorporation of these two verses into Eph. ii. 1–5.

This type of thing is certainly what the human mind does when dealing with phrases and sentences which are extremely familiar and known by heart through constant use. At any rate, when one is freely composing, and at the same time deliberately allowing appropriate quotations from familiar passages of Scripture and hymns, known by heart, to suggest themselves to one's mind, precisely this feature, which we have called 'conflation', constantly appears.

Take, for instance, this sentence used by a speaker in addressing a company of Christians: 'Make sure of the truth as it is in Jesus, and that truth shall make you free.' That sentence is composed of phrases from three different sources, all known by heart by the speaker, who combined them spontaneously, without any deliberate intention, a mental link bringing them together almost automatically in his thoughts:

(i) 'Make sure of truth' is the opening sentence of a hymn.
(ii) 'As the truth is in Jesus' (Eph. iv. 21).
(iii) 'Ye shall know the truth, and the truth shall make you free' (John viii. 32).

The word 'truth' is the common link which associates these three sentences together in the speaker's mind, where they are combined into one new sentence. When we know passages very familiarly they do link themselves up in this way. But would this 'conflation' be as likely to happen if the speaker had not long known these separate sentences by heart, but had merely used them separately in different parts of a letter which he had just been writing? And even if 'conflation' in such circumstances might conceivably have happened once, would it have been likely to be repeated in several places?

The second point worth noting does not concern 'conflation', but its significance for our purpose may be even greater.

In the comparison of Eph. v. 19–20 with Col. iii. 16–17 (see p. 62, where the passages are quoted in full and commented on) we saw how the phrase ἐν ὀνόματι κυρίου Ἰησοῦ was, in Ephesians, part of the exhortation to 'do all in the name of the Lord Jesus'. Immediately following the phrase in Colossians the word εὐχαριστοῦντες occurs; but though it is adjacent in position, it has no link in meaning with the preceding phrase. Yet strangely, in Ephesians, where both ἐν ὀνόματι κυρίου Ἰησοῦ and εὐχαριστοῦντες are reproduced, along with other words from the same context, they are joined together in meaning and grammar, as well as word-sequence, so that now the exhortation reads 'to give thanks in the name of the Lord Jesus'.

The πάντα also from Col. iii. 17 seems to have suffered similar treatment. In Colossians it is part of the phrase 'Do all in the name of the Lord Jesus', but in the mind of the writer of Ephesians it, too, has become linked with *εὐχαριστοῦντες* and the sense of it appears in *πάντοτε* and *πάντων* in Eph. v. 20 (*εὐχαριστοῦντες πάντοτε ὑπὲρ πάντων ἐν ὀνόματι τοῦ κυρίου ἡμῶν 'Ιησοῦ Χριστοῦ τῷ θεῷ καὶ πατρί*).

We must ask ourselves: Is this mechanical reproduction of words, in violation of their original sense, what we should expect of Paul, in a second letter closely modelled on an earlier one and written immediately after it? Would it not rather be the meaning of the words that would linger in his mind? Is it not, on the other hand, just the kind of phenomenon that betrays the hand of an imitator, who can repeat words by heart in a mechanical way, so that sometimes their association with one another becomes, in the new context, strikingly at variance with their meaning in the first place?

This peculiarity and that of 'conflation' will require further examination when we seek to draw our conclusions from these investigations.

IX

THE SIGNIFICANCE OF THEOLOGICAL DIFFERENCES

One further argument emerges from the comparison of Ephesians and Colossians which has a bearing on the question of authorship.

At an earlier stage we noted that one of the arguments which has been used against the Pauline authorship of Ephesians has been the presence of thoughts and expressions which have no precedent in Galatians, Romans, and 1 and 2 Corinthians. We declined, however, to attach to it any great weight. It is true that there may be special instances where the argument may be legitimately employed, but in general it is an untrustworthy argument. It would be hard to define any limits beyond which an alert and vigorous mind could not develop its ideas and vocabulary over the course of a few years or even months, especially when creative movements are afoot.

When Paul lived, the Christian Faith was new to the world. It had no long tradition of creeds or ritual. It was constantly being confronted by new and deadly enemies, and sometimes by equally dangerous friends. It was continually awakening to deeper implications of its message and glimpsing further horizons. It was a time for experiment, in ideas as well as in methods. In these circumstances it is impossible to circumscribe Paul's thoughts and phraseology within the limits of those which he had already used, or foreshadowed, in his earlier epistles. The fact that thoughts about Christ and God's purpose in Christ appear in Colossians and Ephesians in an advanced stage as compared with Galatians and Romans does not by any means disqualify them from being regarded as Paul's.

When, however, differences in theological thought, and in the meaning attached to words, can be shown to exist between Colossians and Ephesians, we are on quite different ground. Differences can be readily allowed for, and even expected, after an interval of months or years. They are not, however, so easily accounted for when no such interval intervenes.

We tried earlier to establish the position that if Paul wrote Ephesians he must have written it so soon after Colossians as to have written it 'at roughly the same time', and we saw that this is a point of view freely acknowledged by those who maintain the Pauline authorship. If, therefore, it can be shown that between Colossians and Ephesians there are such differences as would be most unexpected if the epistles are the work of the same man writing at the same time, with no interval between them to allow for changes to take place in his thought, that will be a formidable argument against Pauline authorship.

That such differences do exist is conceded by at least one who retains, though somewhat hesitantly, the belief that Paul was the writer of Ephesians. C. H. Dodd, comparing Colossians and Ephesians, writes: 'The differences are actually by no means small. Even when the characteristic vocabulary of the two epistles is the same, it is sometimes used with varying shades of meaning, surprising in letters written at one time. . . . The general emphasis and direction of thought are often appreciably different' (*Ab. Com.*, p. 1224).

We must now look at some of these 'differences' and the 'varying shades of meaning' attached to the same words, to determine whether or not they are such as can be reconciled with the idea of their coming from the same author at the same moment in his life. No attempt will be made to draw up an exhaustive list, but only to consider those points of variation which are most significant.

The scholar who attaches most significance to these variations is Dibelius. To him they are the deciding factor in the question of authorship, and it is primarily because of them that he reaches the conclusion that Ephesians cannot have been written by the same author as Colossians. As he himself puts it, it is the comparison of these two epistles which 'provides the point on which a decision can be reached on the question of genuineness'.[1] He is impressed by the relative neglect of the Death of Christ in Ephesians as compared with Colossians and the other Pauline epistles, and the new emphasis on His Exaltation (see p. 20), and also by the new sense attached to the word 'Church'. The most decisive factors for him, however, are those instances where there is a similarity in terminology and yet at the same time a clear difference of thought (KEP, p. 64), instances, that is, where Ephesians reproduces the same words and phrases as Colossians and yet attaches a different meaning to them. In his *Fresh Approach to the New Testament* he expresses the same conclusion: 'What speaks decisively for its spuriousness, and at the same time against the assumption that it is a circular letter

[1] 'Das Verhältnis von Eph zu Col bietet den Punkt dar, von dem aus die Echtheitsfrage zu entscheiden ist' (Dibelius, KEP, p. 63).

sent by Paul to several churches, is its linguistic dependence on Colossians, coupled with a completely different construction of thought' (p. 170).[1] This for Dibelius is conclusive evidence of a different mind at work. Among the instances which he quotes, there are three which he feels to be particularly convincing:

1. *Col.* ii. 19 *and Eph.* iv. 15–16. These two passages have already been quoted to illustrate the manner of the interdependence between the two epistles (p. 61). There can be no doubt that familiarity with Col. ii. 19 is clearly revealed in Eph. iv. 15–16. Both passages insist that Christ is the Head of the Body, and the words which they use to describe the relationship of Head to Body are very similar. In Ephesians the 'Body' of which Christ is the 'Head' is the Church. In Col. ii, however, it is not the Church which is under consideration but the 'cosmic forces' (cf. Col. ii. 10). It is of these that Christ is declared to be the Head, and 'accordingly', writes Dibelius, 'at Col. ii. 19 σῶμα is the Cosmos. What is there applied to the cosmic σῶμα is at Eph. iv. 16 related, with almost exactly the same words, to the Body of the Church.'[2] The same terms, but a different meaning! This, he believes, actually excludes the explanation that the writer is Paul who is here repeating himself.

2. *The use of* ἀποκαταλλάσσω. This word occurs only three times in the New Testament, twice in Colossians (i. 20 and 22) and once in Ephesians (ii. 16). Not only is the use of this rare word indicative that Ephesians is in this context dependent on Colossians, but other correspondences confirm it. Yet the significance of the reconciliation which the word describes is different in Ephesians. In Colossians Paul declares that through the Death of Christ God is reconciling 'all things unto Himself', and particularly those who were 'alienated and hostile' to Him. In Ephesians the emphasis is upon the reconciliation being accomplished between Jews and Gentiles, Christ 'making peace' between them.

Both Moffatt and Goodspeed, as well as Dibelius, feel the weight

[1] H. J. Holtzmann also makes the same point: 'Aber gerade bei dieser verhältnismässigen Selbständigkeit des beiderseitigen Ideenganges befremdet um so mehr, dass in sinnverwandten Stellen beiderseits das gleiche Wortmaterial zu Tage tritt. So ist die Stelle Kol. ii. 11–14 in ihren einzelnen Wortelementen vorhanden in Eph. i. 19–20; ii. 1, 4–6; 11, 15' (ENT, p. 263).

[2] 'Berührungen in der Terminologie trotz Differenz der Gedanken. Den auffallendsten Beleg bietet unsere Stelle im Vergleich zu Col. ii. 19. Zwar ist deutlich, dass κεφαλή und σῶμα Col. i. 18, 24; iii. 15 wie Eph. i. 22, iv. 15 f., v. 23 von Christus und Gemeinde gebraucht werden. Allein in Col. ii. 10, 19 heisst Christus "Haupt" der kosmischen Kräfte; demnach ist σῶμα ii. 19 der Kosmos. Was dort vom kosmischen σῶμα gilt, wird nun Eph. iv. 16 mit fast genau denselben Worten von dem σῶμα der Gemeinde ausgesagt: hier ist also mit denselben Termini eine andere Sache bezeichnet' (Dibelius, KEP, p. 64).

of this argument, and they emphasize that nowhere else in Paul's writings is the Cross of Christ associated with the breaking of the barrier between Jew and Greek, though it is often proclaimed as the instrument of reconciliation between men and God (ILNT, p. 376; ME, p. 37, footnote).

Moreover, as Moffatt points out (ILNT, p. 377), in Colossians it is God in Christ who effects the reconciliation (as in the other Pauline epistles, cf. 2 Cor. v. 18), but in Ephesians 'the function of reconciliation . . . is transferred to Christ Himself'. This, Moffatt claims, is an instance of the 'higher Christology of Ephesians'.

These differences would be of little significance if they existed only between Ephesians and 2 Corinthians, because of the interval of years which separates these epistles; but occurring as they do in two epistles which, on the assumption of Pauline authorship, were written at approximately the same time, they present a real problem.

3. A third passage which for Dibelius tells heavily against Pauline authorship is Eph. iii. 5. This is clearly based on Col. i. 26, and equally clearly is strangely altered.

Eph. iii. 5	Col. i. 26
. . . ἐν τῷ μυστηρίῳ τοῦ Χριστοῦ, ὃ ἑτέραις γενεαῖς οὐκ ἐγνωρίσθη τοῖς υἱοῖς τῶν ἀνθρώπων ὡς νῦν ἀπεκαλύφθη τοῖς ἁγίοις ἀποστόλοις αὐτοῦ καὶ προφήταις ἐν πνεύματι.	*τὸ μυστήριον τὸ ἀποκεκρυμμένον ἀπὸ τῶν αἰώνων καὶ ἀπὸ τῶν γενεῶν —νῦν δὲ ἐφανερώθη τοῖς ἁγίοις αὐτοῦ.*

Both passages declare that God's secret has been long hidden but now at last has been revealed. Colossians says that it has been disclosed to 'His saints', that is, to all God's people in Christ. In Ephesians the same general framework is preserved, but the meaning of the passage is changed by most significant additions. Both Colossians and Ephesians affirm that the secret has now been revealed *τοῖς ἁγίοις*. Ephesians, however, turns *ἁγίοις* into an adjective, and introduces two nouns, *ἀποστόλοις καὶ προφήταις*, to which it serves merely as an epithet. This is a most surprising modification. The people who have been given insight into God's secret are no longer the whole body of Christians, but the much narrower group of the Church hierarchy.

It may be doubted whether Paul would ever have imposed this ecclesiastical restriction on God's revelation. It is in the highest degree unlikely that, having just written Col. i. 26, he would immediately proceed to repeat the same general idea in the same form of words and yet introduce an alteration which so drastically changes the significance of the passage. It is difficult not to agree that here we have what Dibelius describes as 'an ecclesiastical development of Col. i. 26'.[1]

Both Moffatt (ILNT, pp. 376–81) and Dibelius (KEP, pp. 63–5) give other instances of the same kind of thing, but these three will suffice to show that the argument has cogency.

From the same point of view it will repay us to examine in some detail the use made in Colossians and Ephesians of three words which may be said to be characteristic of both epistles. Certainly they are characteristic of Ephesians, and in the case of all three their use in Ephesians seems to be derived from Colossians, as a comparison of the corresponding contexts reveals. The three words are *μυστήριον*, *οἰκονομία*, and *πλήρωμα*.

τὸ μυστήριον

This is one of the characteristic words of Ephesians. It is used six times in the epistle. In Colossians it appears four times, and in all the other Pauline epistles only five times in the singular, though its use in the plural occurs in three other places. An additional instance may be reckoned in 1 Cor. ii. 1, but the evidence of the manuscripts gives stronger support for the alternative reading *μαρτύριον*. But even if *μυστήριον* is read, nothing of significance would be added for our present purpose because it would carry precisely the same meaning as *μυστήριον* six verses later in 1 Cor. ii. 7. Even out of the five in the other Pauline epistles, the one in Rom. xvi. 25 will need to be treated with considerable caution because this final doxology in the epistle to the Romans, where it appears, has come under suspicion. C. H. Dodd writes of it: 'There is ground for the suspicion that it is not an original part of the epistle at all' (MCR, p. 245). It would be out of place here to examine the evidence for this judgement. It is not, however, an isolated opinion, but one which is widely shared by other scholars. Moffatt, for instance, in his translation of the New Testament encloses the passage in brackets. In our investigation, therefore, we must allow for the possibility that this instance of the use of the word is not from the hand of Paul but

[1] '*ἁγίοις* bildet bei Annahme der Echtheit einen Anstoss, den man nicht durch unbeweisbare Hypothesen (Interpunktion nach *ἁγίοις*; *ἁγίοις* oder der ganze Halbvers als Glosse) beseitigen kann. . . . Der Vertreter der Unechtheit dagegen wird in der Stelle eine kirchliche Weiterbildung von Col. i. 26 sehen' (Dibelius, KEP, p. 56).

is part of a passage which has been 'composed on the analogy of Eph. iii. 20–21', and embodies 'certain Pauline ideas familiar from the later epistles' (C. H. Dodd, MCR, p. 245).

Both Abbott and Armitage Robinson agree that Paul's use of the word owes little or nothing to the Mystery Religions. They accept it in its very common meaning of 'a secret', and agree that in the more developed uses of it in Paul's writings it comes to mean 'an open secret', that is, 'a one-time secret which has been disclosed'.

An undeveloped use of the word is found in 2 Thess. ii. 7, where Paul speaks of the 'mystery of lawlessness'. This perhaps is not substantially different from what our generation calls 'the problem of evil'. The word indicates that the true nature of 'lawlessness' is perplexing, so that no wholly satisfactory account of it can be given.

A somewhat similar use appears in 1 Cor. xv. 51, where Paul is trying to find words to suggest the wonderful transformation by which, in the resurrection, the earthly body is replaced by a heavenly body. He cannot pretend to have a complete explanation of it. So he calls it a 'mystery', something not yet fully understood.

In 1 Cor. ii. 7 the chief interest is in 'wisdom', and the reference to 'mystery' is incidental. Paul is disclaiming all human wisdom. Such wisdom as he lays claim to is God's wisdom: *λαλοῦμεν θεοῦ σοφίαν ἐν μυστηρίῳ*. Moffatt takes *ἐν μυστηρίῳ* as adjectival with 'wisdom' and translates: 'the Mysterious Wisdom of God'. If this is right, the meaning is akin to the sentiment in the hymn:

> God moves in a mysterious way
> His wonders to perform.

Others think *ἐν μυστηρίῳ* should be taken with *λαλοῦμεν*. In neither case have we any clear indication of the actual content of the word. Probably it is meant to suggest something which eludes full human comprehension. The centre of interest is, however, the 'Wisdom of God', and it is this which the phrases that follow describe. We do find, however, that certain ideas which in Colossians become explicitly linked with the word *μυστήριον* appear here, though they are rather diffused and ill co-ordinated, and are related to the Wisdom of God, and not to *μυστήριον* (e.g. the idea that it has long been hidden, *ἀποκεκρυμμένην*, and that it is part of God's long-prepared plan, *προώρισεν*).

In Rom. xi. 25 the word *μυστήριον* is used to describe the perplexing means which God is using for the fulfilment of His purposes. The heart of the perplexity is the unwillingness of Israel, God's chosen people, to respond to God's approach in Christ. This is a 'problem' and 'the mystery' of it deepens in view of the happy consequences to which it has apparently led, in the ingathering of the Gentiles.

If Rom. xvi. 25 is included in our consideration, we find that here *μυστήριον* is associated, though still vaguely and inconclusively, with the fact that the Gentiles too have heard the *κήρυγμα* of Jesus Christ, the purpose of which is 'to win them to obedience through the faith' (Weymouth's translation).

The three uses of the word in the plural all occur in 1 Corinthians (iv. 1, xiii. 2, xiv. 2), but there is nothing in the context of any of them to help us to form an exact idea of the meaning attached to the word.

In these earlier letters of Paul, therefore, we find that *μυστήριον* is used to mean some 'problem' or 'perplexity', or some purpose of God which is wholly or partially hidden. There is no consistently worked out significance given to it. What we find in Colossians is therefore all the more impressive, for here we are confronted with a remarkable development in the meaning of the word. The most noticeable fact is that in each of the three contexts (two of the four instances occur in one context, in Col. i. 26–7) it is expressly equated with Christ Himself, and in two of them it is also treated as identical with *λόγος θεοῦ*.

In Col. i. 26–7 the word appears in a context which is affirming that Christ and His gospel are now operative among the Gentiles, but there is no emphasis upon this aspect, indeed the author seems to hurry past it towards the new thought which dominates his mind. This 'new thought' about the meaning of *μυστήριον* is well put by E. F. Scott: 'What the secret consists in is now explicitly stated: "Christ in you, the hope of glory".' 'The mystery of God, hidden from all eternity and now revealed, is the indwelling of Christ in His people, whether Jews or Gentiles' (MCC, pp. 33–4). And the emphasis is far more on Christ and His indwelling than upon the inclusion of the Gentiles. The important truth which emerges from a consideration of the use and meaning of *μυστήριον* in this passage can be expressed in an equation:

ὁ λόγος τοῦ θεοῦ = τὸ μυστήριον = Χριστὸς ἐν ὑμῖν.

The study of Col. ii. 2 is complicated by some doubt about the correct reading, punctuation, and grammatical construction. The most commonly accepted opinion is that the best reading is *τοῦ μυστηρίου τοῦ θεοῦ, Χριστοῦ*, and *Χριστοῦ* should be understood as in apposition to μυστηρίου. This interpretation at any rate accords with the express statement in Col. i. 26–7. So once again we have the equation:

τὸ μυστήριον = Χριστός.

In Col. iv. 3 τὸ μυστήριον is closely related, though not explicitly identified with τοῦ λόγου, and the phrase τὸ μυστήριον τοῦ Χριστοῦ is used. In view of the two preceding passages, it seems certain that E. F. Scott is right when he translates this phrase as 'the mystery consisting in Christ' (MCC, p. 83). So this passage too gives support to the equation already noted.

This, then, is the characteristic meaning of μυστήριον in Colossians, and compared with Paul's earlier uses it is a new and remarkable development. Clearly Paul himself feels that this is so, for he deliberately introduces it three times. For the time being it is an outstanding feature of his thinking. It is an idea which gives him deep satisfaction.

It seems almost certain that in any writing of Paul's, contemporary with Colossians, in which reference was made to μυστήριον, this new significance attached to the word in Colossians would reappear; and we saw that if Ephesians was written by Paul, it must have been written at the same time as Colossians. We should expect, therefore, that the use of μυστήριον in Ephesians would reflect this new development in Colossians. But we do not find this. The word is not equated with Christ, nor is it identified with λόγος θεοῦ. Instead we find something entirely different. It is explicitly and categorically declared that the 'mystery' consists in this newly grasped truth, that the Gentiles are συγκληρονόμα καὶ σύνσωμα καὶ συνμέτοχα τῆς ἐπαγγελίας ἐν Χριστῷ Ἰησοῦ διὰ τοῦ εὐαγγελίου (Eph. iii. 6). Nor can it be claimed that in this Paul is merely returning to an earlier interpretation of the word. It is true that in earlier letters Paul has affirmed that this one-time secret has now been made known to Gentiles as well as to Jews, but never before has Paul made the 'mystery' consist in the equal partnership of Gentiles with Jews in the privileges of the Gospel.

A further and, this time, an entirely new interpretation of the content of the 'mystery' appears at Eph. i. 9, where it is represented as God's purpose ἀνακεφαλαιώσασθαι τὰ πάντα ἐν τῷ Χριστῷ τὰ ἐπὶ τοῖς οὐρανοῖς καὶ τὰ ἐπὶ τῆς γῆς. There is some doubt about the exact meaning of ἀνακεφαλαιώσασθαι, but it probably means 'to reunite'. That is the meaning accepted by E. F. Scott when he comments on this passage as follows: 'So the "mystery", as Paul finally discloses it, is this—that "God proposed to reunite for Himself all things in Christ".'

Armitage Robinson, in his detailed examination of the meaning of μυστήριον in Paul's writings, very much clouds the issue which we are now discussing by treating Ephesians and Colossians under one head and assuming that their use of the word is identical (SPEE, p. 238). The two meanings of the word which he finds in these two epistles are the two which we have noted in Ephesians. They do not, however, appear in Colossians, and Colossians has a different interpretation of its own.

The point we wish to make as a result of this investigation into the meaning of μυστήριον in Paul's writings, and especially in Colossians and Ephesians, is not that Paul was incapable of originating the further interpretations which we find in Ephesians, but that it is unlikely that they would appear so fully developed, so explicit, and so distinct in a writing simultaneous with Colossians. It is equally unlikely that the interpretation which is given so prominent and emphatic a place in Colossians should be entirely ignored in an epistle written approximately at the same time, even though the same word is used several times. Such remarkable changes would require an interval of time. Yet to have to allow for such an interval of time is, apparently, to concede a further argument against Pauline authorship, in view of the other factors already noted in the relationship of Colossians and Ephesians.

The great difference in the significance attached to this word in the two letters is a real difficulty for those who sponsor the Pauline authorship of both.

There is one other occurrence of μυστήριον in Ephesians which must be considered. It is the one in Eph. v. 32. Its use here is quite separate from the main thought of μυστήριον as the Divine Purpose of Universal Reconciliation, for long unknown, but now disclosed in Christ. It is more akin to the use of the word in 1 Cor. xv. 51, where it refers to the Christian's hope of life beyond death in which individual personality will survive; but it is notably different even from this use. It occurs in the passage where the writer is led from an exhortation to husbands and wives on the ordering of their mutual relationships to an illustrative explanation of the relationship between Christ and the Church. The Church is obedient to Christ, and Christ loves the Church. Christ is the Head of the Church, as the husband is the head of the wife. So wives must be obedient to husbands, and husbands must love their wives. Then the writer adds: *τὸ μυστήριον τοῦτο μέγα ἐστίν, ἐγὼ δὲ λέγω εἰς Χριστὸν καὶ [εἰς] τὴν ἐκκλησίαν.* 'This "mystery" is a most important matter, I mean that relating to Christ and the Church' (not the relationship of wives and husbands).

It can be argued that in this case the writer is using the word in the earlier sense, meaning something which is partially but not yet fully understood. Certainly one feels that the writer of Ephesians here introduces an analogy of which he himself has only begun to see the full significance. On the other hand, it can also be argued that quite a new meaning must be given to the word in this instance, and that Jerome was justified in introducing into the Vulgate the Latin word *sacramentum* to translate this particular use of *μυστήριον*. Moffatt (who, by the way, ignores the earlier protest of Abbott in ICC, p. 174, against the incorrect grammar of translating the Greek words as 'This is a great mystery', and against the rendering of *μέγα* as if it expressed 'intensity', whereas 'it properly expresses magnitude') believes that a new meaning is required to represent the word in this context and translates: 'This is a profound symbol.'

This further use of *μυστήριον* contributes nothing to our assurance of Pauline authorship. It may even be felt to tell in the other direction. That at any rate is the significance which Moffatt sees in it. He speaks of it as 'this novel use of *μυστήριον*', and includes it in his list of 'un-Pauline touches' in Ephesians (ILNT, pp. 386–7).

οἰκονομία

Another word which is characteristic of Ephesians is *οἰκονομία*. In the Pauline epistles it occurs only five times, and three of these are in Ephesians. Our immediate purpose is not to consider whether the use made of the word in Ephesians is un-Pauline, but to compare the use of the word in Ephesians with its use in Colossians, and to inquire whether such differences as we find are consistent with the interpretation that these varying uses were employed by the same author at the same time. It will, however, be necessary, as in the consideration of *μυστήριον*, to review briefly the use of the word in the earlier epistles, because if it can be shown that Ephesians differs from Colossians only in that it reverts to some earlier usage, such a difference will have no significance for our purpose. What we must mark is any difference which is not only new as compared with Colossians, but also new as compared with the earlier writings of Paul.

The only use of *οἰκονομία* by Paul, apart from Colossians and Ephesians, is in 1 Cor. ix. 17: *εἰ γὰρ ἑκὼν τοῦτο, μισθὸν ἔχω. εἰ δὲ* ἄκων, οἰκονομίαν πεπίστευμαι. The Revised Version translates the last two words: 'I have a stewardship entrusted to me', and even the modern translations find it difficult to break away from the use of the word 'stewardship', although the meaning of that word has changed in its current modern usages, so that in ordinary speech a steward more often means an attendant than what it means in this context, that is, 'a person entrusted with the management of another's property or interests'. Perhaps the nearest equivalent in the current speech of today is 'assignment'. This is used by newspaper correspondents of a special task entrusted to them by the editor whom they serve. This is exactly the meaning of *οἰκονομία* here. Paul's Master has allotted him a task, and he must see it through successfully, even though it is not to his personal liking, so as to be able to give a satisfactory account when the work is done.

The use of the word in Col. i. 25 is precisely the same as this. Paul is speaking of the Church, and he continues: *ἧς ἐγενόμην ἐγὼ διάκονος κατὰ τὴν οἰκονομίαν τοῦ θεοῦ τὴν δοθεῖσάν μοι εἰς ὑμᾶς πληρῶσαι τὸν λόγον τοῦ θεοῦ, τὸ μυστήριον* . . . . Here the translation 'stewardship' or 'assignment' is quite suitable. It was God's assignment to Paul to bring out the full meaning of God's message for the benefit of his readers, and God's message is then further described as *τὸ μυστήριον*. As in 1 Cor. ix. 17, the stewardship is 'to preach the gospel', though it is here described differently as 'the word of God'. The association of *οἰκονομία* with *μυστήριον* seems, however, to be almost accidental, and it is doubtful if any link between the two would persist in the mind of the author. For the writer of Ephesians, however, these two words have become closely associated, and each of the uses of *οἰκονομία* in Ephesians occurs in conjunction with *μυστήριον*. We have noticed already one instance (see p. 80) where a merely accidental association of words and phrases in Colossians, with no direct sense link at all, is taken up in Ephesians and given an intimate association of meaning. This instance is not so striking as the earlier one, but it raises the same question: Is this transformation of accidental contiguity into a purposeful association more likely to be the work of a second mind, expressing itself in part through borrowed material which is known by heart, or the work of the same mind re-emphasizing certain truths which have recently become clear to it? But even if this repeated association of the two words in Ephesians does not excite any suspicion, the meaning of *οἰκονομία* in Ephesians is so greatly different from that in Colossians (and in 1 Corinthians) as to occasion surprise.

The word is used three times in Ephesians, at i. 9, iii. 9, and iii. 2. They will be considered in that order.

Eph. i. 9: . . . *γνωρίσας ἡμῖν τὸ μυστήριον τοῦ θελήματος αὐτοῦ, κατὰ τὴν εὐδοκίαν αὐτοῦ, ἣν προέθετο ἐν αὐτῷ εἰς οἰκονομίαν τοῦ πληρώματος τῶν καιρῶν, ἀνακεφαλαιώσασθαι τὰ πάντα ἐν τῷ Χριστῷ.*

Here the word does not mean a special assignment which God has entrusted to Paul. Indeed it has nothing to do with Paul or any human agent. It is entirely within the mind of God. It is not dissimilar from the 'planned economy' of which we speak today, the 'planned economy' of God, God's choosing of the right moment to act decisively for the fulfilment of His age-long purpose 'to reunite all things in Christ'.

The same use of the word reappears in Eph. iii. 9, where it is said of Paul that he has been enabled *φωτίσαι τίς ἡ οἰκονομία τοῦ μυστηρίου τοῦ ἀποκεκρυμμένου ἀπὸ τῶν αἰώνων*, and this *οἰκονομία* is adduced as evidence of the *πολυποίκιλος σοφία τοῦ θεοῦ*. The meaning is the same as that in Eph. i. 9. Here we might almost venture to translate it as the 'statesmanship' of God, the supremely wise application of His resources and the perfect timing of His actions so as to obtain His ends. If we prefer a military metaphor to an economic or a political one, we might speak of 'generalship' or 'strategy'. Moffatt calls this the use of *οἰκονομία* in its 'providential aspect' and includes it in his list of 'un-Pauline touches' (ILNT, p. 387).

Both these uses are very far removed from that in Colossians. One would not anticipate so marked a divergence of meaning attached to the same word in two simultaneous pieces of writing by the same author.

In Eph. iii. 2 the wording of the passage is so closely borrowed from Col. i. 25 that we tend to assume that the word *οἰκονομία* is used in precisely the same sense in each case. But a more careful scrutiny reveals that its use in Eph. iii. 2 is identical with the other two instances of its use in Ephesians which have already been examined, and the modification in Ephesians of the phrases borrowed from Col. i. 25 is necessitated by the change of meaning attached to *οἰκονομία*.

Col. i. 25 reads: *κατὰ τὴν οἰκονομίαν τοῦ θεοῦ τὴν δοθεῖσάν μοι εἰς ὑμᾶς.*
Eph. iii. 2 reads: *τὴν οἰκονομίαν τῆς χάριτος τοῦ θεοῦ τῆς δοθείσης μοι εἰς ὑμᾶς.*

The only alteration in Eph. iii. 2 is the addition of an amplifying genitive, of which the author of Ephesians is so fond (i.e. *τῆς* χάριτος). Superficially the modification appears trifling, but it should be noted that the following participle δοθείσης is changed into the genitive, so as to make it describe τῆς χάριτος instead of τὴν οἰκονομίαν. Why? This would be a most unnatural change if οἰκονομία meant the same here as we saw it meant in Colossians. The reason for the change is that in this verse also, as in its other occurrences in Ephesians, οἰκονομία describes the providential dispensation of God (not an assignment to Paul), and so it cannot be described as τὴν δοθεῖσάν μοι. So here again we have the words of Colossians being reproduced in Ephesians, but bearing a different meaning.

πλήρωμα

Another word which is characteristic of Ephesians is πλήρωμα, and we find not only that it is used frequently in this epistle, but also that it is used in an unusual way. Its meaning here is markedly different both from that which we find in Colossians and from that in the earlier epistles. It occurs four times in Ephesians, twice in Colossians, and six times in the other Pauline epistles. Its use in Colossians is notably distinct from the earlier uses. By means of it Paul summarizes a truth of the Christian Faith in an inspired and brilliantly satisfactory way. He himself seems to have felt this, for he uses it twice in precisely the same sense, as though he is re-emphasizing a new statement of the 'truth as it is in Jesus'. He recognizes both the impressiveness and the effectiveness of the word in its new application. Apart from these two illuminating uses of the word, he avoids any further use of it in Colossians.

In these two uses the word has an explicitly theological connotation. Prior to Colossians, it can hardly be said to have been used in a theological sense at all.

1 Cor. x. 26 is a quotation from Ps. xxiv. 1: τοῦ κυρίου γὰρ ἡ γῆ καὶ τὸ πλήρωμα αὐτῆς, where πλήρωμα means 'all the contents'.

Rom. xiii. 10 πλήρωμα οὖν νόμου ἡ ἀγάπη means 'love is the complete observance of the law'.

In Rom. xi. 12. τὸ παράπτωμα of the Jews is described as 'bringing wealth to the world', and their ἥττημα as 'wealth to the Gentiles'. The argument continues: How much greater will be the benefits (for all) at τὸ πλήρωμα αὐτῶν, that is, 'their full restoration'.

In Rom. xv. 29 Paul speaks of his coming ἐν πληρώματι εὐλογίας Χριστοῦ, where the noun followed by a genitive is little more than another way of saying: 'with Christ's full blessing', or 'with the full complement of the blessing of Christ'.

The nearest approach to a theological use in these earlier epistles occurs in two similar passages in Gal. iv. 4 and Rom. xi. 25. In Gal. iv. 4 the birth of Jesus is described as taking place ὅτε δὲ ἦλθεν τὸ πλήρωμα τοῦ χρόνου, that is, at the completion of a stage in God's providential ordering of history.

The use of the word in Rom. xi. 25 seems to be similar to this. Paul is saying that some deadening of spirit has overtaken the people of Israel ἄχρι οὗ τὸ πλήρωμα τῶν ἐθνῶν εἰσέλθῃ. Here, too, the word may mean the completion of a stage in history as God has ordained it. On the other hand, it is more likely to be a resumption of the τὸ πλήρωμα αὐτῶν which precedes it, in verse 12 of the same chapter, and which has been already considered. In this case it will mean the final completion of the in-gathering of the Gentiles, which must be accomplished before the final restoration of the Jews.

So far we have not met any use of the word which is either specially difficult or explicitly theological. The two uses of the word in Colossians are not any more difficult, but they have a very important theological significance. The two passages are:

Col. i. 9: ἐν αὐτῷ εὐδόκησεν πᾶν τὸ πλήρωμα κατοικῆσαι.
Col. ii. 9: ἐν αὐτῷ κατοικεῖ πᾶν τὸ πλήρωμα τῆς θεότητος σωματικῶς.

No doubt this particular use of πλήρωμα was suggested to Paul by the heretical tendencies at Colossae, which he was seeking to counter and discredit. It does not involve any new meaning for πλήρωμα, as compared with the earlier uses, but it is employed in a brilliantly novel association. Its use in Col. i. 9 might be open to some charge of vagueness and ambiguity for modern readers, though the meaning would probably be perfectly clear to its first readers, but its later use in Col. ii. 9 serves as a complete clarification. The sum total of Divine character, it is affirmed, inhabited the human personality of Jesus. It is one of the clearest declarations in Scripture of what we mean by the Divinity of our Lord.

If Ephesians were a writing simultaneous with Colossians, by the same writer, one would naturally expect that any further use of πλήρωμα would reflect this newly expressed and illuminating meaning of the word with its novel theological significance. But we do not find this. Instead, though the word appears four times, and once in the actual phrase in which it occurs in Colossians (πᾶν τὸ πλήρωμα), one looks in vain for its use in the same theological context. No longer is it used to elucidate the relationship of Christ to God, as in Colossians, and in only one of the four instances does it echo any of the earlier uses. Three of the four instances are both quite new and very difficult.

The one instance which bears some resemblance to a pre-Colossians use is in Eph. i. 10. God is spoken of as bringing His purposes to fulfilment in Christ εἰς οἰκονομίαν τοῦ πληρώματος τῶν καιρῶν. The other passage which it resembles is Gal. iv. 4, though one cannot but note that, whereas the meaning in Gal. iv. 4 is clear-cut and unmistakable, here in Ephesians it is neither. It is rather beset with both wordiness and vagueness.

The second use of the word in Ephesians occurs in i. 23: . . . τῇ ἐκκλησίᾳ, ἥτις ἐστὶν τὸ σῶμα αὐτοῦ, τὸ πλήρωμα τοῦ τὰ πάντα ἐν πᾶσιν πληρουμένου. We cannot here enter into a discussion of the meaning of the last six words. They remain an unsolved enigma, and it is still a matter of debate whether the voice of πληρουμένου should be interpreted as Middle or Passive. It may be taken, however, as reasonably certain that the words describe God or Christ. It may even be that the two were so equated in the writer's mind that he did not himself clearly distinguish which he really meant. The important point to notice, however, is that it is not Christ whose significance is explained by πλήρωμα, but the Church.

E. F. Scott contends that the word itself here carries a different meaning from that which it bears in Colossians. There, he claims, it means the 'sum total', whereas here it is 'that which makes up for a deficiency' (MCC, p. 159). Lightfoot and Fritzche claimed that the word was formed from the perfect passive stem of the verb, and so must always carry a passive significance, and must mean 'completeness', and never 'patch'. Lightfoot even tried to substantiate this opinion in the use of the word in Mark ii. 21. Armitage Robinson, however, disputes not only their explanation of the word's origin but also its significance, arguing that it may equally well carry a passive or an active meaning, either 'completeness' or 'that which completes'. We make no judgement on the etymology of the word, but, regarding the meaning it came to have in general use, we believe that Armitage Robinson is right. Often, indeed, these two possible meanings intermingle with each other, just as in English 'completeness' may sometimes be used in the sense of 'that which completes'. The really remarkable thing, however, is not that here an active meaning is given to the word as opposed to the passive meaning in Colossians, but that the word is used to describe not the relationship of Christ to God but of the Church to Christ (or to God). This is indeed most unexpected.

The third use of the word occurs at Eph. iii. 19: ἵνα πληρώθητε εἰς πᾶν τὸ πλήρωμα τοῦ θεοῦ. Here it is the members of the Christian community who are to be filled 'unto all the fulness of God'. The exact meaning is most difficult to ascertain, and commentators discuss at length the various possibilities, and reach different conclusions. All we need to insist on here, however, is that the use of the word is not only unlike the use of the word in Paul's earlier epistles, but quite different from that which is to be found in Colossians.

The fourth appearance of the word is in Eph. iv. 13: *μέχρι καταντήσωμεν . . . εἰς μέτρον ἡλικίας τοῦ πληρώματος τοῦ Χριστοῦ.* Once again the exact meaning of the words has been difficult to determine. The use of *πλήρωμα* is like that in Eph. iii. 19, but unlike the use in Colossians or the earlier epistles. It is noteworthy that here it is to the 'fullness of Christ' that Christians must aspire, whereas in Eph. iii. 19 it was to 'the fullness of God'.

E. J. Goodspeed summarizes the difference between the uses of the word in Colossians and in Ephesians by saying that in Ephesians '*πλήρωμα* is coming to have an ethical rather than a cosmic sense' (ME, p. 51). But it is not our purpose to try to discover the exact meaning of *πλήρωμα*. All that is argued is that if Ephesians and Colossians were written at the same time by the same author, one would expect to find in Ephesians that when the word *πλήρωμα* is used it would bear some of the new significance attached to it in its two occurrences in Colossians; but this we do not find. Moreover, one would not expect that the word would carry the very different significance which it does bear in Ephesians, being used either to explain the relationship of the Church to her Master (not, as in Colossians, of Christ to God) or else to set the goal for the development in experience and character of individual Christians or groups of Christians (as in Eph. iii. 19 and iv. 13). If Paul wrote Ephesians immediately after Colossians these unexpected differences are most difficult to account for.

Remarkable differences have been shown to exist between these two epistles in certain points of emphasis and thought, and in the use of the same words but 'with varying shades of meaning'. These, along with what we have called 'conflation', and the transformation of words, which in Colossians are associated only by being accidentally adjacent in consecutive clauses, into an association of meaning in Ephesians (see p. 80), will need to be taken fully into account in any final conclusions that are reached.

PART III

THE RELATIONSHIP OF EPHESIANS TO THE OTHER PAULINE EPISTLES

X

THE EXTENT OF INTERDEPENDENCE BETWEEN EPHESIANS AND THE OTHER PAULINE EPISTLES

THE interdependence between Ephesians and Colossians is universally admitted, though the significance of it has been variously interpreted. There is, however, no such general agreement about any interdependence between Ephesians and the other epistles of Paul. If, however, the existence of such interdependence can be established, it will clearly have an important bearing on the question of the authorship of Ephesians. If it is no greater in extent or different in manner as compared with the mutual interdependence to be found in other Pauline epistles, then that will be a strong argument for the Pauline authorship of Ephesians. If, however, it can be shown to manifest a greater degree of interdependence, and notable differences in the manner of the interdependence, that must be accounted a powerful argument in favour of the non-Pauline authorship of Ephesians.

One would have thought that this was a question to which an agreed answer could be found by the application of reasonably objective tests. But this does not appear to be so. Competent scholars not only give different answers to this question but even emphatically affirm directly opposite points of view.

A. S. Peake, for instance, sees no evidence at all in Ephesians for any borrowings from any Pauline epistles other than Colossians. This is clear from a passage where he is discussing the possibility that Ephesians is the work of a Paulinist, compiling a new epistle on the basis of large sections borrowed from Colossians. He writes: 'We could understand his attempt to construct a new epistle on the basis of it, though it would not be easy to explain why he did not draw also on the other Pauline epistles' (CINT, p. 52). T. K. Abbott is almost as emphatic. He argues vigorously against those who would ascribe Ephesians to a Paulinist, and makes this point: 'It may be asked . . . how is it that a writer so well acquainted with Pauline thought should have confined his borrowing almost exclusively to the Epistle to the Colossians' (ICC, p. xxiv).

At the other extreme, H. J. Holtzmann claims that one can detect in Ephesians evidence of the writer's familiarity with all the genuine Pauline letters,[1] and von Soden's verdict is that Ephesians is a 'mosaic of Pauline phrases'. This verdict is accepted and elaborated by E. J. Goodspeed, particularly in his book *The Meaning of Ephesians*. On page 8 of that book he writes: 'Ephesians shows abundant use of Romans, 1 and 2 Corinthians, Philippians and Galatians, and a limited but unmistakable use of 1 Thessalonians, 2 Thessalonians and Philemon; it is almost a Pauline anthology; it is altogether built up of Pauline elements.' Commenting on this claim of Goodspeed, A. J. Grieve seems substantially to accept it when he says that not only Colossians is 'reflected' in Ephesians but 'all the other Pauline epistles' are reflected also (SPC, p. 35).

W. L. Knox, too, in PCG, pp. 182–203, where he deals with the Epistle to the Ephesians under the striking title of 'The Ephesian Continuator', instances a number of passages where Ephesians is apparently reproducing thoughts and phrases from the earlier Pauline epistles, and declares that he finds the general solution proposed by Goodspeed 'entirely convincing' (p. 184, footnote).

Those who see in Ephesians the large measure of borrowing from the Pauline epistles which von Soden and Goodspeed claim, naturally interpret it as evidence that the author was a Paulinist, who was intimately familiar with the whole Pauline Corpus in its written form, and freely reproduced from it both words and ideas. Others, however, who recognize similarities but only on a much slighter scale and in more general terms, welcome them as evidence that the same man who wrote the other Pauline epistles also wrote Ephesians. The similarities are cited as proving that the same mind and hand is at work in both cases. A. H. McNeile, for instance, writes: 'It is remarkable . . . how large a number of words in Ephesians and Colossians have New Testament parallels only in 1 and 2 Corinthians. And there are at least 25 thoroughly Pauline words and expressions in Ephesians (found in Romans, 1 and 2 Corinthians, Galatians, Philippians) which do not occur in Colossians'; and these

[1] In ENT, p. 266, H. J. Holtzmann comments on the fact that the author of Ephesians borrows far more extensively from Colossians than from any other of the Pauline epistles, and adds that this is specially remarkable because he does so 'in spite of his demonstrable familiarity with all the genuine Pauline epistles' ('bei nachweisbarer Vertrautheit mit allen echten Plsbriefen').

facts are interpreted as supplying confirmation of the Pauline authorship of Ephesians.

Certainly if Paul wrote Ephesians we should expect to find similarities with his other letters; and still more certainly if a Paulinist, familiar with Paul's letters, wrote Ephesians in the name of Paul we should expect to find similarities. And there is no doubt that many similarities do occur, in spite of the apparently contrary opinion of Peake and Abbott. In consideration of this matter of interdependence, therefore, there are other questions that must be asked if we are to obtain further light on the question of authorship. We must allow that in any case we should expect some measure of similarities, and on the basis of that expectation must inquire: Is there likely to be any discernible difference in the measure or the manner in which Paul himself and a Paulinist imitating Paul would reproduce the similarities? Can we find any tests which will enable us to distinguish the Paulinist from Paul himself? That is now our inquiry, and we will proceed in it by asking a series of questions and trying to answer them: 'What really is the extent of the similarities between Ephesians and the other Pauline epistles?' 'Are they greater than the similarities which exist between a genuine Pauline epistle and the other Pauline epistles?' 'Is the manner of their occurrence in Ephesians different in any way from that found in an admittedly genuine Pauline epistle?'

It is to the first of these questions that we must now give our attention.

The Extent to which the other Eight Pauline Epistles are reflected in Ephesians

In this part of our investigation it will be necessary to make frequent reference to those eight Pauline epistles which remain when Colossians and Ephesians are excepted. For convenience in referring to them these will be described as 'the other eight'. How far these 'other eight' are reflected in Ephesians is an inquiry into which no one has gone so carefully as E. J. Goodspeed. In his *Meaning of Ephesians* he lists in one column the complete text of Ephesians and, in a parallel column, the passages from the 'other eight', which, he claims, are reflected in Ephesians. The multitude of these passages is astounding, and if they are accepted in bulk, they give the impression that Ephesians is indeed little more than a string of Pauline phrases borrowed direct from his other letters. Goodspeed indeed claims that 'out of 618 short phrases into which Ephesians may be conveniently broken for comparison, 550 have unmistakable parallels in Paul, in words or substance'. And elsewhere he claims for these lists of parallels: 'The table appended to my "Meaning of Ephesians" will, I think, satisfy the reader' of the fact that 'Ephesians . . . shows unmistakable acquaintance with all nine of the accepted letters' (INT, p. 214).

When, however, these supposed parallels are examined individually, the impressiveness of this massive list is considerably modified. This is so for three reasons:

1. A great many of these passages, claimed as 'unmistakable parallels', are far from unmistakable. Indeed the similarity is too slight to carry any significance for our purpose. Such instances of possible similarities may be acceptable as further evidence for one who is already, on other grounds, convinced of the non-Pauline origin of Ephesians; but for one who is not so convinced, and who is still looking for evidence on which to found a trustworthy judgement, the inclusion of so many passages which fail to carry conviction is disconcerting. It may even prejudice him against giving a fair consideration to those parallels which are more reliable.

This exaggeration of the favourable evidence is noticeable also in Goodspeed's comparison of Ephesians with Colossians. He claims that 'almost three fifths of Colossians is paralleled in Ephesians' (INT, p. 217). In our calculation, however, in which possible parallels were omitted if in any degree open to doubt, we were content with the estimate of just over one-third.

Similarly, in our comparison of Ephesians with the other eight epistles we find ourselves unable to accept as parallels worthy of affecting our verdict many which Goodspeed records. He instances rather more than 400 passages from the other eight epistles as being reflected in Ephesians. Of these, we find it necessary to omit more than 150 from any calculations we are making as being too uncertain to carry any weight. It is true that they *may* be reflected in Ephesians, but the possibility is so uncertain as to fail to supply any significant evidence for this stage of the inquiry. A mere similarity of thought or the repetition of a single individual word, not in itself remarkable, cannot be cited as evidence of a literary relationship between two documents. Something more like a deliberate quotation or a succession of similar words or ideas is necessary for our purpose.

2. A second consideration, which robs Goodspeed's massive list of parallels of some of its imposing character, is the discovery that several of the passages from the other eight epistles quoted as parallels to Ephesians are also parallels to similar passages in Colos-

sians. This means that the borrowing of Ephesians at these points almost certainly came from Colossians (and *not* from the other epistles) because of the acknowledged dependence of Ephesians upon Colossians, so that the passages cannot also be counted as proving dependence on one of the other epistles. Further, it means that if the same phrase is found both in Colossians and in another epistle, as well as in Ephesians, that phrase is one that Paul was accustomed to use, as part of his 'stock-in-trade', and its appearance in Ephesians need not at all be an indication of borrowing. It is equally open to the interpretation that the author in each case is Paul, and that in Ephesians he is simply using words which he had clearly used on other occasions before.

For this reason, in Appendix I and Appendix VI, the parallels between Ephesians and the other eight epistles are so marked as to show clearly where these parallels coincide with similar passages in Colossians. And for calculation purposes these passages are kept distinct from the others.

3. There are a few other parallels which at first seem highly significant, but which lose their significance when we find that the words concerned have a parallel in more than one of the other eight epistles. For example, the phrase ἐργαζόμενος . . . τὸ ἀγαθόν in Eph. iv. 28 seems so similar to ἐργαζομένῳ τὸ ἀγαθόν in Rom. ii. 10 that we might at first sight be inclined to regard it as probably a deliberate imitation. But when we find in Gal. vi. 10 these words: ἐργαζώμεθα τὸ ἀγαθόν, we realize that the phrase is one of Paul's stock phrases, and its appearance in Ephesians, while of course it may be a deliberate borrowing of a recurrent Pauline phrase which had impressed itself on an imitator's mind, may also be interpreted as evidence that Paul himself is using a phrase he often used.

In Appendix VI therefore it is clearly indicated where a phrase in Ephesians recurs in more than one of the other eight epistles, and for calculation purposes these parallels also are kept separate from the rest.

These three considerations reduce considerably the impressiveness of Goodspeed's lists, and may even lead the student of them to discount the whole argument as a piece of special pleading which is more concerned to win a favourable verdict than to establish an impartial appraisement of the data. This would of course be a most unfair judgement. What makes Goodspeed include in his lists so much more than we are willing at this point to accept is that he himself is already fully convinced of the non-Pauline origin of

Ephesians as he draws up the lists, and so he includes whatever appears to confirm him in his opinion. His presentation is therefore such as to confirm the convinced rather than to convince the sceptical. But arguments which suffice to reassure the persuaded often fail to win those who are unbelievers, and may even repel them.

We must not, however, allow ourselves to be unduly alienated by Goodspeed's inclusion, in his list of parallels, of so many passages which appear to us of no significance for our present purpose, because, even when these unconvincing parallels are removed, there still remains a very large number of others, and some of them exceedingly impressive. Indeed, the smaller number, all of them full of significance, may well carry more weight than the larger number which includes many insignificant items, just as Gideon's 300 proved men were worth more than 30 times their number of unproved men!

If therefore we are looking for evidence that points reliably to Ephesians as the work of an imitator of Paul, writing in Paul's name, we shall scrupulously avoid attaching any significance to parallels which are so slight as to appear improbable. Moreover, we shall clearly indicate those passages where words in Ephesians are paralleled not only by a phrase in Colossians but also by the same phrase in some other Pauline epistle as well, and we shall avoid making them the basis of any argument against Pauline authorship. Nor shall we allow any support for this argument to be claimed from phrases in Ephesians which are reproduced in more than one of the other eight epistles. Even in these instances it may be argued that they are the work of an imitator who is simply availing himself of Pauline phrases which have stamped themselves on his mind by the very fact of their repeated occurrence in the Pauline letters. Since, however, they may with equal justification be interpreted as evidence that it is the same mind, that is the mind of Paul, which is at work in Ephesians as in all the others, it is best, for our present purpose, merely to leave these ambiguous passages out of account. We shall therefore concern ourselves primarily with those phrases in Ephesians which have no parallel in Colossians and are echoed only once in the other eight epistles. With regard to these we must presently ask ourselves whether they are better explained

(*a*) as Pauline phrases which happen to be used again by Paul, as he writes Ephesians, or

(*b*) as Pauline phrases which have so impressed themselves on a careful reader's mind that he reproduces them in an imitative work based mainly on Colossians, but reflecting also what he recalls from the other Pauline epistles.

Before, however, attempting to answer these questions we must attempt to give some indication of the extent to which words and phrases from the other eight Pauline epistles occur in Ephesians.

At this point the reader will be well advised to work carefully through Appendix I, studying the second column where the phrases from the other eight Pauline epistles, which have parallels in Ephesians, are entered. In this column, and in the third column which contains the text of Ephesians, where the similarity is striking the words are undermarked with thin double lines (═══). Less striking, but nevertheless remarkable, similarities are marked with a single thin line (———). Faint similarities are indicated by a dotted line (··········). Those in this last group are, however, not counted in any numerical calculations that are made. Occasionally a possible parallel is included, but without any underlining. This means that it is too uncertain to carry any weight in the argument and yet is considered worthy of mention.

The extent of these parallels can best be indicated in tabular form.

The total number of words in Ephesians is 2,411.

Parallels between Ephesians and Colossians (see p. 57)

Words in Ephesians undermarked with thick lines	387
Words in Ephesians undermarked with less thick lines	251
Words in Ephesians undermarked either with thick or less thick lines	638

This number, 638, represents 26·5 per cent. of the whole.

Parallels between Ephesians and the other Eight Epistles

Words in Ephesians undermarked with double thin lines	313
Words in Ephesians undermarked with single thin lines	389
Words in Ephesians undermarked either with double or single thin lines	702

This number, 702, represents 29·1 per cent. of the whole.

Other calculations, to which reference will be made later in the arguments, may conveniently be listed here:

Words in Ephesians undermarked with both thick and thin lines	211
Words in Ephesians undermarked with thin lines only	491

This number, 491, represents 20·4 per cent. of the whole.

Words in Ephesians, underlined with thin lines only, which have parallels in more than one epistle of the 'other eight': 75, which is 3·1 per cent. of the whole.

Words in Ephesians which have parallels in some other Pauline epistle (i.e. which are underlined with thick, or thin lines, or both): 1,129, which is 46·7 per cent. of the whole.

This last figure, with the percentage it represents, is exceedingly impressive. But our concern now is with the parallels between Ephesians and the other eight Pauline epistles. These amount in all to 702 words. If, however, we discount those also reflected in Colossians, the number is reduced to 491 (20·4 per cent.). Again, if we deduct those words which have more than one parallel in the other eight epistles, that means taking away another 75 words (3·1 per cent.). The result is that the irreducible minimum of significant parallels may be assessed at 416 words (17·3 per cent. of the whole).

It is difficult to draw up any table which accurately represents the measure of interdependence which appears to exist between Ephesians and the individual Pauline epistles. It is easy to count up and say that 54 verses in Romans have parallels in Ephesians and 13 in Philippians. But it is not so easy to be sure that these represent the true proportion of the extent of the dependence. A parallel may be comparatively slight, or it may consist of an extended verbatim similarity, so that in some cases one single verse may provide a larger number of parallels than several other verses together. It follows that a comparison based on the number of verses in which parallels occur may well be misleading, though there is a probability that inequalities such as have been mentioned will be approximately equalized in the sum total. For what it is worth, then, this table of the verses from each individual epistle which are reflected in Ephesians is appended.

Name of epistle	*Number of verses reflected in Ephesians*	*Number of verses reflected twice*	*Number of verses reflected thrice*	*Length of epistle, indicated by number of pages in W. & H.*
Romans	54	9	6	26
1 Corinthians	45	10	1	24
2 Corinthians	20	1	0	16·5
Galatians	15	3	0	8·25
Philippians	13	3	1	6
1 Thessalonians	8	1	0	5·5
2 Thessalonians	1	0	0	3
Philemon	5	0	0	1·25

In general, the table reveals a fairly steady measure of dependence. 2 Thessalonians is the letter least represented, and, in proportion to its length, Philemon is most represented. In view of the close association between Colossians and Philemon, it is not surprising to find that the phrasing of Philemon appears to have influenced considerably the writer of Ephesians. On p. 130 the correspondence between the two can be seen at a glance. Of the others, in proportion to their length, Romans reveals most parallels. 2 Corinthians is reproduced noticeably less than 1 Corinthians.

It will be seen that the total number of parallels between Ephesians and the other eight epistles hardly exceeds the borrowing from Colossians alone. This at first may appear very difficult to explain, and it may have the effect of making the correspondences between Ephesians and the other eight seem slight and unimportant. If, however, the author of Ephesians had known Colossians very intimately before he came to know the other epistles, or if the author was Paul, writing Ephesians immediately after Colossians, or perhaps even after a later re-reading of it, then the far greater correspondence with Colossians has an explanation. And even if, in comparison with the borrowings from Colossians, the reproduction of verses from the others may seem unimpressive, that is an unfair comparison. The true comparison is with the extent of the correspondence which appears between one admittedly genuine letter of Paul and the rest of the Corpus. When this comparison is worked out it is found that Ephesians has a remarkably higher degree of similarities with the other eight Pauline epistles than is found in the case of the others. In this respect Ephesians stands in a category by itself.

XI

COMPARISON BETWEEN EPHESIANS AND PHILIPPIANS

IN THE NUMBER OF WORDS AND PHRASES FOR WHICH PARALLELS CAN BE FOUND IN THE OTHER PAULINE EPISTLES

IN the last chapter we attempted to make an estimate of the extent to which passages from the other eight Pauline epistles are reproduced in Ephesians, and in Appendix I the words underlined with thin lines give indisputable evidence that there are many such passages. We agreed, however, that some measure of correspondence would be expected, whether Ephesians was written by Paul himself or by an imitator. In order to discover whether the measure of the similarities found in Ephesians holds any significance for our present purpose it will first be necessary to try to discover what degree of similarities occur between an admittedly genuine letter of Paul and the rest of the Pauline letters. And while we seek to estimate the extent of the correspondence we shall learn all we can about the character and peculiarities of these correspondences in order that we may later inquire whether they reflect the same character and the same peculiarities as the correspondences in Ephesians. If the measure and the manner both tally approximately with what we find in Ephesians, then that will be a further argument in favour of Pauline authorship. If, however, there are notable differences, that will be an argument on the other side.

A completely satisfactory test would necessitate a careful examination of all the Pauline epistles in order to draw up exhaustive lists of the correspondences between them. These would then have to be assessed on a percentage basis so as to provide a fair basis for comparison in view of the differing length of the epistles. Even then further calculations would be necessary in order to place the results in proper perspective because of the unusually close interdependence between Ephesians and Colossians. The utmost care would have to be taken to make proper but not undue allowance for the large measure of material from Colossians which is reproduced in Ephesians.

It will be necessary, therefore, to remove from our reckonings in the case of Ephesians these correspondences from Colossians and deal only with the similarities with the other eight epistles. If, however, we do this, we must bear in mind that the area from which Ephesians can then draw parallels is less by one epistle than the area open to the other letters. All this considerably complicates the calculations, but it will be necessary to make these adjustments if our estimates are to provide a fair basis for comparison.

Such a detailed study of all the Pauline epistles, and the listing of their similarities one with another, is a separate study on its own and cannot be attempted here. The best substitute for our purpose seems to be to choose one letter which may be regarded as representative of Paul's letters, and treat that as the norm with which Ephesians may be compared. For this purpose Philippians has been chosen, in the belief that it is a typical Pauline letter which probably comes from the same period of Paul's life as Ephesians did, if Ephesians is the work of Paul. In Appendix IV there have been drawn up in parallel columns the passages in Philippians and the passages in the other Pauline epistles which show similarity to each other, and on the basis of these parallels we proceed to our calculations.

In Philippians there are 1,539 words. This makes the epistle about five-eighths the length of Ephesians. The same method of underlining is used in Appendix IV as in Appendix I, that is, verbal correspondences which are more or less exact are undermarked with double lines, and less exact parallels with a single line. The result is that 95 words are marked with double lines and 140 with a single line. So that, in all, 235 words are underlined, and these constitute 15·2 per cent. of the whole.

Since, however, we decided, in view of our special purpose, to discount in Ephesians those parallels which recur in more than one of the other eight Pauline epistles, we must be prepared to do the same in Philippians, so that the basis of comparison remains the same. We find that of the 235 words noted above as being reflected elsewhere in Paul's writings, 84 have parallels in more than one other epistle. These are indicated in Appendix IV by a further broken underlining (------). If these are subtracted from 235, the total left is 151, and this represents 9·8 per cent. of the whole.

If Ephesians is taken as a whole, and all its similarities with all the other nine Pauline epistles, including Colossians, are counted, the differences between it and Philippians are very striking indeed. In Ephesians the total number of words underlined amounted to 46·7 per cent. (see p. 105) and this corresponds with a total in

Philippians which represents 15·2 per cent. If the words are deducted which have more than one parallel in other epistles, the corresponding percentages are 34·9 in Ephesians and 9·8 in Philippians.

Such figures would indeed put Ephesians in a class by itself, but the reason for such complete isolation would be mainly its admittedly close connexion with Colossians, and this is not now the point at issue. So our first step must be to remove from our calculations those words which are reflected only in Colossians. This means that all the words underlined with a thick line only in Appendix I are to be ignored. In order, however, to keep the basis of comparison with Philippians fair, the words which are underlined with a thin line, even if they also have thick undermarkings, will be calculated. The following table gives the comparative figures when this adjustment has been made.

In the table there are four columns, which represent the following calculations:

Column 1: The percentage of words in Philippians which are reflected in the other nine Pauline epistles.
Column 2: The percentage of words in Ephesians which are reflected in the other eight Pauline epistles.
Column 3: The percentage of words in Ephesians reflected in the other eight Pauline epistles, adjusted so as to make allowance for the smaller area from which borrowings may be taken as compared with Philippians.
Column 4: The percentage of words in Ephesians which are reflected in the other nine Pauline epistles, including Colossians.

Column 1 *Philippians*	*Column 2* *Ephesians (without Colossians)*	*Column 3* *Ephesians (adjusted)*	*Column 4* *Ephesians (including Colossians)*
15·2%	29·1%	32·7%	46·7%

If words which have parallels in more than one of the other epistles are not included in the reckoning, the respective percentages work out as follows:

9·8%	26·0%	29·6%	34·9%

For our purpose column 4 may be entirely ignored. The other three columns give figures that are worthy of careful consideration. Those in column 2 are roughly twice as many as those in column 1. That is, the parallels in Ephesians are twice the number of those in Philippians even when full allowance is made for the greater length of Ephesians and the figures calculated in percentages so as to remove any discrepancy that greater length may involve. This suggests very strongly that the explanation which suffices to explain the parallels noted in Philippians, i.e. that they are there as the result of the same author using phrases and thoughts that come naturally to him, is not in itself sufficient to explain the greatly increased number of parallels in Ephesians.

Moreover, the difference between the percentages in columns 1 and 2 does not fully reflect the actual difference which should be reckoned. Philippians has all the other nine Pauline epistles from which to derive parallels for its count, whereas Ephesians has only eight because Colossians has been removed from the reckoning. That is, in pages of Westcott and Hort's edition of the Greek New Testament, Philippians can draw parallels from 83 pages and Ephesians from only 74. So that the figures in columns 2 should be multiplied by 1·12 in order to make them a fair comparison with the figures for Philippians in column 1. This adjusted figure is entered in column 3. Columns 1 and 3 therefore represent the true comparison, and there the differences are even greater than between columns 1 and 2. The parallels in Ephesians now appear as substantially more than twice as many as those in Philippians.

This is a very remarkable difference, and even allowing for the probability that some further parallels in Philippians might be found, if the same intensive study were given to it as has been given to Ephesians so that the margin of difference might be somewhat reduced, the margin is so large as to allow for considerable reduction without being robbed of its significance.

XII

TESTS TO DISTINGUISH BETWEEN PAUL AND A PAULINE IMITATOR

We have tried to measure the extent to which words and phrases from the other Pauline epistles reappear in Philippians and in Ephesians respectively, and our calculations have led us to the conclusion that these parallels occur at least twice as frequently in Ephesians as in Philippians. So large a difference suggests that the explanation which is sufficient to account for the smaller number of parallels in Philippians will not suffice to explain the much greater number in Ephesians. In the case of Philippians, the explanation of the parallels is that the same mind is at work, using phrases and ideas which it is accustomed to use. This explanation alone, however, is hardly sufficient to account for the greatly increased number of parallels which we find in Ephesians.

In this chapter we must give our attention, not to the extent of these parallels, but to their general nature and characteristics. This is clearly a more difficult task than adding up the frequency of their occurrence. Our immediate aim is to characterize the type of parallels which appear in Philippians, and the manner of their occurrence, in order that we may later inquire whether the same characteristics can be found among the parallels in Ephesians. It will, however, help us in our inquiry if we can form some idea of the kind of thing to look for.

So we preface our examination of the parallels in Philippians with these preliminary questions: Are there any tests by which we may hope to distinguish between (i) a genuine writing of Paul, in which he, naturally enough, uses phrases and ideas which he has previously used in other connexions, and (ii) an imitation of a Pauline writing, in which the imitator, genuinely wishing to present what he believes to be the message of Paul, freely allows himself to introduce words and phrases and thoughts which have become familiar to him as a result of careful study of Paul's letters?

It is notoriously difficult to devise such tests. A clever imitator who wishes to escape detection, or who merely wishes to do his work well, may deliberately choose to follow the lines which we should expect to be characteristic of Paul himself. He may quite well be clever enough to avoid almost all of the obvious pitfalls. There are, however, two tests which are worth applying.

1. Let us imagine ourselves in the place of a Pauline disciple who knows Paul's letters, and wishes to write a treatise in the name of Paul and, so far as he can, in the style of Paul, in order to present Paul's message for some special purpose dear to his own heart. He has known Colossians so long and intimately that his mind is thoroughly familiar with every phrase of it. He also knows the other letters, and has read them carefully and been enormously impressed with their insight and wisdom. He wants, in his treatise, to incorporate as much of Paul's phraseology as he can because he aims honestly at representing Paul to his readers.

What should we expect in such a case? We should expect to find that some passages in Paul's writings had influenced him more than others and lingered on more vividly in his mind. As a result, his borrowings from Paul would not be more or less evenly spread over the whole area of his epistles, but certain passages which had made a special impression on his mind would be reflected more than others. Passages of outstanding significance would be likely to be reflected more than less impressive passages. It is true that what he might regard as outstanding need not tally with our ideas, and the special purpose he has in mind might lead him to unexpected choices and rejections. We should, however, anticipate that such a chapter, for instance, as Romans viii would exert a greater influence than, say, Romans x; Romans xii than Romans xiv or xv; 1 Corinthians xv than 1 Corinthians v; and 2 Corinthians v more than 2 Corinthians ix, x, or xi. Moreover, we should expect that the influence of one such impressive passage would not be confined to one solitary, even if remarkable, parallel. Rather there would be repeated parallels, now one phrase from the memorable passage being reflected, and now another, on different occasions throughout the treatise. This phenomenon might not be immediately evident to a reader, perhaps not even after a careful reading of the treatise with the intention of noting its parallels with the Pauline epistles; but if the sum total of the parallels were collected and arranged in order it would then become clear that a large proportion of the parallels were connected with these important passages, and not by any means evenly spread over the whole area of the Pauline Corpus.

This possible characteristic in any list of parallels that may be drawn up will be a point to look for, and where it is found it will have a significant bearing on the question of authorship.

On the contrary, suppose the author to be Paul himself. He is a busy man, who is constantly declaring, explaining, applying his message, as he addresses different congregations of people, or writes to distant companies of Christians. Certainly he would use some of the same phrases and ideas again and again. That we should only expect. But it is very doubtful if he would have any clear verbal memory of what he said on any particular occasion, or what the exact words were which he used in any one letter, especially if that letter had been written months or even years previously. What we, who are able to read and re-read his letters in print, have come to regard as the outstanding passages in his letters would have slipped from his mind no less than the more ordinary chapters. Such coincidences as would occur between a new epistle and his earlier ones would be unintentional and promiscuous. They would not be likely to fall into groups associated with special passages. They would be widely and fairly evenly scattered throughout the other letters and would come just as frequently from unimportant as from important passages.

2. In seeking to differentiate a second test, we will begin again with the imitator. As he built up his work, deliberately allowing Pauline phraseology to mould his style and vocabulary, not only would he be specially influenced by some particular passages, but he would also be inclined to choose, for incorporation in his work, a considerable proportion of striking and memorable words and phrases from the other epistles. This may not be the outcome of deliberate purpose; but rather it would happen to him as to any other reader that the phrases which lodged themselves in his mind would be just these which we have described as 'striking and memorable', and it is these which would be specially likely to be reproduced.

If, on the other hand, Paul is the writer, the points of coincidence are more likely to be the ordinary modes of expression that Paul commonly used. The repetition of one or two striking words might occur, but in the main ordinary phrases in constant use in his writings would be the kind to predominate among the parallels.

These are two tests by which we may hope to be able to distinguish the hand of the imitator from that of Paul himself. Our first inquiry is about their application to Philippians. Do we find what we assumed we should find in the case of a genuine Pauline letter? If so, we shall with more confidence proceed to apply the same tests to Ephesians.

In the case of a genuine Pauline letter, we anticipated that the parallels would be fairly evenly dispersed throughout the other letters, and would not noticeably fall into groups associated with special passages in the other letters. Also, we did not expect to find any predominance of striking phrases among these parallels.

In order to apply the first of these two tests, we have the material ready in Appendix IV, but it will need to be presented in a new arrangement. This new arrangement is provided in Appendix V. In Appendix IV the order of the parallels is based on the order of their occurrence in Philippians. In Appendix V the parallels are listed in the order in which they occur in their own epistle. In this way any group of verses in some other epistle which is unusually frequently reflected in Philippians becomes immediately clear. Columns 2 and 4 are the chief ones for our present purpose. In column 2 the parallels in the other Pauline epistles are listed in the order of their own epistle. In column 1 the parallel passages in Philippians are noted. If the passage in Philippians has more than one parallel in the other letters, the other parallels are noted in column 3. Since, in our treatment of Ephesians, those passages with more than one parallel were largely discounted, for the sake of fairness in comparison, the similar passages in Philippians must also be noted separately from the others. The fourth column is the most relevant of all to our present inquiry. In column 4 are listed the parallels from column 2 which have not been, as it were, cancelled out by further parallels in column 3. Even when an entry has been made in column 3, the opposite entry from column 2 is still, sometimes, carried forward into column 4 if it more nearly represents the corresponding words in Philippians than any of the others.

The first thing to notice in Appendix V is the large proportion of parallels which are entered in column 3. Out of the 71 verses in column 2, no fewer than 36 have further parallels entered in column 3. That is, more than half of the parallels in the list occur in at least two other contexts in the Pauline epistles. At least half of the parallels are therefore immediately evident as phrases that Paul used frequently.

But our primary concern was to find an answer to this question: Are the parallels fairly evenly dispersed throughout the other letters or do they tend to fall into groups associated with certain special passages? A glance down column 4 leaves us in no doubt of the answer. With one or two exceptions, which must be considered further, there is little evidence of passages from the other letters exerting either a sustained or a recurring influence in Philippians. We find approximately what we should have expected in the case of two letters by the same author. The parallels appear to be unrelated to each other.

We must next look briefly at the apparent exceptions to this general impression. It is only to be expected that with 47 entries in column 4, one or two of them would stand near together. So much one would predict. A few coincidences do not disprove a rule. In fact, the exceptions, provided they stand out as exceptions, establish the general truth of the rule. In column 4 it will be seen that brackets are used five times to indicate small groups of verses, from each one of which more than one parallel with Philippians is recorded. There is a sixth bracket in column 2, relating to 2 Cor. xiii. 11. Here, however, each phrase reflected in Philippians has a further parallel in some other letter. Of the five brackets in column 4, two indicate groups of verses from Ephesians; and that perhaps is a matter of significance. The other three groups are Gal. vi. 16–18, Col. iii. 2–15, and 1 Cor. ix. 23–4.

Gal. vi. 16–18. This section includes two parallels, one with Phil. iii. 16 and the other with Phil. iv. 23. Both of them have further parallels in the other Pauline epistles, as noted in column 3. It is true that the parallels from Gal. vi. 16–18 are a trifle nearer than the others, but an examination of them all does not leave in the mind any impression that Gal. vi. 16–18 exercised a twofold influence over the mind of the writer of Philippians. It appears rather that Paul is using phrases which he was accustomed to use, and that two which he happened to use in Philippians happen also to occur in Galatians in adjacent verses.

Col. iii. 2–15. Three parallels with Philippians occur in these verses. If these three parallels all occurred within four or even five verses, they would be impressive. But three in fourteen verses are much less so.

The most impressive of the three groups is 1 Cor. ix. 23–4. 1 Cor. ix. 23 is reflected at Phil. i. 7, and 1 Cor. ix. 24 at Phil. iii. 12–14. This instance is just the kind of thing that one might look for in the work of an imitator. It might be interpreted as the result of these two verses impinging strongly on his mind and being reproduced in his work at two separate points. Had there been any question of the possibility of Philippians being the work of an imitator, it is just such an instance as this which would have aroused suspicion. Even then, only one such instance would have carried no weight by itself. It could have been set aside as a mere coincidence. If, however, several such instances appeared, the plea of coincidence would not avail.

These three groups in Philippians, then, may be taken to represent a kind of average in the number of groups that might be expected as the result of coincidence when there is identity of authorship in all the epistles under consideration. If Ephesians shows only a similar proportion, that will be a further argument in favour of Pauline authorship. If, however, the proportion proves to be noticeably greater, that will cast doubt upon the claim to Pauline authorship.

The second test, also, which we proposed, is substantiated by what we find in Philippians. The parallels there, underlined in Appendix IV, do not abound in phrases and words which might well have impressed themselves vividly on the mind of a reader of the other letters. One or two, which might have been placed in this category, are undermarked with broken lines as well as with thin lines, and this means that they have parallels in more than one place in the other epistles, and so can hardly be put in this class. It may be that ἀποκαραδοκία (i. 20) and σύμμορφος (iii. 21), both of which are used elsewhere by Paul only in Romans, should be included under this head. Perhaps too we should mention the description of his converts as his 'joy and crown' (Phil. iv. 1 and 1 Thess. ii. 9). These three instances, however, are exceptions which confirm the general rule rather than disprove it.

There are also notable parallels between Ephesians and Philippians (i. 11, i. 27, and iv. 15), but the significance of these is ambiguous and will be considered later.

If, on the other hand, to apply our tests from the other side, we turn to the Epistle to the Laodiceans, which is generally admitted to be a post-Pauline attempt to construct an epistle (obviously spurious) in the name of Paul, we find that the hand of the imitator is patently revealed by both the tests indicated above. This epistle is produced as if it were the letter to which Paul refers in Col. iv. 16 as the letter 'from Laodicea'. It is a very short letter, consisting of only twenty verses. It is not known in any Greek original. The Latin version is all which has survived. An English translation is conveniently available in *The Apocrypha of the New Testament* translated by M. R. James (p. 479). It is an attempt to fill an obvious gap in the collected works of Paul. It is little more than an unskilful collection of sayings from the genuinely Pauline epistles. Though it is so very brief, many of the genuine epistles are represented in it by quotations, but it is clear that Philippians dominates the writer's mind, and especially certain passages in Philippians. Ten out of the twenty verses have clear parallels in Philippians. In particular Phil. iv. 4–9 must have impressed itself on the mind of the imitator, for this section is particularly in evidence. Moreover, it is not the ordinary phrasing of the other letters which reappears, but the more striking and memorable phrases. The majority are from Philippians, but not all. Such phrases are: 'For me to live is Christ', 'It is God that worketh in you', 'Filthy lucre', 'Let your requests be made known unto God', 'Whatsoever things are true . . .', 'Rejoice in the Lord'. In this way a clumsy imitator betrays his handiwork.

No such blatant lack of skill is to be looked for in Ephesians, but in a less prominent degree the two features claimed as characteristic of the imitator's hand seem to be discernible. In the next chapter we shall examine the evidence for this.

XIII

THE TESTS APPLIED TO EPHESIANS

We must now turn our attention to Ephesians and apply there the tests we have proposed. We saw that certain correspondences with the other Pauline epistles are to be expected, whether the author be Paul or a later disciple of Paul writing in Paul's name. As between Paul himself and an imitator, however, there would very likely be certain differences in the character of such correspondences. An imitator, for instance, would be likely to use a greater number than Paul himself. He would include a larger proportion of striking phrases from the other letters than Paul would. Also the correspondences would be likely to show familiarity with some of the greater passages from the Pauline epistles, whereas if Paul were the author the correspondences would probably be entirely disconnected from one another and would show no particular association with special passages.

We have already dealt with the first of these tests, and have tried to make some assessment of the extent of such correspondences in Ephesians as compared with a fairly typical Pauline epistle, Philippians. The second test, which is concerned with the proportion of memorable phrases for which parallels can be found in other letters, will be considered later. It is with the test relating to the grouping of the parallels round outstanding passages in the Pauline epistles which must now be considered.

In Appendix I there is provided a text of Ephesians with the parallels from the other epistles noted opposite the phrase in Ephesians to which they correspond. This arrangement of the parallel passages, however, does not help us much in our present investigation. A list needs to be drawn up which includes all these parallels from the other eight Pauline epistles in the order in which they occur in their own epistle, so that an estimate can readily be made as to which are the passages from the other epistles which are most frequently reflected. These, we may presume, will be the passages which have exercised greatest influence on the mind of the writer of Ephesians.

Such a list is provided in Appendix VI. There, in column A are recorded, in the order of their occurrence in their own epistle, the verses which in some measure appear to be reflected in Ephesians.

To the left of this column, in the column marked X, are noted the verses in Ephesians in which they are reflected. If the parallel, noted in column A, is reflected in Colossians as well as Ephesians, the context of the parallel in Colossians is noted in column B. In view of the close relationship between Colossians and Ephesians, it is probable that in these instances it is Colossians rather than the similar phrasing from one of the 'other eight' which has influenced the author of Ephesians. This will make us very cautious about allowing these parallels to count for much in our calculations at this stage, though it does not wholly rule out all of them as of no significance whatever for our purpose. In some cases it may have been the memory of a passage from one of the other eight epistles that was exercising its influence even though the same phrase or one like it appears also in Colossians. But the initial probability is that the dependence is on Colossians, and for present purposes the parallels which are balanced by an entry in column B are discounted.

Column C is also concerned with the duplication of parallels. If the passage in Ephesians is paralleled in more than one of the 'other eight' Pauline epistles, the other parallel verses are recorded in column C. Again, in these instances, there is an initial probability that these are explicable as stock phrases in Paul's vocabulary rather than as evidence of the work of an imitator, and for present purposes are treated with considerable reserve. It is, however, possible that they should be regarded as phrases which, by the very fact of their repetition in the Pauline epistles, have impressed themselves on the memory of a studious reader. In some cases one of these duplicated parallels has some special similarity to Ephesians which the others lack, and in such instances they are not wholly discounted, but are recorded in column D as well as in column C, sometimes with a question-mark following.

Column D records the verses already noted in column A which have no second parallel in column B or column C (apart from the occasional exception just mentioned). It is with the verses listed in this column that our present investigation is primarily concerned, although those in columns B and C should not be entirely ignored.

The brackets in column D indicate those passages and groups of verses in one of the 'other eight' epistles which appear to have recurring parallels in Ephesians, as though the author of Ephesians had a literary acquaintance with the other epistles and had been specially impressed by these passages from which he repeatedly recalls phrases or word-sequences. These are of great importance for our consideration in view of the almost total lack of such 'sustained' parallelism between Philippians and the other Pauline epistles. In Philippians we found parallels with isolated phrases in the other epistles, and identity of authorship was a sufficient explanation. But the same explanation cannot be regarded as adequately accounting for the phenomenon indicated by the brackets in column D of Appendix VI. Whereas in Philippians there were only five brackets, indicating possible groups of influential verses (see Appendix V), and of these four could be largely discounted as insignificant, in Ephesians there are twenty-five groups, and at least twenty of them are significant.

This is so important a test, perhaps the crucial test of the whole of our investigation, that we must give much more detailed consideration to these verses which are grouped into brackets in column D. It is impressive to note the lists themselves in Appendix VI, but, in some cases especially, the bracketed groups become even more impressive when we see them, and their parallels in Ephesians, in the full text, with the corresponding parallels underlined. In view of the importance of this test, we will consider these bracketed groups individually.

Exact similarities are undermarked with double thin lines and less exact similarities with single thin lines. Where some words in Ephesians are more likely to be derived from Colossians, they are undermarked with thick lines. If a phrase recurs in more than one of the other eight Pauline epistles it is also marked with a broken line (-----).

(1) Romans

i. 21–4. . . . διότι γνόντες τὸν θεὸν
οὐχ ὡς θεὸν ἐδόξασαν ἢ ηὐχαρίστη-
σαν, ἀλλὰ ἐματαιώθησαν ἐν τοῖς
διαλογισμοῖς αὐτῶν, καὶ ἐσκοτίσθη ἡ
ἀσύνετος αὐτῶν καρδία. [22] φάσκοντες
εἶναι σοφοὶ ἐμωράνθησαν, [23] καὶ ἤλ-
λαξαν τὴν δόξαν τοῦ ἀφθάρτου θεοῦ
ἐν ὁμοιώματι εἰκόνος φθάρτου ἀνθρώ-
που καὶ πετεινῶν καὶ τετραπόδων
καὶ ἑρπετῶν. [24] διὸ παρέδωκεν αὐτοὺς
ὁ θεὸς ἐν ταῖς ἐπιθυμίαις τῶν καρδιῶν
αὐτῶν εἰς ἀκαθαρσίαν τοῦ ἀτιμάζε-
σθαι τὰ σώματα αὐτῶν.

Ephesians

iv. 17–19. τοῦτο οὖν λέγω καὶ
μαρτύρομαι ἐν κυρίῳ, μήκετι ὑμᾶς
περιπατεῖν καθὼς καὶ τὰ ἔθνη περι-
πατεῖ ἐν ματαιότητι τοῦ νοὸς αὐτῶν,
[18] ἐσκοτωμένοι τῇ διανοίᾳ ὄντες,
ἀπηλλοτριωμένοι τῆς ζωῆς τοῦ θεοῦ,
διὰ τὴν ἄγνοιαν τὴν οὖσαν ἐν αὐτοῖς,
διὰ τὴν πώρωσιν τῆς καρδίας αὐτῶν,
οἵτινες ἀπηλγηκότες ἑαυτοὺς παρέ-
δωκαν τῇ ἀσελγείᾳ εἰς ἐργασίαν
ἀκαθαρσίας πάσης ἐν πλεονεξίᾳ.

This is an instance of what we have called a 'sustained' parallel. It is not just a question of one isolated phrase recurring in Ephesians, but of several phrases from one short passage in Romans being reproduced within three consecutive verses in Ephesians.

It is worth noting the change of subject in *παρέδωκαν* (Eph. iv. 19) as compared with *παρέδωκεν* (Rom. i. 24), where the subject is God. It almost seems as though it may be a silent improvement on the rather harsh expression in Romans, which is capable of unfortunate theological interpretations.

(2) Romans iii. 20–iv. 2

iii. 20. *διότι ἐξ ἔργων νόμου οὐ δικαιωθή-*
σεται πᾶσα σὰρξ ἐνώπιον αὐτοῦ . . . 22 *δικαιο-*
σύνη δὲ θεοῦ διὰ πίστεως Ἰησοῦ Χριστοῦ,
εἰς πάντας τοὺς πιστεύοντας· οὐ γάρ ἐστιν
διαστολή. 23 *πάντες γὰρ ἥμαρτον καὶ ὑστε-*
ροῦνται τῆς δόξης τοῦ θεοῦ, 24 *δικαιούμενοι*
δωρεὰν τῇ αὐτοῦ χάριτι διὰ τῆς ἀπολυτρώ-
σεως τῆς ἐν Χριστῷ Ἰησοῦ· 25 *ὃν προέθετο*
ὁ θεὸς ἱλαστήριον διὰ πίστεως ἐν τῷ αὐτοῦ
αἵματι, εἰς ἔνδειξιν τῆς δικαιοσύνης αὐτοῦ
διὰ τὴν πάρεσιν τῶν προγεγονότων ἁμαρτη-
μάτων ἐν τῇ ἀνοχῇ τοῦ θεοῦ . . . 27 *ποῦ οὖν ἡ*
καύχησις; ἐξεκλείσθη.

iv. 2. *εἰ γὰρ Ἀβραὰμ ἐξ ἔργων ἐδικαιώθη, ἔχει καύχημα.*

Ephesians

i. 19. *τὸ ὑπερβάλλον μέγεθος τῆς δυνάμεως αὐτοῦ εἰς ἡμᾶς τοὺς πιστεύοντας.*

ii. 5. *χάριτί ἐστε σεσωσμένοι.*

ii. 8. *τῇ γὰρ χάριτί ἐστε σεσωσμένοι διὰ πίστεως· καὶ τοῦτο οὐκ ἐξ ὑμῶν, θεοῦ τὸ δῶρον· οὐκ ἐξ ἔργων ἵνα μή τις καυχήσηται.*

i. 7. *ἐν ᾧ ἔχομεν τὴν ἀπολύτρωσιν διὰ τοῦ αἵματος αὐτοῦ τὴν ἄφεσιν τῶν παραπτωμάτων, κατὰ τὸ πλοῦτος τῆς χάριτος αὐτοῦ.*

Eph. ii. 8 is most strikingly similar to the corresponding passage in Romans. It reads almost like a summary of it, with the more general word 'save' substituted for the more technical 'justify'. If the other parallel passages in Ephesians are counted in, then the above passage may be taken as representative of what we have called 'recurring' parallels, for the influence of this single passage in Romans appears to be reflected in three separate contexts in Ephesians.

(3) Rom. v. 1–2	Ephesians
δικαιωθέντες οὖν ἐκ πίστεως εἰρήνην ἔχωμεν πρὸς τὸν θεὸν διὰ τοῦ κυρίου ἡμῶν Ἰησοῦ Χριστοῦ, δι' οὗ καὶ τὴν προσαγωγὴν ἐσχήκαμεν τῇ πιστει εἰς τὴν χάριν ταύτην ἐν ᾗ ἑστήκαμεν, καὶ καυχώμεθα ἐπ' ἐλπίδι τῆς δόξης τοῦ θεοῦ.	iii. 11–12. . . . ἐν τῷ Χριστῷ Ἰησοῦ τῷ κυρίῳ ἡμῶν ἐν ᾧ ἔχομεν τὴν παρρησίαν καὶ προσαγωγὴν ἐν πεποιθήσει διὰ τῆς πίστεως, αὐτοῦ.
	ii. 17–18. εὐηγγελίσατο εἰρήνην . . . ὅτι δι' αὐτοῦ ἔχομεν τὴν προσαγωγὴν οἱ ἀμφότεροι ἐν ἑνὶ πνεύματι πρὸς τὸν πατέρα.

The above parallels strongly suggest that the author of Ephesians had been deeply impressed with this opening passage in Romans v, and so much so that in two separate contexts he repeats its central affirmation of access to God through Christ, and on each occasion includes other different elements from Rom. v. 1–2.

(4) Romans viii. 9–39	Ephesians
viii. 9. ὑμεῖς δὲ οὐκ ἐστὲ ἐν σαρκὶ ἀλλὰ ἐν πνεύματι, εἴπερ πνεῦμα θεοῦ οἰκεῖ ἐν ὑμῖν. εἰ δέ τις πνεῦμα Χριστοῦ οὐκ ἔχει, οὗτος οὐκ ἔστιν αὐτοῦ. [10] εἰ δὲ Χριστὸς ἐν ὑμῖν, . . .	iii. 16. . . . ἵνα δῷ ὑμῖν . . . δυνάμει κραταιωθῆναι διὰ τοῦ πνεύματος αὐτοῦ εἰς τὸν ἔσω ἄνθρωπον, [17] κατοικῆσαι τὸν Χριστὸν διὰ τῆς πίστεως ἐν ταῖς καρδίαις ὑμῶν.
[15] ἐλάβετε πνεῦμα υἱοθεσίας, ἐν ᾧ κράζομεν Ἀββὰ ὁ πατήρ. [16] αὐτὸ τὸ πνεῦμα συμμαρτυρεῖ τῷ πνεύματι ἡμῶν ὅτι ἐσμὲν τέκνα θεοῦ. [17] εἰ δὲ τέκνα, καὶ κληρόνομοι· κληρόνομοι μὲν θεοῦ, συγκληρόνομοι δὲ Χριστοῦ	iii. 6. . . . εἶναι τὰ ἔθνη συγκληρονόμα καὶ σύνσωμα καὶ συνμέτοχα τῆς ἐπαγγελίας ἐν Χριστῷ Ἰησοῦ.
	i. 13–14. ἐν ᾧ καὶ . . . ἐσφραγίσθητε τῷ πνεύματι τῆς ἐπαγγελίας τῷ ἁγίῳ [14] ὅς ἐστιν ἀρραβὼν τῆς κληρονομίας ἡμῶν.
[23] υἱοθεσίαν ἀπεκδεχόμενοι, τὴν ἀπολύτρωσιν τοῦ σώματος ἡμῶν.	i. 4–7. ἐξελέξατο ἡμᾶς ἐν αὐτῷ πρὸ καταβολῆς κόσμου . . . [5] προορίσας ἡμᾶς εἰς υἱοθεσίαν διὰ Ἰησοῦ Χριστοῦ εἰς αὐτόν. . . .
	7. ἐν ᾧ ἔχομεν τὴν ἀπολύτρωσιν.
[28] οἴδαμεν δὲ ὅτι τοῖς ἀγαπῶσιν τὸν θεὸν πάντα συνεργεῖ εἰς ἀγαθόν, τοῖς κατὰ πρόθεσιν κλητοῖς οὖσιν.	i. 11. . . . ἐν ᾧ καὶ ἐκληρώθημεν προορισθέντες κατὰ πρόθεσιν τοῦ τὰ

Rom. viii. 9–39 (*cont.*)	Ephesians (*cont.*)
29 ὅτι οὓς προέγνω, καὶ προώρισεν συμμόρφους τῆς εἰκόνος τοῦ υἱοῦ αὐτοῦ, εἰς τὸ εἶναι αὐτὸν πρωτότοκον ἐν πολλοῖς ἀδελφοῖς· 30 οὓς δὲ προώρισεν, τούτους καὶ ἐκάλεσεν..	πάντα ἐνεργοῦντος κατὰ τὴν βουλὴν τοῦ θελήματος αὐτοῦ.
34. Χριστὸς Ἰησοῦς ὁ ἀποθανών, μᾶλλον δὲ ἐγερθείς, ὅς ἐστιν ἐν δεξιᾷ τοῦ θεοῦ . . . 35 τίς ἡμᾶς χωρίσει ἀπὸ τῆς ἀγάπης τοῦ Χριστοῦ;	20. ἐγείρας αὐτὸν ἐκ νεκρῶν καὶ καθίσας ἐν δεξιᾷ αὐτοῦ. iii. 18–19. ἵνα ἐξισχύσητε καταλαβέσθαι σὺν πᾶσιν τοῖς ἁγίοις τί τὸ πλάτος καὶ μῆκος καὶ ὕψος καὶ βάθος γνῶναί τε τὴν ὑπερβάλλουσαν τῆς γνώσεως ἀγάπην τοῦ Χριστοῦ.
38. πέπεισμαι γὰρ ὅτι οὔτε θάνατος οὔτε ζωὴ οὔτε ἄγγελοι οὔτε ἀρχαὶ οὔτε ἐνεστῶτα οὔτε μέλλοντα οὔτε δυνάμεις 29 οὔτε ὕψωμα οὔτε βάθος οὔτε τις κτίσις ἑτέρα δυνήσεται ἡμᾶς χωρίσαι ἀπὸ τῆς ἀγάπης τοῦ θεοῦ.	i. 21. ὑπεράνω πάσης ἀρχῆς καὶ ἐξουσίας καὶ δυνάμεως καὶ κυριότητος . . . οὐ μόνον ἐν τῷ αἰῶνι τούτῳ ἀλλὰ καὶ ἐν τῷ μέλλοντι.

The phrase *ἀγάπη τοῦ Χριστοῦ* (Eph. iii. 19 and Rom. viii. 35) occurs also in 2 Cor. v. 14, but the context of its occurrence in Romans is more similar to that in Ephesians.

It is noteworthy that these parallel passages in Ephesians fall largely into two groups: (i) Eph. i. 4–11 and (ii) Eph. iii. 16–19. It would appear that as the author of Ephesians writes these two passages, the influence of Romans viii is making itself felt in his thoughts.

(5) Romans xi. 32–xii. 5	Ephesians
xi. 32. . . . ἵνα τοὺς πάντας ἐλεήσῃ. 33 ὦ βάθος πλούτου καὶ σοφίας καὶ γνώσεως θεοῦ· ὡς ἀνεξεραύνητα τὰ κρίματα αὐτοῦ καὶ ἀνεξιχνίαστοι αἱ ὁδοὶ αὐτοῦ.	ii. 4. ὁ δὲ θεὸς πλούσιος ὢν ἐν ἐλέει. iii. 8. τὸ ἀνεξιχνίαστον πλοῦτος τοῦ Χριστοῦ. . . . 10. ἡ πολυποίκιλος σοφία τοῦ θεοῦ.
36. ἐξ αὐτοῦ καὶ δι' αὐτοῦ καὶ εἰς αὐτὸν τὰ πάντα· αὐτῷ ἡ δόξα εἰς τοὺς αἰῶνας· ἀμήν.	iv. 6. εἷς θεὸς καὶ πατὴρ πάντων, ὁ ἐπὶ πάντων καὶ διὰ πάντων καὶ ἐν πᾶσιν. iii. 21. αὐτῷ ἡ δόξα . . . εἰς πάσας

Rom. xi. 32–xii. 5 (*cont.*)	Ephesians (*cont.*)
xii. 1. παρακαλῶ οὖν ὑμᾶς, ἀδελφοί, διὰ τῶν οἰκτιρμῶν τοῦ θεοῦ, παραστῆσαι τὰ σώματα ὑμῶν θυσίαν ζῶσαν ἁγίαν τῷ θεῷ εὐάρεστον, τὴν λογικὴν λατρείαν ὑμῶν· 2 καὶ μὴ συσχηματίζεσθε τῷ αἰῶνι τούτῳ, ἀλλὰ μεταμορφοῦσθε τῇ ἀνακαινώσει τοῦ νοός, εἰς τὸ δοκιμάζειν ὑμᾶς τί τὸ θέλημα τοῦ θεοῦ, τὸ ἀγαθὸν καὶ εὐάρεστον καὶ τέλειον. 3 λέγω γὰρ διὰ τῆς χάριτος τῆς δοθείσης μοι παντὶ τῷ ὄντι ἐν ὑμῖν, μὴ ὑπερφρονεῖν παρ' ὃ δεῖ φρονεῖν, ἀλλὰ φρονεῖν εἰς τὸ σωφρονεῖν, ἑκάστῳ ὡς ὁ θεὸς ἐμέρισεν μέτρον πίστεως. 4 καθάπερ γὰρ ἐν ἑνὶ σώματι πόλλα μέλη ἔχομεν, τὰ δὲ μέλη πάντα οὐ τὴν αὐτὴν ἔχει πρᾶξιν, οὕτως οἱ πολλοὶ ἓν σῶμά ἐσμεν ἐν Χριστῷ, τὸ δὲ καθ' εἷς ἀλλήλων μέλη.	τὰς γενεὰς τοῦ αἰῶνος τῶν αἰώνων· ἀμήν. iv. 1. παρακαλῶ οὖν ὑμᾶς . . . . v. 10. δοκιμάζοντες τί ἐστιν εὐάρεστον τῷ κυρίῳ. v. 17. συνίετε τί τὸ θελημα τοῦ κυρίου. iii. 7. κατὰ τὴν δωρεὰν τῆς χάριτος τοῦ θεοῦ τῆς δοθείσης μοι. iv. 7. ἑνὶ δὲ ἑκάστῳ ἡμῶν ἐδόθη ἡ χάρις κατὰ τὸ μέτρον τῆς δωρεᾶς τοῦ Χριστοῦ. iv. 4. ἓν σῶμα. iv. 25. ἐσμὲν ἀλλήλων μέλη.

Similar words to those of Eph. iii. 21 and Rom. xi. 36, which are underlined with broken rules, appear also at Rom. xvi. 27 and Gal. i. 5; and also παρακαλῶ ὑμᾶς occurs in 2 Cor. x. 1 as well as at Rom. xii. 1 and Eph. iv. 1. But the combined similarity of the two consecutive verses, Rom. xi. 36 and xii. 1, with the two consecutive verses in Ephesians (iii. 21 and iv. 1) is very striking.

The phrase at Rom. xii. 3 recurs three or four times in Paul's epistles, and is not here specially significant, though it is noteworthy that the verses in Eph. iii. 7–10 record three parallels with phrases in this passage from Romans.

The recurrence of the unusual word ἀνεξιχνίαστος in Rom. xi. 33 and Eph. iii. 8 is worthy of note.

(6) 1 Cor. iii. 6–16	Ephesians
iii. 6. ἐγὼ ἐφύτευσα, Ἀπολλῶς ἐπότισεν ἀλλὰ ὁ θεὸς ηὔξανεν· 7 ὥστε οὔτε ὁ φυτεύων ἐστίν τι οὔτε ὁ ποτίζων, ἀλλὰ ὁ αὐξάνων θεός.	ii. 21. ἐν ᾧ πᾶσα οἰκοδομὴ συναρμολογουμένη αὔξει εἰς ναὸν ἅγιον ἐν κυρίῳ.
9. θεοῦ γάρ ἐσμεν συνεργοί· θεοῦ γεώργιον, θεοῦ οἰκοδομή ἐστε. 10	ii. 19–21. ἐστε συνπολῖται τῶν ἁγίων καὶ οἰκεῖοι τοῦ θεοῦ, 20 ἐποι-

1 Cor. iii. 6–16 (*cont.*)	Ephesians (*cont.*)
κατὰ τὴν χάριν τοῦ θεοῦ τὴν δοθεῖσάν μοι ὡς σοφὸς ἀρχιτέκτων θεμέλιον ἔθηκα, ἄλλος δὲ ἐποικοδομεῖ. 11 θεμέλιον γὰρ ἄλλον οὐδεὶς δύναται θεῖναι παρὰ τὸν κείμενον, ὅς ἐστιν Ἰησοῦς Χριστός. 12 εἰ δέ τις ἐποικοδομεῖ ἐπὶ τὸν θεμέλιον	κοδομηθέντες ἐπὶ τῷ θεμελίῳ τῶν ἀποστόλων καὶ προφητῶν, ὄντος ἀκρογωνιαίου αὐτοῦ Χριστοῦ Ἰησοῦ, 21 ἐν ᾧ πᾶσα οἰκοδομὴ συναρμολογουμένη αὔξει εἰς ναὸν ἅγιον ἐν κυρίῳ . . . .
16. οὐκ οἴδατε ὅτι ναὸς θεοῦ ἐστε καὶ τὸ πνεῦμα τοῦ θεοῦ ἐν ὑμῖν οἰκεῖ; εἴ τις τὸν ναὸν τοῦ θεοῦ φθείρει, φθερεῖ τοῦτον ὁ θεός· ὁ γὰρ ναὸς τοῦ θεοῦ ἅγιός ἐστιν, οἵτινές ἐστε ὑμεῖς.	iii. 7. κατὰ τὴν δωρεὰν τῆς χάριτος τοῦ θεοῦ τῆς δοθείσης μοι.

The recurrence of *αὐξάνω* in Eph. ii. 21 as well as in 1 Cor. iii. 7 is probably a mere coincidence. In Eph. iii. 7 we have the same parallel, which has been already noted in Rom. xii. 3. Here the parallel is more exact, but little weight can be attached to it. But the similarities which remain are remarkable.

In Eph. ii. 20, however, the foundation consists of prophets and apostles, which is a notable contrast from the affirmation in 1 Cor. iii. 11.

(7) 1 Cor. iv. 12–16	Ephesians
iv. 12. καὶ κοπιῶμεν ἐργαζόμενοι ταῖς ἰδίαις χερσίν	iv. 28. ὁ κλέπτων μηκέτι κλεπτέτω, μᾶλλον δὲ κοπιάτω ἐργαζόμενος ταῖς ἰδίαις χερσὶν τὸ ἀγαθόν.
14. οὐκ ἐντρέπων ὑμᾶς γράφω ταῦτα, ἀλλ' ὡς τέκνα μου ἀγαπητὰ νουθετῶν	
16. παρακαλῶ οὖν ὑμᾶς, μιμηταί μου γίνεσθε.	v. 1. γίνεσθε οὖν μιμηταὶ τοῦ θεοῦ, ὡς τέκνα ἀγαπητά.

Three separate points of similarity, some of them very close, appear in these two short passages.

(8) 1 Cor. viii. 5–6	Ephesians
viii. 5. καὶ γὰρ εἴπερ εἰσὶν λεγόμενοι θεοὶ εἴτε ἐν οὐρανῷ εἴτε ἐπὶ γῆς, ὥσπερ εἰσὶν θεοὶ πολλοὶ καὶ κύριοι πολλοί, 6 ἀλλὰ ἡμῖν εἷς θεὸς	iii. 14. τούτου χάριν κάμπτω τὰ γόνατά μου πρὸς τὸν πατέρα 15 ἐξ οὗ πᾶσα πατριὰ ἐν οὐρανοῖς καὶ ἐπὶ γῆς ὀνομάζεται.

1 Cor. viii. 5–6 (*cont.*)	Ephesians (*cont.*)
ὁ πατήρ, ἐξ οὗ τὰ πάντα καὶ ἡμεῖς εἰς αὐτόν, καὶ εἷς κύριος Ἰησοῦς Χριστός, δι' οὗ τὰ πάντα καὶ ἡμεῖς δι' αὐτοῦ.	iv. 5. εἷς κύριος, μία πίστις, ἓν βάπτισμα· [6] εἷς θεὸς καὶ πατὴρ πάντων, ὁ ἐπὶ πάντων καὶ διὰ πάντων καὶ ἐν πᾶσιν.

The phrases ἐν οὐρανοῖς, ἐπὶ γῆς (in Eph. iii. 14) are common expressions in Paul and no great importance can be attached to them here, though the conjunction of these two phrases with ὁ πατὴρ ἐξ οὗ in both contexts makes the parallel worthy of being recorded.

(9) 1 Cor. xi. 1–3	Ephesians
xi. 1. μιμηταί μου γίνεσθε, καθὼς κἀγὼ Χριστοῦ . . . . 3. θέλω δὲ ὑμᾶς εἰδέναι ὅτι παντὸς ἀνδρὸς ἡ κεφαλὴ ὁ Χριστός ἐστιν, κεφαλὴ δὲ γυναικὸς ὁ ἀνήρ, κεφαλὴ δὲ τοῦ Χριστοῦ ὁ θεός.	v. 1. γίνεσθε οὖν μιμηταὶ τοῦ θεοῦ, ὡς τέκνα ἀγαπητά, καὶ περιπατεῖτε ἐν ἀγάπῃ καθὼς καὶ ὁ Χριστὸς ἠγάπησεν ἡμᾶς . . . . iv. 16. ὅς ἐστιν ἡ κεφαλή, Χριστός. v. 23. ἀνήρ ἐστιν κεφαλὴ τῆς γυναικὸς ὡς καὶ ὁ Χριστὸς κεφαλὴ τῆς ἐκκλησίας . . . .

The phrase from Eph. iv. 16 has also parallels in Colossians, but it is even closer to the words of 1 Cor. xi. 3.

(10) 1 Cor. xii. 2–6	Ephesians
xii. 2. οἴδατε ὅτι ὅτε ἔθνη ἦτε πρὸς τὰ εἴδωλα τὰ ἄφωνα ὡς ἂν ἤγεσθε ἀπαγόμενοι. [3] διὸ γνωρίζω ὑμῖν ὅτι οὐδεὶς ἐν πνεύματι θεοῦ λαλῶν λέγει ΑΝΑΘΕΜΑ ΙΗΣΟΥΣ, καὶ οὐδεὶς δύναται εἰπεῖν ΚΥΡΙΟΣ ΙΗΣΟΥΣ, εἰ μὴ ἐν πνεύματι ἁγίῳ. [4] διαιρέσεις δὲ χαρισμάτων εἰσίν, τὸ δὲ αὐτὸ πνεῦμα. [5] καὶ διαιρέσεις διακονιῶν εἰσιν καὶ ὁ αὐτὸς κύριος· [6] καὶ διαιρέσεις ἐνεργημάτων εἰσίν, ὁ δὲ αὐτὸς θεὸς ὁ ἐνεργῶν τὰ πάντα ἐν πᾶσιν.	ii. 11. διὸ μνημονεύετε ὅτι ποτὲ ὑμεῖς τὰ ἔθνη ἐν σαρκί . . . ὅτι ἦτε τῷ καιρῷ ἐκείνῳ χωρὶς Χριστοῦ, ἀπηλλοτριωμένοι τῆς πολιτείας τοῦ Ἰσραήλ. iv. 4–6. ἓν σῶμα καὶ ἓν πνεῦμα, καθὼς καὶ ἐκλήθητε ἐν μιᾷ ἐλπίδι τῆς κλήσεως ὑμῶν· [5] εἷς κύριος, μία πίστις, ἓν βάπτισμα, εἷς θεὸς καὶ πατὴρ πάντων, ὁ ἐπὶ πάντων καὶ διὰ πάντων καὶ ἐν πᾶσιν. i. 11. κατὰ πρόθεσιν τοῦ τὰ πάντα ἐνεργοῦντος. i. 23. τὸ πλήρωμα τοῦ τὰ πάντα ἐν πᾶσιν πληρουμένου.

Eph. iv. 4–6 seems to be an excellent summary of three passages from 1 Corinthians: viii. 6, xii. 4–6, and xii. 12. These passages overlap with one another, but each seems to make its own contribution to Eph. iv. 4–6, not least these three consecutive verses from 1 Cor. xii. Eph. i. 11 also contains an echo from 1 Cor. xii. 6.

The words πάντα ἐν πᾶσιν (1 Cor. xii. 6) also occur at 1 Cor. xv. 28.

If it is fair to interpret the opening words of Eph. ii. 11 as a recollection of 1 Cor. xii. 2, it may serve as an early comment on a notoriously difficult verse. It would mean that the author of Ephesians either read ποτὲ in 1 Cor. xii. 2 (instead of ὅτε) or else he understood the passage in that sense.

(11) 1 Cor. xii. 12–13	Ephesians
καθάπερ γὰρ τὸ σῶμα ἕν ἐστιν καὶ μέλη πολλὰ ἔχει πάντα δὲ τὰ μέλη τοῦ σώματος πολλὰ ὄντα ἕν ἐστιν σῶμα, οὕτως καὶ ὁ Χριστός· [13] καὶ γὰρ ἐν ἑνὶ πνεύματι ἡμεῖς πάντες εἰς ἓν σῶμα ἐβαπτίσθημεν εἴτε Ἰουδαῖοι εἴτε Ἕλληνες, εἴτε δοῦλοι εἴτε ἐλεύθεροι, καὶ πάντες ἓν πνεῦμα ἐποτίσθημεν.	iv. 4. ἓν σῶμα καὶ ἓν πνεῦμα . . . [5] εἷς κύριος, μία πίστις, ἓν βάπτισμα. v. 29. καθὼς καὶ ὁ Χριστὸς (θάλπει) τὴν ἐκκλησίαν ὅτι μέλη ἐσμὲν τοῦ σώματος αὐτοῦ. ii. 18. δι' αὐτοῦ ἔχομεν προσαγωγὴν οἱ ἀμφότεροι ἐν ἑνὶ πνεύματι πρὸς τὸν πατέρα.

It may well be that these two further verses from 1 Cor. xii should be considered along with 1 Cor. xii. 2–6 in the preceding section as one large (and very impressive) group with extensive parallels in Ephesians. Perhaps even 1 Cor. xii. 27–8 should be included in this group as well. Since, however, intervals of several verses separate these three smaller groups, it is perhaps less presumptuous to class them as distinct units.

These two verses, at any rate, appear to have recurring parallels in Ephesians.

(12) 1 Cor. xii. 27–8	Ephesians
ὑμεῖς δέ ἐστε σῶμα Χριστοῦ καὶ μέλη ἐκ μέρους. [28] καὶ οὓς μὲν ἔθετο ὁ θεὸς ἐν τῇ ἐκκλησίᾳ πρῶτον ἀποστόλους, δεύτερον προφήτας, τρίτον διδασκάλους, ἔπειτα δυνάμεις,	iv. 4. ἓν σῶμα καὶ ἓν πνεῦμα. iv. 11. καὶ αὐτὸς ἔδωκεν τοὺς μὲν ἀποστόλους, τοὺς δὲ προφήτας, τοὺς δὲ εὐαγγελιστάς, τοὺς ποιμένας καὶ διδασκάλους πρὸς τὸν καταρτισμὸν

1 Cor. xii. 27–8 (*cont.*)	Ephesians (*cont.*)
ἔπειτα χαρίσματα ἰαμάτων, ἀντιλήμψεις, κυβερνήσεις, γένη γλωσσῶν.	τῶν ἁγίων εἰς ἔργον διακονίας, εἰς οἰκοδομὴν τοῦ σώματος τοῦ Χριστοῦ.
	ii. 20. ἐποικοδομηθέντες ἐπὶ τῷ θεμελίῳ τῶν ἀποστόλων καὶ προφητῶν ὄντος ἀκρογωνιαίου αὐτοῦ Χριστοῦ Ἰησοῦ.

Note the conjunction of σῶμα Χριστοῦ with the corresponding list of types of leaders in the Church in both 1 Cor. xii and Eph. iv. 11.

(13) 1 Cor. xiv. 5–26	Ephesians
5. . . . ἵνα ἡ ἐκκλησία οἰκοδομὴν λάβῃ.	iv. 12. . . . εἰς οἰκοδομὴν τοῦ σώματος τοῦ Χριστοῦ, [13] μέχρι καταντήσωμεν οἱ πάντες εἰς τὴν ἑνότητα τῆς πίστεως καὶ τῆς ἐπιγνώσεως τοῦ υἱοῦ τοῦ θεοῦ, εἰς ἄνδρα τέλειον, εἰς μέτρον ἡλικίας τοῦ πληρώματος τοῦ Χριστοῦ, ἵνα μηκέτι ὦμεν νήπιοι . . . .
12. . . . πρὸς τὴν οἰκοδομὴν τῆς ἐκκλησίας ζητεῖτε ἵνα περισσεύητε.	
20. τῇ κακίᾳ νηπιάζετε, ταῖς δὲ φρεσὶν τέλειοι γίνεσθε.	
24. ἐὰν δὲ πάντες προφητεύωσιν, εἰσέλθῃ δέ τις ἄπιστος ἢ ἰδιώτης, ἐλέγχεται ὑπὸ πάντων, [25] τὰ κρυπτὰ τῆς καρδίας αὐτοῦ φανερὰ γίνεται	16. . . . ἐξ οὗ πᾶν τὸ σῶμα . . . τὴν αὔξησιν τοῦ σώματος ποιεῖται εἰς οἰκοδομὴν ἑαυτοῦ ἐν ἀγάπῃ.
26. . . . πάντα πρὸς οἰκοδομὴν γινέσθω.	v. 12. τὰ γὰρ κρυφῇ γινόμενα ὑπ' αὐτῶν αἰσχρόν ἐστιν καὶ λέγειν· [13] τὰ δὲ πάντα ἐλεγχόμενα ὑπὸ τοῦ φωτὸς φανεροῦται . . . .

The phrase εἰς οἰκοδομήν in 2 Cor. x. 8 and xiii. 10 is a closer verbal parallel to the words in Eph. iv. 12 and 16, but in 2 Cor. it is not expressly related to the Church, as it is in 1 Cor. xiv and Eph. iv.

(14) 1 Cor. xv. 9–28	Ephesians
9. ἐγὼ γάρ εἰμι ὁ ἐλάχιστος τῶν ἀποστόλων . . . [10] χάριτι δὲ θεοῦ εἰμι ὅ εἰμι, καὶ ἡ χάρις αὐτοῦ ἡ εἰς ἐμὲ οὐ κενὴ ἐγενήθη.	iii. 8. ἐμοὶ τῷ ἐλαχιστοτέρῳ πάντων ἁγίων ἐδόθη ἡ χάρις αὕτη, τοῖς ἔθνεσιν εὐαγγελίσασθαι.
24. εἶτα τὸ τέλος, ὅταν παραδιδοῖ τὴν βασιλείαν τῷ θεῷ καὶ πατρί,	i. 20. . . . καθίσας ἐν δεξιᾷ αὐτοῦ ἐν τοῖς ἐπουρανίοις [21] ὑπεράνω πάσης

1 Cor. xv. 9–28 (*cont.*)	Ephesians (*cont.*)
ὅταν καταργήσῃ πᾶσαν ἀρχὴν καὶ πᾶσαν ἐξουσίαν καὶ δύναμιν. [25] δεῖ γὰρ αὐτὸν βασιλεύειν ἄχρι οὗ θῇ πάντας τοὺς ἐχθροὺς ὑπὸ τοὺς πόδας αὐτοῦ. [26] ἔσχατος ἐχθρὸς καταργεῖται ὁ θάνατος. [27] πάντα γὰρ ὑπέταξεν ὑπὸ τοὺς πόδας αὐτοῦ. ὅταν δὲ εἴπῃ ὅτι πάντα ὑποτέτακται, δῆλον ὅτι ἐκτὸς τοῦ ὑποτάξαντος αὐτῷ τὰ πάντα. [28] ὅταν δὲ ὑποταγῇ αὐτῷ τὰ πάντα, τότε καὶ αὐτὸς ὁ υἱὸς ὑποταγήσεται τῷ ὑποτάξαντι αὐτῷ τὰ πάντα ἵνα ᾖ ὁ θεὸς πάντα ἐν πᾶσιν.	ἀρχῆς καὶ ἐξουσίας καὶ δυνάμεως καὶ κυριότητος καὶ παντὸς ὀνόματος ὀνομαζομένου οὐ μόνον ἐν τῷ αἰῶνι τούτῳ ἀλλὰ καὶ ἐν τῷ μέλλοντι, καὶ [22] πάντα ὑπέταξεν ὑπὸ τοὺς πόδας αὐτοῦ καὶ αὐτὸν ἔδωκεν κεφαλὴν ὑπὲρ πάντα τῇ ἐκκλησίᾳ, [23] ἥτις ἐστὶν τὸ σῶμα αὐτοῦ, τὸ πλήρωμα τοῦ τὰ πάντα ἐν πᾶσιν πληρουμένου.

It is remarkable that three close verbal correspondences should occur between three consecutive verses in Eph. i and five consecutive verses in 1 Cor. xv.

It may be that Eph. i. 23 is a restatement of a Pauline utterance which seemed unduly to subordinate Christ within the Godhead.

(15) 2 Cor. i. 3–22	Ephesians
3. εὐλογητὸς ὁ θεὸς καὶ πατὴρ τοῦ κυρίου ἡμῶν Ἰησοῦ Χριστοῦ, ὁ πατὴρ . . . ὁ παρακαλῶν	i. 3, εὐλογητὸς ὁ θεὸς καὶ πατὴρ τοῦ κυρίου ἡμῶν Ἰησοῦ Χριστοῦ, ὁ εὐλογήσας . . . .
12. . . . οὐκ ἐν σοφίᾳ σαρκικῇ ἀλλ' ἐν χάριτι θεοῦ, ἀνεστράφημεν ἐν τῷ κόσμῳ.	ii. 3. . . . ἐν οἷς καὶ ἡμεῖς πάντες ἀνεστράφημέν ποτε ἐν ταῖς ἐπιθυμίαις τῆς σαρκὸς ἡμῶν . . . .
22. ὁ . . . θεός, ὁ καὶ σφραγισάμενος ἡμᾶς καὶ δοὺς τὸν ἀρραβῶνα τοῦ πνεύματος ἐν ταῖς καρδίαις ἡμῶν.	i. 13. . . . ἐν ᾧ καὶ πιστεύσαντες ἐσφραγίσθητε τῷ πνεύματι τῆς ἐπαγγελίας τῷ ἁγίῳ, ὅς ἐστιν ἀρραβὼν τῆς κληρονομίας ἡμῶν. iv. 30. καὶ μὴ λυπεῖτε τὸ πνεῦμα τὸ ἅγιον τοῦ θεοῦ, ἐν ᾧ ἐσφραγίσθητε εἰς ἡμέραν ἀπολυτρώσεως.

2 Cor. i. 3 is an exception among the opening paragraphs of the

Pauline letters. All the others, after the initial greeting, continue with a thanksgiving introduced by εὐχαριστέω. The only exception to this is Galatians, where indignant surprise has completely ousted gratitude for the moment, and θαυμάζω replaces εὐχαριστέω. In 2 Cor. i Paul is so full of relief at the passing of a critical situation which had threatened to wreck the church at Corinth that the somewhat formal εὐχαριστέω is insufficient to express his thankfulness for the happy solution that has been found, and appropriately enough he substitutes for it: 'Blessed be God.'

In Ephesians there is no situation of unexpected relief from threatened danger, and so the use of εὐλογητός in Eph. i. 3 appears rather less spontaneous. In each case, it should be noted, the construction is continued by the definite article and the participle.

ἀρραβών recurs in 2 Cor. v. 5, but not elsewhere in Paul, nor in the whole of the New Testament. In 2 Cor. v. 5, however, it is not associated with σφραγίζω. σφραγίζω occurs also at Rom. xv. 28, but in that context it is not associated with either ἀρραβών or the Holy Spirit.

(16) 2 Cor. v. 14–20	Ephesians
v. 14. ἡ γὰρ ἀγάπη τοῦ Χριστοῦ συνέχει ἡμᾶς.	iii. 19. γνῶναι . . . τὴν ὑπερβάλλουσαν τῆς γνώσεως ἀγάπην τοῦ Χριστοῦ.
17. ὥστε εἴ τις ἐν Χριστῷ, καινὴ κτίσις· τὰ ἀρχαῖα παρῆλθεν, ἰδοὺ γέγονεν καινά.	ii. 10. αὐτοῦ γάρ ἐσμεν ποίημα, κτισθέντες ἐν Χριστῷ Ἰησοῦ ἐπὶ ἔργοις ἀγαθοῖς . . . . ii. 15. τὸν νόμον . . . καταργήσας, ἵνα τοὺς δύο κτίσῃ ἐν αὐτῷ εἰς ἕνα καινὸν ἄνθρωπον.
20. ὑπὲρ Χριστοῦ οὖν πρεσβεύομεν.	vi. 20. τὸ μυστήριον τοῦ εὐαγγελίου, ὑπὲρ οὗ πρεσβεύω ἐν ἁλύσει.

The phrase ἡ ἀγάπη τοῦ Χριστοῦ recurs in Rom. viii. 35, and so by itself carries no great weight here.

Also καινὴ κτίσις is used at Gal. vi. 15, but here its association with ἐν Χριστῷ justifies its inclusion as a noteworthy parallel with the two passages from Eph. ii.

The further echo of 2 Cor. v. 20 makes it probable that this impressive passage from 2 Cor. v has lingered in the mind of the writer of Ephesians.

(17) Gal. i. 10–16	Ephesians
10. ἢ ζητῶ ἀνθρώποις ἀρέσκειν; εἰ ἔτι ἀνθρώποις ἤρεσκον, Χριστοῦ δοῦλος οὐκ ἂν ἤμην.	vi. 6. . . . μὴ κατ' ὀφθαλμοδουλίαν ὡς ἀνθρωπάρεσκοι, ἀλλ' ὡς δοῦλοι Χριστοῦ, ποιοῦντες τὸ θέλημα τοῦ θεοῦ ἐκ ψυχῆς . . . .
15. ὅτε δὲ εὐδόκησεν ὁ . . . με . . . καλέσας διὰ τῆς χάριτος αὐτοῦ ἀποκαλύψαι τὸν υἱὸν αὐτοῦ ἐν ἐμοί, ἵνα εὐαγγελίζωμαι αὐτὸν ἐν τοῖς ἔθνεσιν	iii. 8. ἐμοὶ τῷ ἐλαχιστοτέρῳ πάντων ἁγίων ἐδόθη ἡ χάρις αὕτη, τοῖς ἔθνεσιν εὐαγγελίσασθαι τὸ ἀνεξιχνίαστον πλοῦτος τοῦ Χριστοῦ.

The word *ἀνθρωπάρεσκοι* in Eph. vi. 6 is clearly derived from Col. iii. 22, and *δοῦλοι Χριστοῦ* is found also at 1 Cor. vii. 22 and Phil. i. 1, but the association of the two is peculiar to Gal. i. 10 and Eph. vi. 6.

(18) Gal. ii. 9–20	Ephesians
9. γνόντες τὴν χάριν τὴν δοθεῖσάν μοι, . . . δεξιὰς ἔδωκαν ἐμοὶ . . . ἵνα ἡμεῖς εἰς τὰ ἔθνη, αὐτοὶ δὲ εἰς τὴν περιτομήν.	iii. 1. τούτου χάριν ἐγὼ Παῦλος ὁ δέσμιος τοῦ Χριστοῦ Ἰησοῦ ὑπὲρ ὑμῶν τῶν ἐθνῶν—εἴ γε ἠκούσατε τὴν οἰκονομίαν τῆς χάριτος τοῦ θεοῦ τῆς δοθείσης μοι εἰς ὑμᾶς.
15. ἡμεῖς φύσει Ἰουδαῖοι καὶ οὐκ ἐξ ἐθνῶν ἁμαρτωλοί, 16 εἰδότες δὲ ὅτι οὐ δικαιοῦται ἄνθρωπος ἐξ ἔργων νόμου ἐὰν μὴ διὰ πίστεως Χριστοῦ Ἰησοῦ, καὶ ἡμεῖς εἰς Χριστὸν Ἰησοῦν ἐπιστεύσαμεν, ἵνα δικαιωθῶμεν ἐκ πίστεως Χριστοῦ καὶ οὐκ ἐξ ἔργων νόμου.	ii. 8. τῇ γὰρ χάριτί ἐστε σεσωσμένοι διὰ πίστεως· καὶ τοῦτο οὐκ ἐξ ὑμῶν, θεοῦ τὸ δῶρον· οὐκ ἐξ ἔργων ἵνα μή τις καυχήσηται.
20. ὃ δὲ νῦν ζῶ ἐν σαρκί, ἐν πίστει ζῶ τῇ τοῦ υἱοῦ τοῦ θεοῦ τοῦ ἀγαπήσαντός με καὶ παραδόντος ἑαυτὸν ὑπὲρ ἐμοῦ.	v. 2. . . . καθὼς καὶ ὁ Χριστὸς ἠγάπησεν ὑμᾶς καὶ παρέδωκεν ἑαυτὸν ὑπὲρ ἡμῶν. v. 25. . . . καθὼς καὶ ὁ Χριστὸς ἠγάπησεν τὴν ἐκκλησίαν καὶ ἑαυτὸν παρέδωκεν ὑπὲρ αὐτῆς.

The phrase *χάριν τὴν δοθεῖσάν μοι* (Gal. ii. 9 and Eph. iii. 1) is frequently found in Paul's writings. What makes it worth recording here is the unusual *εἰς* with the accusative which follows, to indicate the sphere in which the grace is to be operative. Eph. ii. 8 is more akin to Rom. iii and iv than to Gal. ii, but it shares with Gal. ii the phrase *διὰ πίστεως*. Romans uses only *ἐκ πίστεως*.

The underlined words in Gal. ii. 20 are indeed moving and memorable, and it is significant that they appear twice in Ephesians.

(19) Gal. iii. 14–29	Ephesians
14. . . . *ἵνα εἰς τὰ ἔθνη ἡ εὐλογία τοῦ Ἀβραὰμ γένηται ἐν Ἰησοῦ Χριστῷ ἵνα τὴν ἐπαγγελίαν τοῦ πνεύματος λάβωμεν διὰ τῆς πίστεως.*	i. 13. . . . *ἐν ᾧ καὶ πιστεύσαντες ἐσφραγίσθητε τῷ πνεύματι τῆς ἐπαγγελίας τῷ ἁγίῳ . . . .*
26. *πάντες γὰρ υἱοὶ θεοῦ ἐστε διὰ τῆς πίστεως ἐν Χριστῷ Ἰησοῦ·* 27 *ὅσοι γὰρ εἰς Χριστὸν ἐβαπτίσθητε, Χριστὸν ἐνεδύσασθε· οὐκ ἔνι Ἰουδαῖος οὐδὲ Ἕλλην,* 28 *οὐκ ἔνι δοῦλος οὐδὲ ἐλεύθερος, οὐκ ἔνι ἄρσεν καὶ θῆλυ· πάντες γὰρ ὑμεῖς εἷς ἐστε ἐν Χριστῷ Ἰησοῦ.* 29 *εἰ δὲ ὑμεῖς Χριστοῦ, ἄρα τοῦ Ἀβραὰμ σπέρμα ἐστέ, κατ' ἐπαγγελίαν κληρονόμοι.*	iv. 24. . . . *καὶ ἐνδύσασθαι τὸν καινὸν ἄνθρωπον τὸν κατὰ θεὸν κτισθέντα.*
	ii. 13. *νυνὶ δὲ ἐν Χριστῷ Ἰησοῦ ὑμεῖς οἵ ποτε ὄντες μακρὰν ἐγενήθητε ἐγγὺς ἐν τῷ αἵματι τοῦ Χριστοῦ.* 14 *αὐτὸς γάρ ἐστιν ἡ εἰρήνη ἡμῶν, ὁ ποιήσας τὰ ἀμφότερα ἓν καὶ τὸ μεσότοιχον τοῦ φραγμοῦ λύσας, τὴν ἔχθραν ἐν τῇ σαρκὶ αὐτοῦ* 15 *τὸν νόμον τῶν ἐντολῶν ἐν δόγμασιν καταργήσας, ἵνα τοὺς δύο κτίσῃ ἐν αὐτῷ εἰς ἕνα καινὸν ἄνθρωπον ποιῶν εἰρήνην.*
	iii. 6. *εἶναι τὰ ἔθνη συγκληρονόμα καὶ σύνσωμα καὶ συνμέτοχα τῆς ἐπαγγελίας ἐν Χριστῷ Ἰησοῦ.*

The parallel noted in Eph. iv. 24 does not bear much significance here because it is derived almost entirely from Col. iii. 10.

The three consecutive verses of Eph. ii. 13–15 are very similar in thought to the three consecutive verses in Gal. iii. 26–8, far more so in fact than the underlined words by themselves would suggest.

(20) Philemon	Ephesians
1. *Παῦλος δέσμιος Χριστοῦ Ἰησοῦ.*	iii. 1. *τούτου χάριν ἐγὼ Παῦλος ὁ δέσμιος τοῦ Χριστοῦ Ἰησοῦ.*
4–6. *εὐχαριστῶ τῷ θεῷ μου πάντοτε μνείαν σου ποιούμενος ἐπὶ τῶν προσευχῶν μου,* 5 *ἀκούων σου τὴν ἀγά-*	i. 15. *διὰ τοῦτο κἀγώ, ἀκούσας τὴν καθ' ὑμᾶς πίστιν ἐν τῷ κυρίῳ*

Philemon (*cont.*)	Ephesians (*cont.*)
πην καὶ τὴν πίστιν, ἣν ἔχεις πρὸς τὸν κύριον Ἰησοῦν καὶ εἰς πάντας τοὺς ἁγίους, [6] ὅπως ἡ κοινωνία τῆς πίστεώς σου ἐνεργὴς γένηται ἐν ἐπιγνώσει παντὸς ἀγαθοῦ τοῦ ἐν ἡμῖν εἰς Χριστόν.	Ἰησοῦ καὶ τὴν ἀγάπην τὴν εἰς πάντας τοὺς ἁγίους [16] οὐ παύομαι εὐχαριστῶν ὑπὲρ ὑμῶν μνείαν ποιούμενος ἐπὶ τῶν προσευχῶν μου, [17] ἵνα ὁ θεὸς τοῦ κυρίου ἡμῶν Ἰησοῦ Χριστοῦ, ὁ πατὴρ τῆς δόξης, δώῃ ὑμῖν πνεῦμα σοφίας καὶ ἀποκαλύψεως ἐν ἐπιγνώσει αὐτοῦ . . . .
9. . . . τοιοῦτος ὢν ὡς Παῦλος πρεσβύτης, νυνὶ δὲ καὶ δέσμιος Χριστοῦ Ἰησοῦ	iv. 13. . . . μέχρι καταντήσωμεν οἱ πάντες εἰς τὴν ἑνότητα τῆς πίστεως καὶ τῆς ἐπιγνώσεως τοῦ υἱοῦ τοῦ θεοῦ.
13. . . . ἵνα ὑπὲρ σου μοι διακονῇ ἐν τοῖς δεσμοῖς τοῦ εὐαγγελίου.	vi. 20. . . . τοῦ εὐαγγελίου, ὑπὲρ οὗ πρεσβεύω ἐν ἁλύσει . . . .

In Eph. i. 15–17 there is much similarity with Col. i. 3, 4, 9, but Ephesians follows Philem. 4–6, where Philemon differs from Colossians.

(21) 1 Thess. iv. 5–13	Ephesians
5. καθάπερ καὶ τὰ ἔθνη τὰ μὴ εἰδότα τὸν θεόν	ii. 12. . . . ἦτε τῷ καιρῷ ἐκείνῳ χωρὶς Χριστοῦ . . . ἐλπίδα μὴ ἔχοντες καὶ ἄθεοι ἐν τῷ κόσμῳ.
11. ἐργάζεσθαι ταῖς χερσὶν ὑμῶν.	iv. 28. ἐργαζόμενος ταῖς ἰδίαις χερσὶν τὸ ἀγαθόν.
13. οὐ θέλομεν δὲ ὑμᾶς ἀγνοεῖν, ἀδελφοί, περὶ τῶν κοιμωμένων, ἵνα μὴ λυπῆσθε, καθὼς καὶ οἱ λοιποὶ οἱ μὴ ἔχοντες ἐλπίδα.	ii. 3. . . . καὶ ἤμεθα τέκνα φύσει ὀργῆς, ὡς καὶ οἱ λοιποί.

The words underlined in Eph. iv. 28 (and 1 Thess. iv. 11) are of no significance because a much closer parallel is found at Col. iv. 12.

It is, however, very significant that Eph. ii. 12 links together the two remarkable phrases from 1 Thess. iv. 5 and 13 to describe the condition of the Gentiles.

In addition to these twenty-one passages with recurring or sustained parallels in Ephesians, there are four others which have some claim to be included with the others, but they will be mentioned by context only:

Rom. xiii. 12–14: Eph. iv. 24; v. 8, 11; ii. 3; iv. 24.
Rom. xvi. 25–7: Eph. iii. 9; iii. 3; iii. 20–1.
1 Cor. vi. 9–16: Eph. v. 5; v. 26; v. 31.
Phil. i. 27: Eph. ii. 18–19; iv. 1–3.

These numerous instances in which a single passage from one of the other eight Pauline epistles can be shown either to have several parallels with a similar passage in Ephesians, or else to be echoed at several different places in Ephesians, constitute very strong evidence of literary dependence. It is not the kind of thing one would anticipate if the similarities were due merely to the fact that the same mind was at work on Ephesians as had composed the other letters. It is the kind of thing one would anticipate if the author of Ephesians had had intimate literary acquaintance with the letters.

When we made a test case of Philippians, what we found there was completely different. The parallels with other Pauline letters were isolated and unconnected; there was an almost complete absence of any sustained sequence of similarities, and no single passage could be found in the other letters with recurring echoes in Philippians.

By the application of this test Ephesians is seen to stand apart from Philippians, which we took to be representative of all the genuine Pauline letters. Unless some other admittedly Pauline letter can be shown to have a similar degree and manner of dependence on the others to that which has been found in Ephesians, it must be assumed that Ephesians stands apart also from all other members of the Pauline Corpus, and that the striking peculiarities, noted in this and the preceding chapters, require a different explanation from that which suffices to account for the smaller measure and different kind of similarities which appear in the other epistles.

A further test was suggested on p. 112 for distinguishing between Paul and a Pauline imitator. We argued that an imitator would almost certainly have been impressed, particularly by some of the pre-eminent passages from the letters of Paul, and these passages would exercise a greater influence over his thought and expression than the less outstanding sections. On the other hand, Paul himself, having long forgotten the exact form of what he had written, months or even years before, would use words and phrases that came readily to him through frequent use, but these would not be any more associated with the more important sections of his earlier letters than with the less important.

If, with this test in mind, we review the twenty-one passages from Paul's letters which appear to have exercised the greatest influence upon Ephesians (recorded on pp. 120–33), we find that at least eleven of them are from notably famous chapters (numbers 2, 3, 4, 5, 6, 10, 11, 12, 14, 15, 16), and five others should perhaps be included in the same category (1, 8, 9, 17, 18).[1] This large proportion of the twenty-one seems far greater than can reasonably be accounted for on the grounds of coincidence.

Another distinguishing test was suggested on p. 113. This was derived from the argument that an imitator would not only be specially impressed by outstanding passages, but he would also be most likely to remember and repeat notable and striking phrases, even when these did not occur in specially important contexts. In the case of a genuine Pauline letter, we should expect a far smaller measure of such memorable phrases than in the case of a work by an imitator. Indeed, when we searched Philippians for such phrases, both striking and at the same time not peculiar to Philippians, we could not confidently find any that had an indisputable place in this category (p. 116). The three most likely candidates were: *ἀποκαραδοκία* (Phil. i. 20 and Rom. viii. 19), *σύμμορφος* (Phil. iii. 21 and Rom. viii. 29), and *χαρὰ καὶ στέφανός μου* (Phil. iv. 1 and 1 Thess. ii. 19). There were one or two others which, however, we did not reckon, because they occurred in more than one context in the other letters, as for instance, 'God is my witness'. But it was one of the rules of this consideration, in following the same treatment we had meted out to Ephesians, not to pay much attention to parallels which recur more than once, because the very fact of such recurrence proves them to be 'stock phrases' rather than deliberate imitations.

Before we proceed to examine what number of striking phrases have been taken up into Ephesians from the other epistles it is perhaps worth noting that of the 235 words marked in Philippians as having parallels elsewhere in Paul's epistles, 84 (that is 35·5 per cent.) have parallels in more than one letter. In Ephesians, out of the 702 words with parallels (excluding those from Colossians), only 75 have parallels in more than one letter (that is 10·6 per cent.). The exclusion of Colossians from the reckoning introduces here an element that confuses an accurate comparison, but the difference is certainly remarkable. The higher percentage recorded by Philip-

[1] The following chapters appear to have impressed themselves most on the author's mind: Rom. i, iii, v. 1–11, viii, xii. 1–5; 1 Cor. iii, xii, xv; 2 Cor. i, v. Are they not all among those which most impress all readers?

pians is wholly in line with what we should expect in a genuinely Pauline epistle. It is the stock phrase rather than the striking one which reappears.

Among the parallels noted in Ephesians, not only is there a lower number which have repeated parallels, but there are a great many more than we found in Philippians which fall into the category of 'memorable phrases', of the kind which a careful reader would notice and recall. Here are some of them:

(*a*) Eph. i. 13–14. In 2 Corinthians Paul twice uses the unusual word ἀρραβών in an original sense. In each case it is used with τοῦ πνεύματος, and at 2 Cor. i. 22 is linked with σφραγίζω. This threefold association, as well as the use of ἀρραβών itself, is reproduced at Eph. i. 13–14.

(*b*) Eph. ii. 12 reproduces that pathetic phrase which is used in 1 Thess. iv. 13, ἐλπίδα μὴ ἔχοντες. In each case it is used as a description of the sad plight of the Gentiles, who have not yet received the Christian Gospel.

(*c*) Eph. ii. 18 and iii. 12. This is one of the instances in Ephesians where a phrase from one of the other letters seems to have impressed the writer so much that he repeats it twice in his own epistle. It is the phrase from Rom. v. 2 where Paul says that it is Christ δι' οὗ καὶ τὴν προσαγωγὴν ἐσχήκαμεν. It is Paul's vivid version of the terse Johannine declaration, 'I am the Way'.

(*d*) Eph. ii. 21. In 1 Cor. iii. 16 Paul tells his Christian friends that each one of them is a ναὸς ἅγιος. This same phrase, used with the same application, is found again at this context in Ephesians.

(*e*) Eph. iii. 8. In writing to the Corinthian Church Paul's recollection of the fierce opposition which he at first showed to the Christian Church induces in him a mood of bitter contrition and deep humility, and, in moving words, he disclaims any right to pride of place within the Church: ἐγὼ γάρ εἰμι ὁ ἐλάχιστος τῶν ἀποστόλων (1 Cor. xv. 9). Here, in Eph. iii. 8, the same words are substantially reproduced. We do not wonder that they lodged themselves in a reader's memory. One cannot help feeling, however, that in this new context the words have lost their original, direct simplicity, and even sound, in their artificial exaggeration, somewhat self-conscious and affected.

(*f*) Eph. iii. 8. In this verse there also occurs the phrase τὸ ἀνεξιχνίαστον πλοῦτος τοῦ Χριστοῦ. The repetition of ἀνεξιχνίαστος by itself, from Rom. xi. 33, is noteworthy, but especially so in its association with πλοῦτος, which also is found in the same context in Romans.

(*g*) Eph. v. 2 and v. 25. For very many Christians the poignant words of Gal. ii. 20 ('He loved me and gave himself up for me') have served to express their own sense of personal gratitude to Christ. We are not therefore surprised that the author of Ephesians was similarly moved by them, in fact so much so as to introduce them on two separate occasions into his epistle.

(*h*) Eph. v. 2. It may seem strange to our ears to hear a generous action, prompted by love, described as θυσίαν τῷ θεῷ, ὀσμὴν εὐωδιάς. But that is the phrase which Paul used at Phil. iv. 18, and even though it may not make the same appeal to us as to an ancient reader, we do not doubt that it is a striking phrase, likely to be remembered. It is used again in this verse in Ephesians.

(*i*) Eph. vi. 20. Another Pauline phrase which has caught people's imagination and been the text of many sermons is that from 2 Cor. v. 20: ὑπὲρ Χριστοῦ οὖν πρεσβεύομεν. This, too, is incorporated in Eph. vi. 20.

These do not exhaust the list of memorable phrases borrowed by Ephesians from the other epistles. In fact, some readers would reckon others even more impressive than these. For example, there are the following:

(*k*) 'The fulness of the time', Eph. i. 10, Gal. iv. 4.
(*l*) προορίζειν κατὰ πρόθεσιν Eph. i. 11, Rom. viii. 28.
(*m*) λόγος ἀληθείας Eph. i. 13, 2 Cor. vi. 7.
(*n*) ὁ ἔσω ἄνθρωπος Eph. iii. 17, Rom. vii. 22.
(*o*) 'Man, the head of the woman', Eph. v. 23, 1 Cor. xi. 3.
(*p*) Individual Christians are 'members one of another', Eph. iv. 25, Rom. xii. 5.
(*q*) Individual Christians are members of the Body of Christ, Eph. v. 30, 1 Cor. xii. 12.

All these are just the kind of phrases which would be retained in the mind of a careful reader of Paul's letters. Their presence in Ephesians in such numbers indicates that this test, no less than the others, gives strong evidence in favour of regarding Ephesians as the work of one who was familiar with the letters of Paul in their written form.

XIV

CONFLATION IN EPHESIANS OF PASSAGES FROM THE PAULINE EPISTLES

In our consideration of the manner in which Colossians was used in Ephesians, we noticed (pp. 65–6) how, on numerous occasions, passages in Colossians quite separate from one another were brought together in Ephesians and united in a single sentence. We saw, too, how some common element in the united passages served as a connecting link to establish an association between them in the mind of the writer of Ephesians. We argued that this phenomenon is exactly what one would expect if Ephesians is the work of some follower of Paul, whose mind was saturated with the phraseology of Colossians. Others may argue that precisely this kind of thing might be expected if Ephesians was written by the same author as Colossians. And this might be so. We claimed, however, that whereas occasional instances of this kind are to be expected in two works by the same author, the presence of several such instances would make one suspect the handiwork of a second writer. Moreover, if the number of such instances had to be characterized as 'many', that would be strong, if not conclusive, evidence in favour of an imitator.

The number of instances adduced in the earlier chapter of conflation between separate passages in Colossians did not perhaps exceed a number which could properly be described as 'several'. Our concern here, however, is with instances in Ephesians of the conflation of a passage from Colossians with a passage from one of the other eight Pauline epistles, or else of two or more passages from these other epistles. When these instances are considered and counted, it will be found that they are numerous enough to deserve to be described as 'many'.

Since this is a matter of some importance in our examination of Ephesians, it will be wise for us at this point to look again, and more carefully, at this phenomenon which we have called 'conflation', which we are claiming to be more characteristic of an imitator than of an original writer.

Conflation can sometimes be quite deliberate. A writer or speaker may purposely combine into a single whole two sentences of quite separate origin, because they are both associated in his mind as dealing with the same theme. More often the process is largely or entirely unconscious. The writer or speaker is aware that he is using phrases which are familiar to him, though he could not clearly assign to them their origin, and they link themselves together in his mind spontaneously and almost automatically. Or again, sometimes a writer may think that he is reproducing from some source familiar to him, and without his realizing it, familiar words from another source are incorporated. He has intended faithfully to reproduce his original source, but extraneous matter of a similar nature creeps in without his knowing it.

An instance of the deliberate conflation of Scripture passages is found in the Order of the Administration of the Holy Communion. The Prayer of Consecration, which immediately precedes the distribution of the bread and the wine to the communicants, concludes:

> 'This is my blood of the New Covenant (Testament), which is shed for you and for many for the remission of sins.'

In the Order of Service these are represented as the words of our Lord, but no single one of the accounts of the Last Supper and the institution of the sacrament gives them in exactly this form. They are, in fact, a conflation of all the accounts, representing, in particular, a conflation between the words as they occur in Matthew and in Luke. These two give the fullest records of the words of Jesus on this occasion, and incorporate the shorter sentences in Mark and I Corinthians.

> Mark xiv. 24: 'This is my blood of the new testament which is shed for many.'
> Matt. xxvi. 28: 'This is my blood of the new testament which is shed for many for the remission of sins.'
> I Cor. xi. 25: 'This cup is the new testament in my blood.'
> Luke xxii. 20: 'This cup is the new testament in my blood which is shed for you.'

The above four sentences are quoted from the Authorized Version, since that would represent the same text as was available to the compilers of the Prayer Book.

In the Prayer Book version Matthew is largely followed, but the more direct 'for you' is introduced from Luke.

Since Jesus spoke these words on one special occasion, it is not probable that He Himself used them more than once. Otherwise we might have accepted the variations as the result of slight changes in phraseology on different occasions. They must, however, be due to imperfect human memories. Each writer wished to report the exact words, but the sources on which they relied were not identical, and their recordings of the saying differ. In such a case, the conflation which we find in the Prayer Book version, no doubt intentionally produced, and including all that is important in all the versions, is the most satisfactory form of the words for the special purpose of the celebration of the sacrament. On the other hand, this conflation is precisely the kind of thing that a celebrant of the sacrament, away back in days before Orders of Service were available, but with his mind intimately familiar with the Scripture passages relevant to the great occasion, might find himself using. That little extra from Luke might slip in without his realizing that he was doing more than quote the words from Matthew.

Even apart from the Prayer Book version, the influence of these four parallel sentences upon each other provides an illustration of a similar process at work. Streeter calls it 'assimilation'. The words, as we quoted them, come from the Authorized Version, which was a translation of the Textus Receptus. Since the preparation of that version, however, our knowledge of the original Greek Text of the New Testament has greatly increased because of the discovery and study of earlier and more reliable manuscripts. As a result, it can be said with some confidence that originally the word 'new' did not stand either in Mark xiv. 24 or Matt. xxvi. 28. It has crept into these passages by their 'assimilation' to the corresponding passages from Luke and 1 Corinthians. (Indeed, the whole passage in Luke may have been absent from the original text of Luke; but that is an issue which does not affect our present consideration.) This introduction of the word 'new' into the text would probably not be deliberate. It would be added quite unintentionally by a scribe who knew the passages from Luke and 1 Corinthians so well that it came quite naturally to him to write 'new covenant' rather than just 'covenant'.

This instance of 'assimilation' is far from being unique; it is rather one of hundreds that are found in the various manuscripts of the gospels. Streeter writes: 'Assimilation of parallel passages in the Gospels is the commonest form of textual corruption' (FG, p. 307), and he claims the support of Hort for describing it as 'a principal cause of corruption' (p. 330).

We have made this reference to 'assimilation' because it is due to the same mental processes as 'conflation'. The index in Streeter's book, *The Four Gospels*, reveals many references under each heading. One further instance only will be quoted. Streeter shows (p. 276) how the original version of the Lord's Prayer in Luke xi. 2 ff. is very much shorter than that in Matt. vi. 9 ff. The longer version in Matthew was, however, the one accepted for liturgical use, and so became very familiar to Christians, with the result that gradually, in the later manuscripts of Luke, it supplants the original, shorter version. This did not happen all at once but through a series of stages, the familiar elements in the longer version being added by copyists to the shorter version. In the manuscripts known as A and D, and in the Textus Receptus, the assimilation of the two passages is 'almost complete', but 'the great MSS and the early versions show it at work in a very varied way'.

This means that, where a writer is reproducing one passage in the New Testament, what he writes is very likely to be affected by his intimate acquaintance with other similar passages with which he is familiar, whether from the Bible or from the Church liturgy. This happened quite inadvertently when a copyist was honestly trying to copy what was in front of him. How much more would it be likely to happen when there was no good reason for his trying to avoid it, and, indeed, every reason for encouraging the process, as would be the case if Ephesians is the work of an imitator of Paul who accomplishes his work with the set purpose of summarizing the substance of Paul's teachings and writings.

The same kind of thing happens in our own use of Scripture. For instance, a minister, as he distributes the wine among the communicants, may wish to vary the constant repetition of the words from the Service Book by quoting occasionally appropriate verses from the Bible. In so doing he may find himself saying:

> 'The blood of our Lord Jesus Christ which was shed / for you and for many unto the remission of sins / make you perfect in every good work to do His will.'

This sentence actually consists of three phrases drawn from three different sources. The first ('The blood . . . was shed') comes from the words which the minister is directed to use as he delivers the cup; the second ('for you . . . of sins') is introduced from the preceding prayer of consecration; and the third ('make you . . . His will') is from Heb. xiii. 20, which is frequently used as an appropriate benediction at the conclusion of the Communion Service. The three parts are bound together by both verbal and sense links. The link that joins the first and second parts is 'blood . . . shed', which occurs in both sources from which these parts are drawn. The link which joins the second and third part is still 'the blood of

Christ', for the third phrase, taken from Hebrews, is there immediately preceded by the words 'the blood of the eternal covenant'.

Those whose order of service does not restrict them to set forms of prayer know how often, in spontaneous prayer, materials from Scripture, hymns, and the liturgy become blended together in just this manner which we are calling 'conflation'.

It is precisely this kind of thing which we find in Ephesians. Passages from the other Pauline epistles are associated together in the writer's mind by some common word or idea, and so come to be 'conflated'. It is not merely that phrases used elsewhere in the Pauline epistles are here placed side by side, but some mutual similarity serves as the link that draws them together and blends them in Ephesians into a single sentence. The fact that instances of this kind can be shown to occur, not just as rare and peculiar coincidences, but as a regular feature of Ephesians, constitutes strong evidence of a literary dependence between Ephesians and the Pauline epistles.

There may be those who will argue that these cases of frequent conflation are no more than one would anticipate if Ephesians were a genuine Pauline epistle. It is not, however, enough merely to affirm this opinion, as though its affirmation alone nullified the opposing point of view. It is not a matter of two subjective opinions, each of which has an equal claim with the other to consideration. Those who claim that conflation, to the extent to which we find it in Ephesians, is a natural characteristic of a Pauline epistle must be prepared to demonstrate two things: (1) that similar cases of conflation occur equally frequently in the other Pauline epistles; and (2) that a satisfactory explanation can be found of the fact that it is always passages from two other epistles which are conflated in Ephesians, and not equally passages from Ephesians which are conflated with phrases from another epistle and introduced into a third. Unless these two requirements can be met, mere repudiation of our claim will not be sufficient to disprove it.

We recognized that this phenomenon, which we have called 'conflation', might be expected to occur occasionally in a genuine epistle of Paul. We saw, for instance, that in Philippians, out of 1,539 words, 235 or 15·2 per cent. had parallels in other Pauline epistles. In so large a number we should not be surprised to find one or two instances which present the appearance of conflation. And this is what we do find. In a genuine letter, however, we should expect only a very small number of such instances; and in Philippians the total of such instances amount to two. They are:

(i) Phil. i. 10: εἰς τὸ δοκιμάζειν ὑμᾶς τὰ διαφέροντα.	Rom. ii. 18: . . . δοκιμάζεις τὰ διαφέροντα. Rom. xii. 2: εἰς τὸ δοκιμάζειν ὑμᾶς. . . .

It might almost appear as though the word δοκιμάζω in both the phrases from Romans brought them together and led to their combination in Philippians.

(ii) Phil. ii. 11: ἵνα . . . καὶ πᾶσα γλῶσσα ἐξομολογήσηται ὅτι κύριος Ἰησοῦς Χριστός.	Rom. xiv. 11: καὶ πᾶσα γλῶσσα ἐξομολογήσεται τῷ θεῷ. Rom. x. 9: ἐὰν ὁμολογήσῃς ἐν τῷ στόματί σου κύριον Ἰησοῦν . . . σωθήσῃ.

Here it is the word ὁμολογοῦμαι which might be counted as the link to unite these two phrases from Romans.

It may be merely a coincidence that all four passages which have been apparently conflated in Philippians are taken from Romans. In passing, however, a query may be put: Is it possible that Philippians was written very soon after Romans, when its phrasing had not altogether faded from the writer's memory? Probably, however, it would be wise to treat it as just a coincidence.

The search in Philippians for instances of conflation serves this useful purpose: it provides us with a basis on which to assess what measure of such instances is to be expected in a genuinely Pauline epistle. In comparison with this we must now look at similar instances as they occur in Ephesians.

We saw in Part II ample evidence that the writer of Ephesians was specially familiar with Colossians at the time of writing his epistle. If Paul is the writer, then Ephesians must have been written while the very phrases of Colossians were still fresh in his mind. If it was not Paul, then the author must have been long familiar with Colossians, so that every phrase in it had become part of his own mental equipment. For more than a quarter of Ephesians is composed of words borrowed from Colossians, whereas the total number of words that have parallels in all the other eight epistles is only slightly larger. It is therefore only what we should expect that the instances of conflation in Ephesians should, in very many cases, show dependence, for one of the derived units, upon Colossians. We will consider this group first, where conflation consists of a phrase from Colossians in combination with a phrase from one of the other Pauline epistles.

In previous examinations of illustrative passages we have given most careful attention to the instances drawn from the early chapters of Ephesians. Lest it should be thought that the early chapters provide instances more friendly to our present purpose than the later chapters, we will in this case begin from the end.

(1) Eph. vi. 19–20	Col. iv. 3–4	2 Cor. v. 20
ἐν παρρησίᾳ γνωρίσαι τὸ μυστήριον τοῦ εὐαγγελίου, ὑπὲρ οὗ πρεσβεύω ἐν ἁλύσει, ἵνα ἐν αὐτῷ παρρησιάσωμαι ὡς δεῖ με λαλῆσαι.	. . . λαλῆσαι τὸ μυστήριον τοῦ Χριστοῦ, δι' ὃ καὶ δέδεμαι, ἵνα φανερώσω αὐτὸ ὡς δεῖ με λαλῆσαι.	ὑπὲρ Χριστοῦ οὖν πρεσβεύομεν. 1 Thess. ii. 2 ἐπαρρησιασάμεθα ἐν τῷ θεῷ ἡμῶν λαλῆσαι πρὸς ὑμᾶς τὸ εὐαγγέλιον τοῦ θεοῦ.

It is clear that this passage from Ephesians is based on the parallel words in Colossians. But the matter-of-fact phrase in Col. iv, δι' ὃ καὶ δέδεμαι, is replaced by the equivalent, but more picturesque one, which recalls the memorable words of 2 Cor. v. 20. The words ὑπὲρ οὗ are a natural alternative for δι' ὃ and lead on to πρεσβεύομεν.

The other parallel, with the words in 1 Thess. ii. 2, is less striking, but the introduction of the word παρρησιάζομαι in conjunction with the words λαλῆσαι and εὐαγγέλιον (which serve as the double link) makes it likely that it is more than a coincidence.

(2) Eph. vi. 9	Col. iii. 25	Rom. ii. 11
καὶ προσωποληψία οὐκ ἔστιν παρ' αὐτῷ.	καὶ οὐκ ἔστι προσωποληψία.	οὐ γάρ ἐστι προσωποληψία παρὰ τῷ θεῷ.

There can be no doubt that the main dependence here is on Col. iii. 25, for not only are the words themselves very similar but the whole context of Ephesians at this point is closely parallel to the whole section Col. iii. 22–iv. 1. In the actual form of the phrase in Ephesians it seems probable that the recollection of the notable sentence in Rom. ii. 11 has exercised an influence on the similar words taken over from Colossians.

(3) Eph. vi. 5–6	Col. iii. 22	Phil. ii. 12
οἱ δοῦλοι, ὑπακούετε τοῖς κατὰ σάρκα κυρίοις, μετὰ φόβου καὶ τρόμου, ἐν ἁπλότητι τῆς καρδίας ὑμῶν ὡς τῷ Χριστῷ, μὴ κατ' ὀφθαλμοδουλίαν ὡς ἀνθρωπάρεσκοι, ἀλλ' ὡς δοῦλοι Χριστοῦ.	οἱ δοῦλοι, ὑπακούετε κατὰ πάντα τοῖς κατὰ σάρκα κυρίοις, μὴ ἐν ὀφθαλμοδουλίαις, ὡς ἀνθρωπάρεσκοι, ἀλλ' ἐν ἁπλότητι καρδίας φοβούμενοι τὸν κύριον.	καθὼς πάντοτε ὑπηκούσατε . . . μετὰ φόβου καὶ τρόμου. Gal. i. 10 ἢ ζητῶ ἀνθρώποις ἀρέσκειν ; εἰ ἔτι ἀνθρώποις ἤρεσκον, Χριστοῦ δοῦλος οὐκ ἂν ἤμην.

Once again the main dependence is unquestionably on Colossians. In fact, the correspondence is exceedingly close, though the order of phrases is changed. The only substantial modification is the introduction of two additional phrases into the material taken over from Colossians, and in each case it is a phrase from another Pauline letter which is used to amplify the words of Colossians.

The words *μετὰ φόβου* (Eph.) are equivalent to *φοβούμενοι* (Col.). Such approximate equivalents are characteristic of the relationship between Ephesians and Colossians. What facilitates the substitution of *μετὰ φόβου* is that in Phil. ii. 12 *μετὰ φόβου* is associated with the verb *ὑπακούω* which has just been used in Eph. vi. 5 and *καὶ τρόμου* is also added as further evidence of the influence of the Philippians passage.

In Eph. vi. 6 the words *δοῦλοι Χριστοῦ* have a vague correspondence with *φοβούμενοι τὸν κύριον*, but it is only a very rough equivalent, and in any case the sense of *φοβούμενοι* (in Col. iii. 22) has already been represented in *μετὰ φόβου*. The reason for the introduction of these words becomes apparent from a comparison with Gal. i. 10, where *ἀνθρώποις ἤρεσκον* (a very close equivalent of the adjective *ἀνθρωπάρεσκοι*) is contrasted with *Χριστοῦ δοῦλος*. The recollection of this contrast leads to the latter phrase being introduced at Eph. vi. 6.

(4) Eph. v. 22–3	Col. iii. 18	1 Cor. xi. 3
αἱ γυναῖκες τοῖς ἰδίοις ἀνδράσιν ὡς τῷ κυρίῳ ὅτι ἀνήρ ἐστι κεφαλὴ τῆς γυναικὸς ὡς καὶ ὁ Χρι-	αἱ γυναῖκες, ὑποτάσσεσθε τοῖς ἀνδράσιν, ὡς ἀνῆκεν ἐν κυρίῳ.	παντὸς ἀνδρὸς ἡ κεφαλὴ ὁ Χριστός ἐστιν, κεφαλὴ δὲ γυναικὸς ὁ ἀνήρ.

Eph. v. 22–3 (*cont.*)	Col. i. 18
στὸς κεφαλὴ τῆς ἐκκλησίας, αὐτὸς σωτὴρ τοῦ σώματος.	καὶ αὐτός ἐστιν ἡ κεφαλὴ τοῦ σώματος τῆς ἐκκλησίας.

Eph. v. 22–3 appears to be the result of a conflation of two separate passages from Colossians with a passage from 1 Corinthians; and this third passage serves as the link between the two from Colossians. Col. iii. 18 deals with the relationship between husbands and wives, and thus makes an easy link with 1 Cor. xi. 3, where precisely the same subject is under discussion. The use of κεφαλή then leads to the introduction of Col. i. 18.

Some students have felt that the borrowed phrase from 1 Cor. xi. 3 stands awkwardly in Ephesians, as though it had not arisen spontaneously in the author's thought, but rather had been somewhat unnaturally forced into the context from an outside source. And this may well be what has happened.

(5) Eph. v. 5	Col. iii. 5	1 Cor. vi. 9–10
τοῦτο γὰρ ἴστε γινώσκοντες ὅτι πᾶς πόρνος ἢ ἀκάθαρτος ἢ πλεονέκτης ὅ ἐστιν εἰδωλολάτρης οὐκ ἔχει κληρονομίαν ἐν τῇ βασιλείᾳ τοῦ Χριστοῦ καὶ θεοῦ.	νεκρώσατε . . . πορνείαν, ἀκαθαρσίαν . . . καὶ τὴν πλεονεξίαν ἥτις ἐστὶν εἰδωλολατρία.	ἢ οὐκ οἴδατε ὅτι ἄδικοι θεοῦ βασιλείαν οὐ κληρονομήσουσιν; . . . οὔτε πόρνοι, οὔτε εἰδωλολάτραι . . . οὔτε πλεονέκται . . . βασιλείαν θεοῦ κληρονομήσουσιν.

If there was any doubt that Ephesians was here following Col. iii. 5, the matter would be settled by the inclusion in each of the condemnation of πλεονεξία as idolatry, as well as the great similarity of the list of vices mentioned. But the framework of the sentence in Ephesians seems to be no less influenced by 1 Cor. vi. 9. ἴστε is the equivalent of οἴδατε, and the lists of vices roughly correspond, and each passage is rounded off by the affirmation that these vices have the effect of excluding a man from the Kingdom of God.

Gal. v. 21 has many points of similarity with 1 Cor. vi. 9–10, but lacks some of its likenesses to Eph. v. 5. The introductory οἴδατε is omitted, and πλεονεξία is not included in its list of vices. (See parallels to Eph. v. 5 in Appendix I.)

(6) Eph. v. 1–2	Col. iii. 12–13	Gal. ii. 20
γίνεσθε οὖν μιμηταὶ τοῦ θεοῦ, ὡς τέκνα ἀγαπητά, καὶ περιπατεῖτε ἐν ἀγάπῃ καθὼς καὶ ὁ Χριστὸς ἠγάπησεν ὑμᾶς καὶ παρέδωκεν ἑαυτὸν ὑπὲρ ἡμῶν.	ἐνδύσασθε οὖν, ὡς ἐκλεκτοὶ τοῦ θεοῦ ἅγιοι καὶ ἠγαπημένοι, σπλάγχνα οἰκτιρμοῦ . . . χαριζόμενοι ἑαυτοῖς . . . καθὼς καὶ ὁ κύριος ἐχαρίσατο ὑμῖν.	. . . ἐν πίστει ζῶ τῇ τοῦ υἱοῦ τοῦ θεοῦ τοῦ ἀγαπήσαντός με καὶ παραδόντος ἑαυτὸν ὑπὲρ ἐμοῦ.

Appendix I reveals that two phrases in Eph. v. 1 have parallels in 1 Cor. iv. 14–16. These, however, are not here our concern.

There can be little doubt that Col. iii. 12–13 has influenced Eph. v. 1–2, not only because of the similarities indicated above, but also because of the still clearer evidence of its influence in the last verse of chapter iv. The word ἠγαπημένοι is reflected in ἠγαπητά; the good qualities which the Colossians are urged to 'put on' are summed up in the injunction 'περιπατεῖτε ἐν ἀγάπῃ', and the Lord's gracious dealings (ἐχαρίσατο) becomes His love for them. This appeal to Christ's love for us recalls Gal. ii. 20, a personal confession which had so impressed the author of Ephesians that he introduces it again in v. 25.

(7) Eph. iv. 22–3	Col. iii. 8–10	Rom. xii. 2
ἀποθέσθαι ὑμᾶς . . . τὸν παλαιὸν ἄνθρωπον . . . ἀνανεοῦσθαι δὲ τῷ πνεύματι τοῦ νοὸς ὑμῶν, καὶ ἐνδύσασθαι τὸν καινόν. . . .	ἀπόθεσθε καὶ ὑμεῖς . . . τὸν παλαιὸν ἄνθρωπον σὺν ταῖς πράξεσιν αὐτοῦ, καὶ ἐνδυσάμενοι τὸν νέον τὸν ἀνακαινούμενον.	μεταμορφοῦσθε τῇ ἀνακαινώσει τοῦ νοός.

Ephesians is here repeating from Colossians the thought of the 'old man' being replaced by the 'new man'. The ἀνακαινούμενον of Colossians serves as the link to recall the ἀνακαινώσει of Romans and the words which follow it. The whole phrase slips easily into a context into which it fits so well.

(8) Eph. iv. 17–18	Col. i. 21	Rom. i. 21
τὰ ἔθνη περιπατεῖ ἐν ματαιότητι τοῦ νοὸς αὐτῶν ἐσκοτωμένοι τῇ διανοίᾳ ὄντες, ἀπηλλοτριωμένοι τῆς ζωῆς τοῦ θεοῦ, διὰ τὴν ἄγνοιαν τὴν οὖσαν ἐν αὐτοῖς, διὰ τὴν πώρωσιν τῆς καρδίας αὐτῶν.	καὶ ὑμᾶς ποτε ὄντας ἀπηλλοτριωμένους καὶ ἐχθροὺς τῇ διανοίᾳ.	ἐματαιώθησαν ἐν τοῖς διαλογισμοῖς αὐτῶν, καὶ ἐσκοτίσθη ἡ ἀσύνετος αὐτῶν καρδία.

There can be little doubt that the words ἀπηλλοτριωμένοι τῇ διανοίᾳ in Eph. iv. 18 are borrowed from Col. i. 21, but they occur in a context which is predominantly taken from Rom. i. The link with Rom. i is confirmed by the close similarity between the following verse in Ephesians (iv. 19) and Rom. i. 24. The link that associates these passages from Colossians and Romans in the writer's mind is that each is describing the plight of unredeemed Gentiles.

(9) Eph. iii. 20–1	Col. i. 26	Rom. xvi. 25–7
τῷ δὲ δυναμένῳ ὑπὲρ πάντα ποιῆσαι ὑπερεκπερισσοῦ ὧν αἰτούμεθα ἢ νοοῦμεν κατὰ τὴν δύναμιν τὴν ἐνεργουμένην ἐν ἡμῖν, αὐτῷ ἡ δόξα ἐν τῇ ἐκκλησίᾳ καὶ ἐν Χριστῷ Ἰησοῦ εἰς πάσας τὰς γενεὰς τοῦ αἰῶνος τῶν αἰώνων· ἀμήν.	ἀπὸ τῶν αἰώνων καὶ ἀπὸ τῶν γενεῶν. Col. i. 29 κατὰ τὴν ἐνέργειαν αὐτοῦ τὴν ἐνεργουμένην ἐν ἐμοὶ ἐν δυνάμει.	τῷ δὲ δυναμένῳ ὑμᾶς στηρίξαι κατὰ τὸ εὐαγγέλιόν μου . . . κατὰ ἀποκάλυψιν μυστηρίου . . . μόνῳ σοφῷ θεῷ, διὰ Ἰησοῦ Χριστοῦ, ᾧ ἡ δόξα εἰς τοὺς αἰῶνας τῶν αἰώνων· ἀμήν.

Once again the framework is borrowed from Romans, but the κατὰ following τῷ δὲ δυναμένῳ in Rom. xvi. 25 links up in the writer's mind with the phrase in Col. i. 29, which begins with the word κατά. Also the combination of γενεαί and αἰῶνες in Colossians affects the phrasing of Eph. iii. 21.

(10) Eph. iii. 2	Col. i. 25	1 Cor. iii. 10
τὴν οἰκονομίαν τῆς χάριτος τοῦ θεοῦ τῆς δοθείσης μοι εἰς ὑμᾶς.	κατὰ τὴν οἰκονομίαν τοῦ θεοῦ τὴν δοθεῖσάν μοι εἰς ὑμᾶς.	κατὰ τὴν χάριν τοῦ θεοῦ τὴν δοθεῖσάν μοι.

Eph. iii. 2 seems to be a somewhat wordy combination of the two phrases from Colossians and 1 Corinthians.

(11) Eph. ii. 5	Col. ii. 13	Rom. iii. 24
καὶ ὄντας ἡμᾶς νεκροὺς τοῖς παραπτώμασι συνεζωοποίησεν τῷ Χριστῷ—χάριτί ἐστε σεσωσμένοι.	καὶ ὑμᾶς νεκροὺς ὄντας τοῖς παραπτώμασιν . . . συνεζωοποίησεν ὑμᾶς σὺν αὐτῷ, χαρισάμενος ἡμῖν πάντα τὰ παραπτώματα.	δικαιούμενοι δωρεὰν τῇ αὐτοῦ χάριτι.

Ephesians is here following very closely the form of expression in Col. ii. 13. The χάρις in χαρισάμενος, however, recalls a phrase well known to the writer from Rom. iii. 24, and it leads him to give emphatic expression to the Pauline insistence that our salvation is the achievement of the Grace of God, even though such an utterance is not really germane to this context.[1]

(12) Eph. ii. 1	Col. ii. 13	Rom. vi. 11
καὶ ὑμᾶς ὄντας νεκροὺς τοῖς παραπτώμασιν καὶ ταῖς ἁμαρτίαις ὑμῶν.	καὶ ὑμᾶς νεκροὺς ὄντας τοῖς παραπτώμασιν.	λογίζεσθε ἑαυτοὺς εἶναι νεκροὺς μὲν τῇ ἁμαρτίᾳ.

The link between these two passages is the word νεκρούς. Its association in the author's mind with τῇ ἁμαρτίᾳ in Rom. vi. 11 leads to the inclusion of ταῖς ἁμαρτίαις in Eph. ii. 1, in addition to the phrase borrowed from Colossians. The result is similar to that in (10) above. The conflated expression (τοῖς παραπτώμασιν καὶ ταῖς ἁμαρτίαις) is heavy and overloaded as well as tautological.

It is true that in Rom. vi. 11 the phrase νεκροὺς τῇ ἁμαρτίᾳ carries a very different sense from the corresponding phrase in Col. ii. 13

[1] W. L. Knox comments on this passage: 'Note the insertion of "By grace are ye saved". . . . The whole thought belongs to the Jewish-Christian controversy, not the theme of the Christian 'ascent to heaven'. . . . But it is typical of the continuator (i.e. the author of Ephesians) to feel that grace and works must be dragged in at all costs' (PCG, p. 183).

(and from the same phrase in Eph. ii. 1). In Romans it is used to describe the Christian believer, who is dead to sin, in the sense that he is unresponsive to its enticements. In Colossians, however (and in Ephesians), it describes the unbeliever, who is spiritually dead as the result of sin. Ephesians reproduces the words and meaning of Colossians, while incorporating also the phrase from Romans, in spite of the very different meaning attached to it in its original context. This is not altogether surprising, because the sound of the phrase rather than the specific meaning with which it was used, would be what would linger in the reader's mind.

(13) Eph. i. 21	Col. i. 16	Phil. ii. 9
ὑπεράνω πάσης ἀρχῆς καὶ ἐξουσίας καὶ δυνάμεως καὶ κυριότητος καὶ παντὸς ὀνόματος.	εἴτε θρόνοι εἴτε κυριότητες εἴτε ἀρχαὶ εἴτε ἐξουσίαι.	ἐχαρίσατο αὐτῷ τὸ ὄνομα τὸ ὑπὲρ πᾶν ὄνομα
		1 Cor. xv. 24
		. . . ὅταν καταργήσῃ πᾶσαν ἀρχὴν καὶ πᾶσαν ἐξουσίαν καὶ δύναμιν.

The context in Eph. i. 21 bears very close resemblance to that of Phil. ii. 9. Both are confidently affirming the Exaltation and Supremacy of Christ. The words quoted above from Phil. ii. 9 are preceded, in their context, by the declaration about Christ: διὸ καὶ ὁ θεὸς αὐτὸν ὑπερύψωσεν. This is in meaning equivalent to Eph. i. 20: καθίσας (αὐτὸν) ἐν δεξίᾳ αὐτοῦ ἐν τοῖς ἐπουρανίοις. It is not therefore surprising to find that the measure of the supremacy of Christ is described in Ephesians partly by words taken from Philippians. The phrase ὑπὲρ πᾶν ὄνομα reappears. In this unusual connexion it is not used elsewhere in Paul's writings.

The rest of the great powers, which are now announced as subordinate to Christ, are described in a series of words which bear very close resemblance to 1 Cor. xv. 24, not only in that ἄρχη, ἐξουσία, and δύναμις appear in the same order, but also with the same emphatic addition of πᾶσα. Yet there is no doubt that Col. i. 16 is exercising its influence as well. The verses which follow (Col. i. 17–18) also have parallels in Eph. i. 22–3. Moreover, the unusual word κυρίοτης, used here both by Colossians and Ephesians, is not found elsewhere in the Pauline letters.

Here again we notice the characteristic of Ephesians which has already been pointed out. It is the amplification, even to the extent of wordy tautology, of what has been said elsewhere in the epistles in vivid, short phrases, by the combination of the different elements of all these phrases into one somewhat cumbrous sentence.

(14) Eph. i. 13	Col. i. 5	Rom. i. 16
ἐν ᾧ καὶ ὑμεῖς ἀκούσαντες τὸν λόγον τῆς ἀληθείας, τὸ εὐαγγέλιον τῆς σωτηρίας ὑμῶν, ἐν ᾧ καὶ πιστεύσαντες	προηκούσατε ἐν τῷ λόγῳ τῆς ἀληθείας τοῦ εὐαγγελίου.	τὸ εὐαγγέλιον· δύναμις γὰρ θεοῦ ἐστιν εἰς σωτηρίαν παντὶ τῷ πιστεύοντι.

Once again the main dependence is upon Colossians, and the word εὐαγγέλιον serves as the association which links the words from Col. i. 5 with the memorable definition of the Gospel from Rom. i. 16.

These are not the only instances in which words from Colossians seem to be combined with words from some other Pauline epistle to form a 'conflated' sentence in Ephesians. Other such instances may be found in Appendix I at Eph. i. 10, ii. 15, iii. 9, v. 7, v. 10. A sufficient number, however, has been examined both to illustrate what is meant by 'conflation' and to show that in Ephesians it is not the result of an occasional, curious coincidence, but a regular feature of the epistle.

Besides the frequent instances of conflation between a passage from Colossians and a passage from one of the other Pauline epistles, there are also instances of conflation between passages from two or more of the other epistles. These are not so frequent as those in which Colossians is represented, but this is only what we should anticipate in view of the great extent to which Colossians is reproduced in Ephesians. Nevertheless, they are such as to suggest a literary acquaintance with the other epistles on the part of the author.

(15) Eph. iv. 28	1 Cor. iv. 12	Rom. ii. 10
κοπιάτω ἐργαζόμενος ταῖς ἰδίαις χερσὶν τὸ ἀγαθόν.	καὶ κοπιῶμεν ἐργαζόμενοι ταῖς ἰδίαις χερσίν.	παντὶ τῷ ἐργαζομένῳ τὸ ἀγαθόν. Gal. vi. 10 ἐργαζώμεθα τὸ ἀγαθὸν πρὸς πάντας.

In Eph. iv. 28 the writer is pleading that those who have previously made their living by stealing should now earn their money by working for it. He uses precisely similar words to those in 1 Cor. iv. 12, where Paul is emphasizing his own practice of working for his living instead of expecting support from the churches. The verb ἐργάζομαι may mean not only 'work' but also, in a more general sense, 'do'. Twice in Paul's letters occurs the phrase ἐργάζεσθαι τὸ ἀγαθόν, but it is used in the general sense of 'do good' without any reference to actual work. In Ephesians, however, this phrase is combined with that from 1 Cor. iv. 12, because of the ἐργάζεσθαι which they share in common.

One wonders also whether the adjective ἰδίαις would have been used in Ephesians, apart from the influence of the recollection of the words from 1 Cor. iv. 12.

(16) Eph. iv. 1	Rom. xii. 1	1 Thess. ii. 12
παρακαλῶ οὖν ὑμᾶς ἐγὼ ὁ δέσμιος ἐν κυρίῳ ἀξίως περιπατῆσαι τῆς κλήσεως ἧς ἐκλήθητε.	παρακαλῶ οὖν ὑμᾶς.	. . . παρακαλοῦντες ὑμᾶς . . . εἰς τὸ περιπατεῖν ὑμᾶς ἀξίως τοῦ θεοῦ τοῦ καλοῦντος ὑμᾶς.

We have already seen reasons to believe that Ephesians here represents a recollection of Rom. xii. 1 (pp. 123–4). The use of the three identical words would not in itself prove this, but the further close similarity between the preceding verses in each case (Eph. iii. 21 and Rom. xi. 36) is very strong evidence. The use of the παρακαλῶ, however, recalls to the writer's mind a further context in which the same word occurs, with the result that the thought, and to some extent the actual wording, of that context (1 Thess. ii. 12), are reproduced.

(17) Eph. iii. 8	1 Cor. xv. 9–10	Gal. i. 15–16
ἐμοὶ τῷ ἐλαχιστοτέρῳ πάντων ἁγίων ἐδόθη ἡ χάρις αὕτη, τοῖς ἔθνεσιν εὐαγγελίσασθαι τὸ ἀνεξιχνίαστον πλοῦτος τοῦ Χριστοῦ.	ἐγὼ γάρ εἰμι ὁ ἐλάχιστος τῶν ἀποστόλων . . . χάριτι δὲ θεοῦ εἰμι ὅ εἰμι, καὶ ἡ χάρις αὐτοῦ ἡ εἰς ἐμὲ οὐ κενὴ ἐγενήθη.	. . . εὐδόκησεν ὁ . . . καλέσας διὰ τῆς χάριτος αὐτοῦ ἀποκαλύψαι τὸν υἱὸν αὐτοῦ ἐν ἐμοί, ἵνα εὐαγγελίζωμαι αὐτὸν ἐν τοῖς ἔθνεσιν.

The parallel between Ephesians and 1 Corinthians here is very noticeable. Moreover, at the points where Ephesians differs from 1 Corinthians the wording sounds forced and unnatural, so much so that, apart from any other consideration, doubts have been cast on its genuineness as a Pauline utterance. In 1 Cor. xv. 10 the poignant cry of humiliation is followed by a grateful acknowledgement of the 'grace of God' which was bestowed upon him. The mention of special 'grace' in relation to Paul links up with Gal. i. 15–16, where the gift of God's grace to Paul is associated with God's purpose of using him to evangelize the Gentiles; and this is incorporated in Ephesians.

(18) Eph. iii. 7	Rom. v. 15	1 Cor. iii. 10
οὗ ἐγενήθην διάκονος κατὰ τὴν δωρεὰν τῆς χάριτος τοῦ θεοῦ τῆς δοθείσης μοι.	ἡ χάρις τοῦ θεοῦ καὶ ἡ δωρεὰ ἐν χάριτι τῇ τοῦ ἑνὸς ἀνθρώπου Ἰησοῦ Χριστοῦ εἰς τοὺς πολλοὺς ἐπερίσσευσεν.	. . . κατὰ τὴν χάριν τοῦ θεοῦ τὴν δοθεῖσάν μοι.

The closing phrase in Eph. iii. 7 is a reflection of 1 Cor. iii. 10, but δωρεά, which in Rom. v. 15 stands in close association with χάρις, is introduced to accompany χάρις. Whereas, however, in Romans, δωρεά makes its own contribution to the sentence, and is introduced to add some further content to the meaning of χάρις, in Ephesians it seems to be a further instance of the somewhat laboured accumulation of synonyms, similar to those already noted in (10) and (12).

(19) Eph. i. 13–14	2 Cor. i. 22	Gal. iii. 14
πιστεύσαντες ἐσφραγίσθητε τῷ πνεύματι τῆς ἐπαγγελίας τῷ ἁγίῳ, ὅς ἐστιν ἀρραβὼν τῆς κληρονομίας ἡμῶν.	ὁ . . . θεὸς ὁ καὶ σφραγισάμενος ἡμᾶς καὶ δοὺς τὸν ἀρραβῶνα τοῦ πνεύματος.	. . . ἵνα τὴν ἐπαγγελίαν τοῦ πνεύματος λάβωμεν διὰ τῆς πίστεως.

Eph. i. 13–14 and 2 Cor. i. 22 are clearly parallel to each other, because in each of them there occur the two unusual words σφραγίζομαι and ἀρραβών, and in each case they are associated with the gift of the Spirit. With his usual love of descriptive genitives, however, the writer of Ephesians amplifies the words borrowed from 2 Cor. i. 22 by embodying in his sentence about the Spirit the two-fold idea, from Gal. iii. 14, that the Spirit has been promised, and is received into human life by faith.

To all these instances the convinced believer in the Pauline authorship of Ephesians may be inclined to reply that this is just the kind of interdependence which one would look for among the different writings of the same author. But are they? Our comparison with Philippians failed to produce more than two such instances. This claim, therefore, must be entirely discounted, unless it can be supported by evidence. Such evidence must consist of the demonstration that instances of such conflation occur with equal frequency in the other letters of Paul. Also, it will need to be shown that passages from Ephesians are conflated with passages from other letters; or else an adequate explanation must be found for the fact that it is always in Ephesians that these conflations are found, and not Ephesians which is found so treated in other epistles.

Among the quoted instances of conflation, there are some which seem to be deliberate attempts to compose a comprehensive summary of all Pauline utterances on a particular subject. At Eph. i. 21 the declaration of the supremacy of Christ over every possible rival is composed of elements from three other epistles (see pp. 150–1). At Eph. ii. 12 the sorry condition of the Gentiles, who are without true religion, is described in phrases which are borrowed from three other epistles. There are, in addition, two longer passages which certainly illustrate what we have called 'conflation', but, more than that, they are almost entirely built up of words and phrases taken from the other Pauline epistles, so that they have the appearance of being masterly summaries of Pauline thought as already expressed sporadically in the other letters. It may be argued that it is quite natural for Paul himself to wish to make a full and comprehensive statement of his faith in these particular issues. In view, however, of what we have already seen of conflation, and its probable bearing on the question of authorship, these two passages may well be regarded as best interpreted as the work of one who had studied carefully the writings of Paul. Certainly it is remarkable that the two passages in question should be almost entirely composed of elements derived from the other Pauline epistles.

The two passages we refer to are Eph. ii. 8–9 and iv. 4–6. The dependence of these passages on the other Pauline epistles can be seen in Appendix I, but we will set it forth here more fully. In the first column is given the passage in Ephesians divided up into phrase-units. Opposite these phrase-units, in the second column, is noted the other Pauline context (or contexts) in which this same phrase occurs. In the third column the passages from the other Paulines which are represented in column 2 are quoted in full, with those words underlined which correspond to the phrase-units in column 1.

(20) Eph. ii. 8–9.		
τῇ γὰρ χάριτί	Rom. iii. 24.	Rom. iii. 20. διότι ἐξ ἔργων νόμου οὐ δικαιωθήσεται πᾶσα σὰρξ ἐνώπιον αὐτοῦ.
ἐστε σεσωσμένοι	Rom. iii. 24. Gal. ii. 16.	Rom. iii. 24. δικαιούμενοι δωρεὰν τῇ αὐτοῦ χάριτι (cf. Rom. v. 15).
διὰ πίστεως	Gal. ii. 16. Rom. iv. 16.	Rom. iii. 27. ποῦ οὖν ἡ καύχησις;
καὶ τοῦτο	Rom. xiii. 11. 1 Cor. ii. 2.	Rom. iv. 2. εἰ γὰρ Ἀβραὰμ ἐξ ἔργων ἐδικαιώθη, ἔχει καύχημα.
οὐκ ἐξ ὑμῶν	Rom. iv. 16.	Rom. iv. 16. εἶναι βεβαίαν τὴν ἐπαγγελίαν παντὶ τῷ σπέρματι, οὐ τῷ ἐκ τοῦ νόμου μόνον ἀλλὰ καὶ τῷ ἐκ πίστεως.
θεοῦ τὸ δῶρον	Rom. iii. 12.	
οὐκ ἐξ ἔργων	Rom. iii. 20. Rom. iv. 2. Rom. xi. 6. Gal. ii. 16.	Rom. xi. 6. εἰ δὲ χάριτι, οὐκέτι ἐξ ἔργων. 1 Cor. i. 29. ἐξελέξατο ὁ θεὸς τὰ μὴ ὄντα ἵνα τὰ ὄντα καταργήσῃ, ὅπως μὴ καυχήσηται πᾶσα σάρξ.
ἵνα μή τις	Rom. iii. 27.	Gal. ii. 16. οὐ δικαιοῦται ἄνθρωπος ἐξ ἔργων νόμου ἐὰν μὴ διὰ πίστεως Χριστοῦ Ἰησοῦ.
καυχήσηται	Rom. iv. 2. 1 Cor. i. 29.	

These two verses in Ephesians provide us with the most effective summary we have of the Pauline doctrine of salvation by grace through faith. The words underlined disclose the extent of similarity in phrasing and emphasis with passages in Romans, Galatians, and 1 Corinthians. The starting-point seems to be the declaration of our utter dependence on the grace of God for our justification in Rom. iii. 24. The thought of justification links up with the further truth about justification emphasized in Gal. ii. 16, that it becomes effective on the basis of faith. In Gal. ii. 16 there is also a denial of the false belief that justification can ever be secured as a result of 'what we do' (ἐξ ἔργων). This same point is also made in Rom. iv. 2, where the consequence of this false idea of justification is described as 'self-satisfaction' (καύχημα). This thought is introduced into Ephesians, but the mode of its expression is in a form of words taken from 1 Cor. i. 29.

Eph. ii. 8–9 is therefore built up almost entirely out of phrases already used in the Pauline epistles; but the use of the borrowed phrases is not slavish, and an element of interpretation modifies the borrowing. For instance, in all the contexts in the third column it is 'justification' which is under consideration. In Ephesians it is 'salvation', and the word *δικαιόω* is not used. Perhaps the writer of Ephesians felt that at the time he wrote, and for the Gentile Christians to whom he wrote, the word needed to be interpreted. Ephesians also omits here any reference to the 'law', but the same sense is represented in the phrase *οὐκ ἐξ ὑμῶν*, that is, 'not by our own endeavour and will-power'. This is substantially what Paul meant by the Jewish expression *οὐ . . . ἐκ τοῦ νόμου*, that is, 'not by our scrupulous endeavour to obey the moral standards of the law'. Curiously enough, *δῶρον* is a *ἅπαξ λεγόμενον* in the Pauline writings. Paul prefers in this connexion *δωρεά*, and this word too occurs twice in Ephesians. *καὶ τοῦτο* is not recorded in the parallels in the third column, but it is a thoroughly Pauline phrase.

(21) Eph. iv. 4–6.		
ἓν σῶμα καὶ	Rom. xii. 5. 1 Cor. x. 17. 1 Cor. xii. 12–13.	Rom. ix. 5. *ὁ ὢν ἐπὶ πάντων θεός . . . .* Rom. xi. 36. . . . *ὅτι ἐξ αὐτοῦ καὶ δι' αὐτοῦ καὶ εἰς αὐτὸν τὰ πάντα.* Rom. xii. 5. *οὕτως οἱ πολλοὶ ἓν σῶμά ἐσμεν ἐν Χριστῷ.* 1 Cor. vii. 20. *ἕκαστος ἐν τῇ κλήσει ᾗ ἐκλήθη ἐν ταύτῃ μενέτω.* 1 Cor. viii. 6. *ἀλλ' ἡμῖν εἷς θεὸς ὁ πατήρ, ἐξ οὗ τὰ πάντα, καὶ ἡμεῖς εἰς αὐτὸν καὶ εἷς κύριος Ἰησοῦς Χριστός, δι' οὗ τὰ πάντα.* 1 Cor. x. 17. *ἓν σῶμα οἱ πολλοί ἐσμεν.* 1 Cor. xii. 4–6. *διαιρέσεις δὲ χαρισμάτων εἰσίν, τὸ δὲ αὐτὸ πνεῦμα· καὶ διαιρέσεις διακονιῶν εἰσιν, καὶ ὁ αὐτὸς κύριος· καὶ διαιρέσεις ἐνεργημάτων εἰσίν, ὁ δὲ αὐτὸς θεός, ὁ ἐνεργῶν τὰ πάντα ἐν πᾶσιν.*
ἓν πνεῦμα	1 Cor. xii. 4. 1 Cor. xii. 13.	
καθὼς καὶ	Rom. i. 13. Rom. xv. 7.	
ἐκλήθητε	1 Cor. vii. 20.	
ἐν μιᾷ ἐλπίδι	1 Cor. xiii. 7, 13.	
τῆς κλήσεως ὑμῶν	1 Cor. vii. 20.	
εἷς κύριος	1 Cor. viii. 6. 1 Cor. xii. 5.	
μία πίστις	1 Cor. xiii. 7, 13.	
ἓν βάπτισμα	1 Cor. xii. 13.	
εἷς θεὸς	1 Cor. viii. 6. 1 Cor. xii. 6.	
καὶ πατὴρ πάντων	1 Cor. viii. 6.	

ὁ ἐπὶ πάντων	Rom. ix. 5. Rom. xi. 36.	1 Cor. xii. 12–13. καθάπερ γὰρ τὸ σῶμα ἕν ἐστιν καὶ μέλη πολλὰ ἔχει, πάντα δὲ τὰ μέλη τοῦ σώματος πολλὰ ὄντα ἕν ἐστιν σῶμα, οὕτως καὶ ὁ Χριστός· καὶ γὰρ ἐν ἑνὶ πνεύματι ἡμεῖς πάντες εἰς ἓν σῶμα ἐβαπτίσθημεν . . . καὶ πάντες ἓν πνεῦμα ἐποτίσθημεν.
καὶ διὰ πάντων	Rom. xi. 36.	
καὶ ἐν πᾶσιν.	1 Cor. xii. 6. Rom. xi. 36.	

Eph. iv. 4–6 is built up almost entirely of words and phrases derived from 1 Corinthians, and mainly from chapters viii and xii, though there may be echoes from Romans. There are only two phrases which have no clear parallel elsewhere, and they are ἐν μιᾷ ἐλπίδι and μία πίστις. The words ἐλπίς and πίστις appear prominently enough in Paul's letters, but it is not actually specified elsewhere that Christians share a single hope and a single faith. These two words, in combination with ἀγάπη, make up the famous triad which is always associated with the name of Paul. Their most notable appearance together is in 1 Cor. xiii. 13, but this is by no means an isolated case. They occur also in 1 Thess. i. 3 and v. 8. In 1 Cor. xiii ἀγάπη is not only declared to be the greatest of the three, but also it embraces the other two within itself (cf. 1 Cor. xiii. 7: ἡ ἀγάπη . . . πάντα πιστεύει, πάντα ἐλπίζει.) Here, in Eph. iv. 4–6, the whole context is an exaltation of ἀγάπη as the controlling characteristic of a Christian community. Eph. iv. 3, which immediately precedes, reads: ἐν ἀγάπῃ σπουδάζοντες τηρεῖν τὴν ἑνότητα τοῦ πνεύματος ἐν τῷ συνδέσμῳ τῆς εἰρήνης.

In the lists in Appendix VI there is a notable absence of specific parallels with 1 Cor. xiii, which one would have thought would be a chapter to impress any reader and assert its influence on any imitator. Here, however, is the debt of Ephesians to 1 Cor. xiii: ἀγάπη is declared to be the essential element in the maintenance of peace and unity in the Christian community, and the eulogy of ἀγάπη leads to the emphasis on its two satellites, hope and faith.

These two impressive summaries of Pauline teaching are not in themselves evidence of non-Pauline authorship. They may be Paul's own considered attempt to give a comprehensive statement of his faith in these matters. In view, however, of the abundant evidence of what we have called 'conflation' in Ephesians, the question is raised whether these summaries are not best explained as the work of one who had studied very carefully the thought and phrasing of Paul's letters, and then set himself to give final and universal expression to great Pauline truths, mainly in Pauline words, and yet avoiding those which would not be equally intelligible to Gentile as to Jewish Christians.

We may summarize the conclusions of this chapter thus:

1. Conflation is certainly the kind of thing one would expect in the work of a Pauline imitator; it is less certainly what one would anticipate in a genuinely Pauline letter.
2. It occurs hardly at all in Philippians, which has been taken as representative of the Pauline epistles. Its occurrence in Ephesians far exceeds this.
3. There is a complete absence in the other letters of instances where passages from Ephesians have been conflated with words from another letter to make a new combination.

In these respects, therefore, Ephesians stands apart from the genuinely Pauline epistles, and its peculiarities require special explanation.

PART IV

THE DATE OF EPHESIANS

IT now remains to explore every avenue which may lead to information about the date of Ephesians. Answers must be given to the following questions: Does the evidence drive us back to a date so early that we are left with no alternative but to regard the epistle as genuinely Paul's? Or does it allow for, perhaps even demand, a later date? If so, what is the latest permissible date? Within the permitted limits, does an earlier or a later date accord better with the general character of the contents of the epistle?

To find answers to these questions the external evidence will first be examined. The general significance of this evidence has been referred to in Part I, but a fuller treatment is now required. This must include not only the evidence of the Apostolic Fathers and their immediate successors, but also that of the writings within the New Testament itself which seem to reflect acquaintance with Ephesians, or possibly to be reflected in it. Revelation, the Pastoral Epistles, Acts, and 1 Peter will demand special attention. The elucidation of their relationship to Ephesians will throw light on other New Testament issues as well as on our present problem. The section will conclude with an inquiry whether the contents of the epistle are more appropriate to a date within the lifetime of Paul or later in the first century.

XV

EXTERNAL EVIDENCE FOR THE DATE OF EPHESIANS

THE strongest bulwark in the defence of the Pauline authorship of Ephesians has been the unanimous testimony of the external evidence in its favour. From earliest times Ephesians has had its place in the collection of Paul's letters. No scrap of evidence can be produced to suggest anything but the closest possible association with the name of Paul and with his other letters. In consequence of this, we have already insisted that any alternative theory, claiming for it a non-Pauline origin, must be able to offer some convincing explanation of this complete unanimity amongst the earliest Christian writers. For this reason even the opponents of Pauline authorship have had to concede for it a date before A.D. 100. The facts entirely support B. W. Bacon's judgement that 'Ephesians is surpassed by scarcely any other New Testament writing beside 1 Corinthians in explicit attestation from the earliest times' (INT, p. 116). Nor is Charteris in any way overstating the case when he writes: 'The testimony of the early Church is unanimous in favour of the Pauline origin of the Epistle' (C, p. 237). These are the circumstances which lead J. Knox to speak of the 'two apparently contradictory facts which create the problem of Ephesians: (1) that the internal evidence overwhelmingly suggests that Paul did not write this letter, and (2) that the external evidence equally strongly indicates that he did' (MNT, pp. 58–9).

In view of the general agreement of scholars on the significance of this external evidence, it will not be necessary here to go into details except at points where their opinions have varied. The evidence which is not included here may be found, stated in full with great impartiality by the Oxford Committee, in NTAP, and also, with a smaller degree of caution, by Abbott in ICC, pp. ix–xiii.

Irenaeus in Gaul *c.* A.D. 185 explicitly quotes Eph. v. 30, 'We are members of His body', as being the words of the 'Blessed Paul in the epistle to the Ephesians' (*Adv. Haer.* v. 2. 3).

Clement of Alexandria *c.* A.D. 200 quotes Eph. v. 21–5 (at *Strom.* iv. 65) and Eph. iv. 13–15 (at *Paed.* i. 18) as words of 'the apostle' to the Ephesians, and the contexts leave no room for doubt that the 'apostle' is Paul.

The Muratorian Canon, which is usually dated about A.D. 200 and associated with Italy, also includes Ephesians in its list of Pauline epistles.

These three explicit attestations may be taken as representative of Gaul (and probably Asia Minor too), Alexandria, and Rome at the end of the second century.

We do not, however, have to wait till the end of the second century for such clear testimonies. About the middle of that century, Marcion included Ephesians in his private selection of Christian writings which he declared worthy to rank as Scripture. It is true that he called it 'Laodiceans', and no wholly satisfactory explanation of his use of this name, which is peculiar to him, has been found. There is, however, no doubt that the epistle is the same as that which we know as Ephesians. Excerpts quoted from it make this quite certain. Indeed Tertullian inveighs against him for so unjustifiably introducing an unfamiliar title for a familiar epistle. What Tertullian has to say about Marcion is not always very fair, but that need not concern us now. All that matters here is that Tertullian's fiery onslaught on Marcion's heresy makes it perfectly clear that both Marcion and Tertullian knew Ephesians, and knew it as a Pauline letter, even though they disagreed about the name by which it was known and the address to which it was sent.

Marcion was active both in Asia Minor and at Rome, and Tertullian was a prominent figure in north-west Africa. We can therefore conclude that before A.D. 150 Ephesians was not only known but confidently treated as a member of the Pauline Corpus in Africa, Asia Minor, and Rome. For though Marcion was accused of misusing and tampering with the known letters of Paul, he was never charged with introducing spurious letters into their number.

These are the earliest explicit references to Ephesians as the work of Paul. There are, however, clear indications that earlier writers were familiar with Ephesians, though they do not specifically ascribe it to Paul. We may take it as certain that those who quoted it did so on the understanding that they were quoting words of Paul. Abbott, after quoting evidence that early writers were acquainted with Ephesians, continues: 'When we add to this the fact that it professes to be St. Paul's, we are fairly justified in saying that evidence of its reception is evidence of its genuineness' (ICC, p. ix). This, however, is stating it too strongly. It is not necessarily true that evidence of its reception can be taken as evidence of its genuineness.

All we can say is that it is evidence that those who quote it accept its genuineness. It tells us nothing about the reliability of their information.

Polycarp

It has long been customary to treat Polycarp's letter to Philippi as a single letter, written to introduce the collection of the letters of Ignatius which the Philippian Church had asked for. It was therefore felt that it could be dated within a year or two of A.D. 110. P. N. Harrison, however (in PEP), has shown grounds for believing that this apparently single letter is in reality two, one a very short one which actually accompanied the letters of Ignatius, and a much longer one which was written very much later, perhaps even as late as A.D. 140. His arguments have not won universal acceptance and need not be taken as conclusive. C. H. Dodd, for instance, in his commentary on the Johannine Epistles (p. xii) writes: 'Dr. Harrison dates the later letter about 135–7; but his arguments for so late a date are not conclusive. It might well be ten or fifteen years earlier. Indeed, there seems no cogent reason why the interval between the first letter and the second may not have been measured in months rather than years.' We cannot here pretend to make a decision on this disputed issue. Since, however, it is in this longer letter that most of the echoes of the New Testament books are found, it is well to remember that this evidence may be valid only for A.D. 140 and not for the earlier date.

The Oxford Committee, whose errors are never in the direction of rashness, agreed that it was 'very probable' that Polycarp's letter shows acquaintance with Ephesians. That was the judgement of the whole committee. P. V. M. Benecke, however, who was responsible for presenting the evidence to the committee and recording its findings, in his own personal comments reveals a larger measure of confidence than this rather non-committal verdict suggests, and P. N. Harrison regards it as 'certain' that Polycarp was familiar with Ephesians.

The two most significant instances of correspondence between the two writings are:

(i) Pol. i. 13	Eph. ii. 8
εἰδότες ὅτι χάριτί ἐστε σεσωσμένοι, οὐκ ἐξ ἔργων ἀλλὰ θελήματι θεοῦ διὰ Ἰησοῦ Χριστοῦ.	*τῇ γὰρ χάριτί ἐστε σεσωσμένοι διὰ πίστεως· καὶ τοῦτο οὐκ ἐξ ὑμῶν, θεοῦ τὸ δῶρον· οὐκ ἐξ ἔργων.*

On this Benecke comments: 'The words εἰδότες ὅτι seem to imply a consciousness in Polycarp that he is making a quotation; the two passages agree verbally, except for the absence in Polycarp of some unessential words; and it is to be noted that the sharp Pauline antithesis of faith and works is not characteristic of the Apostolic Fathers generally.'

(ii) Pol. xii. 1	Eph. iv. 26
Modo, ut his scripturis dictum est, Irascimini et nolite peccare, et Sol non occidat super iracundiam vestram.	ὀργίζεσθε καὶ μὴ ἁμαρτάνετε· ὁ ἥλιος μὴ ἐπιδυέτω ἐπὶ παροργισμῷ ὑμῶν.

At this point in Polycarp we are dependent upon a Latin version of his letter. It is not likely that his reference to 'Scriptures' can mean Ephesians. It is rather a recognition that the quotation is derived from the Old Testament. The significant point is that it is not one quotation but a combination of two. The first part comes from Ps. iv. 5 and the second from Deut. xxiv. 15. It is, of course, conceivably possible that two writers might make this same combination independently, but the combination is so unexpected that it must be regarded as highly probable that Polycarp derived the association of the two passages from Ephesians. Benecke's opinion is: 'The collocation of the two passages in Polycarp is almost certainly due to Ephesians.'

Other similarities have also been pointed out, but these two alone make it reasonably sure that Polycarp knew this epistle.

Ignatius came from Syria to Asia Minor on his way to martyrdom in Rome about A.D. 110. His letters were written from Asia Minor. It is therefore possible that such knowledge as he had of Paul's epistles was acquired during his short stay in Asia Minor. More probably his acquaintance with the letters dated from his ministry in Syria, but we cannot assume that this was so.

There is no doubt that Ignatius knew 1 Corinthians. His echoes of it are so frequent that W. R. Inge thinks that 'Ignatius must have known this epistle almost by heart. . . . Echoes of its thought and language pervade the whole of his writings.' The evidence of his use of Ephesians is less clear. Nevertheless the Oxford Committee regard it as 'very probable' that he knew Ephesians, and this is certainly not an exaggerated estimate.

There are several slight instances of correspondence, noted by the

Committee, which need not here be considered. The most convincing parallels are:

(i) Ignatius: Pol. v. 1	Eph. v. 25
τοῖς ἀδελφοῖς μου παράγγελλε ἐν ὀνόματι Ἰησοῦ Χριστοῦ ἀγαπᾶν τὰς συμβίους, ὡς ὁ Κύριος τὴν ἐκκλησίαν.	οἱ ἄνδρες, ἀγαπᾶτε τὰς γυναῖκας, καθὼς καὶ ὁ Χριστὸς ἠγάπησε τὴν ἐκκλησίαν (cf. v. 29).

(ii) Ignatius: Eph. i. 1	Eph. v. 1
μιμηταὶ ὄντες θεοῦ.	γίνεσθε οὖν μιμηταὶ τοῦ θεοῦ.

The most natural explanation of both these similarities is that Ephesians was influencing the thought of Ignatius. The Oxford Committee, curiously enough, attach little significance to (ii), but the idea contained there is unique to Ephesians among the Pauline writings, and though it is implied in the teaching of Jesus (e.g. Matt. v. 44–8), this blunt expression of it is distinctly daring. For this reason it seems very likely that Ignatius is reproducing an expression he has remembered.

The inscription of Ignatius' letter to the Ephesians also has a series of similarities with Eph. i. 3–14, which can hardly be regarded as purely accidental. Zahn calls them 'not very certain echoes', and that may be true, but the association of so many of them in a short passage is impressive. The inscription is as follows, and the words underlined are those which also occur in Paul's epistle to the Ephesians, i. 3–14:

τῇ εὐλογημένῃ ἐν μεγέθει θεοῦ πατρὸς πληρώματι, τῇ προωρισμένῃ πρὸ αἰώνων εἶναι διὰ παντὸς εἰς δόξαν παράμονον ἄτρεπτον, ἡνωμένῃ καὶ ἐκλελεγμένῃ ἐν πάθει ἀληθινῷ ἐν θελήματι τοῦ πατρὸς καὶ Ἰησοῦ Χριστοῦ τοῦ θεοῦ ἡμῶν, τῇ ἐκκλησίᾳ τῇ ἀξιομακαρίστῳ τῇ οὔσῃ ἐν Ἐφέσῳ, πλεῖστα ἐν Ἰησοῦ Χριστῷ καὶ ἐν ἀμώμῳ χαρᾷ χαίρειν.

Another group of words to which some scholars have attached great significance is that from Ignatius' Eph. xii, where he speaks of the Ephesian Christians as *συμμύσται Παύλου τοῦ ἁγιασμένου*. Some have seen in this a reference to the prominence of *μυστήριον* and its significance in Paul's epistle to the Ephesians. Abbott (ICC, p. xi) declines to interpret it in this way, and certainly if this were the only evidence of acquaintance with Ephesians, it would be exceedingly precarious. In view, however, of the other similarities, it is far from improbable that the words do bear some such significance. Taking them all together, we would not dissent from W. R. Inge's summary of their significance: 'It may be considered almost certain that the correspondences are not accidental.'

Hermas too has correspondences with Ephesians that appear to be more than accidental. The Oxford Committee estimate it as 'very probable' that Hermas was acquainted with this epistle. There is no reference which is beyond doubt, but there are at least two passages in Ephesians which appear to have exercised an influence upon this later writer.

In Mandate X we find such phrases as these:

ii. 2: ἡ λύπη . . . λυπεῖ τὸ πνεῦμα τὸ ἅγιον.

ii. 4: ἡ ὀξυχολία λυπεῖ τὸ πνεῦμα.

ii. 5: ἆρον οὖν ἀπὸ σεαυτοῦ τὴν λύπην καὶ μὴ θλῖβε τὸ πνεῦμα τὸ ἅγιον τὸ ἐν σοὶ κατοικοῦν.

These seem to reveal a recollection of Eph. iv. 30: μὴ λυπεῖτε τὸ πνεῦμα τὸ ἅγιον. J. Drummond, spokesman of the Oxford Committee in this section, comments: 'In view of the originality and boldness of the phrase in Ephesians, it seems likely that Hermas is developing in his own way a phrase that has lodged in his mind.'

In Similitude IX there appear to be echoes of Eph. iv. 3–6:

Similitude IX	Eph. iv. 3–6
xiii. 5. οἱ πιστεύσαντες . . . ἔσονται εἰς ἓν πνεῦμα καὶ ἓν σῶμα . . . [7] ἓν πνεῦμα καὶ ἓν σῶμα. xvii. 4. λαβόντες οὖν τὴν σφραγῖδα μίαν φρόνησιν ἔσχον καὶ ἕνα νοῦν, καὶ μία πίστις αὐτῶν ἐγένετο καὶ [μία] ἀγάπη. xviii. 4. . . . ἔσται ἡ ἐκκλησία τοῦ θεοῦ ἓν σῶμα, μία φρόνησις, εἷς νοῦς, μία πίστις, μία ἀγάπη.	. . . ἐν ἀγάπῃ . . . ἓν σῶμα καὶ ἓν πνεῦμα . . . ἐν μιᾷ ἐλπίδι . . . εἷς κύριος, μία πίστις, ἓν βάπτισμα, εἷς θεός . . . .

J. Drummond adds: 'These passages have all the appearance of being imitated from Ephesians.'

The other instances are less convincing than these two, but these two alone suggest that Hermas knew Ephesians. Hermas may be taken as representative of the Christian community at Rome in the earlier part of the second century. His date cannot be fixed with certainty. Streeter (PC, p. 98) decides in favour of A.D. 97–110, but others prefer a rather later period.

The Epistle of Barnabas is an Alexandrian work, which is usually accorded an early date, though few would now regard it as coming from the Barnabas of whom we read in Acts. Streeter (PC, p. 98) does not attempt to fix the date more definitely than between A.D. 78 and 120.

Abbott does not cite Barnabas at all as evidence of early familiarity with Ephesians, and the Oxford Committee hesitates to characterize it even as 'probable' that Barnabas reveals acquaintance with it, though they regard it as possible.

In Barnabas vi. 11 there is a passage which describes forgiveness as involving 'renewal', 're-creation', 're-moulding', and in xvi. 8 the same thoughts reappear, along with the words καινός and κτίζω. This is undoubtedly similar to Eph. ii. 10, where re-born Christians are described as God's ποίημα, κτισθέντες ἐν Χριστῷ, and to Eph. iv. 22 ff., where Christians are said to be 'renewed' and 'created anew', and the words καινός and κτίζω are also used. The ideas were, however, an essential part of the Christian message, and by no means peculiar to Ephesians. It should be noted, however, that Abbott-Smith in his *Lexicon of the Greek New Testament* confines the use of κτίζω, in the sense of 'a divine operation on the soul', to three instances in Ephesians, and the combination with καινός is also peculiar to Ephesians. We do find, however, at 2 Cor. v. 17 and Gal. vi. 15 the same idea, and substantially the same words, in the phrase καινὴ κτίσις.

The peculiar expression in Eph. iii. 17 which describes Christ as κατοικεῖν ἐν ταῖς καρδίαις ὑμῶν may be echoed in the similar phrase ἐν ἡμῖν κατοικεῖν which appears at least three times in Barnabas, in xvi. 8–10 and vi. 14.

In Eph. ii. 21 f. the Christian community is described as ναὸς ἅγιος, in which Christians are built up together (συνοικοδομεῖσθε) εἰς κατοικητήριον τοῦ θεοῦ ἐν πνεύματι. The word κατοικητήριον occurs in no other Pauline letter, and only once elsewhere in the New Testament. It is significant, therefore, that in Barnabas xvi. 8–10 God is spoken of as dwelling in our κατοικητήριον, and in association with it appear the words πνευματικὸς ναὸς οἰκοδομούμενος τῷ κυρίῳ. The association of these words also reappears at vi. 15: ναὸς γὰρ ἅγιος, ἀδελφοί μου, τῷ κυρίῳ τὸ κατοικητήριον ἡμῶν τῆς καρδίας. It is true that some of these ideas are to be found also in 1 Cor. iii. 16 f., but there they are not associated with κατοικητήριον, nor is κατοικέω used to describe the indwelling of Christ.

One questions whether such similarities are adequately accounted for by appealing to a common fund of Christian ideas on which all Christian writers could draw. J. V. Bartlet believes that the evidence 'points to a source beyond common Christian tradition, and to a knowledge of the Pauline writings themselves'; and as compared with the claims of 1 Corinthians, he concludes: 'Ephesians has the advantage over 1 and 2 Corinthians in several ways.' That seems to be a fair assessment of the evidence.

1 *Clement*

Abbott quotes four passages from 1 Clement which, he believes, clearly reveal acquaintance with Ephesians. The Oxford Committee is much less confident. In fact, in their judgement it is improbable that the similarities between the two epistles are due to any literary relationship. They acknowledge that these similarities are considerable, but are disposed to ascribe them to the common use of the same liturgical forms. Our knowledge of these early liturgical forms is slight, and we cannot name with confidence a date when they were first in general use.

We record the more noticeable points of similarity in the two epistles, and though it may be argued that they are the kind of phrases which would be incorporated in liturgical forms, it is probably easier to explain them on the assumption that Clement had read Ephesians than in any other way.

1 Clem. xxxvi. 2	Eph. i. 18
διὰ τούτου ἠνεῴχθησαν ἡμῶν οἱ ὀφθαλμοὶ τῆς καρδίας· διὰ τούτου ἡ ἀσύνετος καὶ ἐσκοτωμένη διάνοια ἡμῶν ἀναθάλλει εἰς τὸ φῶς.	πεφωτισμένους τοὺς ὀφθαλμοὺς τῆς καρδίας ὑμῶν.
	Eph. iv. 18
	ἐσκοτωμένοι τῇ διανοίᾳ ὄντες.
	Cf. Rom. i. 21. ἐσκοτίσθη ἡ ἀσύνετος αὐτῶν καρδία.
1 Clem. lix. 3	
ἀνοίξας τοὺς ὀφθαλμοὺς τῆς καρδίας ἡμῶν εἰς τὸ γινώσκειν σε.	

The phrase οἱ ὀφθαλμοὶ τῆς καρδίας sounds familiar enough to us, but in the New Testament it is peculiar to Ephesians. The second phrase ἡ ἀσύνετος καὶ ἐσκοτωμένη διάνοια is more reminiscent of Rom. i. 21, which also includes the adjective ἀσύνετος. Ephesians, however, may claim some influence in the preference of διάνοια to καρδία; also the form of the participle ἐσκοτωμένη (as against ἐσκοτισμένη) is the form used in Ephesians, at any rate in the MSS. ℵ A B P46.

1 Clem. xlvi. 6–7	Eph. iv. 4–7
ἢ οὐχὶ ἕνα θεὸν ἔχομεν καὶ ἕνα Χριστὸν καὶ ἓν πνεῦμα τῆς χάριτος τὸ ἐκχυθὲν ἐφ' ὑμᾶς; καὶ μία κλῆσις ἐν Χριστῷ; ἵνα τί διέλκομεν καὶ διεσπῶμεν τὰ μέλη τοῦ Χριστοῦ, καὶ στασιάζομεν πρὸς τὸ σῶμα τὸ ἴδιον, . . . μέλη ἐσμὲν ἀλλήλων.	ἓν σῶμα καὶ ἓν πνεῦμα, καθὼς καὶ ἐκλήθητε ἐν μιᾷ ἐλπίδι τῆς κλήσεως ὑμῶν· εἷς κύριος, μία πίστις, ἓν βάπτισμα· εἷς θεὸς καὶ πατὴρ πάντων· ἑνὶ δὲ ἑκάστῳ ἡμῶν ἐδόθη ἡ χάρις κατὰ τὸ μέτρον τῆς δωρεᾶς τοῦ Χριστοῦ.
	Eph. v. 29–30
	ὁ Χριστὸς . . . ὅτι μέλη ἐσμὲν τοῦ σώματος αὐτοῦ.
	Cf. Rom. xii. 5. οἱ πολλοὶ ἓν σῶμά ἐσμεν ἐν Χριστῷ, τὸ δὲ καθ' εἷς ἀλλήλων μέλη.
1 Clem. xxxviii. 1	Eph. iv. 25
σωζέσθω οὖν ἡμῶν ὅλον τὸ σῶμα ἐν Χριστῷ 'Ιησοῦ, καὶ ὑποτασσέσθω ἕκαστος τῷ πλησίον αὐτοῦ.	. . . λαλεῖτε ἀλήθειαν ἕκαστος μετὰ τοῦ πλησίον αὐτοῦ.
	Cf. Rom. xv. 2. ἕκαστος ἡμῶν τῷ πλησίον ἀρεσκέτω.

Clem. xlvi. 6–7 has obvious similarities to Eph. iv. 4–7, and one would be inclined to assume that the later writer had availed himself of the earlier. It is, however, true that these passages represent exactly the kind of material that would first be used in short statements of belief, which might come to have wide currency among the early Christian communities. It is reasonably certain that Clement knew Romans, and where a similarity may be derived from either Ephesians or Romans, it is safer to give the preference to Romans. For instance the phrases μέλη ἐσμὲν ἀλλήλων and ἕκαστος τῷ πλησίον, though each with similarities in Ephesians, must be ascribed rather to Romans.

1 Clem. lxiv. 1	Eph. i. 4–5
ὁ ἐκλεξάμενος τὸν κύριον Ἰησοῦν Χριστὸν καὶ ἡμᾶς δι' αὐτοῦ εἰς λαὸν περιούσιον.	ἐξελέξατο ἡμᾶς ἐν αὐτῷ . . . προορίσας ἡμᾶς εἰς υἱοθεσίαν διὰ Ἰησοῦ Χριστοῦ.

The similarity between these two passages is obvious, but the thought expressed is not so unusual as to imply interdependence. The word ἐκλέγομαι, however, is not used elsewhere in Paul's writings of the Divine choice of human agents. There may therefore be some significance in the parallels.

One cannot, however, be quite confident that Clement knew Ephesians, but on the whole these similarities can probably best be accounted for on the assumption that he did.

The other three writings in the Apostolic Fathers, known as the 'Didache', 2 Clement, and Diognetus, afford no significant evidence that they either knew or did not know Ephesians.

The evidence of the Apostolic Fathers, therefore, establishes the conclusion that almost certainly Ephesians was known to Polycarp, Ignatius, Hermas, and Barnabas, and probably to 1 Clement. This means not only that Ephesians must have been produced before these men wrote, but also that it must have been in circulation long enough to win recognition and to reach the Christian centres where they worked. Opinions will differ upon the number of years required for such a development. Usually, in the early days of the Church, it seems to have been a rather slow process, but in certain circumstances a few years would have been sufficient.

Hort's verdict on the significance of the Apostolic Fathers for the date of Ephesians was: 'It is all but certain on this evidence that the epistle was in existence by 95 A.D.' (PRE, p. 118). If 1 Clement has in fact been influenced by Ephesians, then the date might probably be brought forward to A.D. 90.

XVI

EVIDENCE FROM REVELATION AND THE PASTORAL EPISTLES

EVIDENCE for the date of Ephesians comes not only from the early Christian writings which lie outside the New Testament but from those within it also. The ones most likely to afford help in this matter are Revelation, the Pastoral Epistles, 1 Peter, and Acts.

Some may wish to add the Johannine literature. The author of these books (or, it may be, authors) was very probably acquainted with Paul's teaching, and it is likely that he knew the epistles, though this would be more difficult to prove. Goodspeed, however, claims that it can be shown that the author was actually acquainted with each one of the ten epistles, and he quotes the 'elaborate study' of A. E. Barnett in *The Use of the Letters of Paul in Pre-Catholic Christian Literature* as confirmation of this claim. It may be doubted whether such proof could be provided in each individual case, although there is little reason to doubt that he did know the Pauline letters. But even if it could be shown that this author had read Ephesians, it would add little to the knowledge of the date of Ephesians already acquired from the Apostolic Fathers, for it would not necessitate a date earlier than A.D. 90.

The evidence of 1 Peter and Acts is elusive and its significance is problematical. It will require detailed examination in later chapters. The bearing of Revelation and the Pastoral Epistles on our inquiry is much clearer.

Revelation

R. H. Charles in his commentary on Revelation (ICC) is quite confident that Ephesians was known to the author. His verdict is: 'Quite decidedly . . . our author had the Gospels of Matthew and Luke before him, 1 Thessalonians, 1 and 2 Corinthians, Colossians, . . . Ephesians, and possibly Galatians, 1 Peter and James' (vol. i, pp. lxxxiii ff.). The passages in Revelation which according to Charles reflect acquaintance with Ephesians, and on which he bases his unhesitating judgement, are as follows:

(1) Rev. iii. 21	Eph. ii. 6	Luke xxii. 30
ὁ νικῶν, δώσω αὐτῷ καθίσαι μετ' ἐμοῦ ἐν τῷ θρόνῳ μου ὡς κἀγὼ ἐνίκησα καὶ ἐκάθισα μετὰ τοῦ πατρός μου ἐν τῷ θρόνῳ αὐτοῦ.	ἡμᾶς . . . καὶ συνήγειρεν καὶ συνεκάθισεν ἐν τοῖς ἐπουρανίοις ἐν Χριστῷ 'Ιησοῦ.	καθήσεσθε (v.r. καθίσεσθε) ἐπὶ θρόνων.

The Epistles make frequent reference to Christ Himself, sitting at the right hand of God in Heaven, but Eph. ii. 6 alone seems to speak of Christians as sharing in this privilege. Rev. iii. 21 is therefore a closer parallel to Eph. ii. 6 than might appear at first sight. The force of the συν- in συνεκάθισεν may perhaps be represented in Revelation by the words μετ' ἐμοῦ, and the words ἐν τῷ θρόνῳ αὐτοῦ (Rev.) convey the same meaning as ἐν τοῖς ἐπουρανίοις ἐν Χριστῷ 'Ιησοῦ (Eph.).

It may be claimed that these words in Rev. iii. 21 show a greater resemblance to Luke xxii. 30, and therefore should be regarded as dependent on that passage rather than Ephesians. In the Lukan context, however, the whole thought is different, even though the word θρόνος is used; moreover, κάθημαι appears instead of καθίζω. It is true that καθίσεσθε stands in the Received Text, but it is not supported by the more reliable manuscripts.

(2) Rev. vii. 2-3	Eph. iv. 30	2 Cor. i. 22
εἶδον ἄγγελον . . . ἔχοντα σφραγῖδα θεοῦ ζῶντος, καὶ ἔκραξεν . . . λέγων Μὴ ἀδικήσητε τὴν γῆν μήτε τὴν θάλασσαν μήτε τὰ δένδρα, ἄχρι σφραγίσωμεν τοὺς δούλους τοῦ θεοῦ ἡμῶν ἐπὶ τῶν μετώπων αὐτῶν.	τὸ πνεῦμα ἅγιον τοῦ θεοῦ ἐν ᾧ ἐσφραγίσθητε εἰς ἡμέραν ἀπολυτρώσεως. Eph. i. 13 ἐν ᾧ καὶ πιστεύσαντες ἐσφραγίσθητε τῷ πνεύματι τῆς ἐπαγγελίας τῷ ἁγίῳ, ὅς ἐστιν ἀρραβὼν τῆς κληρονομίας ἡμῶν.	. . . ὁ καὶ σφραγισάμενος ἡμᾶς καὶ δοὺς τὸν ἀρραβῶνα τοῦ πνεύματος ἐν ταῖς καρδίαις ἡμῶν.

Abbott-Smith (MNT) indicates that only in these four contexts in the New Testament is σφραγίζω used in the sense of 'sealing', with the purpose of giving a mark 'for distinction'. It may be that Ephesians is here indebted to 2 Corinthians. It would seem more natural, therefore, to ascribe any debt that Revelation may owe here to the Pauline epistles to 2 Corinthians. Charles, however, adds a special footnote (p. lxxxv) to argue that it is Ephesians which has exerted the influence.

In some texts of Revelation *σφραγίζω* is printed as if it were a quotation from the Old Testament and its source is indicated as Ezek. ix. 4. If this were so, it might be Ezekiel, and not Ephesians, which here suggests the word to the author of Revelation. But *σφραγίζω* is not used in the text of Ezekiel, though the general sense is similar. Instead we find *δὸς σημεῖον ἐπὶ τὰ μέτωπα*.

The use of the word *σφραγίζω*, therefore, and the similarity of its meaning may be taken as suggesting a recollection of Ephesians.

(3) Rev. xviii. 4	Eph. v. 11
. . . *ἵνα μὴ συγκοινωνήσητε ταῖς ἁμαρτίαις αὐτῆς.*	*καὶ μὴ συγκοινωνεῖτε τοῖς ἔργοις τοῖς ἀκάρποις τοῦ σκότους.*

The only other use of *συγκοινωνέω* in the New Testament is at Phil. iv. 14, where the context is quite different from either of the above. The two passages quoted are clearly very similar, and one might well spring from the recollection of the other.

(4) Rev. xxii. 21	Eph. vi. 23–4
ἡ χάρις τοῦ κυρίου Ἰησοῦ μετὰ πάντων.	*εἰρήνη τοῖς ἀδελφοῖς καὶ ἀγάπη μετὰ πίστεως ἀπὸ θεοῦ πατρὸς καὶ κυρίου Ἰησοῦ Χριστοῦ· ἡ χάρις μετὰ πάντων.*

The concluding greetings in some other Pauline epistles are very similar, but those which most resemble Rev. xxii. 21 insert *ὑμῶν* with *πάντων*. It may be, therefore, that Revelation is here adopting the less direct formula of benediction from Ephesians.

Other echoes of Ephesians in Revelation may be heard at:

(5) Rev. iv. 11: *ἔκτισας τὰ πάντα* (cf. Eph. iii. 9).
(6) Rev. xxi. 14: *θεμελίους δώδεκα . . . δώδεκα ἀποστόλων* (cf. Eph. ii. 20).
(7) Rev. xviii. 20: *οἱ ἀπόστολοι καὶ οἱ προφῆται* (cf. Eph. ii. 20).

We may question whether these similarities are such as to bear out fully Charles's confident affirmation that the author of Revelation 'quite decidedly . . . has Ephesians before him'. The evidence cannot be said unmistakably to confirm this opinion. In fact, if no other Pauline epistles had influenced Revelation, we might well have felt justified in explaining these similarities as mere coincidences. There is, however, good reason to believe that others were known to the author, and so it is probable that these parallels, indicated above, may be interpreted as pointing to the author's acquaintance with Ephesians.

The Pastoral Epistles

P. N. Harrison in his *Problem of the Pastoral Epistles* is convinced that these epistles reveal literary acquaintance with most, if not all, of Paul's letters, and certainly of Ephesians. On pp. 171–2 he gives an extensive list of passages in the Pastorals which he believes reflect passages in Ephesians. He indicates ten such passages in 1 Timothy, five in 2 Timothy, and five in Titus. In addition to these twenty, in the margin of the full text of the Pastoral Epistles, printed at the end of the book, thirteen other possible, but less impressive, parallels are noted. It will suffice here to record a few of the clearer instances, since these alone will substantiate Harrison's claim:

(1) 1 Tim. i. 14	Eph. vi. 23
ὑπερεπλεόνασεν δὲ ἡ χάρις τοῦ κυρίου ἡμῶν μετὰ πίστεως καὶ ἀγάπης τῆς ἐν Χριστῷ Ἰησοῦ.	*εἰρήνη τοῖς ἀδελφοῖς καὶ ἀγάπη μετὰ πίστεως ἀπὸ θεοῦ πατρὸς καὶ κυρίου Ἰησοῦ Χριστοῦ. ἡ χάρις μετὰ πάντων.*
(2) 1 Tim. i. 15	Eph. iii. 8
ἁμαρτωλοὺς . . . ὧν πρῶτός εἰμι ἐγώ· ἀλλὰ διὰ τοῦτο ἐλεήθην . . .	*ἐμοὶ τῷ ἐλαχιστοτέρῳ πάντων ἁγίων ἐδόθη ἡ χάρις αὕτη . . .*
(3) 1 Tim. i. 16	Eph. ii. 7 (cf. iv. 2)
ἵνα ἐν ἐμοὶ πρώτῳ ἐνδείξηται Ἰησοῦς Χριστὸς τὴν ἅπασαν μακροθυμίαν . . .	*ἵνα ἐνδείξηται ἐν τοῖς αἰῶσιν τοῖς ἐπερχομένοις τὸ ὑπερβάλλον πλοῦτος τῆς χάριτος αὐτοῦ ἐν χρηστότητι ἐφ' ὑμᾶς ἐν Χριστῷ Ἰησοῦ.*
(4) 1 Tim. iii. 16	Eph. v. 32
καὶ ὁμολογουμένως μέγα ἐστὶν τὸ τῆς εὐσεβείας μυστήριον.	*τὸ μυστήριον τοῦτο μέγα ἐστίν . . .*

(5) 2 Tim. i. 9–10	Eph. iii. 9–11
. . . θεοῦ, τοῦ σώσαντος ἡμᾶς καὶ καλέσαντος κλήσει ἁγίᾳ, οὐ κατὰ τὰ ἔργα ἡμῶν ἀλλὰ κατὰ ἰδίαν πρόθεσιν καὶ χάριν, τὴν δοθεῖσαν ἡμῖν ἐν Χριστῷ Ἰησοῦ πρὸ χρόνων αἰωνίων, φανερωθεῖσαν δὲ νῦν διὰ τῆς ἐπιφανείας τοῦ σωτῆρος ἡμῶν Χριστοῦ Ἰησοῦ καταργήσαντος μὲν τὸν θάνατον φωτίσαντος δὲ ζωὴν καὶ ἀφθαρσίαν διὰ τοῦ εὐαγγελίου.	καὶ φωτίσαι τίς ἡ οἰκονομία τοῦ μυστηρίου τοῦ ἀποκεκρυμμένου ἀπὸ τῶν αἰώνων ἐν τῷ θεῷ τῷ τὰ πάντα κτίσαντι, ἵνα γνωρίσθῃ νῦν ταῖς ἀρχαῖς καὶ ταῖς ἐξουσίαις ἐν τοῖς ἐπουρανίοις διὰ τῆς ἐκκλησίας ἡ πολυποίκιλος σοφία τοῦ θεοῦ, κατὰ πρόθεσιν τῶν αἰώνων ἣν ἐποίησεν ἐν τῷ Χριστῷ Ἰησοῦ . . .
(6) 2 Tim. ii. 1	Eph. vi. 10
σὺ οὖν, τέκνον μου, ἐνδυναμοῦ ἐν τῇ χάριτι τῇ ἐν Χριστῷ Ἰησοῦ.	ἐνδυναμοῦσθε ἐν κυρίῳ καὶ ἐν τῷ κράτει τῆς ἰσχύος αὐτοῦ.
(7) 2 Tim. ii. 15	Eph. i. 13
τὸν λόγον τῆς ἀληθείας.	τὸν λόγον τῆς ἀληθείας.
(8) Titus i. 5	Eph. iii. 1 and 14
τούτου χάριν.	τούτου χάριν.
(9) Titus ii. 5	Eph. v. 21–2
ὑποτασσομένας τοῖς ἰδίοις ἀνδράσιν.	ὑποτασσόμενοι ἀλλήλοις . . . αἱ γυναῖκες τοῖς ἰδίοις ἀνδράσιν.
(10) Titus iii. 3–7	Eph. ii. 3–7
ἦμεν . . . ποτε καὶ ἡμεῖς . . . ἐπιθυμίαις . . . χρηστότης . . . οὐκ ἐξ ἔργων . . . ἔσωσεν ἡμᾶς διὰ λουτροῦ . . . διὰ Ἰησοῦ Χριστοῦ . . . πλουσίως . . . τῇ ἐκείνου χάριτι.	καὶ ἡμεῖς . . . ποτε . . . ἐν ταῖς ἐπιθυμίαις . . . ἤμεθα . . . πλούσιος ὢν . . . τὸ . . . πλοῦτος τῆς χάριτος αὐτοῦ ἐν χρηστότητι ἐφ' ἡμᾶς ἐν Χριστῷ Ἰησοῦ. τῇ γὰρ χάριτί ἐστε σεσωσμένοι . . . οὐκ ἐξ ἔργων. Eph. v. 26: καθαρίσας τῷ λουτρῷ.

This last instance is particularly impressive, and perhaps by itself conclusive.

The passages in Eph. ii. 3–10 and iii. 1–11 seem to have been particularly influential upon the mind of the compiler of the Pastoral Epistles.

The lack of an agreed date for either Revelation or the Pastoral Epistles makes it difficult to assess the exact significance of their evidence. If Revelation could be dated definitely within the period of the Neronian persecution, and if it could be asserted that it unmistakably echoes Ephesians, then so early a date for Ephesians would demand that it be treated as Pauline. But the echoes are not so clear as to be unmistakable, and it is probable that Revelation was written in the time of Domitian rather than Nero. F. B. Clogg's judgement, based on all the relevant evidence, is that it is 'most probable that the book in its present form was written in A.D. 90–96' (INT, p. 292). This date for Revelation therefore does not require an earlier date for Ephesians than the evidence of the Apostolic Fathers does. It provides further confirmation, however, that Ephesians was known and influential in Asia Minor by A.D. 90 or very soon after.

Clogg's estimate of the date of the Pastorals is that 'the three cannot be later than A.D. 110, and are more likely to have been written near the end of the first century' (INT, p. 123). P. N. Harrison argues for a date later than A.D. 110, and explains the similarities between the Pastorals and Ignatius as due, not to Ignatius' knowledge of the Pastorals, but to the influence of Ignatius on the compiler of the Pastorals. Whether we accept the earlier or the later date, these epistles also confirm what has been learnt from the Apostolic Fathers and Revelation, that Ephesians was known and valued in Asia Minor soon after A.D. 90.

XVII

THE RELATIONSHIP BETWEEN EPHESIANS AND 1 PETER

THE similarities between these two epistles are so numerous and so close that the majority of scholars are agreed that they cannot be merely the result of coincidence or even of mutual familiarity with a common tradition of Christian teaching. Only some measure of literary dependence, it is felt, is sufficient to account for the words and expressions, thoughts and groups of thoughts, which these two epistles have in common. One might justifiably anticipate, therefore, that a careful comparison of the corresponding passages would throw light upon the problem of the date and authorship of Ephesians. One obstacle, however, holds up every advance. It is the uncertainty concerning the date and authorship of 1 Peter. If that could be regarded as fixed and settled, then from that point of stability we could proceed to confident affirmations about other writings with which it has literary relationships. But we are not in a position to assume an agreed date for 1 Peter. Scholars are about equally divided over it. One group confidently affirms that its claim to Petrine authorship is genuine, and ascribes it to the closing years of Peter's life. Another group with equal confidence ascribes it to a date towards the end of the first century, and regards it as pseudonymous. Others admit that there is much to be said on each side, and leave the issue open. Perhaps the majority of modern scholars are inclined to reject the Petrine authorship, as does F. W. Beare in the most recent exposition of the epistle (1947), but for English readers this is considerably offset by the resolute defence of it which E. G. Selwyn included in his commentary. We cannot pretend here to pronounce on the correct solution, nor can we attempt to enter into an exhaustive study of the relevant arguments and assess their validity. Every student will have his own opinion, but so long as it holds no more secure status than that of a personal judgement on a disputed issue, it is insufficient to use as a premiss from which to proceed to conclusions on other matters.

In all our consideration of these two epistles, therefore, we are dealing with two unknowns—the date and authorship of Ephesians, and the date and authorship of 1 Peter. It is unlikely that we shall be able to solve a simple equation in which there are two unknowns. No matter how clearly we may be able to define the relationship between these two epistles, its bearing upon the authorship of Ephesians will be ambiguous so long as the date of 1 Peter may be regarded as either *c.* A.D. 60 or *c.* A.D. 95. Until the date of either 1 Peter or Ephesians can be fixed, an examination of their relationship will be inconclusive. At the present stage it is indeed likely to produce evidence that will affect the dating of 1 Peter more than that of Ephesians. If, of course, one is persuaded that a post-Pauline date for Ephesians has been established, then this investigation will have a direct bearing on the date of 1 Peter.

If we assume that there is literary dependence between these two epistles, the ambiguity of the relationship is shown by the four possibilities which confront us:

(*a*) If 1 Peter is genuinely the work of Peter, and can at the same time be shown to exhibit an acquaintance with Ephesians, that will be tantamount to a conclusive proof that Ephesians is genuinely a Pauline epistle.

(*b*) If 1 Peter is genuinely the work of Peter, and if, on the other hand, it can be demonstrated that it is Ephesians which displays knowledge of 1 Peter, then Ephesians will be almost certainly post-Pauline.

(*c*) If, however, 1 Peter is of post-Petrine origin, and is dependent on Ephesians, then Ephesians may be either Pauline or post-Pauline.

(*d*) If 1 Peter is of post-Petrine origin, and is also demonstrably prior to Ephesians, then the post-Pauline origin of Ephesians would be established.

It may be possible to resolve the question of priority between these two epistles, and that will at any rate reduce the four possibilities to two, but until a decision can be reached between a Petrine and non-Petrine origin, it will remain impossible for us to reduce farther the two possibilities to a single one. We may not therefore anticipate conclusive evidence from this study of the relationship of these two epistles, but it must be undertaken for what it is worth, since our investigation would be incomplete without it.

Several scholars have drawn up lists of the parallels between these two epistles, though no two lists exactly coincide. Among them are Abbott in ICC, pp. xxiv–xxvii, where he is largely indebted to the earlier lists which H. J. Holtzmann printed in his *Kritik*; F. H. Chase in HDB, vol. iii, p. 788; Moffatt in ILNT, pp. 381–3; and

McNeile in INT, pp. 158–9. All these correspondences, and others, are indicated in Appendix I. The closeness of each individual parallel is shown by underlinings thus: in wavy lines (〰〰) for verbal identity or for very close similarity, and an oblique dotted line (⁄⁄⁄⁄⁄⁄⁄⁄) for a smaller degree of similarity.

The extent and closeness of these similarities have led almost all scholars to believe that some degree of literary dependence must exist between the two epistles. Moffatt may be taken as summarizing the consensus of opinion, as well as expressing his own conclusion, when he writes that the points of correspondence are 'more than coincidences due to the common store of early Christian thought' (ILNT, p. 382).

There are those, however, who stop short of claiming literary interdependence. Salmon, for instance, argues that the similarities between 1 Peter and Romans are probably due to Peter's knowledge of that Pauline letter. Realizing, however, the difficulties in the way of assuming that Peter could also have read Ephesians, he accounts for the similarities between it and 1 Peter by supposing that Peter would have constant opportunities of hearing Paul speak and converse during his last Roman imprisonment, that Paul would speak of the subjects that were engaging his mind at that time, and so the subject-matter and phraseology of Ephesians would often sound in Peter's ears, and not unnaturally his letter would reflect this (HDB, iii, p. 789). One cannot regard this as a convincing explanation.

Zahn prefers to trace the marks of Pauline influence in 1 Peter to the part that Silvanus played in its composition. He is regarded not merely as Peter's amanuensis, but rather as a responsible literary agent, acting under Peter's direction and entrusted with a large measure of creative responsibility. He assumes, with most others, that this Silvanus is the same man as the friend of Paul who bore that name.

E. G. Selwyn also, in his recent, noteworthy commentary on 1 Peter, while acknowledging the close similarities in the letter with Ephesians, is unwilling to account for them on the grounds of direct literary dependence. He believes that the large part taken by Silvanus in the writing of the letter may be taken to explain some of the marks of Pauline influence; but his main argument is that before A.D. 60 there were in common use throughout the churches standardized codes of belief and conduct, and that these helped to shape some of the sections in both these letters, and so established these similarities. It would not be disputed that such codes probably did exist towards the end of the first century, but that they were in common use as early as A.D. 60 is much to be doubted. If there is a proved similarity between some of these codes and Paul's letters, it is at least as likely that it was the letters which helped to shape the codes as that the codes are reproduced in the letters. The statistics and lists of parallels which Selwyn has drawn up are certainly impressive, and if 1 Peter can confidently be accepted as Petrine in origin, a strong argument may be framed from them in support of the existence of early catechetical codes. An equally valid explanation of the parallels would be that Paul's letters were the original pattern, and that all the rest, including 1 Peter, were indebted to that influential model. Such an explanation would almost certainly exclude the possibility of recognizing 1 Peter as genuinely Petrine, but that does not *ipso facto* rule the explanation out of court, for we have seen that a large percentage of scholars, if not actually the majority, on quite general grounds question the Petrine authorship. Selwyn's judgement on the early date of the codes is based on the prior judgement on the early date of 1 Peter, but that is an insecure judgement on which to base other conclusions.

Moreover, lists of verbal parallels do not exhaust the similarities between these two epistles. The similarities are discernible in the whole structure, outlook, and atmosphere. Hort's judgement is cited with approval by several writers: 'The connexion, though very close, does not lie on the surface. It is shown more by identities of thought and similarity in the structure of the two epistles as wholes than by identities of phrase' (*1 Peter*, p. 5). Dibelius implies the recognition of the same characteristics when he writes: 'In regard to content, 1 Peter belongs in the neighbourhood of Ephesians' (FA, p. 186), and E. G. Selwyn also writes:

> 'It is not a question of detailed parallels . . . but of certain broad underlying assumptions and factors in the situation which are common to both. We get the impression from both epistles of a floodtide which has been running strongly in the Church, and accounts for much in the temper and atmosphere of each. . . . Behind both epistles flows the tide of the Church's unity and expansion. The great issue of Jew and Gentile has been settled. . . . 1 Peter rejoices no less than St. Paul (in Ephesians) . . . in the redemption, the call, the new inheritance, the salvation, and in the Church, which represents and embodies these, even in its sufferings and trials.'

He notes also 'the triumphant theme of praise and benediction with which this epistle [1 Peter] like Ephesians, opens' and 'the note of the glorious expansion of the Church' on which they both end (IP, pp. 39–40).

Indeed some scholars have been so impressed not only by what Selwyn calls the 'general climate of feeling and thought' which marks both these epistles, but also by the closer parallels which will be indicated, that they have even suggested that the same author may have been responsible for the writing of both of them. Harnack, for instance, urged that Paul should be credited with the writing of 1 Peter as well as of Ephesians, and Seufert, while not wishing to claim Paul as the common author, argued that one man was the writer of both, and was inclined to name Silvanus for the honour. No other scholars have taken up these suggestions, but they serve to show the great community of thought and expression which has been recognized in these two epistles. It is very questionable whether catechetical tables can be held responsible for so wide and diffuse a similarity, in addition to the more obvious verbal correspondences.

The great majority of scholars choose a course between the two extremes of denying literary relationship and of advocating identity of authorship. They are persuaded that some measure of literary dependence must be admitted. The names of those who hold such a point of view are too numerous to record. As a judicial summary of the position, the words of P. N. Harrison may be quoted: 'It is generally agreed that the many points of close contact between 1 Peter and Ephesians prove literary dependence one way or the other. But to which of them we should assign the priority is still a matter of debate' (PTE, p. 299).

It is to this issue which is 'still a matter of debate' that we must now turn. It is true that no final decision on it has been reached, but it would not be true to say that each side has equally numerous supporters. There are important names among those who claim priority for 1 Peter, but numerically a far longer list can be drawn up of scholars who maintain that the priority belongs to Ephesians. Of these Jülicher, Harnack, Chase, Hort, Peake, Holtzmann, Abbott, and E. F. Scott are only some of the names. A few are content to leave the matter quite open. Peake mentions only two scholars as having maintained the priority of 1 Peter. He writes: 'B. Weiss has attempted to show that the letter [1 Peter] was written before any of Paul's letters, and that so far as there is dependence, it is of Paul on Peter, and not of Peter on Paul. In this he is followed only by Kuhl, and the theory may be safely set aside' (CINT, p. 91). Shortly after this judgement was recorded, a further advocate for the priority of 1 Peter appeared in the person of J. Moffatt (ILNT, pp. 337–8 and p. 382), and he gives the names of several other scholars, besides the two named by Peake, who have maintained that point of view (p. 337). One cannot say how far Moffatt was influenced in this judgement by his confident conclusion that Ephesians must be given a post-Pauline date, and his inclination to regard 1 Peter as genuinely Petrine. In his treatment of 1 Peter, which precedes that of Ephesians, he leaves the question of priority open: 'Either Peter knew Ephesians, or, if the latter is post-Pauline, the author of Ephesians was probably acquainted with the Petrine pastoral' (p. 338). Under his treatment of Ephesians, however, he writes: 'Unless both are assigned to the same author, the probabilities on the whole point to an acquaintance on the part of "auctor ad Ephesios" with the simpler 1 Peter, if on other grounds the latter is attributed to Peter, and Ephesians assigned to a Paulinist' (p. 382). In support of this position, Moffatt names one or two parallels where the words in Ephesians are said to be less natural and less germane to their context than they are in 1 Peter. But his interpretation of the relationship is at variance with that of most scholars, and his own words suggest that it is not based primarily on an examination of the relationship, but rather on prior conclusions concerning date and authorship.

On the other hand, those who maintain the priority of Ephesians have in all probability been in some measure influenced by their presupposition that Ephesians is a genuine Pauline letter, and the improbability that Paul would borrow from a Petrine letter in the composition of one of his own. Moreover, it is generally acknowledged that 1 Peter reflects acquaintance with Romans, and is indebted especially to Romans xii. It is almost incredible that Paul used 1 Peter in writing his epistle to the Romans. Holtzmann pours scorn on the proposition that 'the most original of all New Testament writers' should be thought of as 'laboriously gleaning' exhortations from 1 Peter. Most scholars therefore are content to assume that Peter at Rome was himself influenced by the weighty correspondence of his brother-apostle to the city of his adoption. If one other than Peter, in a later generation, wrote 1 Peter, the assumption of his dependence on Romans becomes more than ever probable.

Since this is so, and since there is interdependence also between Ephesians and 1 Peter, it is probable that the explanation of it is the same as that for the interdependence between Romans and 1 Peter.

The great weakness in all these judgements about the priority of one or the other of these two epistles is that they are to some extent based on earlier judgements about genuineness and date. These, however, are the very questions to which we are seeking an answer, and so in attempting to assess accurately the relationship between the epistles we must scrupulously avoid any presuppositions on these other matters, and try to examine the evidence with open mind. Without even letting the question arise: 'Which view of the relationship will favour my views on authorship and date?' we must examine the parallel passages, and inquire if in the manner of the similarity there is anything which will enable us to settle the dispute about priority.

We shall not attempt to investigate each parallel in detail, but only those which appear to have a bearing on the issue before us.

First of all, mention should be made of the words and phrases in 1 Peter which appear also in Ephesians but not in any other of the Pauline epistles. Of themselves these will not carry us far in our investigation, but they supply some objective evidence for the opinions, already quoted, of Hort, Selwyn, and Dibelius, that the two epistles 'breathe the same atmosphere'.

The following words appear nowhere else in the New Testament except in these two epistles:

εὔσπλαγχνος as descriptive of Christian character (1 Pet. iii. 8; Eph. iv. 32).

ἀκρογωνιαῖος as descriptive of the place of Christ in any truly Christian structure (1 Pet. ii. 6; Eph. ii. 20).

The following words and phrases in Ephesians and 1 Peter are used also in some of the late books of the New Testament, but not in the other Pauline epistles, nor in Mark:

πρὸ καταβολῆς κόσμου (1 Pet. i. 20; Eph. i. 4).

διάβολος (1 Pet. v. 8; Eph. iv. 27, vi. 11).

πάροικος (1 Pet. ii. 11; Eph. ii. 19). There is a curious difference in the use of this word in these two contexts. In 1 Peter it is used to describe what a true Christian ought to be in this world, a kind of resident alien, aware of the impermanence of his stay here, and so unattached to what has significance only for this earthly life, to its possessions and passions. In Ephesians, however, it is used in a bad rather than a good sense, to describe what the Gentiles once were, before they were brought into the family of the Church, outsiders and unaccepted aliens, though this former inferiority of status has now been entirely annulled by the death of Christ.

ποιμήν (Eph. iv. 11); *ποιμαίνω* (1 Pet. v. 2), used not of Christ Himself but of Christian pastors.

ἄφθαρτος (1 Pet. iii. 4); *ἀφθαρσία* (Eph. vi. 24), used to signify what is pure and untarnished in the moral sense, and not, as is more usual in the New Testament, immortal and incorruptible in a metaphysical sense.

περιποίησις (Eph. i. 14; 1 Pet. ii. 9) in a passive sense, meaning 'possession', as distinct from the active meaning of 'acquisition' in 1 Thess. v. 9 and 2 Thess. ii. 14.

ποικίλος (1 Pet. iv. 10); *πολυποίκιλος* (Eph. iii. 10), used somewhat daringly to describe an attribute of God, in one case His Grace, and in the other His Wisdom.

ἀσωτία (1 Pet. iv. 4; Eph. v. 18) of profligate conduct unworthy of a Christian.

The pre-Christian condition of unbelievers is described in both epistles, firstly as 'ignorance' (1 Pet. i. 14; Eph. iv. 18), and secondly as 'vanity' (1 Pet. i. 18; Eph. iv. 17).

More relevant to our present purpose of fixing the priority on one epistle or the other, and of deciding what degree of probability may be assigned to Selwyn's theory of their mutual dependence upon Church codes, are the following five corresponding passages, which will be examined in some detail.

(*a*) 1 Pet. i. 3	Eph. i. 3	2 Cor. i. 3
εὐλογητὸς ὁ θεὸς καὶ πατὴρ τοῦ κυρίου ἡμῶν Ἰησοῦ Χριστοῦ, ὁ κατὰ τὸ πολὺ αὐτοῦ ἔλεος ἀναγεννήσας ἡμᾶς εἰς ἐλπίδα ζῶσαν δι᾽ ἀναστάσεως Ἰησοῦ Χριστοῦ ἐκ νεκρῶν	εὐλογητὸς ὁ θεὸς καὶ πατὴρ τοῦ κυρίου ἡμῶν Ἰησοῦ Χριστοῦ ὁ εὐλογήσας ἡμᾶς . . . . Eph. ii. 4 ὁ δὲ θεὸς πλούσιος ὢν ἐν ἐλέει, . . . ἡμᾶς νεκροὺς τοῖς παραπτώμασι συνεζωοποίησεν τῷ Χριστῷ.	εὐλογητὸς ὁ θεὸς καὶ πατὴρ τοῦ κυρίου ἡμῶν Ἰησοῦ Χριστοῦ ὁ . . . παρακαλῶν . . . .

We noted in our earlier comparison of Eph. i. 3 and 2 Cor. i. 3 that this opening phrase of eleven words is identical in both letters.

In 2 Corinthians it springs naturally and appropriately from the great sense of relief which Paul is feeling at the settlement of what had threatened to become a permanent rift in his relationship with the Corinthian Church. In comparison, the same words in Ephesians appear at any rate rather less spontaneous.

It is remarkable that these eleven identical words should reappear in the opening sentences of 1 Peter, and one would at first be inclined to assume that one author had borrowed an impressive phrase from the other. In that case, the borrower would almost certainly be the author of 1 Peter, unless it is argued that 1 Peter was written before 2 Corinthians, and that the apparently spontaneous cry of relief in 2 Cor. i. 3 was in fact merely an imitation of 1 Pet. i. 3. If we grant that 2 Cor. i. 3 is probably original, it must be admitted that the author of Ephesians, whether Paul himself or one deliberately following Paul's letters as his model, would be much more likely to reproduce a phrase which was already familiar in 2 Corinthians than to appropriate the same phrase from 1 Peter.

Selwyn declines to recognize in this similarity any evidence of interdependence, and discounts any special significance that others may derive from it by saying that it 'represents a common form of expression' (IP, p. 462). It is true that in the Psalms one occasionally finds a very similar association of words, e.g. *εὐλογητὸς κύριος ὁ θεὸς τοῦ Ἰσραήλ, ὁ ποιῶν θαυμάσια μόνος* (Ps. lxxi. 18, LXX). Such remembered phrases would be influential in shaping the Christian cry of gratitude in 2 Cor. i. 3. It is, however, questionable whether it is justifiable to ascribe the use of these eleven identical words in 1 Peter to 'a common form of expression', unless one is fully assured that 1 Peter could not possibly have had acquaintance with Ephesians or 2 Corinthians.

If, in this same general context in 1 Peter, there was no trace of any other similarity with Ephesians, the matter would not be pressed, because admittedly these eleven words are of the kind that might readily become a liturgical formula, though there is insufficient evidence to claim with confidence that this had actually taken place in the common usage of the Church within the lifetime of Paul and Peter. There are, however, in the same context, other similarities with Ephesians which are too numerous to be merely accidental.

The first of these to be noted is the construction of the article with the participle, persisting throughout several verses, and alternating with the use of the relative pronoun. This occurs in both 1 Pet. i. 3–12 and Eph. i. 3–14.

Secondly, in each case the paragraph which follows opens similarly, with an inferential διό in 1 Pet. i. 13 and διὰ τοῦτο in Eph. i. 15.

Moreover, in the same context in each epistle there is included an emphasis on 'hope' (1 Pet. i. 3; Eph. i. 18) in association with 'inheritance' (1 Pet. i. 4; Eph. i. 18) and 'the power of God' (1 Pet. i. 5; Eph. i. 19), which is pre-eminently manifest in the Resurrection of Christ (1 Pet. i. 3; Eph. i. 20). This sequence of similarities establishes a striking coincidence between 1 Pet. i. 3–5 and Eph. i. 18–19 (see Appendix I at Eph. i. 18).

Further, 1 Pet. i. 3, with its declaration that the mercy of God has given new life to men through Christ's resurrection, is substantially equivalent to Eph. ii. 4–5. The meaning of these passages corresponds even more closely than the actual words.

Even if the two epistles contained no other points of coincidence, the resemblance of these opening verses would make it probable that there had been some measure of interdependence, over and above familiarity with a common tradition, and that in this relationship of dependence the priority is with Ephesians.

(*b*) 1 Pet. i. 10–12	Eph. iii. 2–6	Col. i. 26–7
περὶ ἧς σωτηρίας ἐξεζήτησαν καὶ ἐξηραύνησαν προφῆται οἱ περὶ τῆς εἰς ὑμᾶς χάριτος προφητεύσαντες, ἐραυνῶντες εἰς τίνα ἢ ποῖον καιρὸν ἐδήλου τὸ ἐν αὐτοῖς πνεῦμα Χριστοῦ προμαρτυρόμενον τὰ εἰς Χριστὸν παθήματα καὶ τὰς μετὰ ταῦτα δόξας· οἷς ἀπεκαλύφθη ὅτι οὐχ ἑαυτοῖς ὑμῖν δὲ διηκόνουν αὐτά, ἃ νῦν ἀνηγγέλη ὑμῖν διὰ τῶν εὐαγγελισαμένων ὑμᾶς ἐν πνεύματι ἁγίῳ.	εἴ γε ἠκούσατε τὴν οἰκονομίαν τῆς χάριτος τοῦ θεοῦ . . . [4] ἐν τῷ μυστηρίῳ τοῦ Χριστοῦ, ὃ ἑτέραις γενεαῖς οὐκ ἐγνωρίσθη τοῖς υἱοῖς τῶν ἀνθρώπων ὡς νῦν ἀπεκαλύφθη τοῖς ἁγίοις ἀποστόλοις αὐτοῦ καὶ προφήταις ἐν πνεύματι . . . [6] ἐν Χριστῷ Ἰησοῦ διὰ τοῦ εὐαγγελίου.	τὸ μυστήριον τὸ ἀποκεκρυμμένον ἀπὸ τῶν αἰώνων καὶ ἀπὸ τῶν γενεῶν . . . νῦν δὲ ἐφανερώθη τοῖς ἁγίοις αὐτοῦ.

As will be seen from these columns, there is a substantial similarity between 1 Pet. i. 10–12 and Eph. iii. 2–6. In each the purpose of God is declared to have been long hidden, but now His gracious dealings with His people are proved by the disclosure of this purpose in the Gospel of Christ, which has come to us ἐν πνεύματι. The 'prophets' are introduced into each passage, but in two different senses. In 1 Peter they are the Old Testament prophets, who failed to grasp the true purpose of God; in Ephesians they are the Christian prophets, who were the chosen vehicles of its open declaration.

These resemblances are too close to be casually dismissed as mere coincidences due to the common Gospel tradition on which each writer depended. Nor, in this case, can it be argued that each passage is derived from some standardized catechetical code, for the subject-matter is not of the type that would appear either in a liturgical formula or an ethical code.

If, however, literary interdependence must here be conceded, priority must certainly be accorded to Ephesians, for Ephesians in this passage is undoubtedly dependent upon Colossians. This, we believe, was established in an earlier chapter. If this is so, then Ephesians here cannot be derived from 1 Peter, and so it must be that 1 Peter is derived from Ephesians. Nor can it be argued, if anyone should attempt this expedient, that perhaps 1 Peter was derived from Colossians at this point, for though the passage in 1 Peter includes some words which are common to both Ephesians and Colossians, several others have their equivalent only in the passage in Ephesians.

(*c*) 1 Pet. ii. 2–6	Eph. ii. 18–22	Rom. v. 2
. . . ἵνα ἐν αὐτῷ αὐξηθῆτε εἰς σωτηρίαν, εἰ ἐγεύσασθε ὅτι χρηστὸς ὁ κύριος. πρὸς ὃν προσερχόμενοι . . . καὶ αὐτοὶ ὡς λίθοι ζῶντες οἰκοδομεῖσθε οἶκος πνευματικὸς εἰς ἱεράτευμα ἅγιον . . . ἀκρογωνιαῖον.	δι' αὐτοῦ ἔχομεν προσαγωγὴν οἱ ἀμφότεροι ἐν ἑνὶ πνεύματι πρὸς τὸν πατέρα· ἄρα οὖν οὐκέτι ἐστὲ ξένοι καὶ πάροικοι, ἀλλὰ . . . οἰκεῖοι τοῦ θεοῦ, ἐποικοδομηθέντες ἐπὶ τῷ θεμελίῳ . . . ὄντος ἀκρογωνιαίου αὐτοῦ Ἰησοῦ Χριστοῦ, ἐν ᾧ πᾶσα οἰκοδομὴ συναρμολογουμένη αὔξει εἰς ναὸν ἅγιον ἐν κυρίῳ, ἐν ᾧ καὶ ὑμεῖς συνοικοδομεῖσθε εἰς κατοικητήριον τοῦ θεοῦ.	δι' οὗ καὶ τὴν προσαγωγὴν ἐσχήκαμεν. 1 Cor. iii. 12 εἴ τις ἐποικοδομεῖ ἐπὶ τὸν θεμέλιον . . . 16 ὁ γὰρ ναὸς τοῦ θεοῦ ἅγιός ἐστιν, οἵτινές ἐστε ὑμεῖς. Cf. also Gal. vi. 10 and 1 Cor. iii. 9. Col. ii. 19 . . . ἐξ οὗ πᾶν τὸ σῶμα διὰ τῶν ἁφῶν καὶ συνδέσμων ἐπιχορηγούμενον καὶ συμβιβαζόμενον αὔξει τὴν αὔξησιν τοῦ θεοῦ. Col. ii. 7 ἐποικοδομούμενοι ἐν αὐτῷ.

In these two short sequences of verses (1 Pet. ii. 2–6 and Eph. ii. 18–22) we find that the following ideas are shared: the Christian's access to God through Christ; the thought that this privilege should lead on, in the Christian's life, to some fuller experience (αὐξάνω); this developing experience is represented by the figure of a house under construction, a house which is to be a holy shrine, in which the chief corner-stone is to be Christ Himself.

It would be most unusual, even within a community whose thought was shaped by a common experience, for two entirely independent writers to incorporate so many similar ideas into so short a space. Some measure of interdependence, or mutual dependence upon some common source, is required to explain it.

If we assume some kind of literary dependence, does this passage help us to establish to which of the two priority belongs? Or does it help us to decide for or against the alternative explanation that church codes and formulae lie behind the similarities?

In an earlier chapter we saw that Ephesians was based on Colossians, and that Colossians is in large measure reproduced in Ephesians. In view of this it is clear that certain elements in Eph. ii. 18–22, and some of them parallel to parts of 1 Pet. ii. 2–6, are derived from Colossians. For instance, ἐποικοδομηθέντες and ἐν ᾧ . . . συνοικοδομεῖσθε are reproduced in Ephesians from the pattern of ἐποικοδομούμενοι ἐν αὐτῷ in Col. ii. 7; and similarly the association of the two ideas of the harmony within the structure and its development (αὐξάνω) reflect the influence of Col. ii. 19. It cannot, therefore, be argued that these particular elements in the passage from Ephesians are derived from 1 Peter.

Moreover, other words and thoughts in Eph. ii. 18–22 which have parallels in 1 Pet. ii. 2–6 are found in earlier letters of Paul. The thought of access to God (through Christ) occurs in Rom. v. 1–2, and, moreover, in words with a closer resemblance to Eph. ii. 18 than the words of 1 Pet. ii. 2 bear. Again, the figure of speech which likens a Christian community to a ναὸς ἅγιος occurs in 1 Cor. iii. 6 (cf. also 2 Cor. vi. 16), and there is also a parallel in Eph. ii. 20 with 1 Cor. iii. 12.

If Paul is the writer of Ephesians we cannot accuse him of dependence upon 1 Peter for the use of words and phrases which he has already shown to be part of his own vocabulary by his use of them in earlier letters. If, on the other hand, the author is a later admirer of Paul, who is aiming at representing the Pauline teaching in summary for a subsequent generation, and for this purpose freely drawing on the thought and vocabulary of the genuine letters, we must surely assume that these Pauline elements are derived direct from these letters rather than appropriated through the mediating agency of 1 Peter.

These corresponding passages, therefore, provide additional support for the priority of Ephesians.

It is true that the subject-matter of Eph. ii. 18–22 is of the kind that might be used for didactic and liturgical purposes, and therefore it has been argued that the similarity with 1 Pet. ii. 2–6 is due to the influence of the same church codes on both authors; but the manner of the relationship of the Ephesian passage to Colossians and the other Pauline letters precludes this explanation. If Paul wrote Ephesians, he is here saying over again what he has already said elsewhere; if a Paulinist, he is allowing Paul's own words and thoughts to re-emerge in his epistle. In view of this relationship to the genuine Pauline epistles, it is as unconvincing to argue that Ephesians here is dependent upon church codes as it is to claim that it is borrowing from 1 Peter.

(*d*) 1 Pet. iii. 22	Eph. i. 20–1	Col. ii. 12
. . . δι' ἀναστάσεως Ἰησοῦ Χριστοῦ, ὅς ἐστιν ἐν δεξιᾷ θεοῦ, πορευθεὶς εἰς οὐρανόν, ὑποταγέντων αὐτῷ ἀγγέλων καὶ ἐξουσιῶν καὶ δυνάμεων.	. . . ἐν τῷ Χριστῷ, ἐγείρας αὐτὸν ἐκ νεκρῶν καὶ καθίσας ἐν δεξιᾷ αὐτοῦ ἐν τοῖς ἐπουρανίοις ὑπεράνω πάσης ἀρχῆς καὶ ἐξουσίας καὶ δυνάμεως καὶ κυριότητος.	συνηγέρθητε διὰ τῆς πίστεως τῆς ἐνεργείας τοῦ θεοῦ τοῦ ἐγείραντος αὐτὸν ἐκ νεκρῶν. Col. iii. 1 . . . οὗ ὁ Χριστός ἐστιν, ἐν δεξιᾷ τοῦ θεοῦ καθήμενος. Col. i. 16 εἴτε κυριότητες εἴτε ἀρχαὶ εἴτε ἐξουσίαι.

Between these two passages from 1 Peter and Ephesians there is this striking community of ideas: God's power to save, demonstrated and proved by His raising of Christ from the dead, and Christ's exaltation to God's right hand, and His effective authority over every other kind of power in the universe.

It is true that these points of emphasis are just the ones that might well have been given a place in early statements of belief in Christ, and there is a prima-facie case for the claim that some such statement lies behind these two parallel passages, in which substantially the same affirmations are reproduced, though in somewhat different words. Selwyn is quite confident in his assertion that they 'derive from liturgical sources' (p. 462).

A preliminary hesitation in accepting this categorical predication of their origin arises from the variety of the wording. Catechisms and liturgies teach people fixed forms of words rather than ideas of such flexibility that they can be variously expressed in different words. If liturgical formulae lay behind these two passages, we should expect to find the reproduction of set phrases of identical words in greater degree than is the case here.

There is, however, a stronger argument against deriving these words from a community catechism or a standardized liturgy. It is this: that here, as in the other passages examined, Ephesians is clearly derived from Colossians. Its combination of separate phrases from Colossians, to which we gave the name 'conflation', is characteristic of the way in which Ephesians has used Colossians.

Certainly there can be no doubt that ἐγείρας αὐτὸν ἐκ νεκρῶν (Eph. i. 20) is derived from Col. ii. 12. Not only are the words themselves identical, but the preceding verses in each case show a considerable measure of interdependence (see Appendix I at Eph. i. 19). The parallels with Col. iii. 1 and Col. i. 16 are also fairly clear evidence of dependence.

Once again, therefore, it can be said with confidence that, since Ephesians here is derived from Colossians, it cannot be derived also from 1 Peter, and the relationship can best be explained by regarding 1 Peter as the borrower.

Moreover, since the combination of these three separate elements from Colossians is original to Ephesians, it cannot be maintained that Ephesians is here derived from church codes, and still less that Colossians is reproducing them, because in Colossians the combination of elements has not yet been effected. It may be argued with some justification that Ephesians influenced the formation of these codes of belief and conduct, and that these influenced the author of 1 Peter. The simpler explanation, however, is that the author has read carefully the epistle to the Ephesians, and certain thoughts and phrases from it have impressed themselves on his mind.

The evidence of this passage, in fact, even more than that of the others already considered, is fatal to the theory that Ephesians is borrowing from 1 Peter, and almost equally effectively refutes the alternative theory that both are dependent on codes in common use, although it is to this passage that advocates of this explanation appeal with special confidence.

(*e*) *Ethical Counsel*

E. G. Selwyn in his contention that the similarities between 1 Peter and Ephesians are not due to any direct dependence, but to mutual acquaintance with standardized codes which had come into general use throughout the Christian communities, relies particularly on the similarity in general pattern and in actual wording which is to be found in the ethical teaching of these two epistles. If, however, it is claimed that Ephesians is in these sections merely reproducing ethical codes already familiar in the Church, then the same must be true of Colossians, for in these sections Ephesians follows exactly the pattern of Colossians, merely amplifying what had already been written in the earlier letter.

The following columns show how exactly Ephesians keeps to the general outline of Colossians in these sections:

Subject	*Colossians*	*Ephesians*	*Subject*	*1 Peter*
General counsel .	iii. 5	iv. 25	General counsel .	ii. 1
γυναῖκες . .	iii. 18	v. 22	οἰκέται . .	ii. 18
ἄνδρες . . .	iii. 19	v. 25–33	γυναῖκες . .	iii. 1
τέκνα . . .	iii. 20	vi. 1	ἄνδρες . .	iii. 7
πατέρες . .	iii. 21	vi. 4	General counsel .	iv. 12
δοῦλοι . . .	iii. 22	vi. 5	πρεσβύτεροι . .	v. 1
κύριοι . . .	iv. 1	vi. 9	νεώτεροι . .	v. 5

It will be seen from these columns that Ephesians gives counsel to the same groups of people as Colossians, and treats them in precisely the same order. Almost all the sections in Ephesians are enlarged by the inclusion of additions to what is found in Colossians, but the bulk of what is given in Colossians is incorporated into Ephesians, and very often in the identical words. In Appendix I the words in Colossians which are reproduced in Ephesians are underlined, and in the sections of Colossians listed above (Col. iii. 18–iv. 1), out of 117 words in all, 81 are underlined as having equivalents in the corresponding sections in Ephesians. There is no doubt that in these sections Ephesians is largely derived from Colossians.

If, therefore, the similarities between 1 Peter and Ephesians at this point are to be explained as due to mutual dependence on church codes, it is clear that Colossians must equally be dependent on them; and if 1 Peter is dependent on them, then 1 Peter should show an even closer correspondence with Colossians than with Ephesians, and in any divergence between Colossians and Ephesians, 1 Peter should follow Colossians, since Ephesians is following Colossians rather than the original code. We do not, however, find that 1 Peter is closer to Colossians than to Ephesians, but in every case of difference is closer to Ephesians. Even apart from this, it is almost incredible that Paul when he wrote Col. iii. 5–iv. 1 was laboriously reproducing teaching which was already familiar in the standardized instructional codes of the Church. Much stronger evidence than that which has so far been produced will be required to give conviction to any claim that these sections of Colossians are other than the spontaneous utterance of an inspired writer addressing himself to a particular situation.

It will be seen that in spite of a superficial similarity, 1 Peter does not follow the same order as Ephesians and Colossians, nor does it use the same term of address for some of the groups named. The blunt and perhaps offensive word δοῦλοι is replaced by οἰκέται, and κύριοι, πατέρες, and τέκνα are omitted. Curiously enough a second section of general counsel is introduced at iv. 12, before the concluding paragraphs addressed to πρεσβύτεροι and νεώτεροι. This is one of the considerations—and the doxology in iv. 11, which may be interpreted as the conclusion of the original letter—which led Streeter to the belief that iv. 12–v. 14 represented a different piece of writing from i. 1–iv. 11.

The actual points of correspondence in these ethical sections are as follows:

(i) 1 Pet. ii. 1	Eph. iv. 25, 31	Col. iii. 8
ἀποθέμενοι οὖν πᾶσαν κακίαν καὶ πάντα δόλον.	ἀποθέμενοι τὸ ψεῦδος . . . σὺν πάσῃ κακίᾳ.	ἀπόθεσθε . . . ὀργήν, θυμόν, κακίαν, βλασφημίαν . . . μὴ ψεύδεσθε.

Ephesians is here derived from Colossians, though with that adaptation which the author constantly uses. If 1 Peter is linked with these in some kind of literary dependence, it is clearly to Ephesians rather than Colossians that it is indebted; moreover, the indebtedness is to Ephesians rather than to an hypothetical code, which if it influenced Ephesians must have done so primarily through Colossians. This is clear, because the similarities between Ephesians and 1 Peter are not confined to those elements which Ephesians has reproduced from Colossians.

There are, both in 1 Peter and in Ephesians, the participial form of ἀπόθεσθαι, the use of πᾶσα with κακία, and the use of the noun rather than a second verb in the prohibition of falsehood, whereas Colossians differs in these particulars from both of them.

(ii) 1 Pet. ii. 18	Eph. vi. 5	Col. iii. 22
οἱ οἰκέται, ὑποτασσόμενοι ἐν παντὶ φόβῳ τοῖς δεσπόταις.	οἱ δοῦλοι, ὑπακούετε τοῖς κατὰ σάρκα κυρίοις μετὰ φόβου.	οἱ δοῦλοι, ὑπακούετε κατὰ πάντα τοῖς κατὰ σάρκα κυρίοις . . . φοβούμενοι τὸν κύριον.

The general meaning of 1 Peter and Ephesians is here the same, but there is considerable divergence in the wording. On this instance alone one would not suspect any literary interdependence. Since, however, it has been claimed that such similarity as there is bears witness to the influence of a church code upon both passages, it must be insisted again that Ephesians is here clearly derived from Colossians.

It is, moreover, most improbable that the ethical injunctions in Colossians are the product of codes in common use. If it were true, however, it should mean that 1 Peter is closely related to Colossians, and less so to Ephesians, since Ephesians is certainly at least one remove from the code, being influenced by it only via Colossians. This is not what we find. Verbally 1 Peter is unlike both Colossians and Ephesians, but it is nearer to Ephesians in one point: the insistence on respect for one's master is expressed not by the verbal form φοβούμενοι but by the noun φόβος. Any influence from any known document that helped to shape 1 Peter in this verse came almost certainly from Ephesians.

One further point is worth noting, though it need not be pressed. In the verse following 1 Pet. ii. 18, in which servants are urged to show obedience, not only to reasonable masters, but to awkward ones as well, we read: τοῦτο γὰρ χάρις εἰ διὰ συνείδησιν θεοῦ ὑποφέρει τις λύπας πάσχων ἀδίκως. Since συνείδησις in the New Testament (with one possible exception at Heb. x. 2) always means 'conscience', both the Authorized and Revised Versions here translate, 'for conscience towards God', that is, 'because of a conscientious sense of duty towards God'. Moffatt and some other modern translators and commentators are dissatisfied with this interpretation. They prefer to give to συνείδησις the meaning 'consciousness', which is common enough outside the New Testament. Moffatt translates: 'from a sense of God', and W. H. Bennett (GE, p. 219) paraphrases: 'through the inspiration and strength due to a consciousness of His presence'.

Whichever rendering we choose, by itself it seems a curious phrase in this connexion. It may be that a clue to its real meaning may be found in Ephesians, and that the author of 1 Peter is seeking in this phrase to represent concisely something that lingers in his mind from Eph. vi. 8. There the motive for obedience to masters is introduced by εἰδότες ὅτι, which may be represented by διὰ συνείδησιν (see Appendix I). The motive itself is expressed as follows: ἕκαστος ἐάν τι ποιήσῃ ἀγαθόν, τοῦτο κομίσεται παρὰ κυρίου (cf. also εἰδότες ὅτι . . . in Eph. vi. 9).

It is at any rate a possible explanation of this rather curious phrase in 1 Pet. ii. 19 that the author was intending to summarize in a phrase the motive, as he remembered it, expressed in Eph. vi. 8 more fully and explicitly. If so, then this may be regarded as supporting evidence for the priority of Ephesians.

Additional Note. A further point of current interest may be raised. In E. G. Selwyn's commentary on 1 Peter a long appendix is added by D. Daube (pp. 467–88) in which the writer seeks to show that J. H. Moulton was in error in holding the opinion that in the Common Greek of the first century the absolute use of the participle may bear an imperatival sense (cf. *A Grammar of New Testament Greek*, vol. i, pp. 180 ff., 223 ff.). He interprets the imperatival use of the participle in the New Testament as due to the influence of standardized codes whose phrasing was dominated by Aramaic or Hebrew idiom. H. G. Meecham in an article on 'The Use of the Participle for the Imperative in the New Testament' joins issue with Daube and seeks to show that Moulton's view can be substantiated from the papyri (*Expository Times*, vol. lviii, No. 8, pp. 207–8).

If our contention, that 1 Peter is here following Ephesians rather than church codes, can be established, it may be argued that ὑποτασσόμενοι is felt by the author to be a sense-equivalent of the imperative ὑπακούετε in Ephesians. If so, this may be cited as evidence that a participle could be used to express the meaning of an imperative.

Evidence in the same direction may be found also in sections (iii) and (iv) which follow.

Daube, however, would give a different explanation. On p. 488 of Selwyn's commentary he writes: 'It is important to note that 1 Peter occasionally has the imperative participle where Paul has not (1 Pet. iii. 1 against Eph. v. 22 and Col. iii. 18; 1 Pet. ii. 18 against Eph. vi. 5 and Col. iii. 22). This puzzle may be solved in many ways. Slightly differing codes may have been drawn upon by different writers; or Paul may have made, or used, a better translation than others.'

(iii) 1 Pet. iii. 1	Eph. v. 22	Col. iii. 18
ὁμοίως γυναῖκες ὑποτασσόμεναι τοῖς ἰδίοις ἀνδράσιν.	ὑποτασσόμενοι ἀλλήλοις . . . αἱ γυναῖκες τοῖς ἰδίοις ἀνδράσιν ὡς τῷ κυρίῳ.	αἱ γυναῖκες, ὑποτάσσεσθε τοῖς ἀνδράσιν ὡς ἀνῆκεν ἐν κυρίῳ.

In view of the constant dependence of Ephesians upon Colossians, there can be no doubt that in this verse Ephesians is reproducing Colossians. Their common use of the phrase ὡς . . . κυρίῳ at the end makes this clear. 1 Peter is also closely similar to both Ephesians and Colossians, but its resemblance is closer to Ephesians, as is shown by the use of ἰδίοις to qualify ἀνδράσιν. Moffatt points to 'this remarkable ἰδίοις in Ephesians' as evidence that the author of Ephesians was familiar with the similar wording of 1 Peter (ILNT, p. 383). In view, however, of the immediate dependence of Ephesians on Colossians and the other evidence already quoted for the priority of Ephesians (in relationship to 1 Peter) it is a simpler explanation of the presence of this strange ἰδίοις in both epistles to assume that 1 Peter is revealing acquaintance with Ephesians.

(iv) 1 Pet. iii. 7	Eph. v. 25	Col. iii. 19
οἱ ἄνδρες ὁμοίως συνοικοῦντες κατὰ γνῶσιν.	οἱ ἄνδρες, ἀγαπᾶτε τὰς γυναῖκας.	οἱ ἄνδρες, ἀγαπᾶτε τὰς γυναῖκας.

Here the only similarity between 1 Peter and Ephesians is that each addresses a specific piece of advice to 'husbands'. It is, however, clear that if this is to be interpreted as evidence of dependence, it cannot be Ephesians which is dependent on 1 Peter, because Ephesians is here exactly reproducing the words of Colossians.

(v) Some may wish to argue that πρεσβύτεροι and νεώτεροι in 1 Pet. v. 1 and 5 are variants of πατέρες and τέκνα in Eph. vi. 1 and 4, just as οἰκέται is a variant of δοῦλοι. But this cannot be substantiated. In Ephesians πατέρες and τέκνα relate to the internal ordering of the individual family, whereas πρεσβύτεροι and νεώτεροι relate to the life of the Church. Nor is there any evidence that 1 Peter is in any way dependent on the πατέρες and τέκνα sections of Ephesians.

There is, however, an interesting parallel between 1 Pet. v. 5 and Eph. v. 21 (the section of general counsel):

1 Pet. v. 5	Eph. v. 21	Col. iii. 20
ὁμοίως, νεώτεροι ὑποτάγητε πρεσβυτέροις· πάντες δὲ ἀλλήλοις τὴν ταπεινοφροσύνην ἐγκομβώσασθε.	ὑποτασσόμενοι ἀλλήλοις ἐν φόβῳ Χριστοῦ ...	
	Eph. vi. 1	
	τὰ τέκνα, ὑπακούετε τοῖς γονεῦσιν ὑμῶν ἐν κυρίῳ.	τὰ τέκνα, ὑπακούετε τοῖς γονεῦσιν . . . ἐν κυρίῳ.

These two *τέκνα* sections in Ephesians and Colossians are almost identical in wording, but they are wholly unrelated to 1 Pet. v. 5. This passage, however, has a similarity to Eph. v. 21, where humble respect and even deference towards each other is required of Christians. It is doubtful how far these words should be regarded as part of 1 Peter's address to the *νεώτεροι*. The *πάντες* probably widens the address to include all Christians. Grammatically *ἀλλήλοις* may not be closely linked with *ὑποτάγητε*, but the sense of the verb is almost certainly carried forward to the pronoun. The appearance of several variant readings in the manuscripts bears witness to the ambiguity of the grammatical construction.

If, however, we see the association of these words in both 1 Peter and Ephesians as evidence of interdependence, it would be an improper deduction to claim that Ephesians is here dependent on 1 Peter, for these words in Ephesians merely reproduce similar, if not verbally identical, exhortations to be found in Paul's earlier writings: e.g. Gal. v. 13, *διὰ τῆς ἀγάπης δουλεύετε ἀλλήλοις* and Rom. xii. 10, *τῇ τιμῇ ἀλλήλους προηγούμενοι*. It is not likely that Ephesians would need to borrow from 1 Peter thoughts which had already appeared in Galatians and Romans. If it is pointed out that there is a verbal similarity between 1 Peter and Ephesians closer than that between Ephesians and the parallels from Galatians and Romans, that can only be interpreted as meaning that 1 Peter is echoing Ephesians rather than either of the other two.

It will be seen from Appendix I that there are other parallels between Ephesians and 1 Peter besides those given special consideration here. But the others do not add anything to what these instances have already demonstrated—that where Ephesians is most like 1 Peter, it is still more like Colossians, and is clearly derived from Colossians rather than 1 Peter. If, therefore, there is interdependence, it must be that 1 Peter has reproduced remembered phrases and thoughts from Ephesians.

The conclusions of this chapter may be summarized as follows.

1. The general opinion of the great majority of scholars should be accepted, that there are similarities between these two epistles which cannot be satisfactorily accounted for merely on the basis either of coincidence or of a common Christian tradition.

2. If there is direct literary dependence of one epistle on the other, it is undoubtedly Ephesians which is prior to 1 Peter, because, where the two are similar, Ephesians is often derived from Colossians, or if not derived from Colossians, can be shown to be reproducing phrases already used in earlier Pauline epistles.

3. The alternative suggestion, persuasively argued by E. G. Selwyn, that standardized church codes have imposed something of their form and phraseology on both epistles, is unlikely for the same reason, that where the influence of the code on Ephesians is said to be most noticeable, it can be shown that Ephesians is in fact derived from Colossians. If a church code is ultimately responsible for the similarities between Ephesians and 1 Peter, it must have influenced Ephesians through Colossians. If, however, the same code has influenced 1 Peter direct, it should mean that 1 Peter stands closer to Colossians than to Ephesians. But this is in no case true. Where Ephesians differs from Colossians, 1 Peter resembles Ephesians more closely than Colossians.

Moreover, in one case of similarity, and one most confidently claimed as due to the influence of liturgical forms (Eph. i. 19), the passage in Ephesians can be shown to be an entirely original combination of three separate elements from different parts of Colossians. If it is original to Ephesians, then its appearance in 1 Peter can only be due to borrowing.

The evidence, therefore, establishes the priority of Ephesians, and favours the direct dependence of 1 Peter upon Ephesians rather than their mutual dependence on church codes.

As was said in the opening paragraph of the chapter, these conclusions do not give us much help in solving the problem of the authorship of Ephesians. It is true, of course, that if 1 Peter could be confidently ascribed to Peter's lifetime, the fact of the priority of Ephesians would be an almost conclusive argument for its Pauline authorship; but the authorship of 1 Peter cannot be so confidently affirmed. On the other hand, if Ephesians is to be dated about

A.D. 90, then the non-Petrine authorship of 1 Peter is established, since it must be subsequent to Ephesians. Even if Ephesians is regarded as Paul's own last letter, it remains very difficult to understand how Peter could be so familiar with it as to reproduce phrases from it in his own epistle.

The results of this comparison of the two letters are therefore ambiguous in their bearing upon the date and authorship of Ephesians. They have, indeed, a more direct contribution to make to the solution of the problem of the authorship and date of 1 Peter. The fact, however, that Ephesians is prior to 1 Peter does, of course, mean that Ephesians must be dated at any rate earlier than the latest possible date ascribable to 1 Peter. But this is not a very helpful clue, for the earliest writer of whom we can confidently affirm that he knew 1 Peter is Polycarp. It is much less sure that Ignatius or 1 Clement knew it. This external evidence, therefore, does not entitle us to claim for it a date much before A.D. 140. Those scholars who reject the Petrine authorship usually ascribe it to the reign of Trajan (A.D. 98–117). The fact that Ephesians must be earlier than this does not add anything to what we already knew about the date of the epistle on other grounds.

If, however, a conclusion is reached to date Ephesians about A.D. 90, the fact that 1 Peter shows dependence on it will have a most significant relevance to our verdict on its date and authorship.

Addendum

It may be a conceivable explanation of the relationship between Ephesians and 1 Peter to argue that 1 Peter may be regarded as the earlier, on the grounds that the author of Ephesians, while mainly relying on Colossians, has 'conflated' with his excerpts from Colossians phrases from 1 Peter, as he has 'conflated' passages from the Pauline epistles. I do not personally regard this as the correct solution because 1 Peter's borrowings from Ephesians sometimes include elements borrowed by Ephesians from Colossians, and also because of the dependence of 1 Peter on Eph. i. 19, which is an original combination of separate elements from Colossians.

If, however, it were the true explanation, it would be fatal to the view that Paul wrote Ephesians, for it is incredible that Paul, writing Ephesians immediately after Colossians, should incorporate several echoes from 1 Peter, whereas in the earlier epistle no such echoes appear.

XVIII

THE RELATIONSHIP BETWEEN EPHESIANS AND ACTS

In seeking to assess the significance of any relationship that may be discovered between Ephesians and Acts, we find ourselves confronted by similar difficulties to those which we encountered in the case of 1 Peter. This is because the date of Acts is also a matter of disagreement. Some have argued that since its narrative stops short of the death of Paul, therefore it must have been written before his execution. Others have pointed to the lateness of the earliest external testimony to its existence. Polycarp is the first to show any acquaintance with it. On this and other grounds it is argued that a date well on in the second century is more appropriate. Both these views of the date are, however, unusual. The great bulk of scholars believe that Acts was written about the same time as the Gospel according to Luke, and so ascribe it to a date about A.D. 85. This will be assumed as the probable date of Acts, though other possibilities are not ignored.

Among the unanswered problems which beset Acts is the question of its relationship to the letters of Paul. There is not the slightest suggestion in Acts that Paul, whose missionary activities are the theme of more than half the book, ever wrote a letter, or enjoyed any reputation in the Church as a writer of letters. It is not easy to imagine how a writer in A.D. 85 could recount at such length the enterprising campaigns of Paul in many different centres of Christian activity and yet make no allusion to his letters to the churches. It becomes even more difficult if a still later date is claimed for Acts. Goodspeed, as we have seen, provides his own answer to the problem by assuming that Paul's letters were forgotten for a generation following his death, and were sought out and published only as a result of the new interest in Paul generated by the thrilling story in Acts. On this theory, therefore, the author of Acts wrote in complete ignorance of the existence of these letters.

If this explanation cannot be accepted, the problem of the silence of Acts on this matter remains.

It is certain that Acts contains no explicit reference to Paul as a writer of letters. Is it, however, equally sure that the author had no acquaintance whatever with his letters? Are there not words, or phrases, or passages in Acts which compel us to believe that the author was familiar with them?

The almost unanimous verdict of scholars is that Acts in no way reflects any acquaintance with them.[1]

An exception to this consensus of opinion is found in H. J. Holtzmann. In his *Einleitung in das Neue Testament* (p. 405) he gives as one of his grounds for ascribing a comparatively late date to Acts the author's knowledge of Romans, Corinthians, Galatians, Ephesians, Thessalonians, and Hebrews.[2] Unfortunately he does not provide evidence to substantiate this opinion, apart from the assertion that three passages in Acts represent a deliberate modification of statements in Galatians. It is true that there are apparent divergences of historical data between Acts and Galatians, but most scholars see in these differences clear evidence, not that the author of Acts was contradicting Paul, but that he was ignorant of what had been written in Galatians and was doing his best to make a coherent story out of such material as was available to him.

In opposition to this isolated judgement of Holtzmann, the great majority of scholars agree with Harnack in maintaining the other point of view. Peake gives cautious expression to it: 'The author (of Acts) does not seem to have used the Epistles in constructing his story, for it would be difficult to explain if he had done so why he should not have availed himself of much of the material to be found there' (CINT, p. 130). Moffatt is more explicit and emphatic:

> 'So far as the internal evidence suggests, Luke did not use any of Paul's epistles; his acquaintance with Paul's movements and ideas is drawn from oral tradition or personal reminiscence, not from the reading of his correspondence. Some critics (e.g. Soltau) consider that the Pauline speeches as well as the narratives are drawn from materials provided by the Epistles . . . but there is no real evidence to render this a necessary hypothesis.'

It is also worthy of note that Sanday and Headlam in their commentary on Romans (ICC) deal fully with words and phrases in Romans which reappear in other writings in the New Testament or in some way seem to have exercised an influence over another

[1] Cf. Harnack (BAP, p. 7): '. . . weil in der Apostelgeschichte die Benutzung keines Paulusbriefes nachgewiesen werden kann.'

[2] 'Für verhältnissmässig spätere Datirung werden Gründe geltend gemacht wie: (1) Kenntniss von Rm, Kor, Eph, Th und Hbr, auch von Josephus, (2) bewusste Zurechtlegung von Gal. i. 17–24 in ix. 26–30; Gal. ii. 1–10 in Acts xv. 1–33; Gal. ii. 11 f. in Acts xv. 35–39.'

writer, but do not indicate one single parallel in Acts (pp. lxxiv–lxxxv).

We may assume, therefore, that Acts provides no evidence of its author's acquaintance with the Pauline epistles as a whole. But does this apply to Ephesians in particular?

Our concern in this chapter is to discover what resemblances exist between Acts and Ephesians, and to inquire:

(*a*) Do they amount to evidence of interdependence?
(*b*) If so, do they suggest that the author of Acts knew Ephesians?
(*c*) Or, alternatively, that the author of Ephesians knew Acts?
(*d*) If the similarities fall short of establishing interdependence, do they nevertheless suggest that both writings sprang from the same period in the development of the Christian Church?

Our primary interest is in Acts. But it is usually agreed that Luke–Acts constitutes a single unit appearing in two parts, so that it will be wise to include parallels in Ephesians with Luke as well as with Acts, since these too may make some contribution to the solving of our problem.

First of all we give a list of the words which are peculiar to Luke–Acts and Ephesians, and which do not appear elsewhere in the New Testament.

	Luke–Acts	*Ephesians*
ἀπειλὴ	Acts iv. 29; ix. 1	vi. 9
ἐργασία	Acts xvi. 16, 19; xix. 24, 25; Luke xii. 58	iv. 19
ὁσιότης	Luke i. 75	iv. 24
πανοπλία	Luke xi. 22	vi. 11, 13
πατριά	Luke ii. 4; Acts iii. 25 (LXX)	iii. 15
πολιτεία	Acts xxii. 28	ii. 12
συγκαθίζω	Luke xxii. 55	ii. 6
(τὸ) σωτήριον	Luke ii. 30; iii. 6; Acts xxviii. 28	vi. 17
φρόνησις	Luke i. 17	i. 8
χαριτόω	Luke i. 28	i. 6

It is fairly impressive that out of the fifty or so words in Ephesians which are not used elsewhere in the Pauline writings, ten appear in Luke–Acts, but not elsewhere in the New Testament. Five of these, however, are found in the Gospel and not in Acts, and some of them are used in Luke–Acts in a different sense from that given to them in Ephesians. It cannot, therefore, be argued from the vocabulary alone that there is any kind of direct dependence, though it may be urged that the mutual use of these words, not elsewhere found in the New Testament, indicates that both writings belong to the same general stage in the developing experience of the Church.

We will proceed to consider the parallels between Ephesians and Luke–Acts which extend to more than a single word. Some are very slight, and are only included because others have wished to attach significance to them. Some, on the other hand, are more than slight, and we must try to determine what measure of significance can justifiably be assigned to them.

The parallels between Ephesians and Luke will be listed first, and it is noticeable that these are fewer in number and slighter in dimension than those between Ephesians and Acts.

(*a*) Luke i. 75	Eph. iv. 24
λατρεύειν αὐτῷ ἐν ὁσιότητι καὶ δικαιοσύνῃ ἐνώπιον αὐτοῦ . . .	. . . τὸν καινὸν ἄνθρωπον τὸν κατὰ θεὸν κτισθέντα ἐν δικαιοσύνῃ καὶ ὁσιότητι τῆς ἀληθείας.

In the preceding list of words we noted that ὁσιότης occurs in the New Testament only in these two contexts. That by itself is a small matter, but its use in each case in association with δικαιοσύνη is remarkable.

It is true that the same two words are associated in Deut. ix. 5 (LXX), but not so closely as here, and there is no evidence that their association was in any way customary.

(*b*) Luke ii. 14	Eph. i. 5
ἐπὶ γῆς εἰρήνη ἐν ἀνθρώποις εὐδοκία (or εὐδοκίας).	προορίσας ἡμᾶς εἰς υἱοθεσίαν διὰ Ἰησοῦ Χριστοῦ εἰς αὐτόν, κατὰ τὴν εὐδοκίαν τοῦ θελήματος αὐτοῦ.

Moffatt sees a link between these two passages in the declaration that 'men are the objects of the divine εὐδοκία', and he claims significance for the similarity (ILNT, p. 383). The word εὐδοκία is, however, found elsewhere in Luke and also in Paul, so that it is improbable that any argument for interdependence can be based on its use in these sentences.

(*c*) Luke xi. 34	Eph. v. 13
ὅταν ὁ ὀφθαλμός σου ἁπλοῦς ᾖ, καὶ ὅλον τὸ σῶμά σου φωτεινόν ἐστιν· ἐπὰν δὲ πονηρὸς ᾖ, καὶ τὸ σῶμά σου σκοτεινόν.	τὰ δὲ πάντα ἐλεγχόμενα ὑπὸ τοῦ φωτὸς φανεροῦται. πᾶν γὰρ τὸ φανερούμενον φῶς ἐστιν.

Some have claimed a significant resemblance between these two passages, but beyond the very common contrast between darkness and light, which finds a place in many books of the New Testament, they have very little in common.

(*d*) Luke xii. 35	Eph. vi. 14
ἔστωσαν ὑμῶν αἱ ὀσφύες περιεζωσμέναι.	στῆτε οὖν περιζωσάμενοι τὴν ὀσφὺν ὑμῶν ἐν ἀληθείᾳ.

Moffatt includes this parallel in his list of 'affinities' between these writings (ILNT, p. 384). Certainly the phrase 'gird up your loins', used in a metaphorical sense, is found in the New Testament only in these two passages and in 1 Pet. i. 13. One cannot deny that Luke's record of these words of Jesus may have influenced the author of Ephesians, but the recurrence of the phrase can be explained on other grounds. The writer may have had knowledge of this word of Jesus apart from Luke; or he may have been using a phrase which was in common use. Certainly it occurs in the LXX (e.g. Exod. xii. 11, Jer. i. 17, &c.), though usually in a literal sense.

(*e*) Luke xii. 47	Eph. v. 17
ἐκεῖνος δὲ ὁ δοῦλος ὁ γνοὺς τὸ θέλημα τοῦ κυρίου αὐτοῦ καὶ μὴ ἑτοιμάσας ἢ ποίησας πρὸς τὸ θέλημα αὐτοῦ δαρήσεται πολλάς.	συνίετε τί τὸ θέλημα τοῦ κυρίου.
	Eph. vi. 6
	ὡς δοῦλοι Χριστοῦ ποιοῦντες τὸ θέλημα τοῦ θεοῦ ἐκ ψυχῆς.

Of the two passages from Ephesians, vi. 6 is the closer to Luke xii. 47. If v. 17 is derived from any other part of the New Testament, it will be from Rom. xii. 2 (δοκιμάζειν . . . τί τὸ θέλημα τοῦ θεοῦ). It is true that in Eph. v. 17 κυρίου takes the place of θεοῦ, but it does not require the influence of Luke to account for the interchanging of these two interchangeable words.

Appendix I reveals that Eph. vi. 6 is derived in part from Col. iii. 23, but not in the particulars in which it resembles Luke xii. 47. The common elements between Luke and Ephesians here are, however, in such general use ('slave' and 'doing the will of the Lord') that it is impossible to claim them as evidence of interdependence. Moreover, as in (*d*), if this word of Jesus has influenced the author of Ephesians, it may have been known to him apart from Luke's record of it.

(*f*) Luke xv. 13	Eph. v. 18
ζῶν ἀσώτως.	ἀσωτία.

The word ἀσωτία is not found in Paul's epistles, but there is no good reason for claiming that its use here is derived from Luke.

(*g*) Luke xv. 24	Eph. ii. 5
οὗτος ὁ υἱός μου νεκρὸς ἦν καὶ ἀνέζησεν.	καὶ ὄντας ἡμᾶς νεκροὺς τοῖς παραπτώμασιν συνεζωοποίησεν τῷ Χριστῷ.

The fact that Eph. ii. 5 is an almost exact repetition of Col. ii. 13 precludes the possibility of any dependence on Luke, though even apart from this one would have doubted it.

Moffatt notes (ILNT, p. 384) that Resch (*Paulinismus*, pp. 273–4) 'gives a long list of parallels between Eph. ii. 1–19 and Luke xv. 11–32', but refrains from expressing any opinion on it. McNeile, however, while acknowledging that the comparison of the two passages has devotional value, declares that 'they can hardly be imagined to have any literary connexion', and in this surely he is right (INT, p. 157).

(*h*) Luke xxi. 15	Eph. vi. 13
ἐγὼ γὰρ δώσω ὑμῖν στόμα καὶ σοφίαν, ᾗ οὐ δυνήσονται ἀντιστῆναι ἢ ἀντειπεῖν ἅπαντες οἱ ἀντικείμενοι ὑμῖν.	ἀναλάβετε τὴν πανοπλίαν τοῦ θεοῦ, ἵνα δυνηθῆτε ἀντιστῆναι ἐν τῇ ἡμέρᾳ τῇ πονηρᾷ καὶ ἅπαντα κατεργασάμενοι στῆναι.

There is a certain similarity between these passages, and in each of them there appears the combination of the two words δύνασθαι ἀντιστῆναι, but it is difficult to imagine that this constitutes any literary connexion.

There is nothing in these eight parallels which cannot be accepted as due to coincidence, or at most to a common atmosphere of Christian thought. If, however, it is claimed that one writing reflects acquaintance with the other, on this evidence the priority must be accorded to Luke. Six of the parallels are concerned with recorded words of Jesus. It is true that these may have been affected both in their selection and in their phraseology by the circumstances of the early communities who preserved them, but it is highly improbable that the wording of Ephesians was influential in shaping them. It is much more likely that the words of Jesus, whether mediated through the third Gospel or by other means, influenced the author of Ephesians.

The points of coincidence between Acts and Ephesians are both more frequent and more significant.

(i) Acts i. 9

καὶ ταῦτα εἰπὼν βλεπόντων αὐτῶν ἐπήρθη, καὶ νεφέλη ὑπέλαβεν αὐτὸν ἀπὸ τῶν ὀφθαλμῶν αὐτῶν.

Luke xxiv. 51

καὶ ἐγένετο ἐν τῷ εὐλογεῖν αὐτὸν αὐτοὺς διέστη ἀπ' αὐτῶν ⟦καὶ ἀνεφέρετο εἰς τὸν οὐρανόν⟧.

Eph. iv. 8–10

διὸ λέγει· ἀναβὰς εἰς ὕψος ᾐχμαλώτευσεν αἰχμαλωσίαν, ἔδωκεν δόματα τοῖς ἀνθρώποις. τὸ δὲ ἀνέβη τί ἐστιν εἰ μὴ ὅτι καὶ κατέβη εἰς τὰ κατώτερα μέρη τῆς γῆς; ὁ καταβὰς αὐτός ἐστι καὶ ὁ ἀναβὰς ὑπεράνω πάντων τῶν οὐρανῶν.

Eph. i. 20

καθίσας ἐν δεξιᾷ αὐτοῦ ἐν τοῖς ἐπουρανίοις.

The fact that the Ascension is specifically emphasized in Ephesians is regarded by Moffatt as one of the affinities between this epistle and Luke–Acts. No other Pauline epistle refers to it, nor does either Mark or Matthew make mention of it (cf. J. Denney, DB, vol. i, p. 161). This has been claimed as evidence of the post-Pauline date of Ephesians. It is capable also of being interpreted as indicating acquaintance with Luke–Acts. It should be noted that in Luke xxiv. 51 the words enclosed in brackets are of doubtful textual authority, and if these are removed, the Ascension is not explicitly affirmed by Luke in the Gospel, though the preceding words may well imply it. The only unmistakable description of the Ascension is in Acts i. 9. References to it occur elsewhere in the New Testament, as for instance in the fourth Gospel (at vi. 62, &c.), Heb. iv. 14, 1 Pet. iii. 22, 1 Tim. iii. 16, but it is probable that all these are subsequent to both Acts and Ephesians.

Although Paul is emphatic in his affirmation of the Exaltation of Christ, he makes no explicit mention of the Ascension. It may be argued from this omission that Paul (and Mark and Matthew also) did not know the story of the Ascension as the means by which Christ entered into His glory; or it may be claimed that for them it was the Exaltation which was the important thing, and the process of its attainment a matter of small significance in comparison. Whether Paul's failure to mention the Ascension means his ignorance of it we may never know, but Eph. iv. 8–10 in which it is emphasized is in its phrasing much closer to Phil. ii. 9–11 than to Acts i. 9.

Goodspeed makes a good deal of this passage in Ephesians, emphasizing, however, not so much the presence of the Ascension doctrine as the inclusion of the doctrine of the Descensus ad Inferos. This, he claims, is a derivative of the Ascension doctrine, and therefore a period of reflection must intervene between the first affirmation of the Ascension in Acts and this tentative suggestion of the Descensus in Ephesians.

This may be so. Certainly there is no trace of the doctrine of the Descensus in the earliest Christian records. But it cannot be said with complete confidence that Ephesians does here teach this doctrine. A good case can be made for the interpretation which makes 'he came down' refer to the Incarnation, and 'the lower parts of the earth' mean not the infernal regions, the parts lower than the earth, but the regions of the earth which are lower than the heavenly spheres. This would make Eph. iv. 10 into an emphatic declaration that the Heavenly Christ, exalted to the right hand of God, is indeed the very same as the Jesus Christ who was known to men in a human body.

Actually in Ephesians neither of these possible alternatives seems particularly appropriate to the argument of the passage, so that the test of relevance to the context does not help us to decide which is the more likely to be correct.

(ii) Acts ii. 4, 15	Eph. v. 18
4. καὶ ἐπλήσθησαν πάντες πνεύματος ἁγίου, καὶ ἤρξαντο λαλεῖν ἑτέραις γλώσσαις . . . 15. οὐ γὰρ ὡς ὑμεῖς ὑπολαμβάνετε οὗτοι μεθύουσιν.	μὴ μεθύσκεσθε οἴνῳ ἐν ᾧ ἐστιν ἀσωτία, ἀλλὰ πληροῦσθε ἐν πνεύματι λαλοῦντες ἑαυτοῖς ψαλμοῖς . . .

The resemblance between these two passages is remarkable. In both it is implied that there is a certain similarity between a man who is intoxicated and one who is filled with the Holy Spirit. This is so peculiar that it might be argued that Eph. v. 18 reflects acquaintance with the hostile allegation in Acts ii. 13. That is at any rate a possibility. One could not, however, countenance any claim for literary dependence in the other direction. This passing phrase in Eph. v. 18 can hardly be put forward as the origin of the contemptuous sneer in Acts ii. 13. The word ἀσωτία is not a common one in the New Testament. Only Titus and 1 Peter use it, apart from Ephesians. Its equivalent adverb, ἀσώτως, however, appears in Luke xv. 13.

Another resemblance reinforces the claim that Ephesians here reflects acquaintance with Acts. It is the phrase 'being filled with the Spirit'. This is not a Pauline phrase. Apart from this one instance it is, in the New Testament, entirely confined to Luke–Acts. It occurs three times in Luke (i. 15, 41, 67) and five times in Acts (ii. 4, iv. 31, ix. 17, xiii. 9, 52). It is true that only at Acts xiii. 52 is the verb πληρόω used. Elsewhere it is πίπλημι. But the adjective πλήρης, in the phrase 'full of the Holy Spirit', is found at Luke iv. 1, Acts vi. 3, 5, vii. 55, xi. 24 (but not elsewhere in the New Testament). This solitary appearance in Ephesians of a phrase otherwise confined to Luke–Acts lends itself to the interpretation that the influence of Acts is here to be felt. Its association in each writing with an implied resemblance to drunkenness supports that interpretation.

Whether λαλοῦντες in Eph. v. 19 in any way reflects a recollection of λαλεῖν in Acts ii. 4 is more questionable.

(iii) Acts vii. 55

εἶδεν δόξαν θεοῦ καὶ Ἰησοῦν ἑστῶτα ἐκ δεξιῶν τοῦ θεοῦ καὶ εἶπεν· Ἰδοὺ θεωρῶ τοὺς οὐρανοὺς διηνοιγμένους καὶ τὸν υἱὸν τοῦ ἀνθρώπου ἐκ δεξιῶν ἑστῶτα τοῦ θεοῦ.

Acts ii. 32–5

τοῦτον τὸν Ἰησοῦν ἀνέστησεν ὁ θεός, οὗ πάντες ἡμεῖς ἐσμεν μάρτυρες· τῇ δεξιᾷ οὖν τοῦ θεοῦ ὑψωθεὶς . . . οὐ γὰρ Δαυεὶδ ἀνέβη εἰς τοὺς οὐρανούς, λέγει δὲ αὐτός·

εἶπεν κύριος τῷ κυρίῳ μου
κάθου ἐκ δεξιῶν μου
ἕως ἂν θῶ τοὺς ἐχθρούς σου
ὑποπόδιον τῶν ποδῶν σου.

Eph. i. 20

ἐγείρας αὐτὸν ἐκ νεκρῶν καὶ καθίσας ἐν δεξιᾷ αὐτοῦ ἐν τοῖς ἐπουρανίοις.

Col. iii. 1

τὰ ἄνω ζητεῖτε, οὗ ὁ Χριστός ἐστιν ἐν δεξιᾷ τοῦ θεοῦ καθήμενος.

Rom. viii. 34

τίς ὁ κατακρινῶν; Χριστὸς Ἰησοῦς ὁ ἀποθανών, μᾶλλον δὲ ἐγερθείς, ὅς ἐστιν ἐν δεξιᾷ τοῦ θεοῦ, ὃς καὶ ἐντυγχάνει ὑπὲρ ἡμῶν.

There are similarities between Acts and Ephesians in these passages, but probably they represent a common means by which faith in Christ found expression in those early days. The fact that the affirmation of the Exaltation of Christ to God's right hand finds a place in both Romans and Colossians shows that the belief was accepted before the time of Luke–Acts. Ephesians is here closely following Colossians, and agrees with Colossians in two particulars against Acts: Christ is described as seated, not standing, and His relationship to God is described in the words ἐν δεξιᾷ τοῦ θεοῦ not ἐκ δεξιῶν. So there is no question of Ephesians being here dependent on Acts.

Nor is there the slightest need to imagine that Acts is dependent on Ephesians. Acts ii. 34–5 is quoting from Ps. cx. 1. But this use of the quotation is not original to Acts. It appears at Mark xii. 36, and also at Matt. xxii. 44 and Luke xx. 42. Heb. i. 13 also uses it. We need not doubt that it was Jesus who first drew His followers' attention to it, and it probably stood in the Book of Testimonies[1] in common use among the early Christians. Its presence in both Mark and Paul shows that the doctrine it supports was an element in Christian belief at a very early date.

These passages, therefore, in spite of similarity, provide no evidence of interdependence; the similarity is due to their authors' common acceptance of the belief of the Church.

(iv) Acts iii. 25

ὁ θεὸς . . . λέγων πρὸς Ἀβραάμ· καὶ ἐν τῷ σπέρματί σου ἐνευλογηθήσονται πᾶσαι αἱ πατριαὶ τῆς γῆς.

Luke ii. 4

. . . διὰ τὸ εἶναι αὐτὸν ἐξ οἴκου καὶ πατριᾶς Δαυείδ.

Eph. iii. 15

. . . τὸν πατέρα, ἐξ οὗ πᾶσα πατριὰ ἐν οὐρανοῖς καὶ ἐπὶ γῆς ὀνομάζεται.

πατριά is one of those words whose use in the New Testament is restricted to Ephesians and Luke–Acts. It may be nothing more than a curious coincidence that the occurrence of this word in both Ephesians and Acts is associated with the words πᾶσα and γῆς. A keen advocate might claim this indicates the influence of Acts upon Ephesians. Certainly, if there is more than coincidence here, it cannot be that Ephesians has influenced the author of Acts, for in Acts its appearance is due to a quotation from the LXX.

(v) Acts x. 34

ἐπ' ἀληθείας καταλαμβάνομαι ὅτι οὐκ ἔστιν προσωπολήμπτης ὁ θεός.

Eph. vi. 9

καὶ προσωπολημψία οὐκ ἔστιν παρ' αὐτῷ.

[1] G. D. Kilpatrick challenges the whole idea of the Book of Testimonies, writing: 'It is improbable that Rendel Harris's theory is sound' (OM, p. 66; see also p. 4). But the persuasive arguments of Rendel Harris will require a larger measure of disproof before being abandoned.

The words in Acts x. 34, affirming God's impartiality, are usually printed as a quotation from the Old Testament. In their general sense they reproduce the sentiment of both Deut. x. 17 and 1 Sam. xvi. 7, but they are not an exact quotation. The word *προσωπολήμπτης* does not occur in either of these Old Testament contexts.

The corresponding noun is used by Paul both in Rom. ii. 11 and Col. iii. 25, and James also uses it (and the cognate verb) in ii. 1 and ii. 9. The adverb *ἀπροσωπολήμπτως* occurs in 1 Pet. i. 17.

Eph. vi. 9 is clearly derived in the main from Col. iii. 25, so that we may rule out any suggestion that it was at all influenced by Acts. It is equally unlikely that there was any influence in the opposite direction.

This affirmation about God was probably one of the common battle-cries of the early Christian community against those who claimed status and privilege with God on the basis of their membership among the people of Israel. John the Baptist is recorded as inaugurating the declaration of this truth about God when he poured scorn on those who felt that, because they were 'sons of Abraham', they were God's favourites (Luke iii. 8). The fact that it appears in two different epistles of Paul (apart from Ephesians) suggests that this particular expression of the truth was one of Paul's watchwords. The author of Acts may conceivably have remembered it from his association with Paul, but it is most unlikely that he needed to derive it from Ephesians.

(vi) Acts xiii. 1	Eph. ii. 20
ἦσαν δὲ ἐν Ἀντιοχείᾳ κατὰ τὴν οὖσαν ἐκκλησίαν <u>προφῆται</u> καὶ διδάσκαλοι.	*ἐστὲ συνπολῖται τῶν ἁγίων . . . ἐποικοδομηθέντες ἐπὶ τῷ θεμελίῳ τῶν <u>ἀποστόλων</u> καὶ <u>προφητῶν</u> . . .*
Acts xv. 6	Eph. iv. 11
συνήχθησάν τε οἱ <u>ἀπόστολοι</u> καὶ οἱ πρεσβύτεροι.	*καὶ αὐτὸς ἔδωκεν τοὺς μὲν <u>ἀποστόλους</u>, τοὺς δὲ <u>προφήτας</u>, τοὺς δὲ εὐαγγελιστάς, τοὺς δὲ ποιμένας καὶ διδασκάλους.*

The passages in Acts make mention of both apostles and prophets, who also appear in association in both of the passages from Ephesians. But this resemblance is insufficient to suggest any interdependence. Apostles, prophets, and teachers are all named in Paul's epistles as well as in Ephesians, and also elsewhere in the New Testament. They were recognized leaders in the Christian communities from earliest times.

(vii) Acts xiii. 10	Eph. iv. 27
υἱὲ διαβόλου.	μήδε δίδοτε τόπον τῷ διαβόλῳ.

The word διάβολος is not found in Paul's epistles, and its presence in Ephesians is used as an argument for a post-Pauline origin. The appearance of the word in Acts may be claimed as evidence that Acts and Ephesians belong to the same period in the development of Christian thought and phraseology, but it is not evidence of literary dependence.

(viii) Acts xv. 11	Eph. ii. 7–8
Peter: διὰ τῆς χάριτος τοῦ κυρίου Ἰησοῦ πιστεύομεν σωθῆναι καθ' ὃν τρόπον κἀκεῖνοι.	. . . τὸ ὑπερβάλλον πλοῦτος τῆς χάριτος αὐτοῦ ἐν χρηστότητι ἐφ' ἡμᾶς ἐν Χριστῷ Ἰησοῦ. τῇ γὰρ χάριτί ἐστε σεσωσμένοι διὰ πίστεως.
Acts xvi. 31	
Paul and Silas: πίστευσον ἐπὶ τὸν κύριον Ἰησοῦν, καὶ σωθήσῃ σὺ καὶ ὁ οἶκός σου.	

Both these passages in Acts are admirable statements of what we normally regard as the Pauline emphasis, and in them there are obvious similarities with Eph. ii. 7–8: the grace of Jesus Christ is that which accomplishes men's salvation through their faith in Him. Indeed it is probably true to say that these verses in Ephesians bear a closer resemblance to these two passages in Acts than to the similar passages from the other Pauline epistles, for the closest parallels elsewhere in Paul's writings are those which speak of justification rather than salvation.

This in itself is an insufficient ground for claiming interdependence between Acts and Ephesians, but the preference for salvation as a substitute for justification may well point to a date later than Paul's lifetime, when the issue, as Paul first faced it, had rather changed its form.

(ix) Acts xx. 19	Eph. iv. 2	Col. iii. 12
δουλεύων τῷ κυρίῳ μετὰ πάσης ταπεινοφροσύνης καὶ δακρύων καὶ πειρασμῶν τῶν συμβάντων μοι ἐν ταῖς ἐπιβουλαῖς τῶν Ἰουδαίων.	ἀξίως περιπατῆσαι... μετὰ πάσης ταπεινοφροσύνης καὶ πραΰτητος μετὰ μακροθυμίας, ἀνεχόμενοι ἀλλήλων.	ἐνδύσασθε . . . ταπεινοφροσύνην, πραΰτητα, μακροθυμίαν, ἀνεχόμενοι ἀλλήλων.
	Eph. vi. 7	Col. iii. 23–4
	δουλεύοντες ὡς τῷ κυρίῳ καὶ οὐκ ἀνθρώποις.	ἐργάζεσθε ὡς τῷ κυρίῳ καὶ οὐκ ἀνθρώποις . . . καὶ τῷ κυρίῳ Χριστῷ δουλεύετε.

This is the first of several similarities between this section of Acts (xx. 17–38) and Ephesians. Moffatt specifies four of them, and gives it as his judgement that 'significance attaches to certain traits of phraseology' (ILNT, p. 384). But there are more than four.

The similarities between Ephesians and Acts xx. 19 are of peculiar interest, because Ephesians is clearly based very closely on Colossians.

The two phrases in Acts xx. 19 which are parallel to phrases in Ephesians are *μετὰ πάσης ταπεινοφροσύνης* and *δουλεύων τῷ κυρίῳ*. The word *ταπεινοφροσύνη* in Ephesians, along with the words and phrases that immediately follow it, is clearly derived from Col. iii. 12. But the fact that it is used both at Acts xx. 19 and Eph. iv. 2 along with *μετὰ πάσης* is noteworthy. In each case it is the only use of the word in each book, and that the exact phrase should be repeated in each case is unexpected. Those who are eager to prove that Ephesians is secondary to Acts might claim that here the author, familiar with Acts, and particularly with these verses in Acts xx. 17–38, is conflating phrases from his various sources, as we have already seen that he does among the Pauline epistles.

The other phrase which the passages have in common is *δουλεύων τῷ κυρίῳ*. Here Ephesians is clearly derived from Col. iii. 23–4, though it should be noted that the phrase occurs elsewhere at Rom. xii. 11 and also, with a slight difference, at 1 Thess. i. 9. There is no reason whatever, therefore, for supposing that Ephesians here is borrowing from Acts. Perhaps the best explanation of the phrase in Acts is that the author is either well acquainted with Paul's ways of speech, and so able to incorporate this and other characteristic phrases in his reported speech, or else is able to remember the speech so accurately as to be able not only to give its general sense but even to reproduce exactly some of its very words.

(x) Acts xx. 21	Eph. i. 15	Col. i. 4
διαμαρτυρόμενος . . . τὴν εἰς θεὸν μετάνοιαν καὶ πίστιν εἰς τὸν κύριον ἡμῶν Ἰησοῦν.	. . . ἀκούσας τὴν καθ' ὑμᾶς πίστιν ἐν τῷ κυρίῳ Ἰησοῦ.	. . . ἀκούσαντες τὴν πίστιν ὑμῶν ἐν Χριστῷ Ἰησοῦ.

'The faith in our Lord Jesus Christ' appears in each context. Ephesians, however, is derived from Colossians and cannot be claimed as dependent on Acts. The phrase is one in constant use in Paul's writings. Its presence in Acts may best be explained, as in the case of δουλεύων τῷ κυρίῳ in (ix), as the result of the author's faithful representation of Pauline idiom.

(xi) Acts xx. 24	Eph. iii. 2, 7	Col. i. 23, 25
. . . ὡς τελειώσω τὸν δρόμον μου καὶ τὴν διακονίαν ἣν ἔλαβον παρὰ τοῦ κυρίου Ἰησοῦ διαμαρτύρασθαι τὸ εὐαγγέλιον τῆς χάριτος τοῦ θεοῦ.	εἴ γε ἠκούσατε τὴν οἰκονομίαν τῆς χάριτος τοῦ θεοῦ τῆς δοθείσης μοι εἰς ὑμᾶς . . . διὰ τοῦ εὐαγγελίου, οὗ ἐγενήθην διάκονος κατὰ τὴν δωρεὰν τῆς χάριτος τοῦ θεοῦ.	. . . τοῦ εὐαγγελίου . . . οὗ ἐγενόμην ἐγὼ Παῦλος διάκονος . . . ἡ ἐκκλησία, ἧς ἐγενόμην ἐγὼ διάκονος κατὰ τὴν οἰκονομίαν τοῦ θεοῦ τὴν δοθεῖσάν μοι εἰς ὑμᾶς.

In these two passages from Acts and Ephesians we find four common elements: (1) the declaration that Paul is fulfilling a διακονία (as a διάκονος) and (2) that this has been laid upon him by God (or Christ) and not taken up on his own initiative; (3) the association of this διακονία with the Gospel and (4) with the grace of God. The first three of these four appear also in Col. i. 23, 25, and there is no doubt that Ephesians in this context is dependent on Colossians rather than Acts.

Does this large measure of similarity imply, therefore, that the author of Acts knew Ephesians? The one item of the four in Ephesians which is not derived from Colossians is one which appears elsewhere in Paul's writings. For instance in Gal. i. 15–16 it is God's grace which has equipped Paul to preach the Gospel, so that what Acts has in common with Ephesians is not peculiar to Ephesians among the Pauline epistles.

Does it mean, then, that the author of Acts knew the Pauline epistles and is reproducing ideas from them? It would suggest this explanation, unless it is, as we have already mentioned in other connexions, that the author of Acts has access to the very things that Paul said on this one occasion or was accustomed to say on similar occasions.

(xii) Acts xx. 27	Eph. i. 11
οὐ γὰρ ὑπεστειλάμην τοῦ μὴ ἀναγγεῖλαι πᾶσαν τὴν βουλὴν τοῦ θεοῦ ὑμῖν.	. . . ἐκληρώθημεν προορισθέντες κατὰ πρόθεσιν τοῦ τὰ πάντα ἐνεργοῦντος κατὰ τὴν βουλὴν τοῦ θελήματος αὐτοῦ.

The word βουλή is used four times in Luke–Acts of the divine purpose. Elsewhere in the New Testament it bears this meaning only in Heb. vi. 17 and Eph. i. 11.

(xiii) Acts xx. 28	Eph. iv. 11
προσέχετε ἑαυτοῖς καὶ παντὶ τῷ ποιμνίῳ, ἐν ᾧ ὑμᾶς τὸ πνεῦμα τὸ ἅγιον ἔθετο ἐπισκόπους ποιμαίνειν τὴν ἐκκλησίαν τοῦ θεοῦ, ἣν περιεποιήσατο διὰ τοῦ αἵματος τοῦ ἰδίου.	αὐτὸς ἔδωκεν . . . τοὺς μὲν ποιμένας . . . εἰς οἰκοδομὴν τοῦ σώματος τοῦ Χριστοῦ. (Cf. Eph. i. 22: . . . τῇ ἐκκλησίᾳ, ἥτις ἐστὶν τὸ σῶμα αὐτοῦ.) Eph. i. 14 ἐσφραγίσθητε τῷ πνεύματι τῆς ἐπαγγελίας τῷ ἁγίῳ, ὅς ἐστιν ἀρραβὼν τῆς κληρονομίας ἡμῶν εἰς ἀπολύτρωσιν τῆς περιποιήσεως. Eph. i. 7 ἀπολύτρωσιν διὰ τοῦ αἵματος αὐτοῦ . . . .

In Acts xx. 28 there is a sequence of uncommon words and ideas which, curiously enough, reappear in Ephesians.

The metaphor of 'flock' and 'shepherd', meaning the church and the Christian pastor, does not occur in the other Pauline epistles, but it is found both in Acts and in Ephesians.

περιποίησις and περιποιοῦμαι are both rare words in the New Testament, being used only eight times altogether. In Acts and Ephesians there occurs one instance each, and in each case it is associated with the Holy Spirit.

Its single occurrence in Ephesians (i. 14) is found in connexion with ἀπολύτρωσις, and ἀπολύτρωσις, seven verses earlier (i. 7), is joined with διὰ τοῦ αἵματος αὐτοῦ. In Acts xx. 28 the verb περιποιοῦμαι is used in conjunction with διὰ τοῦ αἵματος. This reference to the blood of Christ as effective for man's salvation is unique in Acts.

Also its use with the preposition διά is worth noting. The more usual expression elsewhere in the New Testament is ἐν with the dative.

These coincidences are certainly remarkable. It is perhaps claiming too much to say that they are significant. They may be only coincidences; or they may be accounted for by assuming that the author of Ephesians had made himself familiar with Paul's address to the Ephesian elders at Miletus, as it appears in Acts, in the same way that he had studied Paul's epistles, and so thoughts and words from it slipped easily into his epistle.

(xiv) Acts xx. 32	Eph. i. 18
καὶ τὰ νῦν παρατίθεμαι ὑμᾶς τῷ κυρίῳ καὶ τῷ λόγῳ τῆς χάριτος αὐτοῦ τῷ δυναμένῳ οἰκοδομῆσαι καὶ δοῦναι τὴν κληρονομίαν ἐν τοῖς ἡγιασμένοις πᾶσιν.	εἰς τὸ εἰδέναι . . . τίς ὁ πλοῦτος τῆς δόξης τῆς κληρονομίας αὐτοῦ ἐν τοῖς ἁγίοις. Eph. iv. 12, 16 εἰς οἰκοδομὴν (cf. Eph. ii. 20, 21).

We have seen that κληρονομία is one of the characteristic words of Ephesians, where it is used, not in its normal sense of an inheritance from a deceased benefactor, but to describe the Christian's share in the blessings of Christ's Kingdom. The only use of the word in this latter sense in Paul's writings, apart from Ephesians, is Col. iii. 24. The word does not occur elsewhere in Acts. It is peculiar that it should here be used in the sense always given to it in Ephesians, and also in association with the same group of words ('among the saints').

It should be noted that the last six passages from Acts, (ix)–(xiv), all occur within twenty consecutive verses (xx. 17–38). When each is considered individually, in isolation from the others, the correspondences with Ephesians may appear as little more than curiosities. But when six passages, all of which contain 'curious' coincidences with Ephesians, stand so near together, one wonders whether 'coincidence' is the correct description of them, especially when it is noted that this passage of twenty verses is the record of Paul's farewell address at Miletus to the elders *from the church at Ephesus*.

(xv) Acts xxi. 8	Eph. iv. 11
. . . εἰσελθόντες εἰς τὸν οἶκον Φιλίππου τοῦ εὐαγγελιστοῦ, ὄντος ἐκ τῶν ἑπτά	καὶ αὐτὸς ἔδωκεν τοὺς μὲν ἀποστόλους, τοὺς δὲ προφήτας, τοὺς δὲ εὐαγγελιστάς, τοὺς δὲ ποιμένας καὶ διδασκάλους.

The word εὐαγγελιστής is used in the New Testament only in these two instances and in 2 Tim. iv. 5. Its presence in these three writings, and in no others, may be taken as indicating that they share a common background and a common historical situation.

It is worth noting that all five church 'officials', listed in Eph. iv. 11, have their equivalent in Acts, though only three of the five are mentioned in the Pauline epistles.

(xvi) Acts xxvi. 16–18	Eph. i. 18	Col. i 12–14
Jesus to Paul: εἰς τοῦτο γὰρ ὤφθην σοι, . . . ἀνοῖξαι ὀφθαλμοὺς αὐτῶν, τοῦ ἐπιστρέψαι ἀπὸ σκότους εἰς φῶς καὶ τῆς ἐξουσίας τοῦ Σατανᾶ ἐπὶ τὸν θεόν, τοῦ λαβεῖν αὐτοὺς ἄφεσιν ἁμαρτιῶν καὶ κλῆρον ἐν τοῖς ἡγιασμένοις πίστει τῇ εἰς ἐμέ.	. . . πεφωτισμένους τοὺς ὀφθαλμοὺς τῆς καρδίας ὑμῶν, εἰς τὸ εἰδέναι ὑμᾶς . . . τίς ὁ πλοῦτος τῆς δόξης τῆς κληρονομίας αὐτοῦ ἐν τοῖς ἁγίοις. Eph. ii. 2 περιεπατήσατε . . . κατὰ τὸν ἄρχοντα τῆς ἐξουσίας τοῦ ἀέρος . . . . Eph. v. 8 ἦτε γάρ ποτε σκότος, νῦν δὲ φῶς ἐν κυρίῳ. Eph. i. 7 ἐν ᾧ ἔχομεν . . . τὴν ἄφεσιν τῶν παραπτωμάτων.	εὐχαριστοῦντες τῷ πατρὶ τῷ ἱκανώσαντι ὑμᾶς εἰς τὴν μερίδα τοῦ κλήρου τῶν ἁγίων ἐν τῷ φωτί· ὃς ἐρύσατο ἡμᾶς ἐκ τῆς ἐξουσίας τοῦ σκότους καὶ μετέστησεν εἰς τὴν βασιλείαν τοῦ υἱοῦ τῆς ἀγάπης αὐτοῦ, ἐν ᾧ ἔχομεν τὴν ἀπολύτρωσιν, τὴν ἄφεσιν τῶν ἁμαρτιῶν.

The most remarkable feature of these passages is not the series of items in which Ephesians is similar to Acts, but the large measure of agreement between Acts and Colossians. This is the more impressive because it is in each case comprised in a single sentence. It is difficult to know how this similarity can be most satisfactorily accounted for.

The passage in Acts is that part of Paul's defence before Agrippa where he is describing the commission laid upon him by Christ. It is a succinct and clear-cut announcement. Paul's task is to be:

1. To open men's eyes.
2. To turn them from darkness to the light.
3. To turn them from Satan to God.
4. To enable them to accept forgiveness from God through Christ.
5. To give them their rightful place among God's people.

All of these reappear in Ephesians, but not together and not very distinctly. In Colossians the last four appear in a single sentence.

The word ἄφεσις is common in Luke–Acts, but it is not found in Pauline writings except at Col. i. 14 (and Eph. i. 7), and there, as in Luke–Acts, it is associated with τῶν ἁμαρτιῶν and not as in Eph. i. 7 with παραπτωμάτων.

The phrase which describes the converted man as having a 'rightful place among the saints' is also puzzling. Acts and Colossians agree against Ephesians in using κλῆρος instead of κληρονομία. Ephesians and Acts agree against Colossians in following the noun with a prepositional phrase (ἐν τοῖς . . .). Ephesians and Colossians agree against Acts in preferring the adjective ἁγίοις to the passive participle ἡγιασμένοις.

If Acts is here dependent on any known literary source, that source must be Colossians rather than Ephesians. One cannot, however, feel satisfied that this is the correct explanation. It may well be that Luke had heard Paul state his commission from Christ in words very similar to those which he is able to reproduce in Acts. If so, it is not surprising that echoes of these words occur also in Colossians.

(xvii) Acts xxviii. 20	Eph. vi. 20
εἵνεκεν γὰρ τῆς ἐλπίδος τοῦ Ἰσραὴλ τὴν ἅλυσιν ταύτην περίκειμαι. Acts xxviii. 31 . . . κηρύσσων τὴν βασιλείαν τοῦ θεοῦ καὶ διδάσκων τὰ περὶ τοῦ κυρίου Ἰησοῦ Χριστοῦ μετὰ πάσης παρρησίας ἀκωλύτως.	ἐν παρρησίᾳ γνωρίσαι τὸ μυστήριον τοῦ εὐαγγελίου, ὑπὲρ οὗ πρεσβεύω ἐν ἁλύσει ἵνα ἐν αὐτῷ παρρησιάσωμαι ὡς δεῖ με λαλῆσαι.

In Eph. vi. 20 the author is reproducing the substance of Col. iv. 3–4. At two points, however, he departs from the phrasing of Colossians, though he keeps the sense of the passage. At each of these two points, where a change is introduced the change establishes a link with the closing sentences of Acts. The noun ἅλυσις (otherwise not found in Paul's writings) is used to represent the meaning of δέδεμαι in Col. iv. 3, and παρρησιάσωμαι (recalling μετὰ πάσης παρρησίας of Acts xxviii. 31) replaces φανερώσω in Col. iv. 4.

If Acts had influenced the author of Ephesians, it is not improbable that the closing sentences of the book, which are descriptive of Paul's imprisonment, should be reflected in the closing words of the epistle.

It is unlikely that it was Acts which here borrowed from Ephesians, for ἅλυσις is a common word in Luke–Acts, and so is παρρησία. On the other hand, παρρησιάζομαι is predominantly a Lukan word in the New Testament, being used seven times in Acts and only twice elsewhere (1 Thess. ii. 2, and here at Eph. vi. 20).

How can the significance of these points of resemblance between Acts and Ephesians be most satisfactorily assessed?

Those who have tried to demonstrate that the author of Acts was acquainted with Paul's epistles as a whole have failed to prove their case because of the almost complete absence of similarities of thought and phrase. Between Ephesians and Acts, however, we have seen that there are points of correspondence which cannot be dismissed as insignificant coincidences. No other Pauline epistle provides so many. None is so closely related to Acts as Ephesians is.

There are several possible explanations of this relationship. It is conceivable that the author of Acts did know Ephesians, even though he was ignorant of the other Pauline epistles. Or it may be that he knew Ephesians so much better than the others that it alone exercised an influence upon him. Another possible explanation is that the author of Ephesians was familiar with Acts. A third explanation suggests that both writings sprang from the same period in the development of the Christian Church, and perhaps even from the same area. Others may be content to affirm that the similarities are no more than one might legitimately anticipate in two wholly unrelated Christian writings of the first century.

Before we proceed to choose the most likely of these four explanations it will be well to pause to consider the significance of the two passages in Acts, examined in paragraphs (xi) and (xvi). In these two passages, especially in the later one, we find that Acts is similar to Ephesians in passages where Ephesians is clearly derived from Colossians. This means that at these points at least it will not do to explain the similarities merely by claiming that the author of Ephesians is borrowing from his recollections of Acts. Does this mean that we are driven, as an alternative, to the conclusion that Acts is here clearly dependent on Ephesians? There are considerations that make this improbable. In paragraph (xi), for instance, the similarities to Ephesians are in particulars which reappear in other Pauline epistles, and in paragraph (xvi) Acts is noticeably closer to the parallel passage in Colossians than to that in Ephesians. Indeed, if this were not just one isolated instance, it might be cited as evidence that the author of Acts knew Colossians, and availed himself of Paul's words as written there. In view, however, of the fact that no other instances of this kind occur, another explanation is more probable.

It should be noticed that both these two passages appear in addresses given by Paul: (xi) occurs in his farewell words to his Ephesian friends at Miletus, and (xvi) in his defence before Agrippa. Moreover, they both fall within the 'we-sections' of the travel diary which has been incorporated in Acts. It is true that the second passage is not usually included in these sections and the pronoun 'we' is not used, but the incident lies between 'we-sections' in such a way as to suggest that the diarist was present at the events related. Both passages therefore are addresses of Paul at which the diarist may have been himself present. He may have sensed the importance of the occasions, and made notes as he listened; or he may have become so familiar with the main features of Paul's message and his mode of expressing it that he could reproduce it accurately, even in the very words he used. At any rate the close similarity between Acts and Colossians at these points is probably best explained as the result of the accurate reporting in Acts of the actual words of Paul.

Many scholars who recognize that similarities do exist between Acts and Ephesians regard them as confined to the passage in Acts xx where the author records the meetings of Paul with the Ephesian elders at Miletus. Moffatt, for instance, mentions no other parallels but these. He believes that 'significance attaches to them', though he does not precisely specify what that significance is. F. B. Clogg, also, writes: 'There are affinities between Ephesians and Acts, particularly in Paul's address to the Ephesian elders at Miletus, but that may support the trustworthiness of Luke's summary of the address, rather than cast doubt upon the genuineness of Ephesians' (INT, p. 97). McNeile takes a similar line: 'The parallels would be sufficiently accounted for if St. Paul wrote Ephesians, and if St. Luke obtained a more or less trustworthy summary of the contents of his address at Miletus' (INT, p. 158).

This explanation does not, however, do justice to those similarities with Ephesians in other parts of Acts, nor to these parallels where Ephesians is at variance with the common Pauline usage as we know it in his other epistles. Such parallels are, for instance, the emphatic assertion of the Ascension in Ephesians; the use of the phrase 'filled with the Spirit', and its curious association with drunkenness; the combination of the rare word πατριά with πᾶσα and $\gamma\hat{\eta}$; the appearance in Acts of all the 'officials' named in Eph. iv. 11, though two of them are not mentioned elsewhere in Paul's letters; the use of the peculiar phrase 'inheritance among the saints'.

These parallels, and others like them, are not covered by the explanation suggested by McNeile and Clogg because they do not occur in those parts of Acts where the author is reporting a speech of Paul's. If some measure of interdependence is to be assumed between the two writings to account for these similarities, it cannot be Acts which is reproducing Pauline ideas, because these ideas are not Pauline but Lukan. If there has been borrowing, it must have been in the other direction.

It is even doubtful whether the similarities in Paul's speech at Miletus are adequately accounted for on the grounds favoured by Clogg and McNeile. These writers accept the Pauline authorship of Ephesians and recognize the parallels between it and Paul's farewell address at Miletus to the men of Ephesus. Neither suggests that the author of Acts is here drawing on what Paul wrote to the Ephesians. Their contention is that the similarities are adequately accounted for if we assume that Paul wrote Ephesians and the author of Acts accurately reported his speech at Miletus. But why, it must be asked, should this speech bear close resemblance to what Paul wrote to the Ephesians rather than to some other epistle? Presumably an interval of several years intervened between the speech and the writing of the epistle. If the speech in Acts resembled Pauline style in general, we could take that as an indication of Luke's faithfulness in reporting. But why should its chief resemblances be with one particular letter, and that letter one which is not confidently ascribed to Paul? The fact that each is addressed to Ephesians may appear to give the reason. But it is no reason at all. Paul would not adopt a modified style of address for the Ephesian Church which was different from his mode of speaking or writing to others.

Let us look therefore at the alternative explanation, and let us suppose that the author of Ephesians was a Christian who lived in the neighbourhood of Ephesus and wrote predominantly for his fellow Christians of that area; and that he wrote in the presence both of the Pauline epistles and of Acts. What section of Acts would be most likely to have claimed his closest attention? Would it not be precisely this speech of Paul to the leaders of the church at Ephesus? If he knew Acts, would it not be probable that this section would leave its impress on him even more than others? If, moreover, we found evidence of 'conflation' between this section of Acts and Colossians (as in paragraph (ix), for instance), would not that be one further example of the method which the author used in his treatment of his sources?

The fact that the similarities to Ephesians in Acts nowhere come so thick and fast as in Paul's address at Miletus cannot therefore be used to support Pauline authorship of Ephesians. The similarities in the speech to other Pauline epistles (as in paragraph xi) are evidence of Luke's accuracy, but the fact that Ephesians shows so many more parallels requires some other explanation.

We have noted the various items of similarity between Acts and Ephesians, and have tried to estimate the significance of some of the more important of them. We must now ask: How can the whole range of the similarities best be accounted for?

There are four possibilities:

(*a*) The first ascribes them to coincidence, claiming that they are no greater than one might legitimately expect in any two Christian writings of the first century. This, however, is surely inadequate, because the similarities here are far greater than those which elsewhere exist between independent writings of the first century. Moreover, many of the phrases in Ephesians which have parallels in Acts had already been noted as peculiar because of their departure from normal Pauline usage. It is very doubtful indeed whether this explanation is adequate to the facts of the case.

(*b*) The second suggested explanation is that the author of Acts was acquainted with Ephesians, and so at liberty to reflect words and phrases from it. No doubt some of the similarities are amenable to this explanation, but not all. This explanation can perhaps be defended in combination with (*a*) above by saying that some of the similarities can be explained by assuming that Luke knew Ephesians and that the rest are due to coincidence.

But still the question would remain: Why, among all the Pauline epistles, does Ephesians alone provide these parallels with Acts, and at the same time make such heavy demands on the possibilities of coincidence?

(*c*) The third possibility: May it be that these similarities are better explained on the ground that Ephesians is a later writing than Acts, whose author wrote under the influence of Acts? The points, already noted, where Ephesians is at variance with normal Pauline usage, and yet in harmony with Acts, suggest that such an explanation is possible. The passages considered in paragraphs (i), (ii), (iv), (ix), (xiii), and (xvii) all provide evidence which points in that direction, and the parallels in Paul's address at Miletus in Acts xx are more readily explicable on that assumption.

(*d*) Or, fourthly, may it be that there is no literary interdependence at all? Perhaps a sufficient explanation can be given if we may assume that both writings originated not only in the first century, but within the same decade (e.g. A.D. 80–90), and perhaps even in the same area. Their similarities would then be due to the fact that the authors breathed the same spiritual atmosphere and knew the same stage in the developing life of the Church. Paragraphs (vii), (viii), (xii), (xiii), and (xv) favour this explanation.

Just as (*a*) and (*b*) may be combined into a joint explanation, so may (*c*) and (*d*). A positive answer to (*c*) would not be inconsistent with the acceptance of the suggestion in (*d*). In fact, in view of the earlier evidence against a date for Ephesians later than A.D. 90, the acceptance of it as of later date than Acts would also require for it a date within the decade when Acts appears to have been written.

If the evidence viewed in this chapter is considered quite independently of any other evidence, the explanations suggested in (*c*) and (*d*) appear more probable than the others. Certain features of the relationship between Acts and Ephesians stubbornly resist being fitted into (*a*) and (*b*).

If, however, (*b*) is chosen as the most probable explanation, it will mean that Ephesians must be regarded as Pauline, but (as in the case of (*a*) also) a further inquiry will be necessary to discover why Ephesians, alone among the Pauline epistles, has this curious relationship to Acts.

If (*c*) is correct, it will require for Ephesians a date subsequent to Acts, that is later than A.D. 85. If (*d*) is correct, it will require a date for Ephesians within the decade A.D. 80–90 or thereabouts. In view of earlier evidence for the date of Ephesians, the acceptance of (*c*) and (*d*) would have the result of enabling us to fix the date within the five years A.D. 85–90.

XIX

INTERNAL EVIDENCE

H. J. Holtzmann accuses the epistle to the Colossians of having a 'double-face' ('Doppelgesicht', ENT, p. 265), because in some respects it appears to him to be thoroughly Pauline, and in others distinctly un-Pauline. We may question the accuracy of this charge as applied to Colossians, but it is certainly appropriate to Ephesians. For there we find, on the one hand, an abundance of words, phrases, and ideas already familiar to us in the other Pauline epistles, and, on the other hand, intermingled with them, words, phrases, and ideas which not only are unfamiliar to us in Paul's other epistles but have also marked affinities with Christian writings which belong to the close of the first century. These un-Pauline characteristics would have led to the conclusion that Ephesians should be classed with Hebrews as an epistle mistakenly ascribed to Paul, were it not that, unlike Hebrews, it includes so much that is unmistakably Pauline, and also specifically claims to have been written by Paul. It is these two features in the internal evidence of the epistle which have prevented any general abandonment of its Pauline authorship.

The extent of the Pauline material in Ephesians can be seen in Appendix I, where the words in Ephesians which echo phrases from other Pauline letters are clearly marked. They are, as we have seen, very numerous, and advocates of Pauline authorship point to them confidently as incontrovertible evidence of the Pauline nature of the epistle.

That these constitute genuine Pauline material cannot be denied, but there may be another explanation than that which ascribes them directly to Paul. A legitimate claim can be made that they should be regarded as deliberate borrowing by a later Paulinist from the genuine letters. There are peculiarities in the extent of their occurrence and the manner of their appearance in Ephesians which may be held to substantiate this claim. But the Pauline features are indisputably there, and used so naturally, for the most part, that it may well be urged that it is incredible that they have been laboriously pieced together by a later compiler.

The second feature in Ephesians which speaks emphatically for Pauline authorship is its explicit use of Paul's name, both in the opening greeting and in the body of the epistle. If it occurred only in the greeting, it might without difficulty be ascribed to a later hand. A greeting can easily be added or varied. But Paul's name is worked into the fabric of the epistle, and in such a way that it cannot be explained away as a later insertion. The whole section Eph. iii. 2–13 springs out of the mention of Paul's name at iii. 1. Nor is it plausible to argue that this whole section has been inserted at a later date, with the one purpose of claiming Pauline authority for the epistle, because in it we find the same dependence on Colossians that we have noted as characteristic of the epistle, and also the same echoes of earlier epistles.

Those therefore who argue that Ephesians is post-Pauline must frankly recognize it as deliberately pseudonymous. It is not that the name of Paul has been fathered on to it by a later editor. The name was introduced by the author.

This raises the whole matter of the strange use of pseudonymity by early Christian writers. To us in the twentieth century it appears less than honest, and we find it disconcerting. It is, however, clear that it did not present the same problem to people of Biblical times. It is found in the Old Testament. Writings are attributed to David, Solomon, Isaiah, and Daniel which must have been written long after their time. Among the apocryphal literature of New Testament days we find gospels, epistles, acts, and apocalypses which claim, without any justification, the authority of such great names as Peter, Paul, and Barnabas. Even in the New Testament itself there is at least one case of pseudonymity. Few scholars today would care to argue that 2 Peter is the work of the apostle.

Because of this somewhat irresponsible use of great names, which marked the early days of the Christian era, we find that those scholars who maintain the Pauline authorship of Ephesians do not attempt to base their arguments on its use of Paul's name. E. F. Scott, for instance, acknowledges that pseudonymity is 'the manner approved by ancient literature' (LNT, p. 179), a judgement in which Moffatt entirely concurs (ILNT, pp. 40–4).

An illuminating comment by Tertullian helps us to understand this practice. He writes: 'The Gospel which was published by Mark may also be maintained to be Peter's, whose interpreter Mark was, . . . since it is allowable that that which pupils publish should be regarded as their masters' work' (*Adv. Marcion.* iv. 5). We may therefore regard the practice as a pupil's acknowledgement of the debt he owes to a revered master.

Moreover, if Ephesians is indeed not only an attempt to produce a faithful presentation of Paul's teaching, but is also constructed largely out of actual phrases and thoughts derived from Paul's epistles, an anonymous writer would feel less compunction than ever about ascribing it to Paul, since everything of value in it was felt to come from Paul.

These two facts therefore, which are strong arguments for the Pauline authorship, are also amenable to other explanations. The Pauline elements may be present as a result of deliberate borrowing from the genuine letters, and Paul's name may be used as a pseudonym according to a commonly accepted convention of that time. But it still remains true that the letter claims specifically to be written by Paul, and includes a large number of undoubtedly Pauline words, phrases, and ideas, and uses them for the most part in a thoroughly Pauline way.

On the other hand, however, there are many items in the epistle which are more easily explicable on the assumption that the author wrote many years later than Paul. These may be divided into two groups:

(i) Those which do not appear to be congruous with what we know of Paul and his writings from other sources.
(ii) Those which, though not patently out of place in a genuinely Pauline epistle, are certainly more appropriate to a post-Pauline writing.

The presence of these elements has been one of the principal factors in the problem of Ephesians. Jülicher noticed them as he tried in vain to solve the puzzle. He writes: 'Many separate points in the epistle would certainly become more intelligible on the assumption that it was written by a disciple of the Apostle' (INT, p. 72). It is to these points that we must now give our attention, and seek to determine what weight should be attached to them.

In the chapters on the Findings of the Past we indicated those items which belong to group (i), that is, those which have been felt to be incompatible with Pauline authorship. These include the use of the words διάβολος and ἠγαπημένος (of Christ), the consistent use of the word ἐκκλησία to mean the Church Universal, the insistent plea for unity within the Church, the elimination of the expectation of the Second Advent. These, and similar features, are not easy to reconcile with Pauline authorship, but they would be entirely natural in a writing produced towards the end of the first century.

It is not our intention in this chapter to re-tread this ground which has been already covered, but rather to concentrate on the items in the second group. So we ask: What passages in Ephesians are particularly appropriate to an origin late in the first century? Goodspeed claims that the right solution of the problem of Ephesians, when formulated, will be found to 'illumine' both many individual items in the epistle and also the epistle as a whole. If therefore it is found that light is shed on the meaning of many passages by the assumption of a late date, that may be interpreted as evidence in its favour.

Let us suppose therefore that the epistle may be regarded as the product of a devoted admirer of Paul about a generation after his death, and let us inquire what items in the epistle are 'illumined' by such an assumption. It may be that they should be interpreted as evidence that at these points the author is allowing the mentality and atmosphere of his own day to distort the Pauline approach which he is trying to adopt.

Goodspeed, more than any other writer, has studied the epistle from this particular point of view. His book, *The Meaning of Ephesians*, is largely a development of this theme. Several of the points raised in this chapter are there dealt with in much greater detail.

1. This epistle is not addressed to any specific community. The name of Ephesus came to be attached to it at a later stage in its history. Moreover, it is not directed to any definite situation. In these particulars it is unique among the Pauline epistles. Attempts have been made to find for it a satisfactory place among them by ascribing these peculiarities to unusual circumstances. It is said to have been a circular letter, addressed to no one particular church, but to a group of churches, perhaps in Asia Minor, which were of a predominantly Gentile nature, and, that for some reason not clearly known, it aimed at presenting a comprehensive statement of Paul's faith and teaching.

There is something artificial and improbable about this suggestion. Even if he were writing to people that he did not know personally, would his letter have been so vague and indefinite, without any suggestion that the churches addressed were composed of real people? The epistle to the Colossians is written to Christians not known personally to Paul, but there is nothing vague about his approach to them. Moreover, this circular theory assumes that Paul made several copies of his letter, and left blanks in them for the insertion of the name of individual churches, as if to disguise the fact that the letter was a circular. It is not easy to imagine Paul doing this. Certainly it is not the way he sent a message to a group of churches on an earlier occasion. His epistle to the Galatians is a circular letter addressed to several different churches in a specific area, but he does not adopt any device to hide the fact that he is addressing them collectively. He writes simply: 'Paul an apostle . . . and all the brethren that are with me, unto the churches of Galatia' (Gal. i. 1).[1]

A similar straightforward approach might have been expected in a second circular letter, with some indication that it is a circular letter, and that certain churches in a named area are addressed in it.

The opening verses of Ephesians are therefore a difficulty for supporters of Pauline authorship. On the assumption, however, of the later date, the difficulties vanish. The absence of any specific address becomes understandable, for such an epistle would be addressed to all who would read it. The absence also of any indication of a local situation either in Paul's life or in the churches addressed is explained.

2. A second peculiarity which presents difficulties on the basis of Pauline authorship is the inexplicable vacillation between 'you' and 'we' at certain points in the epistle. One or two instances will be noted:

(*a*) i. 12–14. In i. 3–12 the author is extolling the wise and generous purpose of God toward 'us'. We assume that by 'us' he means Christian people in general. God has blessed 'us', chosen 'us', and foreordained 'us'; He has given 'us' redemption and understanding of His purposes. Then suddenly at the end of verse 12 'we' is used in opposition to 'you', so that we must now interpret 'we' as Paul and his circle of friends, and 'you' as the people to whom he writes. The 'we' is further defined as 'those who had before hoped in Christ' as distinct from 'you', who 'heard the word of truth', 'believed', and 'were sealed with the Holy Spirit of Promise'. Then in verse 14 the first person again replaces the second, and the Holy Spirit is described as the pledge of 'our' inheritance. It is difficult to escape the conclusion that 'we' is being used ambiguously, sometimes to mean all Christians (including both the writer and the recipients of the letter) and sometimes only Paul and his immediate circle as distinct from the recipients. If not, then we are compelled to believe that all references to 'us' in verses 3–14 are intended to signify Paul and his

[1] The inclusion of the phrase 'with all that call upon the name of the Lord Jesus Christ in every place' at 1 Cor. i. 2 (so too at 2 Cor. i. 1) makes the Corinthian epistles into circulars also. But it is probable that this phrase was introduced later when these epistles stood first among the genuinely Pauline epistles in the Pauline Corpus.

friends as opposed to those whom he is addressing. Yet if this paragraph is to be so circumscribed in its application, we wonder, first, why it is not made plainer, and second, whether something valuable is not lost by such a narrowing down of its scope. Yet this must be the meaning if verses 12–13 are to be consistent with the rest of the passage.

(*b*) Again in ii. 1–10 we find this peculiar interchanging of 'you and 'we'. The passage opens: 'And *you,* when *ye* were dead through *your* trespasses and sins, in which aforetime *ye* walked . . .'. Then, before the sentence is complete, the pronoun is changed. The same sentence continues at ii. 3: 'among whom *we* also all once lived', and then seems to get lost. The author tries to find his way again by repeating at ii. 5 the opening words of the paragraph, but with a change of pronoun. Now it reads 'when *we* were dead through our trespasses . . .'. Then suddenly at ii. 8 the 'you' is reintroduced: 'by grace have *you* been saved through faith'. But at ii. 10 it is 'we' again: 'For *we* are His workmanship.'

No consistent meaning can be attached to this changeable use of the pronouns.

When at last we reach ii. 11–22, for the first time a clear distinction is indicated in the significance of 'we' and 'you': 'you' is defined as 'the Gentiles in the flesh', and 'we' is by implication the Christians who by birth were Jews. It may be possible to read back this distinction of meaning into some of the earlier passages, but it certainly cannot be applied consistently throughout ii. 1–10, and probably not elsewhere either. But even if it could, we should be forced to ask: If Paul is the writer, and if this is the distinction between 'you' and 'we' which he meant his readers to understand from the beginning, why did he not make it clear at a much earlier stage, instead of leaving it till half-way through the second chapter?

(*c*) Other similar, sudden changes of pronoun appear throughout the epistle, as, for instance, at v. 2: 'Christ also loved *you,* and gave Himself up for *us*', where apparently there is no real difference in the significance of the two pronouns.

This apparently purposeless variation is hard to understand if Paul wrote the epistle. It would at any rate be a little less difficult to account for in a pseudonymous writing of the second generation of Christians, for the author who tries to write in the name of Paul ('we') is himself among those for whom the epistle is being written ('you'). In a case where the writer is trying to identify himself with the supposed author, whereas in fact he feels himself to be one of those who are being addressed, a certain confusion in the use of these pronouns would not be unexpected.

The same kind of thing occurs in Heb. xiii. 20–21: 'The God of peace . . . make *you* perfect . . . working in *us* that which is well-pleasing in His sight.'

3. If it was a post-Pauline writer who composed Ephesians in the name of Paul, Paul would probably represent to him two groups of Christians, as distinct from the groups to which he himself belonged:

(*a*) The first generation of Christians, and
(*b*) The converts from the Jewish race.

In contrast, the writer would feel that he himself and the people for whom he writes are Christians of the second generation, and also Gentiles by birth.

This twofold significance appears in the use of 'we' when it is distinctly opposed to 'you'. The former interpretation occurs in i. 12, where 'we' is suddenly thrown into opposition to 'you', and is further described as τοὺς προηλπικότας ἐν τῷ Χριστῷ. The Revised Version gives a non-committal translation: 'we who had before hoped in Christ'. This leaves it to the reader to decide what is meant by 'before'. Abbott discusses the possible meanings which may be derived from it, but does not claim to know the correct one. Either it means 'before you' or 'before the birth of Christ'. In the first case Paul is represented as contrasting himself, as one of the earliest believers, with Christians of a later date. In the second, he identifies himself with those Christians who were Jews by birth, and his meaning is that the Jews as a people had been for centuries before the birth of Jesus eagerly hoping for the coming of One who was to be their Christ. E. F. Scott prefers this second alternative (MCC, p. 148), but Weymouth and Moffatt in their translations choose the first, interpreting the words as meaning: 'we who were the first to put our hopes in Christ'.

This surely is the right rendering. Although the distinction between 'us' as Jewish Christians and 'you' as Gentile Christians emerges clearly enough later at ii. 11, there has been nothing in the epistle up to this point to prepare us for it. One can only impose that meaning on this passage by reading back into it a contrast which is not introduced until later in the epistle. The contrast involved here in 'before' is surely that 'we' were brought into the Christian life before 'you'. Paul, of course, had a perfect right to say this to any of his converts. He does not, however, draw that distinction elsewhere, and we may ask whether within Paul's lifetime there was any sense of the community of Christian people being divided into earlier and later generations.

It is, however, just the kind of difference one would expect to find in a post-Pauline writing. This deferential reference to the first believers would be entirely in place from one who himself belonged to a later generation, and also the description of his own contemporaries, in contrast, as 'those who had heard the word of Truth'.

Nor would this interpretation in any way exclude the distinction which appears later between Jewish Christians ('we') and Gentile Christians ('you'), for the earliest believers were mainly of the Jewish race and the later believers almost entirely of Gentile origin.

4. i. 17–18: '... that the God of our Lord Jesus Christ, the Father of Glory, may give unto you a spirit of wisdom and revelation in the knowledge of him; having the eyes of your heart enlightened, that ye may know what is the hope of his calling, what the riches of the glory of his inheritance in the saints.'

The verses are part of a prayer in which the writer asks that God will grant his readers a full appreciation of the supreme value of their Christian Faith. It is true that any Christian writer sending a message to any group of Christians may express this sentiment. It has, however, a special appropriateness to the second generation of Christians, and the words used to express it do not sound quite like Paul. To begin with, they are used to deplore lukewarmness and halfheartedness. These, however, were not the failings of the Pauline churches. Excess of enthusiasm, gross disregard for moral obligations, and mistakes arising from imperfect understanding of their new faith characterize the errors which Paul tries to correct in his letters, but not a tepid coolness. On the other hand, we know that this was the very fault which roused the outspoken condemnation of the authors of Hebrews and Revelation.[1]

The very word which is used in Ephesians to describe the Christian Faith may be significant. It is called their 'inheritance'. The word κληρονομία is elsewhere used in Paul's letters only of an actual family legacy (with the exception of Col. iii. 24, where the exact meaning is difficult to determine). It would, however, be an appropriate word for Christians of the second generation to use to describe the faith which had been handed down to them. More significant than the word 'inheritance' are the words used to describe the content of the inheritance—wisdom, revelation, knowledge, and en-

[1] Rev. ii. 4 denounces this fault in the church in *Ephesus*.

lightenment. It is true that these words occur in Paul's writings, but not grouped together consecutively. On the other hand, they are just the kind of words which became common currency towards the end of the first century. 'We feel that we are on our way to the Johannine view of religion, with its emphasis on light, knowledge and truth', writes Goodspeed of this passage (ME, p. 27).

5. Some have sensed an un-Pauline point of view in ii. 3. It is not so impressive as some of the others, but may be mentioned. The 'we' is taken to signify Jewish Christians as opposed to Gentile Christians, though the distinction is not precisely made until eight verses later. It is on this understanding urged that the writer is accusing non-Christian Jews of the same degrading immoralities as the Gentiles, although Paul recognizes that the Jews are not guilty of the same vicious excesses which he condemns in the Gentiles (cf. Rom. i and ii). Here, however, no difference is acknowledged in the moral quality of their pre-Christian lives, and this attitude is felt to be more characteristic of a Greek writer, later than Paul, than of Paul himself. Goodspeed, for instance, writes: 'This is the sign manual of a Greek hand, and the mark of a later time, when the difference between heathen and Jewish ethical backgrounds was no longer keenly felt in the Church. The writer is a Greek Christian; in this verse the disguise slips for a moment, and he acknowledges his own heathen past, or at least extraction' (ME, p. 32).

6. Earlier, reference was made to the difficulty for Pauline authorship involved in the comment on circumcision in ii. 11–12. Hort felt it to be so acute that he took the utmost care to try to supply a satisfactory explanation. Abbott too is at some pains to account for the scornful epithets applied to circumcision. Writing of one of these, *χειροποιήτου*, he is bound to acknowledge that it is 'clearly depreciatory', indicating 'a merely external and artificial thing'. This is felt to be an extreme expression for Paul; so Abbott adds: 'But he is far from depreciating circumcision, in its true significance, as the sign of membership of the commonwealth of God' (ICC, p. 56). Yet this is precisely what the author appears to be doing. It may be therefore that this attitude of unveiled contempt for 'so-called' circumcision, an institution for which Paul felt reverence, even though he denounced a superficial reliance on it, belongs more naturally to a later stage in the life of the Church than that provided within Paul's lifetime.

Further evidence of a late date is also furnished in these two verses. For Paul, as for all Jews, mankind was divided into two groups, Jews and Gentiles. In the Christian Church there were Jewish Christians and Gentile Christians, and Paul was proud of his special commission to champion the cause of the Gentile Christians. These verses, however, appear to reflect a different background. The writer seems to think of mankind as divided into three groups: Jews, Gentiles, and Christians, or perhaps we should say into two groups, Christians and non-Christians, and the non-Christian group can be further subdivided into Jews and Gentiles. Within the Church, however, the old rivalry of Jew and Gentile is a thing of the past. It is no longer customary to speak of Jewish and Gentile Christians, but just of Christians, and to reserve the name 'Gentile' for someone who is neither a Jew nor a Christian. Once a Gentile became a Christian, he was no longer regarded as a Gentile. This seems to be implication in ii. 11–12, which Weymouth translates:

> 'Therefore, do not forget that *formerly* you were Gentiles as to your bodily condition. You were called the Uncircumcision by those who style themselves the Circumcised—a circumcision in the body made by hands. *At that time* you were living apart from Christ . . .'.

The assumption behind these words seems to be that Christians are no longer to be thought of as Gentiles. If they were Gentiles 'formerly', that is by origin, as Christians they are so no longer. 'At that time' must mean 'when they were Gentiles', a status which has been cancelled out by their acceptance of the Christian Faith.[1] Aristeides in the second century in his *Apology* calls the Christians a new race; and some of the early martyrs when asked of what race they were refused to give any answer other than 'Christianus sum'. The germ of this idea seems to be present in these verses in Ephesians.

It is true that at iii. 1 the Pauline manner of speaking is resumed, and his readers are all called 'Gentiles', but it is possible that at ii. 11 a writer of about A.D. 90 has inadvertently permitted the thought of his own day to creep into his attempt to speak in the name of Paul. This interpretation does at any rate illumine an otherwise obscure sentence.

There may also be significance in the injunction to 'remember' (ii. 11). The word is certainly used elsewhere in Paul's writings, but not, as here, to recall the past. On other occasions it means to 'keep in mind', and is used to call attention to his own sufferings in the

[1] It is true that 1 Cor. xii. 2 seems to use the name Gentiles in a similar sense; but both the text and the interpretation are so uncertain that it is unwise to base any argument on it.

cause of Christ, the needs of others, or some counsel which had been given on another occasion. Here alone it means: 'Cast your mind back', and it appears to imply a well-advanced stage in Christian development. This provides one further parallel between Ephesians and Hebrews, for there we read: 'You must *remember* those early days when you were first enlightened . . .' (x. 32). The implication in both passages is that Christians can now look back over many years to the early days of the faith, and derive valuable lessons from the past.

7. From ii. 11 (and from other passages also) it appears that the writer assumes that the church or churches which he addresses are wholly Gentile. It is true that, even in Paul's day, one individual church here and there may have been composed entirely of people of Gentile origin, but it certainly could not have been true of the churches as a whole, nor yet of any large group of churches. It was usually the Jews of the town to whom the first appeal in any new missionary enterprise was made, and converts from their number often became the nucleus of the future church. If Paul therefore addressed a letter to Christians generally (as the encyclical theory suggests) or even to the Christian churches in a specified area (as the circular theory assumes), it would have to take into account the presence of at any rate some members of Jewish origin.

E. G. Selwyn comments on this issue: 'It is doubtful . . . whether there were many churches in the first century outside Palestine, at any rate in the larger centres of population, of which the members were wholly Jewish or wholly Gentile, though in most of them Jews were probably in the majority' (IP, p. 44). We may doubt whether Selwyn is right in assuming the predominance of Jewish Christians in the churches of Asia Minor and Greece, at any rate as late as the closing years of the century, but we agree that very few indeed would, in the time of Paul, be exclusively Gentile.

Since, however, those addressed in Ephesians are spoken of as wholly Gentile stock, that may be taken as a further indication of a date late in the century.

8. In Eph. ii. 14 it is declared of our Lord that He has 'broken down the middle wall of partition, that is the enmity' (τὸ μεσότοιχον τοῦ φραγμοῦ λύσας, τὴν ἔχθραν), which Weymouth translates as 'the hostile dividing wall'. This is a vivid metaphor, announcing that Christ has overcome the old hostility between Jew and Gentile, and, within the Christian community, effected a complete reconciliation

between them. 'The literal reference', writes Weymouth in a note on this passage, 'is to the stone wall in the Temple beyond which no Gentile might advance into the inner court.' E. F. Scott, too, so interprets it, and makes mention of the discovery in 1871 of one of the notices which used to warn Gentiles that for those who trespassed within the barrier the penalty would be death (MCC, p. 171). He thinks that such an implication is especially probable, because it was an alleged offence against this prohibition which led to the disorder as a result of which Paul was taken into custody by the Roman authorities.

Goodspeed endorses this explanation of the words, but, unlike Scott, argues that so clear an affirmation of the destruction of the barrier would be almost impossible so long as the actual barrier was still standing immune in the Temple; because, no matter how effectively the psychological barrier, which it represented, had been demolished by Christ in the experience of those who acknowledged His Lordship, it would have been inappropriate to describe the spiritual change under this particular metaphor, if that offensive symbol of arrogant exclusiveness still flaunted itself at Jerusalem for all to see. 'It is its actual destruction', he writes, 'that suggests its figurative use here' (ME, p. 37). He therefore claims that this association of the reconciliation of Jews and Gentiles 'in Christ' with the destruction of this actual material barrier must imply a date after its demolition, that is, a date later than A.D. 70 when the Temple, barrier and all, was razed to the ground.

9. A long parenthesis begins at iii. 2. It does not end until iii. 13. Then at iii. 14 the opening phrase of iii. 1 is repeated and the appeal is resumed.

The contents of this parenthesis have been felt to provide difficulties for advocates of Pauline authorship. It is largely concerned with Paul himself, and exalts his insight, special gifts, and achievements. Many students have been perplexed by the tone of complacency and self-congratulation, and also, side by side with it, a somewhat artificial depreciation of himself. E. F. Scott is clearly not wholly comfortable about it, and interprets its inclusion in the letter thus: 'As he speaks of the Gospel, Paul is led to reflect on his own right to teach it' (MCC, p. 181). And later he feels he must defend Paul against the charge of arrogance to which this passage exposes him (p. 184).

If, however, Ephesians is the work of a later admirer of Paul, a certain heightening of effect is to be expected. In such a case both the exaltation of Paul's discernment and also the exaggeration of his self-abasement cease to be a problem. It becomes easier on the one hand to account for the self-assured reminder of his 'understanding in the mystery of Christ', and on the other hand for the almost abject servility of the description of Paul as 'less than the least of all the saints' (iii. 8). There is an air of unreality about a prominent preacher who begins his discourse by an exaggerated disclaimer of his ability to speak adequately to the occasion. One doubts very much whether Paul was the kind of man to be guilty of such insincerity. We know that at 1 Cor. xv. 9 a cry of anguished penitence broke from him: 'I am the least of the apostles. I am not worthy to be called an apostle, for I persecuted the Church of God.' That is spontaneous and genuine. But can the same be said of Eph. iii. 8? Is not H. J. Holtzmann right to call it a 'doppelte Steigerung in pejus von 1 Cor. xv. 9' (*Kritik*, p. 50)? A further stage in this process appears in 1 Tim. i. 15, for there Paul is made to castigate himself not as 'the least of the Christians' but as the 'chief of sinners'.

Perhaps iii. 4 and iii. 8 are the two passages in Ephesians which we should be glad, for Paul's own sake, to believe that he did not write.

10. Eph. iii. 3–4. *ἐγνωρίσθη μοι τὸ μυστήριον καθὼς προέγραψα ἐν ὀλίγῳ, πρὸς ὃ δύνασθε ἀναγινώσκοντες νοῆσαι τὴν σύνεσίν μου ἐν τῷ μυστηρίῳ τοῦ Χριστοῦ.*

It is not easy to suggest a satisfactory explanation of this passage on the basis of Pauline authorship. Goodspeed, however, claims that his own theory provides not only an adequate but even an illuminating interpretation. The difficulties primarily arise from the uncertainty of the precise meaning to be attached to (*a*) *προέγραψα*, (*b*) *ἀναγινώσκοντες*, and (*c*) *ἐν ὀλίγῳ*.

(*a*) If *προέγραψα* stood by itself, the previous writing to which it refers could mean either the preceding chapters of Ephesians, or the epistle to the Colossians, or Paul's earlier letters to the other churches. The difficulty lies in reconciling these meanings with (*b*) and (*c*). It is not possible to interpret it as an epistolary aorist, because of the prefix *προ-*.

(*b*) *ἀναγινώσκοντες*. It is most natural to associate this participle closely with *προέγραψα*, and to understand that what Paul has already written is what his readers are soon to read. For this reason alone it is most improbable that the writer means that it is the prophetic parts of the Old Testament which are to be read, although this has been suggested.

It is important to notice that we are dealing with a participle in the present tense. Some of the explanations of προέγραψα come to grief on this tense of the participle. For instance, it could not be made to refer either to the preceding chapters of the same epistle or to an earlier letter already familiar to the readers. For such a meaning Paul would have used the participle in the aorist tense. The same objection applies to the interpretation which makes the reference apply to the Old Testament, unless the argument is not so much from what the reader has already seen there, as from what he may still find if he will turn to it.

The only possible explanation on the basis of Pauline authorship seems to be that which applies the word to Colossians, which is thought of as written before Ephesians, but as not likely to reach the recipients of Ephesians until they have read their own epistle. To us who know Colossians and the instructions there for an interchange of letters, this may appear a completely satisfactory explanation. But how would the first readers of this epistle know that this was the meaning? Surely if Paul had meant this, he would have been more explicit, and given some warning here, as he did in Colossians, that another letter of his, written to a nearby church, would soon be made available to them.

None of these explanations therefore is free from real difficulty. Goodspeed's, on the other hand, presents little difficulty so far as this particular passage is concerned, apart from the ἐν ὀλίγῳ which must be considered next. Of the passage as a whole Goodspeed writes: 'The language unmistakably points to a *later* reading of an earlier writing of Paul's. And what would be more natural, if the collected letters of Paul followed?' For the use of προγράφω in this sense (that is, referring to an earlier letter), he quotes not only the authority of Chrysostom, but an identical use from the Oxyrynchus Papyri, No. 291. 'Here emerges', he continues, 'the purpose of Ephesians as the Introduction to the collected letters. . . . The readers of Ephesians are expected to read Paul's letters, and find in them, as the writer of Ephesians has done, the proof of his deep understanding of the Christian faith' (ME, pp. 41–2).

This certainly is an ingenious explanation of the aorist tense in προέγραψα combined with the present tense in ἀναγινώσκοντες. But does ἐν ὀλίγῳ fit in equally well?

(*c*) Goodspeed does not explain the meaning of this expression, nor does he suggest how it can be fitted into his theory. Superficially at any rate it does not seem particularly suitable as a description of the whole collection of Paul's letters. It would be much more appropriate to the epistle to the Colossians only. For this epistle is brief enough to warrant the description ἐν ὀλίγῳ, and it deals specifically with τὸ μυστήριον. If Ephesians—whether in association with all the other Pauline epistles or only with Colossians—were regarded as addressed to a limited constituency, among whom Colossians was already familiar, that might appear to be a possible explanation. But since this interpretation assumes that the readers have a previous acquaintance with Colossians, we should expect an aorist rather than a present tense for the participle.

It is, however, difficult to have to apply ἐν ὀλίγῳ to the whole Pauline Corpus. It is hardly natural to describe all that Paul there says about Christian doctrine and ethics in the whole nine epistles as 'sketchy' or 'in small compass'. It may, however, have been a characteristic of the literary style of that day for a man to speak in this slightly depreciatory way of his own writing, even though it is not strictly appropriate. There is some evidence that this might have been the case. For instance, in Heb. xiii. 22, after thirteen substantial chapters, the writer refers to what he has written in these words: διὰ βραχέων ἐπέστειλα ὑμῖν. Even 1 Peter cannot be described as a particularly short letter, but the same apologetic note appears in v. 12: δι' ὀλίγων ἔγραψα. So this way of speaking may be just a mannerism of the time, little more than a recognized courtesy, as applicable to a hundred pages of Pauline letters as to twenty-five in Hebrews.

If this does not commend itself as a satisfactory explanation of ἐν ὀλίγῳ as applied to all the Pauline letters, it may be argued, perhaps more plausibly, that the writer is not referring to the letters as a whole, but only to those parts in them which deal with the μυστήριον, since it is Paul's understanding of this which is being emphasized. Certainly, as compared with what is said in Ephesians on this subject, all other references, even including those in Colossians, are sketchy and slight. It may reasonably be claimed that Paul's treatment of the μυστήριον apart from Ephesians is ἐν ὀλίγῳ.

If ἐν ὀλίγῳ can be explained in one or other of these two ways, then these two verses (iii. 3–4) may be said to favour some such explanation as Goodspeed proposes. It does at any rate do justice to the present tense of the participle ἀναγινώσκοντες in association with the aorist tense and the prefix of προέγραψα. Apart from the possibility that Paul is the writer, and that he is referring here to Colossians—and this we saw is beset with difficulties—the most satisfactory explanation is that the writer is aware that epistles previously written by Paul are now available for those who care to read them.

11. Eph. iii. 5: 'The holy apostles and prophets.' This phrase has already been commented on, both in the review of the Findings of the Past and in the comparison between Ephesians and Colossians. The association of apostles and prophets, apart from other church officials, is significant and especially in view of the epithet 'holy'. It undoubtedly presents difficulties for those who wish to fit it into Paul's lifetime, whereas it would be wholly unobjectionable in a context written after A.D. 85. In view of similar phrases in Luke i. 70, Rev. xviii. 20, and 2 Pet. iii. 2, there is good ground for accepting it as characteristic of the vocabulary of the second generation of Christians.

Moreover, the same is true of the meaning behind the words. C. H. Dodd interprets this as follows: 'The Church is built upon the twofold foundation of the apostles and prophets, the apostles representing the authority of primary witness to the Gospel facts, while prophets represent the living guidance of the Spirit by which the facts were apprehended in ever fuller meaning and scope' (JE, p. 105). This interpretation commends itself as probably the right one. One wonders, however, if Paul, or any writer before A.D. 65, would have felt the apostolic authority in need of support or correction. Paul himself was so sure of his own apostolic authority that no criticism or abuse could undermine his confidence. It is very doubtful whether, in allocating authority in the Christian Church, he would have felt the need to associate prophets with apostles, as though they added something which the apostles could not supply. As an expression of the attitude of the second generation of Christians, at a time when the apostles had long been dead, it is altogether appropriate.

12. Eph. iii. 14–21. This brief paragraph is one of the gems in the rich treasury of Ephesians, and the doxology at the end is one of the noblest in the New Testament.

Some elements in the passage are more appropriate to a date about A.D. 90 than to A.D. 60. Ephesians, as we have said, consistently uses the word 'church' in its universal sense and never in its local meaning. But here it is something more which distinguishes its use from that in the other Paulines. In iii. 21 an unusual atmosphere surrounds the word, which points to an advanced stage of development. Abbott interprets this passage: 'The Church then is that by whose greatness and perfection the δόξα of God is exhibited, as it is also exhibited in Christ Jesus' (ICC, p. 104). Of these verses Goodspeed writes that the Church is given a 'liturgical function' and acclaimed as 'the channel of man's praise to God'. Whichever meaning is adopted, it is a use of the word 'church' which would be entirely natural by A.D. 90, but somewhat surprising in A.D. 60.

The words πᾶσα πατριά in iii. 15 have harassed commentators. Abbott (ICC, p. 93) insists that the only possible translation is: 'From whom every family in heaven and on earth is named'. But he adds: 'We should rather have expected the apostle to say "the whole family", which would require πᾶσα ἡ πατριά.' Many commentators indeed force this meaning into the words, even though there is no article to justify it. Abbott turns his back resolutely against such a rendering, though with obvious reluctance. 'Grammatically it cannot be maintained', he insists (ICC, p. 94). His reluctance is caused by the lack of any satisfactory meaning that can be suggested for the words without the article.

The word πατριά is not a particularly rare word. Abbott interprets its significance in the Septuagint as applied to those 'descended from a common ancestor, narrower in meaning than φυλή, and wider than οἶκος'. In the New Testament only Luke–Acts uses it, apart from Ephesians, and the use there coincides with that of the Septuagint. Abbott feels himself driven to the following interpretation, which is neither satisfactory nor germane to the context: 'By the πατριαί on earth are doubtless meant the nations, with the fundamental division into Jews and Gentiles; by those in heaven, angels regarded as belonging to certain groups or "tribes"' (ICC, p. 94). E. F. Scott accepts what is substantially the same interpretation.

Because of the unsatisfactory nature of this interpretation many commentators have imported a meaning of their own into πατριά and have tried to make it mean 'fatherhood': 'God is the Father from whom all fatherhood is named.' E. F. Scott says that this is the usual explanation in most modern commentaries. But there is no evidence that the word ever meant 'fatherhood', and, in any case, to quote Scott: 'The idea with which Paul is thus credited is strange and hardly intelligible' (MCC, p. 193).

Goodspeed has a new suggestion to make for the significance of πατριά, which enables us to retain its natural meaning of 'family' and to translate it, as it should be translated here, as 'every family'. He claims that it is here used to indicate the individual church. Since the usual word for church, ἐκκλησία, is in this epistle used only for the Universal Church, it is a reasonable suggestion that some other word is needed to describe the individual church, and it seems likely that this is the significance of πατριά here. If so, it has the additional advantage of throwing light on the interpretation of οἰκοδομή in ii. 21, where the omission of the article has caused perplexity, just as in this context. Probably there the πᾶσα οἰκοδομή means every individual church and the ναὸν ἅγιον the whole Universal Church.

This twofold reference to the individual churches which compose the One Church has a bearing on an argument which was cited earlier in defence of Pauline authorship. There it was claimed that though Ephesians contains a strong plea for unity, it is always in reference to unity between individuals, and not between sections or communities, and therefore it is an error to associate Ephesians with the pleas for unity against the sects which were common towards the end of the first century. If, however, this proposed interpretation of πατριά is right, it means that the individual church is not overlooked, and in ii. 21 at any rate its orderly place in the united whole is given great emphasis.

It is difficult to find an English rendering of πατριά which immediately conveys the meaning here suggested. If we use 'every family', that does not at once suggest that the individual Christian community is meant, though it can be given that significance in a commentary. Nor is it easy to keep the association of words which is found in the original between πατήρ and πατριά. Since each church is called a πατριά because all its members have found a common brotherhood in their experience of the One Father, it may be that the best we can do will be to translate as 'brotherhood', in some such way as this: 'from whose Fatherhood every Christian brotherhood, in heaven and on earth, derives its name'.

The reference to 'families in heaven' has baffled commentators. It was difficult to find a meaning for the family on earth, but impossible to discover one for the family in heaven. Goodspeed's suggested solution of the meaning of πατριά may not wholly solve the problem of the heavenly πατριαί, but it does offer a less unlikely explanation than some of the others. The writer thinks of each church group as consisting of a community of 'brothers', some of whom are in heaven and some on earth. It is one of the first examples of that line of thought which led to the doctrine of the Church as both Triumphant and Militant, as it finds expression, for instance, in the hymn of Charles Wesley:

> One family we dwell in Him,
> One Church, above, beneath.

Such a thought of the Church is probably more appropriate to the second than the first generation of Christians. It is true that even as early as the Thessalonian letters Paul had to face problems arising from the death of members of the Christian community before the expected Second Coming of Christ. But this approach to the problem is something quite different from what we find in Paul's letters, and indeed is hardly consistent with earlier Pauline eschatology, which appears to envisage a 'long-deferred final judgement'. It is more in harmony with the attitude to these matters which we find in Revelation, where each church is thought of as having a guardian angel, or even with the Johannine picture of a 'hospitable Father's house awaiting the Christian'.

This explanation of the verse is of course open to question, but it may well prove the least unsatisfactory of the suggested interpretations. It would fit easily enough into the atmosphere of A.D. 90, but less easily within Paul's lifetime.

13. Eph. iv. 1–16

(*a*) ἑνότης. This word, twice used in Ephesians (at iv. 3 and iv. 13), does not occur elsewhere in Paul's writings, nor, indeed, in the rest of the New Testament. On the other hand, significantly, it is used seven times in the letters of Ignatius. The word itself therefore has clear associations with the end of the century. But more than that, the plea for unity within the body of the world-wide Church, which this word is used to enforce, is wholly in keeping with the atmosphere of that period. In those crucial years various sectarian tendencies were threatening to divide and weaken the Church. Verse 14, with its warning against 'being tossed about and swirled around by every wind of doctrine', fits exactly the need of that time. Indeed the whole passage is an elaboration of the extreme necessity of preserving unity in the Church. It reflects the same spiritual atmosphere as that implied in the solemn warning of Acts xx. 29–30, that 'grievous wolves will enter in among you and not spare the flock'. Similar verses in Revelation (e.g. ii. 6, 15, &c.) are also directed against these disintegrating tendencies, and Ignatius faced them in still more formidable forms.

This repeated use of the word and the plea it enforces would be entirely appropriate in a writing thirty years later than Paul.

(*b*) *Descensus ad Inferos* (Eph. iv. 8–10). It is usually believed that these three verses not only imply a doctrine of the Ascension, but also make explicit reference to the related doctrine of the descent of Christ into Hades in the interval between His death and resurrection.

It is agreed that in no other Pauline letter is mention made of the Ascension, and certainly there is no other hint of the Descent. Indeed it has been claimed that Paul's letters could not have contained any reference to them, for the simple reason that the doctrine of the Ascension was only formulated for the first time in Acts i. 9, and the doctrine of the Descent, being a derivative of it, came later still.

This argument, however, is not accepted by all. Some claim a much earlier date for both these doctrines, and point to 1 Pet. iv. 6 in support of their claim, for there the doctrine of the Descent is clearly propounded. Others again do not accept the early date of 1 Peter, and find the presence of the doctrine there proof rather of the lateness of the epistle than of the earliness of the doctrine.

Others even question whether we need to see in this passage in Ephesians any reference at all to the Descent. They contend rather that the writer is alluding to the Incarnation, and that the Descent to 'the lower parts of the earth' means only, as the hymn puts it, that 'He came down to earth from heaven'.

Whatever may be the correct interpretation, this at any rate is certain: the perplexing words would cause no problem at all if they could be ascribed to the end rather than to the middle of the century.

(*c*) A further element in the paragraph which appears to reflect a date later than Paul is the specialization which is evident among the church officials. In Eph. iv. 11, for instance, the terms 'evangelist' and 'pastor' appear, and these are not used elsewhere in the New Testament except by writers who represent this later period.

This section (iv. 1–16) is therefore remarkable for these three features: the emphasis on the need for unity within the Church, the inclusion of what appears to be the Doctrine of the Descent into Hades, and the specialized functions of the Church officials. So significant does Goodspeed regard these particular items that he writes: 'If there were nothing else in the epistle to point to a date late in the first century, these three striking features would suffice; they are so concrete, distinctive and specific.'

14. We find that in this epistle there are more emphatic and explicit directions for the proper upbringing of the children of Christian parents than occur elsewhere in Paul's works. They are not easy to reconcile with Paul's expectation of an early end to the present world order. Against this it can be argued that Paul's own early thoughts underwent a change, and that this change is re-

fected in Ephesians. Whether this is so or not, it is undeniable that this admonition to Christian parents would be entirely in place in a writing of A.D. 90 and there no one would question its propriety.

It would not be true to say that all these items present real difficulties for the Pauline authorship of Ephesians. Some of them do, but others represent only slight divergences from normal Pauline usage, and in themselves need not be regarded as very significant. But of all of them it can be said that they would be entirely at home in a context belonging to about A.D. 90. Such a date would have the effect not only of removing all difficulties connected with them, but even of investing them with a special appropriateness.

If this can be said of so many separate individual items in the epistle, what of the epistle as a whole, its theme and message? Can it be said to be more appropriate to the condition of the Church in A.D. 90 than in 60? Or would its message be inapplicable to a community consisting largely of Christians of the second generation?

For all Paul's epistles, except Ephesians, it is possible to enumerate their main topics and outline their theme and message. But this is not so with Ephesians. It is notoriously difficult to isolate its theme or to find any outline or argument. Commentators who have made the attempt have arrived at different results. The epistle really appears to be a somewhat confused set of variations on three related themes:

1. An affirmation, that in Christ and His Gospel there is a completely adequate answer to all human need.
2. A plea, that Christians shall avail themselves to the full of what is theirs through Christ.
3. An exhortation, that they shall conduct themselves worthily of what they have received through Christ.

These three themes are not developed in orderly sequence, but they intermingle and blend. The only time a clear outline appears is when the author follows and expands the exhortations derived from Colossians (Eph. v. 22–vi. 9), and in these expanded exhortations affirmation and plea find their place also.

These three points might have formed the main themes of an address by any Christian teacher to any Christian audience at any time. But they are particularly applicable to Christians whose faith has come to them, not fresh from the hand of God, but mediated by some venerated tradition, and who have lost, if they ever had, that first 'careless rapture' of a new-born soul.

In every age since that of the Apostles we can be confronted by the characteristics of 'second-generation Christians'. They are not peculiar to the closing years of the first century. They can be found today on the mission field in men and women whose parents, rescued out of degraded paganism into the Christian faith, became 'new creatures in Christ'. Their children, however, have heard the name of Christ from their earliest years, and have accepted Him, partly, at any rate, as a result of parental example and precept rather than as the outcome of an altogether personal and life-changing discovery. They can also be found in our own churches, in the lives of men and women whose parents entered the Christian life by some memorable experience of the Grace of God which transformed the whole quality of their lives, but who themselves have been familiar with Christian teaching from childhood. Their danger is that they take for granted the amazingly wonderful and precious things of the Christian faith. They know them by name, but not in their reality. But knowing their name, they are deluded into thinking they know the reality also, and so are unaware of their poverty. They do not fully appreciate all that Christ may mean to them. They have not appropriated for themselves what He has to offer. Their faith is valued in some half-hearted way as if it were some precious work of art, which their father had come to love years before and had sacrificed much in order to buy. In a general sort of way they know it is valuable, but they have never been arrested by its beauty or its matchless worth, and certainly have never 'sold all that they had' in order to possess it. Such Christians need to be awakened to the great privileges of their faith, and they need to be exhorted to live worthily of them, for they are more prone to carelessness and compromise than their fathers had been.

This epistle therefore, with its reiterated affirmations, pleas, and exhortations, is entirely appropriate to the special needs of Christians of the second generation, and may even be said to become 'illumined' if it is interpreted as addressed to them.

XX
CONCLUSIONS

It is now necessary to summarize and review the conclusions to which our investigation has led us.

In the prolonged debate about the authorship of Ephesians the arguments based on vocabulary, style, and doctrine had reached a tantalizing state of equilibrium. It was impossible to say with confidence to which side the balance tilted. Moreover, these arguments had been worked out fully, and little of value could be added to them. If new evidence of a weighty nature was to be found, some different approach had to be tried. The way which seemed most likely to lead to new and significant facts was a thorough investigation of the relationship between Ephesians and the other Pauline epistles, with special reference to the admittedly close relationship with Colossians.

Ephesians and Colossians

The following features were found to mark the relationship between these two epistles:

1. Their relationship is exceedingly close, far closer than that existing between any other two epistles of Paul. More than a quarter of the words in Ephesians are found in Colossians. More than a third of the words in Colossians reappear in Ephesians. This measure of interdependence cannot be accounted for by saying that it is due merely to their identity of authorship. One of these epistles must have been deliberately based on the other.

2. There are good reasons for believing that Colossians is the earlier of the two, and that it is Ephesians which is based on Colossians.

3. The manner of this borrowing is remarkable. Though so much of Colossians is reproduced in Ephesians, there is hardly a trace of mechanical reproduction. It is extremely rare for as many as five consecutive words in Ephesians to correspond exactly with five consecutive words in Colossians. Even where the substance of a passage from Colossians is reproduced in Ephesians, some variations are introduced, so that the correspondence is less than identical. This absence of identical sentences suggests that Ephesians is not the work of a writer who copied from a document open in front of

him. It points rather to an author who knew the earlier writing so well that he was able to reproduce from memory many of its phrases and word-sequences. This is borne out by the way in which the phrases from Colossians appear in Ephesians in a completely different order.

There is, however, one noteworthy exception to the general rule that no long passage is identically copied. This is at Eph. vi. 21–2, where a prolonged sequence of words is reproduced verbatim from Col. iv. 7–8. This, however, is the only instance among all the many parallels which requires us to assume that the author of Ephesians turned at this point to his copy of Colossians and deliberately made an extract from it. Apart from this, what Ephesians owes to Colossians is not at all the debt of a transcriber to his prototype. Rather it leads us to think that the substance of Colossians was already in the mind of the writer of the later epistle, and that in it he was drawing, not on what he saw written before him, but on what was stored up in his memory.

4. This estimate of the manner in which the author of Ephesians has availed himself of Colossians is confirmed by another characteristic of their relationship. Quite frequently two phrases, widely separated in Colossians, are combined in Ephesians. Some word or thought, common to the two passages, serves to link them in the mind of the author. It is a process similar to what in Gospel criticism is called 'conflation'. This is the very thing we all do with material which we know by heart, such as lines from hymns or verses of Scripture. It would not have happened so often in Ephesians unless the writer had known Colossians very intimately, and had absorbed its contents into his thoughts.

5. Another feature of this relationship is that important words are taken over from Colossians, often in conjunction with other words from the same context, and yet in Ephesians they are made to carry a different significance. Instances of this have already been extensively commented on, and only the more important examples need be recalled here:

(*a*) The word *σῶμα* in Eph. iv. 16 appears in the same general context of words as in Col. ii. 19. But whereas in Colossians it appears to mean the Cosmos (so Dibelius insists), in Ephesians it is applied to the Church.

(*b*) The word *ἀποκαταλλάσσω* is used in the New Testament only in Ephesians and Colossians. Its use in Ephesians is clearly derived from Colossians, but its significance has been changed. In Colossians it describes the reconciliation of man and God, and it is the direct achievement of God Himself by means of the death of Christ. In Ephesians it is applied to the reconciliation, not of man to God, but of Jews and Gentiles, and it is the direct work of Christ.

(*c*) In Col. i. 26 it is declared that God's ultimate disclosure of His long-hidden secret (*μυστήριον*) was made to 'the saints' (*τοῖς ἁγίοις*). In Eph. iii. 5 the same thought is expressed, but the words *ἀποστόλοις καὶ προφήταις* are added. This has the effect not only of making *ἁγίοις* into an adjective instead of a substantive but of seriously distorting the meaning of the passage, by drastically reducing the scope of God's revelation of His purpose.

(*d*) In Colossians the *μυστήριον* is consistently equated with Christ, the Word of God. In Ephesians, though the word is used even more frequently, the significance attached to it is always entirely different.

(*e*) In Colossians the word *πλήρωμα* is twice used. It seems to have been one of the catchwords of the false teachers at Colossae. Paul daringly adopts it for his own purposes, and turns it to an inspired use. He declares that the truth about the *πλήρωμα* is that the whole *πλήρωμα* of God is to be found in Christ. But when the word appears in Ephesians there is no trace of its use with this significance.

(*f*) Another word which in Ephesians is clearly borrowed from Colossians and yet used very differently is *οἰκονομία*. It is used in Colossians with the same meaning as it has in Paul's other epistles. It signifies the special task or assignment which God has entrusted to Paul. This objective significance of the word is, in Ephesians, replaced by a subjective one. It comes to mean God's wise planning or generalship, something which is entirely within the mind of God Himself.

6. A further peculiarity in the relationship of these two epistles appears at Eph. v. 19–20. The author is clearly following very closely what he remembers of Col. iii. 16–17. This passage reads: 'Whatsoever ye do, do all in the name of the Lord Jesus, giving thanks to God the Father through Him.' Here the phrase 'in the name of the Lord Jesus' has no sense-connexion with the verb 'giving thanks', which follows it. They are two phrases which accidentally are placed adjacent to one another, but without any connexion whatever in meaning. Yet when these same words are in substance reproduced in Ephesians, it is not their meaning which is retained but the words divorced from their original meaning.

The phrase 'in the name of the Lord Jesus' is not used, as in Colossians, to describe the motive of all our conduct, but is added, rather pointlessly, to the verb 'give thanks', and the readers are urged to 'give thanks always for all things in the name of the Lord Jesus Christ to God, even the Father'. This is a curious instance of the merely accidental association of words prevailing over the meaning which they were originally used to convey.

Ephesians and the other Pauline Epistles

1. There are very extensive similarities between Ephesians and the other Pauline epistles. If all the words in Ephesians which have parallels in the other letters are underlined, they amount to 46·7 per cent. of the words in the epistle. Since, however, it is admitted that a special relationship of dependence exists between Ephesians and Colossians, if the relationship of Ephesians with the other epistles is to be fairly estimated, the parallels with Colossians should be omitted from the calculation. If these are excluded, it is found that the words in Ephesians with parallels in the other letters amount to 29·1 per cent. of the total number of words in the epistle.

2. There are parallels with all the epistles, with the possible exception of 2 Thessalonians. This letter is certainly represented least, and, interestingly enough, the one represented most, in proportion to its length, is Philemon.

3. In order to have a standard of comparison it is necessary to select one of the admittedly genuine epistles and mark in it, also, all the parallels that can be found with Paul's other letters. Philippians seemed as suitable as any to be chosen for this purpose.

The words in Philippians which have parallels in other Pauline epistles amount to 15·2 per cent. of the whole (in comparison with the figure of 29·1 per cent. for Ephesians). The exclusion of parallels from Colossians, however, reduces the range in which parallels to Ephesians may be found to 74 pages (in WH) as compared with 83 available to Philippians. If allowance is made for this, the figure of 29·1 per cent. should be increased to 32·7 per cent.

This means that the parallels in Ephesians are more than double those in Philippians (32·7 per cent. compared with 15·2 per cent.).

4. Not only is the number of parallels considerably higher in Ephesians, but the manner of their appearance is significantly different. For instance, the parallels noted in Ephesians tend to group themselves around specific passages in the other epistles. The following passages, for example, have exercised a *sustained* influence on

Ephesians: that is, several echoes of each one reappear within a single passage in Ephesians:

Rom. i. 21–4	(cf. Eph. iv. 17–19)
Rom. iii. 21–iv. 2	(cf. Eph. ii. 8)
1 Cor. iii. 9–16	(cf. Eph. ii. 19–20)
1 Cor. xv. 24–8	(cf. Eph. i. 20–3)
Philemon 4–6	(cf. Eph. i. 15–17)

Other passages exercise a *recurring* influence in Ephesians; that is, phrases from them reappear at several places in Ephesians. Such passages are: Rom. v. 1–2; Rom. viii. 9–39; Rom. xii. 1–5; 1 Cor. xi. 1–3; 1 Cor. xii. 12–13; 2 Cor. v. 14–20; Gal. ii. 20.

It will further be noticed that included in these two groups of influential passages is a large proportion of passages which any reader familiar with Paul's epistles would recognize as worthy to be counted among the great passages in the Pauline epistles and most likely to be remembered.

In contrast, the parallels in Philippians are not at all like this. There is no instance of a passage from any other letter appearing to exercise either a *sustained* or a *recurring* influence, with the possible exception of an odd case which is clearly no more than a coincidence.

5. Moreover, compared with Philippians, memorable phrases from the other letters appear much more frequently in Ephesians.

6. There are also many instances of what we have called 'conflation'. Phrases from different epistles are brought together in Ephesians. In many cases Colossians is the source of one of the two phrases so combined, but not in every case. The number of such instances is far in excess of what can be found in Philippians.

7. In at least two cases this process of 'conflation' is elaborated to combine not two phrases but many. The result is what appears to be a deliberate attempt to present a kind of summary of all that has been said in the earlier epistles on some particular theme. Two such passages are Eph. ii. 8–9 and iv. 4–6.

The Kind of Author presupposed by these Considerations

These features of the relationship of Ephesians with the other Paulines point to certain facts about its author. Any final theory regarding him must do justice to them.

1. He was a person who knew Colossians so well as to know it almost by heart. Probably, however, he did not know it completely by memory, otherwise there would have been more lengthy quotations of the exact words. But he knew it well enough for its words

and phrases and ideas to be readily reproduced and combined in new associations.

2. He also wrote with a copy of Colossians ready to hand, for though he did not use it for writing the epistle as a whole, he must have had it to turn to at Eph. vi. 21–2 in order to transcribe Col. iv. 7–8. So large a measure of exact repetition requires such an explanation.

3. Though he freely availed himself of the vocabulary of Colossians, he did not always use the words with the same meaning. New meanings are imposed upon them. Also, phrases which in Colossians merely stand next to each other, but in different clauses, and with no association of meaning, are in Ephesians also found together, but are now not merely adjacent; they have been combined into a new relationship of meaning.

4. This author also had an intimate acquaintance with what Paul had written in earlier epistles, for familiar phrases from them reappear in Ephesians, and in far greater number than is the case with Philippians.

5. He seems to have some special attachment to the epistle to Philemon. He not only uses phrases from it, which in itself is unusual, for this little letter was often completely ignored, but in proportion to its length, more phrases from it occur in Ephesians than from any other letter (apart from Colossians).

6. The whole of the epistle has often been characterized as a kind of summary of Pauline teaching. There are one or two passages in particular which certainly appear to be deliberate summaries of certain aspects of it. This comprehensiveness was probably part of the intention of the author.

Whether our decision be in favour of Pauline authorship or not, these features of the relationship must be accounted for. We must now ask whether they, and other features of this relationship with the other letters, can better be fitted into a theory which retains Pauline authorship or one that abandons it.

Pauline Authorship in view of these Considerations

It is not necessary here to repeat the arguments in favour of Pauline authorship. It is sufficient to recall that they rely chiefly on the unanimity of the external evidence in its favour. It is clear that Ephesians was known and quoted as a Pauline letter as early as were Romans and 1 Corinthians. In the earliest known forms of the Pauline Corpus it had an assured place. Much of its phraseology and teaching is recognizably Pauline, and it makes a specific claim to have been written by Paul.

Moreover, some of the features which characterize the relationship of Ephesians with the other Paulines fit readily into an assumption of Pauline authorship. The preponderant use of Colossians, for instance, and the flexible manner in which its phrases are regrouped and modified is just what might be expected if Paul wrote Ephesians immediately after finishing Colossians, while what he had just written was still fresh in his mind. The earlier letter would also be at his elbow, and he could easily turn to it and copy out the exact words which he had used about Tychicus, who was to be the bearer of both letters. Indeed he was to carry three, for that to Philemon about Onesimus was already written. This, too, would be fresh in his mind and able to influence what he wrote in Ephesians. It may also have been that in writing Ephesians Paul was not addressing one particular church but preparing a kind of encyclical epistle for Christians generally, or for a number of churches within a certain area. Perhaps, also, as he wrote, he deliberately made it his aim to produce a comprehensive statement of the Christian message as he understood it and preached it. In such an epistle (or homily) he would not be addressing himself to a particular situation or wrestling with some definite error; it would not be his task to apply his Gospel to some pressing problem of the day. Rather, he would deliberately say what he had often said before, and use the words and phrases which he was accustomed to use in his preaching and writing. It is not impossible that he retained copies of his earlier letters, and feeling that this general letter was likely to be a kind of final testament, had re-read them in prison before beginning to write, so that what he wrote revealed an unusual degree of repetition from them.

Some such reconstruction of the circumstances of its production is necessary if Ephesians is to be fitted into Paul's lifetime.

In order to account for the un-Pauline features in the epistle, some writers have suggested that Paul used an amanuensis, as we know he often did, but in this case left more than usual to the exercise of his discretion. This explanation is, however, unlikely for two reasons: firstly, contrary to Paul's custom, no other name is associated with his in the greetings of this epistle; and if a man was competent to be entrusted with the responsibility of writing a letter in Paul's name, he would have been a colleague worthy of being mentioned in the greeting. Nor is there any reference in the letter to suggest that an amanuensis was being used, though such references are found elsewhere (Col. iv. 18, Gal. v. 11). Secondly, and more important, an amanuensis would not have been able to incorporate the material of Colossians in the peculiar manner in which we find it actually accomplished. Merely to have copied out Colossians at Paul's dictation would not have produced the necessary degree of familiarity with it.

T. W. Manson admits only two possible solutions of the problem of Ephesians on the basis of its authenticity. We may explain it, he writes, 'either (with Marcion) as the letter to the Laodiceans referred to in Col. iv. 16, or as a circular letter, similar to that in Rev. i–iii, intended to be read in a number of Asian churches' (CB, p. 112). Of the two the second is more probable.

The chief difficulty about identifying Ephesians with the epistle to the Laodiceans is that Paul's relationships with the church at Laodicea appear to have been similar to those which he had with Colossae. He was not the founder of the church, nor had he visited it. In a letter to such a church we should have expected an approach similar to the one in Colossians. But the epistle to the Ephesians is much more impersonal. It is hardly credible that it was written to any particular church, even one unknown to Paul, and written at the same time as he wrote to the church at Colossae, a church also unknown to him personally.

If it is a Pauline writing, we appear to be driven to the conclusion that it was a circular letter, written near the end of his days. Almost certainly it must be accepted as Paul's last letter, and therefore written from Rome, because an earlier date does not allow for the marked development of outlook which characterizes this epistle in comparison with the earlier letters, nor does it accord with the apparent repetition from the earlier epistles. Further, it must have been written within a few hours of the completion of Philemon and Colossians, and dispatched at the same time, by the same messenger. It has the appearance of being a final statement by Paul, a comprehensive summing up of the Gospel which he had been called to preach, and which he had found adequate to meet every moral need and to answer every intellectual perplexity.

The facts of the case drive us to this solution as the most probable within the lifetime of Paul. There are, however, serious objections to it. Some are applicable to this particular solution, and others to any solution which is based upon the assumption of Pauline authorship.

The objections to this particular solution of the problem are as follows:

(i) What we read in the epistle to Philemon does not at all imply that Paul was in the frame of mind in which he would set himself to write a 'last will and testament'. Rather he was then expecting an early release from prison. This is clear from his request that accommodation should be kept ready for him, since it was his intention to visit Philemon and his family immediately upon his release. Yet if Ephesians is Pauline, it is contemporary with Philemon.

(ii) This intimation to Philemon that Paul expects to pay him an early visit strongly supports the Ephesian origin of Philemon (and therefore of Colossians). So casual a mention of a forthcoming visit from a distance of some hundreds of miles seems a little odd. Moreover, the implication behind Philem. 13–14 is an unmistakable request that Philemon will not only deal mercifully with the runaway slave but, in addition, send him back to Paul, to 'minister unto him in the bonds of the Gospel'. It was a very long way from Rome to Colossae. Even if it is possible that Paul might send back Onesimus all that distance, is it likely that he would do so with an implied request that he should be immediately returned to him in Rome? Were the Christians of those days so affluent, and with such a leisurely disregard of time, that Onesimus could be sent from Rome to Colossae, merely to be sent back again? The journey from Ephesus would be trivial by comparison. If it was from Rome that Paul wrote, surely he would have adopted a method of negotiating Philemon's consent to his keeping Onesimus without the expense in time and money involved in the long double journey to Asia and back. If, however, Philemon and Colossians have to be brought within the period of Paul's Ephesian ministry, Ephesians must be brought to this earlier date also. In these circumstances it would be difficult to regard it as the last of his epistles, a kind of final summing up of his message.

(iii) Would the fact that Paul was writing a circular letter cause him to omit all reference to its destination, even in general terms? We have in Galatians an instance of how he wrote and addressed a letter intended to be sent to a group of churches in a certain area. Gal. i. 2 tells us that the letter is meant for 'the churches of Galatia'. If Ephesians was intended, as T. W. Manson very reasonably suggests, as a circular to be read in a number of Asian churches, would not its address probably have been somewhat similar?

There are, therefore, real difficulties in the way of treating Ephesians as an epistle by Paul, written by him consciously as his last, from his imprisonment in Rome, and addressed as a circular to a group of churches. These arguments, however, against this particular solution are inconsiderable in comparison with other arguments which tell against the acceptance of any solution of the problem which is based on the assumption of Pauline authorship. These arguments are derived from our study of the relationship of Ephesians, firstly with Colossians, and secondly with the other Pauline epistles. When taken in conjunction with the arguments from vocabulary, style, and doctrine they are formidable.

Difficulties for Pauline Authorship arising from the Relationship of Ephesians with Colossians

1. The literary relationship requires that if Paul wrote Ephesians he wrote it *immediately* after Colossians, while its subject-matter and phraseology were still fresh in his mind. The mode of its reproduction and the identical reference to Tychicus, bearer of both letters, necessitate this assessment of the relationship. Some of the words derived from Colossians are, however, used with a different significance. It becomes almost incredible that Paul, having just written Colossians, should have immediately used the same words over again, often in the same general context, and yet have departed so strangely from the meaning which the words originally conveyed.

It is this fact that the same words are used with different meanings which is for Dibelius the decisive factor in his rejection of Pauline authorship.

2. We noticed that widely separated phrases in Colossians are in Ephesians combined into a single unit because of some common element which serves to link them together. We called this 'conflation', and we found that it was a characteristic feature of the way in which Ephesians had used Colossians.

We have no means of testing how often this phenomenon might have appeared in two unquestionably genuine letters of Paul, written within a few hours of each other. It is, however, very doubtful if it would have happened as frequently as we find it happening in Ephesians.

It is undoubtedly the kind of thing which our minds tend to do with material which has become very familiar to us by constant reading or repetition. People whose minds are steeped in the Bible and Hymn Book sometimes pray in sentences which are built up of words and phrases derived from these sources. One letter, written immediately after another, would probably reproduce much of the earlier one, but we question whether this particular phenomenon of 'conflation', beyond an occasional coincidence, would characterize the relationship. It is at any rate more readily explicable on the assumption that the author of Ephesians knew Colossians almost by heart, through repeated hearing or reading, than that his knowledge of it was due to the fact that he had himself just written it.

3. The way in which Col. iv. 16–17 is reproduced in Eph. v. 19–20 is very peculiar. The phrase 'in the name of Jesus' is wrenched from the word to which it very appropriately belongs in Colossians ('do all in the name of the Lord Jesus'), and is artificially associated with 'giving thanks', a verb which is adjacent to it in Colossians, but not attached to it by any sense-link at all. It is an instance of the mere contiguity of words prevailing over their meaning. An imitator might be guilty of this, but it is not what Paul would have done if he were letting his thoughts, already expressed in Colossians, find utterance again in Ephesians. For him undoubtedly the meaning would predominate over the mere words used to express it. He would have been much more likely to express the same sentiment in somewhat different words than to use the same words to say something quite different and at the same time less pointed and less appropriate.

A well-known hymn by John Keble contains this verse:

> The trivial round, the common task,
> Will furnish all we ought to ask;
> Room to deny ourselves, a road
> To bring us daily nearer God.

In this verse 'a road' is a second object of 'furnish'. It has no connexion in sense with the verb 'deny'. If we heard someone quote the third line by itself as an independent unit: 'Room to deny ourselves a road', as though 'a road' were something we should deny ourselves, we should feel this to be a sorry mutilation of the real meaning of the words of the poet. Yet this has been known to happen. It happens, however, only in the mind of one who has memorized the words and recalls the sound of them rather than the sense. Such a violation of the meaning is something which the author himself could not possibly have perpetrated, certainly not within a few hours of composing the hymn. Yet it is something similar to this which occurs in Eph. v. 20.

Zahn shrewdly suggests how the hand of the imitator may be detected. He writes:

> 'In order to prove that Ephesians is a forgery, based either entirely or for the most part on a genuine letter to the Colossians, conclusive evidence must be adduced to show that ideas and words in Colossians were misunderstood or intentionally misinterpreted by the imitator, or clumsily copied, and used in the wrong place. For these are the

characteristics of all known forgeries of this sort, at least all ancient forgeries' (INT, p. 501).

Though the word 'forgery' is unnecessarily offensive, and 'imitation' should be preferred, these suggested tests are very much to the point. It is precisely because we do find in Ephesians, in its relationship to Colossians, what Zahn says we should anticipate in the work of an imitator that it appears so difficult to maintain its Pauline authorship. In Ephesians the words of Colossians are sometimes 'misunderstood' and 'misinterpreted' and sometimes 'clumsily copied and used in the wrong place' (though perhaps in this case 'remembered' should take the place of 'copied').

A dilemma confronts us: if Ephesians is by Paul, it must have been written immediately after Colossians. Many features of the literary relationship require this. On the other hand, there are features of the relationship which demand that the epistle, if by Paul, must have been written only after the lapse of a considerable interval of time. Only so can the changes in the use of words and the artificial reproduction of word-sequences in such a way as to do violence to their original meaning be accounted for.

It is doubtful if this dilemma can be resolved on the basis of Pauline authorship.

Some try to surmount these difficulties, and to account for the fact that the author appears to use Colossians as though he had largely memorized it, by claiming that Paul probably retained a copy of Colossians, and after a considerable interval, when the issues that had led to its being first written had ceased to be of pressing importance, took it up again, read it over, and meditated on it before using it as the basis of a more general statement on similar but not identical lines.

This, however, is far from convincing. It is not in keeping with what we know of Paul to think of him turning up an old letter after a long interval in order to find inspiration and material for a further statement of his message. What is, however, almost conclusive in eliminating this theory of an intervening period of time between the two letters is the passage in each epistle which makes reference to Tychicus. Eph. vi. 21–2, as we have seen, provides the one prolonged verbatim reproduction of a passage from Colossians (iv. 7–8). If Paul wrote both letters at the same time and dispatched them together by the hand of Tychicus, it is not unnatural that he should, in the second letter, copy out word for word what he had written about the messenger in the earlier letter. But that he should do this after the lapse of many months, even if by a strange coincidence Tychicus happened to be available to carry the second letter, is highly improbable. In such a case he might well have commended Tychicus, perhaps even in words bearing a general resemblance to his earlier commendation, but he would not have copied out the identical words.

The dilemma therefore remains, and its difficulty for Pauline authorship remains. If Paul wrote both epistles, they must have been written together; and yet the differences in doctrine and the use of words make it impossible that they were written together. The solution of the dilemma seems to lie only in the abandonment of Pauline authorship.

Difficulties for Pauline Authorship arising out of the Relationship of Ephesians with the other Pauline Epistles

1. The parallels between Ephesians and the other Pauline epistles (apart from Colossians) are exceedingly numerous. They amount to more than twice the number of similar parallels in Philippians, which may be taken as representative of the genuine epistles. The parallels in Philippians are explained by the fact that it and the other epistles are the work of the same mind, and so naturally enough the same words and phrases are sometimes used. This explanation, which suffices to account for the smaller number of parallels in Philippians, cannot be regarded as adequate to explain the far greater number in Ephesians. Some further explanation is required.

2. The manner in which these parallels appear in Ephesians is very different from what we find in Philippians. In Philippians they are haphazard and obviously accidental. No single passage from the other epistles seems to have exercised more influence than another. There is nothing to suggest that outstanding passages have been remembered and partially reproduced. In Ephesians quite the contrary appears. There are 'sustained' parallels with certain passages, and also 'recurring' parallels with others, as though these passages lingered on in the mind of the author. Moreover, these passages are often precisely those which readers today, as in other days, remember because of their outstanding significance.

3. In Philippians there was an almost complete absence of striking and memorable phrases repeated from the other epistles. In Ephesians such phrases occur frequently.

4. In Ephesians widely separated phrases from Colossians are 'conflated'. So too are phrases from the other epistles. Since the

influence of Colossians on Ephesians is so predominant, it is not unnatural that the conflation often consists of one phrase from Colossians and one from another epistle. Sometimes, however, it consists of two phrases from the other epistles. It may be urged that this is exactly what may be expected in the writings of the same author. But this is not so. There is an almost complete absence of this peculiarity from Philippians. The one or two odd cases which do occur are obviously coincidences. Those in Ephesians, however, are far too numerous to be explained as coincidences. It is very doubtful if phrases from letters which we have written months earlier do lodge in our minds so securely as to lead to this phenomenon. On the other hand, as we have seen, it is just the kind of thing that our minds do with material which is exceedingly familiar to us.

These features of Ephesians in its relationship to the other epistles, in which it differs so significantly from Philippians, are difficult to account for on the basis of Pauline authorship. On the other hand, they are precisely what we should anticipate in the work of a later writer who had read and re-read the collected letters, and who had been particularly moved by certain outstanding passages in them, and whose mind had retained some of the more striking phrases.

It may be objected that this comparison between Philippians and Ephesians is misleading; that Ephesians is not an ordinary letter, and so cannot be compared with Philippians, which is; and that Ephesians probably represents a much later period in Paul's life than Philippians and therefore will in certain respects be different. If indeed Ephesians is to be regarded as the last of Paul's writings, written from Rome, if it is to be accepted more as a homily in epistolary form than a real letter; and if we may assume that it was composed deliberately by Paul to represent a final summary of the message of his Gospel, as he had come to understand it in its fullness; and if, on the other hand, Philippians is to be dated in the Ephesian ministry, perhaps even earlier than 1 Corinthians,[1] then it may be justifiably argued that what appears in the one should not be taken as a precedent for what to expect in the other.

There is no doubt that these arguments may be held to account for some of the differences between these two epistles, but they have little bearing on the actual issues before us. Paul would not be more likely to quote from or echo his own previous letters in a homily than in another church letter. Nor would such echoes as do occur in a homily be noticeably different in character from those in a

[1] So Michaelis, DP, p. 62, and others also.

letter. Neither would an earlier date for Philippians account for these differences. It is true, of course, that Philippians could not reflect letters still unwritten; but we should expect that these later letters as well as Philippians would contain personal mannerisms, so that certain parallels would be found between them. So the measure of interdependence would remain relatively constant, whether the letter was early or late. Even if Ephesians is the last of Paul's writings and Philippians one of the earliest it would not explain the particular points of difference before us.

In actual fact, however, if Ephesians is by Paul it probably comes from the same period of Paul's life as Philippians. Until recently both were confidently dated in his last Roman imprisonment. Claims for an earlier Ephesian imprisonment, however, from which some or all of the imprisonment epistles were written, have been made and strongly argued.[1] If, however, Philippians is to be assigned to this Ephesian period, so in all probability must be Colossians and Philemon, and with them Ephesians also. It is true that some scholars are inclined to divide the group of imprisonment epistles and assign some to Ephesus and others to Rome. F. B. Clogg, for instance, believes that Philippians may be ascribed to an Ephesian imprisonment, but that the others more naturally belong to the Roman period (INT, p. 80). A. D. Nock, on the other hand, prefers it the other way round, assigning Colossians and Philemon to the earlier occasion and Philippians to Rome (SP, p. 221). He treats Ephesians as post-Pauline, and so does not need to fit it into Pauline chronology. It is not impossible that the group should be split up, but the strength of the arguments in favour of Ephesus depends on all three,[2] and the grounds for dividing them are very unconvincing. One of the main arguments for ascribing Colossians and Philemon to the Roman period has been that they belong to the same group as Ephesians, and where Ephesians is placed, they too must be. Ephesians, however, by its doctrinal differences from the earlier letters, demands a place at the end of Paul's life. Some of those who maintain its Pauline authorship admit that this would have to be abandoned if there were no other place for it within Paul's lifetime except at so early a stage as the Ephesian ministry. It is the need of postponing Ephesians to the latest possible date in Paul's life, and the fact that Colossians and Philemon must be grouped

[1] By G. S. Duncan in *St. Paul's Ephesian Ministry*, J. H. Michael in *Philippians* (Moffatt Commentary), and W. Michaelis in *Die Datierung des Philipperbriefes*.

[2] That is, Philippians, Colossians, and Philemon. Ephesians is quite neutral in the matter, except that its advanced type of teaching requires as late a date as possible.

with it, that has been one of the main arguments against their Ephesian origin. If Ephesians were left out of account, Colossians and Philemon would naturally be associated with Philippians in whichever imprisonment the evidence most favoured, and the main obstacle to the earlier of the alternative dates would be removed.

Ephesians, therefore, if Pauline, in all probability belongs to the same period in Paul's life as Philippians, whether it be the imprisonment at Rome or at Ephesus. This means that Philippians is admirably suited to be treated as a standard by which Ephesians may be measured and tested. The differences, therefore, in their relationships with the other Pauline epistles, both in degree and in manner, must be accorded their full significance.

Unless it can be shown that these peculiarities, which have been noted in Ephesians in its relationship with the other epistles, occur also in the genuine letters, and no less frequently, then it must be accepted as an established fact that Ephesians stands in a class apart from the other epistles. If this great difference is to be accounted for on the basis of Pauline authorship, the only possible explanation seems to be that, in some way or other, Paul, before the end of his life, was able to re-read, and deeply ponder over, all his earlier letters shortly before writing this epistle. What P. N. Harrison writes of the Pastoral Epistles might equally well be applied to Ephesians:

> 'We have not found between any one genuine epistle and the others anything like the same series of composite links connecting the Pastorals with them all. Indeed so numerous and striking are these verbal agreements that it becomes a very serious question whether Paul himself would have been able, or likely, to reproduce, purely from memory, such a variety of extracts from letters which he had dictated seven or eight years previously. Supposing that the Pauline authorship of the Pastorals were fully established, we should almost feel driven to conclude that the Apostle obtained, or retained, copies of his own earlier letters, and refreshed his memory of their contents before setting to work on the Pastorals' (PPE, p. 89).

The 'composite links' with the other epistles are certainly more apparent in the case of the Pastorals than in that of Ephesians, but what Harrison says here of the Pastorals is true also of Ephesians, if in a somewhat less obvious degree.[1]

[1] Von Soden noted these 'composite links' between Ephesians and the other Paulines, and because of them decisively rejected Pauline authorship. He wrote (of Ephesians): 'It is true that every sentence contains verbal echoes of Pauline epistles; indeed, except where ideas peculiar to the epistle come to expression, it is simply a

To suppose that Paul was in a position to read his collected works before his death is so improbable that it need not be treated as a sober alternative until some claim for it, based on evidence, is seriously made.[1]

These arguments against Pauline authorship which spring only from the consideration of the relationship of the epistle with the other epistles are in themselves formidable. When taken in conjunction with the other arguments based on style, vocabulary, and doctrine (which alone have seemed decisive to some) they may well appear conclusive.

Non-Pauline Authorship

The balance of evidence appears to favour a post-Pauline origin for Ephesians. The abandonment of Pauline authorship, however, presents certain difficulties which must be frankly faced. We must be prepared to explain the emphatic use of Paul's name in the body of the letter. We must recognize that its authenticity was never for a moment in doubt in the early Church, that it was quoted as Paul's as early as Romans and was given an unquestioned place in the first Pauline Corpus. Other epistles whose traditional authorship has been questioned lack some of the assurance with which Ephesians is invested. Hebrews, for instance, does not claim to be by Paul; the Pastorals were missing from the collection of letters which Marcion used; 1 Peter does not appear to be quoted until as late as Polycarp, and is not named in the Muratorian Canon. But none of these doubts affect Ephesians. Moreover, the epistle on the whole is thoroughly Pauline, both in outlook and vocabulary.

Explanations, however, can be suggested. The use of Paul's name may be the earliest instance in the New Testament of the prevalent practice of pseudonymity. It appears elsewhere in the New Testament, and in the Old Testament, and is characteristic of the apocryphal literature. In some cases pseudonymity seems to us to be something less than honest, but this charge need not be levelled against Ephesians. If the writer deliberately derived what he wrote

mosaic of Pauline phraseology. But this very fact makes it impossible to ascribe the letter to one who was of so original a spirit and so rarely repeated himself as St. Paul' (HECL, p. 294).

[1] Harnack rejects the suggestion as most unlikely, to say the least. He writes: 'Hat etwa Paulus selbst seine Briefe gesammelt oder ist das schon bei seinen Lebzeiten geschehen? Das ist sehr unwahrscheinlich, um nicht mehr zu sagen. . . . Es gibt schlechterdings keine Notiz und keine Spur, Paulus selbst habe seine Briefe gesammelt' (BAP, pp., 6–7).

from the epistles which Paul had written, and did so that he might the more faithfully represent Paul to a subsequent generation, it might well have been less honest in his case to pass the result off under his own name than to acknowledge it as Paul's.

The presence of Pauline doctrine may be explained as the work of a Pauline disciple, who greatly reverenced his master and felt that a timely reaffirmation of the essentials of his teaching was urgently needed in the life of the Church. The fact that so many genuine Pauline words and phrases appear is probably due to his skilful incorporation of remembered phrases from the other letters with which he was familiar.

The early acceptance of the epistle and its immediate inclusion in the Pauline Corpus must mean that in some important area it had become established as a Pauline letter before the Corpus in its final form reached the area, or else it appeared as a member of that Corpus when it was first collected.

The predominant use of Colossians has been difficult to explain. Why should a post-Pauline writer choose this minor epistle on which to base his writing? The answer seems to be that for some reason the writer had been familiar with this letter for a long time before the others came to his notice, so that its phrases and ideas, already well established in his mind, dominated what he wrote.

The Date

If the writer is post-Pauline, we must try to fix the date as accurately as possible. We saw that the external evidence does not permit a date much later than A.D. 90. Even if we are not persuaded that the uncertain echoes of Ephesians in 1 Clement prove that author's acquaintance with the epistle, the less disputable evidence from other early Fathers compels us to accept a date within a year or two of A.D. 90 at the latest. Two writings also within the New Testament, Revelation and the Pastoral Epistles, both show a knowledge of Ephesians, and thus confirm that at the latest the date cannot be much after A.D. 90. The internal evidence of the epistle itself is completely in harmony with the suggestion that the epistle originated in the last decade of the first century.

If A.D. 92 may be accepted as the *terminus ad quem*, have we any evidence by which to fix the *terminus a quo*? Apart from the use of Paul's name, which we interpret as pseudonymous, there is nothing that positively requires a date before A.D. 90. But is there anything that makes A.D. 90 more probable than A.D. 70 or 80? The internal evidence, as we have said, fits in better with the later years of the century, but apart from this there is little to help except the problematical relationship between Acts and Ephesians. We saw that the evidence of Acts, though not conclusive, is favourable to an assumption that the author of Ephesians wrote subsequently to Acts, knew Acts, was influenced by some of its striking phrases, and was familiar with some of its notable passages relating to Paul, especially that one in which Paul is most closely associated with the leaders of the Ephesian Church. There are similarities too remarkable to be wholly ascribable to mere coincidence. Moreover they are definitely not amenable to the explanation that they are due to Luke's acquaintance with Ephesians (if we may assume that Luke is the author of Acts). If one has influenced the other, it is Acts which has influenced the author of Ephesians. If we could confidently assume that this was so, and also that the most commonly favoured date (*c.* A.D. 85) for Acts is approximately correct, then the date of Ephesians could be most satisfyingly pin-pointed within a period of five years or so. It would mean that we could ascribe Ephesians to the short period between A.D. 87 and 92.

Though the lower limit cannot be as confidently fixed as the upper one, some date within this period of five years may be accepted as very probable.

The Author

It now remains to combine our earlier general conclusions about the author of Ephesians with these later ones which have led to the opinion that the author was someone other than Paul. The facts about him, and the way he went to work appear to be as follows:

(i) He wrote this epistle between the years A.D. 87 and 92.

(ii) He had long known the epistle to the Colossians, and had pondered over it so intimately that its thoughts and phrases had become part of the equipment of his own mind. He also knew Philemon very well, and could draw freely from its contents.

(iii) In a lesser degree he was familiar with all the letters of Paul now in the New Testament, and by his use of phrases and thoughts from them reveals that his imagination had been particularly fired by some of the greater passages, and these especially had impressed themselves on his memory.

(iv) His purpose appears to have been to produce a comprehensive statement of Pauline teaching. All the main items of his teaching are welded into this exhaustive summary.[1] Certain passages in

[1] There is one curious omission. No direct reference is made to the Sacrament of the

the epistle in fact seem to be deliberately constructed so as to include all that Paul had taught, fragmentarily and at various points in his other letters, on a particular subject (cf. Eph. ii. 8–9 and iv. 4–6).

(*a*) Of set purpose this broad and general statement is completely *detached from specific problems.* Paul's greatest utterances of faith arise mainly out of his attempts to offer Christian solutions to concrete problems in the churches. His declarations of truth are usually related to actual situations in the life of some individual church, and on the surface they may seem to be predominantly of merely local interest. This writer seems to aim at a general statement of the truth of the Christian Gospel, as interpreted by Paul, in its timeless and essential aspects, apart from any application of it to particular situations.

(*b*) In this statement, so far as possible, Paul's actual words from his letters are used and skilfully built up into what reads like an original composition. Here and there, however, there is an *element of interpretation* as though the writer was concerned to impart to his readers not so much the words which Paul had written as the meaning he had wished to convey. It is apparently for this reason that the word 'justify' is omitted and replaced by 'save', even in the passage Eph. ii. 8–9, where the substance of what Paul said elsewhere about justification is faithfully reproduced. Moreover, in Ephesians it is not dependence on the law which is condemned as failing to offer men a basis for right relationship with God, but dependence on ourselves (οὐκ ἐξ ὑμῶν instead of οὐ . . . ἐκ τοῦ νόμου). The meaning is the same, but the change of expression is significant.

The author makes it clear in the epistle that he is addressing himself to Gentiles only. There seem to be no Jewish Christians at all in his thoughts. But Gentiles without any background of synagogue teaching or fellowship with Christians of Jewish origin would find references to 'justification' and the 'law' bewildering. So the author reinterprets these words with predominantly Jewish associations, and substitutes for them words which would convey the same meaning to Gentile readers. If the writer was himself a Gentile, as certain phrases in the epistle suggest, when hints of his own identity peep through the façade of Pauline authorship, he would himself realize the need for such a measure of reinterpretation and be well equipped to provide it.

W. F. Howard, in assessing the relationship of the Fourth Gospel to the primitive tradition, writes that in this Gospel we find an

Body and Blood of Christ, though it may be included by implication. This omission needs to be faced in any exposition of the Epistle.

'explicative emphasis' (CJ, pp. 22–4); that is, what is implicit in the Synoptic Gospels is made explicit in the Fourth. We find a similar emphasis in Ephesians in its relationship with the other Paulines. Stig Hanson (in UCNT, p. 71) makes reference to Gal. iii. 13, and adds: 'This thought is most clearly expressed in Eph. ii. 15.' It appears to be almost a characteristic of Ephesians that in it some aspects of Pauline thought find their clearest expression.

It is this faithfulness to Paul's words, and in some cases an even greater faithfulness to his meaning, that entitles the author to use Paul's name without exposing himself to the accusation of 'forgery'.

(*c*) He takes the opportunity of emphasizing aspects of Paul's teaching which seemed to him particularly *relevant to the needs of his own day*. One such point of emphasis is the Unity of the Church. This truth, while implicit in Paul's own writings, had become of vital importance for the later generation of Christians for whom Ephesians was written. In affirming and making it central the writer exalts a doctrine of the Church which not only helped the churches to become One Church and gave guidance in those early days towards a truly Christian ideal, but also still today stimulates our hopes and kindles our aspirations.

(*d*) He aims also at tactfully introducing not only the teaching of Paul but also his name and reputation to a community among whom, apparently, he was not at all well known, and commending him as a teacher of great understanding and worthy of the utmost reverence (Eph. iii. 1–13).

Such are the conclusions about our author and the purpose with which he wrote which emerge from our investigation. They constitute the skeleton of any theory which is constructed about the author and the circumstances in which he did his work. When, however, we begin to clothe this skeleton with flesh, we find ourselves venturing into the realm of conjecture, and so far it has been our aim to avoid conjecture and limit ourselves to those conclusions which may be legitimately drawn from the evidence available. It may, however, be permissible to attempt a cautious reconstruction of the circumstances which gave rise to this epistle, provided that what is added to these conclusions as outlined above is treated as surmise, and not vested with a degree of probability which it does not merit.

Reconstruction

Somewhere in the province of Asia about the year A.D. 90 there was living a Christian who owed a great personal debt to Paul and felt for him a regard amounting to veneration. He remembered him as a great man of God, an outstanding ambassador of Christ. It grieved him that other Christians, who had not known Paul personally, failed to appreciate his supreme greatness as an exponent of Christ. Even his name was in danger of being forgotten by this later generation (Eph. iii. 2). And yet how badly they needed a leader of his clarity of vision and his deep experience of the Grace of God in Christ! The message of Christ, as proclaimed in the generation after Paul's death, had tended to become but a diluted version of the full, life-transforming Gospel which he had so fearlessly proclaimed. To this disciple, looking back with regretful longing to the days of the first missionary enthusiasm of the Church, Paul seemed to be the apostle who beyond all others had grasped 'the truth as it is in Jesus'. To him it seemed that the Church of his day needed nothing so much as to hear afresh this truth, in the fullness and with the clarity and vigour with which Paul had declared it.

This Christian was of Gentile birth, and he did not forget that Paul had been the outstanding champion of the Gentiles within the Christian movement (Eph. iii. 1–2). The fact that now the majority of Christians were of Gentile birth, and that the old friction between them and Jewish Christians was a forgotten thing of the past, he knew, though others had forgotten it, was largely the achievement of Paul (Eph. iii. 6). This Apostle had been raised up of God in order that the Church might break free from the hampering chains of Judaism by which many had wished to restrain her restless, adventurous spirit of expansion. He before others had sensed that the mysterious purpose of God included Gentiles no less than Jews, and on complete equality with Jews. He more than others possessed that inner sensitiveness of spirit which gave him in special measure 'understanding in the mystery of Christ' (Eph. iii. 4).

Because of his devotion to Paul, this later disciple treasured a copy of Paul's letter to the Colossian Church. It was the only church letter written by Paul to which he had access. It is probable that he himself belonged to the area of Colossae and had some connexion with the church there. At any rate, he had made himself familiar with this writing of his loved master, and had obtained his own copy of it. He had read it so often that he knew it almost by heart.

There was, however, another letter of Paul's which he knew, and knew very intimately. It was not a church letter in the ordinary sense, but a semi-private one, addressed to Philemon. This, too, he had read so often that some of its sentences were almost as familiar to him as the passages from Colossians. His intimate acquaintance with this short note may not seem surprising in view of its close connexion with the letter to Colossians. They were both sent to the same area of Asia Minor, and anyone who knew the one might be expected to know the other. But, on the other hand, it seems to be unusual for this little personal letter to be given any kind of special notice by anyone. Most writers, even those who display considerable knowledge of Paul's letters as a whole, ignore this one. This Christian, however, knew it well and valued it highly. Since this is so exceptional it does perhaps justify us in asking whether it may not be that he had some personal acquaintance with the family to whom it was sent. It may even be that he, because of his known attachment to Paul, had been entrusted with the custody of it.

For a long time, apparently, these two letters were the only writings of Paul which he knew. In time, however, other letters, written to churches in other areas, came to his notice. Greedily he read them. His mind drank in the living truth that spoke from their pages. It seemed as though, once again, the actual voice of the great apostle was sounding in his ears. Here was spiritual treasure in far larger measure than was preserved in the two short letters he already knew. Some of the outstanding passages he read again and again. Striking phrases expressing important truths resounded in his thoughts. The whole gamut of the Christian Gospel seemed to be covered in one letter or another. Moreover, some points of emphasis which he found there were just the ones needed in the churches of his own day: the clear enunciation that it is not in man to be able to achieve or earn his own salvation, which can only be received from the hands of God as a free, undeserved gift; the declaration of the essential unity of the individual churches within the One Church, and of the fundamental truths which bound them into this Unity.

He believed that no one had seen so deeply into the essentials of the Faith as Paul, and here and there, throughout these letters, the exposition of these essentials was to be found. He longed that these should be made easily accessible to all thoughtful readers. It is true that the collected letters, recently brought to his notice, would become more generally known. But would every reader be sure of discerning the heart of the message when, for the most part, it emerged almost accidentally from Paul's treatment of apparently unimportant issues belonging to times long past and places far distant? Of course the two letters already known to him must be given their place alongside the others, but he would add another, one that he himself would prepare from the other letters, in which the essential message of the Gospel would be declared quite apart from any practical difficulties or local problems with which it was so often entangled in the other letters.[1]

So he set himself to draw up a comprehensive summary of Paul's message; but since he wanted it above everything else to be a genuine statement of Paul's message, he used as far as possible phrases from the actual letters as he was able to call them to mind. It was to be Paul who spoke through what he wrote. The only liberty he took was that of occasional interpretation. Where a Pauline word had been derived from Jewish beliefs and practices, and so sounded strange, if not unintelligible, to his readers, he substituted a less technical word to represent the same meaning. Naturally, since he had known Colossians so much longer than the others, that letter predominated in what he wrote, but all the others known to us made their contribution. He must have had before him the Pauline letter collection which we know today.[2]

This Christian must have been in a position of key importance in the Church. Only so could what he wrote have come to be included along with Colossians and Philemon in the collection of Paul's epistles. Indeed, even the inclusion of Philemon seems to demand some special explanation. It was not a natural thing for so personal a letter to be given a place among the church letters.

Judging from this restatement of Pauline faith which he prepared, we are inclined to believe that he had also read Acts and been considerably influenced by it. We cannot say with confidence that it exerted over him the precise influence which Goodspeed suggests. That is in the realm of speculation. It is, however, quite probable that the new interest in Paul, awakened by the story of his missionary work in Acts, suggested that the right moment had arrived to bring Pauline material to people's notice.

It is significant that, though echoes of Lukan phrases from Acts occur several times in Ephesians, the passage in Acts which has most similarities with Ephesians is that which records Paul's fare-

[1] It is probable that a liturgical as well as an editorial interest prompted the writer, in that his work was done not so much for the benefit of private readers as for worshipping congregations. This restatement of Paul's faith and teaching is admirably fitted to be read as part of an act of worship before a company of praying people. The somewhat rhetorical style is perhaps best explained as due to this purpose which Ephesians was designed to fulfil.

[2] A. D. Nock writes: 'What he gives is mainly a Pauline mosaic, and may involve a use of lost Pauline epistles in addition to those which we know' (SP, p. 230). It is, however, unlikely that Pauline letters which were known as late as A.D. 90 would be lost after that date.

well address to the elders from Ephesus who had come to meet him at Miletus. This is not surprising, because a man of Colossae, or of that neighbourhood, who had risen in church circles to a position so important that he was able to influence the form in which the Pauline letters were circulated in that province must have had close connexions also with Ephesus, the chief church of that area. Therefore that particular speech of Paul's in Acts would be of peculiar interest to him, and would be given special attention.

This raises the question of the people to whom this epistle which later became known as 'Ephesians' was originally addressed. Because of the author's association with Ephesus, we may assume that his first readers would be the Christians of the area of which Ephesus was the head. It is true that it was issued without any name attached to it. Our earliest manuscripts (including the Chester-Beatty papyrus) give the title 'To the Ephesians', but omit the name of any church in the opening greeting. This is apparently how Tertullian knew the epistle. Marcion must have known it before even the title was added, because, by an ingenious guess, he identified it with the unknown letter associated with the church of Laodicea in Col. iv. 16. Once the absence of an address was felt to be awkward, its early association with Ephesus would lead to its present title being added, and once the title had been accepted, it was an easy step to insert the name of the church in the opening greeting, on the pattern of the other epistles. Though, therefore, there is reason to believe that Pauline authorship, in the strict sense of the word, may have to be relinquished, it is probable that the traditional address of the epistle is approximately correct, and that it was originally written primarily for the Christians in the province of which Ephesus was the chief city.

Our reconstruction has suggested how Ephesians was written, and how it came to have an undisputed place in the earliest known form of the Pauline Corpus. Goodspeed has proposed a more detailed and imaginative explanation, but in the present state of our knowledge we shall be wise to proceed with caution.[1] But whatever explanation is the correct one, something must be suggested to

[1] It will be clear that our reconstruction has much in common with Goodspeed's theory. Any attempt, however, to form a considered estimate of his account of the way the Pauline Corpus was first brought together, and of the special place ascribed to Ephesians in it, lies beyond the scope of this present book. Those who wish to examine the matter further should consult Goodspeed's *Introduction to the New Testament*, chapter xiii. J. Knox, also, in his book on *Marcion and the New Testament* deals with the Pauline Corpus in chapter iii and corroborates the theory which Goodspeed has put forward.

account adequately for the early acceptance of Ephesians within the Pauline Corpus.

Concerning the identity of the author we are probably wise to be content to say that we do not know who he was. The introduction of the name of Tychicus, however, at Eph. vi. 21–2 and the unusually long verbatim reproduction of words from Colossians (iv. 7–8) require some explanation. Moffatt is content to account for them in this way: 'The solitary reference to concrete conditions (vi. 21–22) is adapted from Colossians, in order to lend "vraisemblance" to the writing' (ILNT, p. 393). It is doubtful if this can be considered adequate. Why should this verse alone be included? Why not, instead of it, or in addition, some of the greetings which follow in Col. iv. 10–18? If *vraisemblance* is the only motive, why does the quotation from Colossians stop short at the name of Onesimus in Col. iv. 9? W. L. Knox believes that this reference to Tychicus may be a thinly veiled hint at the identity of the author, and that it is Tychicus to whom we owe the composition of this epistle. This is not impossible, though the omission of the name of Onesimus, and also of the word σύνδουλος as descriptive of Tychicus, when apart from that omission all the rest of the long sentence is reproduced verbatim, suggests that it is no more likely than Goodspeed's guess that the author was Onesimus.

We cannot say who is the author, but this special mention of Tychicus seems to require some explanation more convincing than Moffatt's. May it not be that at the time when the epistle was written Tychicus was still living as an old man in the neighbourhood of Ephesus, and was known both to the author and to the Christians of that area; that the proposal to write the epistle in Paul's name was submitted to his judgement and gained his consent, and that his approval of the finished work as a worthy presentation of Paul's message was indicated by the inclusion of Paul's earlier reference to him as 'a faithful minister', well able to represent Paul? If so, then this epistle comes to us as a kind of authorized reaffirmation of the Pauline message.

Even if this epistle must be viewed as a pseudonymous work, it is not unworthy to bear the name of Paul. Not only is it built up of largely Pauline materials, but it faithfully represents the Pauline message, edited a little to make it immediately intelligible and applicable to the time for which it was prepared, but so true to the spirit of Paul and his insight into the Gospel that it has deservedly been regarded as the quintessence of Paulinism. If we may not, in strict accuracy, call it the Epistle of Paul, we might term it 'The Gospel according to Paul', because in it all the most important elements in Paul's interpretation of the Christian message find their proper place, and some receive their clearest and most memorable expression.

XXI

THE BEARING OF AUTHORSHIP ON THE VALUE OF THE EPISTLE

We have seen that Ephesians is in many ways a thoroughly Pauline composition. It reproduces Paul's phrases and thoughts, not mechanically or unimaginatively, but with insight and understanding. It is a faithful presentation of the Gospel according to Paul the Apostle. But apparently it was not actually the work of his own hand nor the direct product of his own mind.

What is the effect of such a conclusion on our view of the value of the epistle? Does it divest it of that greatness which has been generally accorded to it? If so, does it mean that the New Testament itself has in some measure been impoverished? Or may we claim that the epistle, even without the authority of Paul's name, has lost none of its real value? Is it even possible that its value may have been enhanced, and that the change has in fact produced more gains than losses?

Of one thing we may be sure: if our conclusion is the correct one, we need not fear its consequences, for the truth, however unpalatable it may be at the first taste, or however disturbing to treasured opinions, is really only gain. Robert Rainy, on the occasion when George Adam Smith was charged with heterodoxy, said: 'When I see evidence for facts, they are God's facts, and they will only be my help in the end, if I can duly make use of them' (P. C. Simpson, *Life of Rainy*, ii, p. 269).

That must be our approach. If the evidence points to a post-Pauline date for Ephesians, no matter how unwelcome that verdict may be in the first place it must be humbly accepted in the confidence that if such is the truth of the matter it will indeed be our 'help in the end'. But can we see at this present moment any way in which such a verdict may prove an actual gain rather than a serious loss?

It must be freely admitted that the abandonment of the Pauline authorship of Ephesians would for many be accompanied by an initial sense of grievous loss. So it was when scholars provided demonstrable proof that the Epistle to the Hebrews could no longer be attributed to Paul. But the loss proved to be only apparent, and further consideration has led us to view it as substantial gain. In consequence we see that the Christian Faith is established on an even broader base than we had thought, and for that reason is the more securely founded. Its truth is less dependent on the authority of one man, outstandingly great though that one man is. The presence of non-Pauline Hebrews in the New Testament has proved that certain points of emphasis, which anti-Pauline critics were disposed to reject as a peculiar and false interpretation of the Christian Faith, a 'misleading Paulinism' as they called it, are not at all the private preserve of Paul but part of the rich heritage of the whole Church.

So too when the three Pastoral Epistles had to be acknowledged as, in large part at any rate, a post-Pauline production, the conclusion was associated with an initial sense of loss. But in this instance too, further consideration has led us to view it as an actual gain. It has given us a clearer discernment of Paul's distinctive thought. We have no longer to attempt to reconcile all the pedestrian and sometimes platitudinous sentiments of the Pastorals with the vivacious and brilliant thoughts of Paul. Moreover, it enables us to find in the Pastorals valuable evidence for the condition of the Church at the end of the first century. It shows us the Church leaders accommodating the pure gold of the Gospel as Paul offers it to men to the practical needs of the developing Church and to the human frailty of the men and women within it.

In the case of Ephesians, may it not also be that what appears as an initial loss may prove to be an ultimate gain? May there not be compensating gains which will more than counterbalance the losses? We can already discern in what direction some of these gains may lie.

1. Just as the removal of the Pastorals from the genuine Pauline writings led to a more precise delineation of Paul's distinctive thought, so in this case we should expect a further clarification of the exact pattern of Pauline theology. Certain features which have hitherto had to be included, although incompatible with the rest, would no longer need to be forced into a system to which they do not belong. In this way the scheme of Pauline thought would be relieved of some things which had proved very hard for it to assimilate.

2. At the same time we should expect, even more confidently, to find a measure of gain along the same general lines as gain was felt to accrue when Hebrews was isolated from the Pauline Corpus. It would mean that a further witness had been found, within the canon of the New Testament, to the essential truth of the Gospel as Paul proclaimed it, and yet sufficiently independent of Paul to

represent a new mind of deep spiritual insight adding its authority to the main points of the Gospel message as presented in Paul's epistles, for, as C. H. Dodd puts it, the author of Ephesians, if he is to be regarded as other than Paul, is 'an original and powerful thinker' (*Ab. Com.*, p. 1224).

There is no doubt that Marcion had a deep appreciation of the truth of Paul's interpretation of the Christian Faith, though he fell into the error, common enough among new and enthusiastic converts, of disparaging the old and familiar in comparison with the new instead of gratefully regarding it, as Paul did, as 'a tutor to bring us to Christ'. We have no criticism to offer of Marcion's very restricted canon of the New Testament, except that it was not based broadly enough, and did not adequately acknowledge our debt of gratitude to the antecedents of Christianity. The whole of his canon is included in ours, and is a highly valued part of it. But the Third Gospel and the Pauline epistles, precious though they are, constitute by themselves a more assailable authority than the much broader canon of the Church. The testimony of two witnesses has been greatly strengthened by the addition of many others, substantially independent of each other, and yet confirming the same central truths.

From a similar point of view it may be argued that the discovery within the accepted canon of the Church of another authoritative voice, which, while echoing much that is already familiar through the Pauline epistles, does so with a resolute note of personal confirmation, is gain rather than loss because the truth of the Gospel is seen to rest on the testimony of one further independent witness, and the basis of authority is found to be in that measure broader and therefore stronger.

3. In the third place, if Ephesians has to be regarded as a non-Pauline epistle, this conclusion may lead to a further gain by compelling us to re-think and restate what we believe about the inspiration and authority of the Bible, and especially to discover how that authority is constituted and on what it is based. Even those who are most vividly aware of the presence of that authority find themselves at a loss to describe exactly what is its source.

In the formation of the canon an apostolic name was the password which gained entry, though some have argued that the real test was faithfulness to apostolic doctrine, and that an apostolic name was readily accorded to an early writing which reliably set forth that doctrine. The apostolic name, however, has continued to be associated with authority, so that the forfeiture of that name raises acutely the right of such a book to its place in the canon and to our veneration as Scripture.

No doubt there is a measure of truth in this reverence for personalities, but we are convinced that it is a misleading approach to the problem. Certainly a master is more likely to produce a great picture than an unknown artist. It does not follow, however, that every picture by the recognized master is worthy of the highest acclamation, nor, on the other hand, is every work by an unknown artist to be denied anything better than a second-rate status. The greatness of the picture, rightly assessed, does not lie in the personality or fame of the painter but in the picture itself. So it is with the authority of Scripture. As a general rule what an apostle wrote is more likely to be the truth than a piece of writing with no claim to apostolic origin. But this is a rule which has many exceptions. The authority of any single writing lies, not in its author, but in the measure of truth to be found in it, and the extent to which it is able to open the minds of its readers to the apprehension of that truth, so that in its light they see light.

The recent publication of several books on this very subject shows that men's minds are exercised by it and are aware of the need of some restatement. If Ephesians is to be regarded as bereft of its apostolic authorship, it may help to bring to a focus some of the crucial issues. For it is universally agreed that in Ephesians we have one of the great books of the New Testament. It has exercised, and rightly exercised, a very great influence in the Christian Church. It has been the means of opening men's minds to the truth about God, and providing them with words by which the truths they have apprehended may be adequately expressed. It is an inspired book, and a book which has wielded and still wields weighty authority. But wherein does this authority lie, if there is no apostolic name to sustain it? It may be that for these very reasons Ephesians will provide a kind of test case by which any restatement of the theory of inspiration and authority may be put to the proof.

4. Fourthly, if Ephesians is to be dated about A.D. 90, it occupies a position of critical importance in the history of the proclamation of the Gospel.

This 'original and powerful thinker' who is its author is one who stands in the direct line of spiritual succession from Paul. Paul in his day had seen to the very heart of the Gospel. Others had seen part of the truth, or had seen it less clearly. To him it had been given to grasp the essential message of the Grace of our Lord Jesus Christ with a clarity and depth of understanding given to very few others.

He never wearied in his task of proclaiming it, and defending it against all who wished to reduce or obscure its essential originality or who tried to make its majestic grandeur less humiliating to human pride. Both the truth of the Gospel and Paul, its champion, had many enemies, not only outside the Church, but within it as well. Even among those who were Church leaders there were some who felt that in the achievement of salvation more emphasis than Paul was accustomed to allow should be placed upon human effort and less on the Divine initiative. This had been part of the contention of the Judaizers, who wished the Gospel of Christ to be a supplement to Judaism and not a substitute for it. That particular perversion of the Gospel had been effectively countered by Paul, but the mentality from which it had derived its support still persisted. Had it been allowed to prevail, the essential note of the Gospel might have been smothered under humanistic moralizings. Its emphasis was: 'Be obedient to the laws of God, and thereby you will attain to salvation.' Salvation was represented as a reward for good conduct.

Paul had withstood with might and main this tendency to make salvation dependent on human achievement, because he well knew the weariness and futility of seeking salvation in that way. He had insisted with all the emphasis in his power that salvation was the free gift of God through Christ, the work of the Grace of God, appropriated by an act of faith, and not achieved by human effort or 'good works'.

In the generation that followed Paul we find this Pauline emphasis losing ground. Paul's words are reproduced, but often with a hollow sound, as though the writers are honouring Paul with their lips, but their hearts are far from him. In the Pastoral Epistles, for instance, except so far as a few Pauline phrases are somewhat mechanically repeated, this Pauline emphasis on grace and faith (in the true Pauline sense) has largely disappeared. The same is true of 1 Clement. Anderson Scott writes of that epistle: ' "Sin", "faith", in the sense which Paul gives to the word, and "reconciliation" fall into the background.' The death of Christ has ceased to be central, and 'the Holy Spirit has lost all its vitalising force. . . . It is hard to resist the conclusion that either Clement did not know the Pauline Gospel as a "divine force unto salvation" or that he had rejected it' (RG, pp. 23–4). Clement actually makes the affirmation: 'We are saved by works and not by words', and that may be accepted as a summary of his attitude. Paul emphasized the importance of Christian conduct, and he put no value on mere words, but he could never have said that we are saved by works, not even in protest against an overvaluation of mere words. Nor would anyone who understood Paul's message have allowed himself to use that misleading sentence. It denies an elemental truth which Paul had been prepared to champion against all comers and at any cost.

This tendency away from the Gospel emphasis is not peculiar to the Pastorals and 1 Clement. It appears to be indicative of the general direction of Christian thought at that time. Anderson Scott attributes this in part to the fact that the only Scriptures available at that time for nourishing the faith of Christian people were the Scriptures of the Old Testament, and in them the spirit of legalism often obscures the emphasis on grace. Whatever the explanation, there is little doubt of the fact. The Gospel of the free grace of God, offered to man not on the grounds of his worthiness but of his need, as proclaimed by our Lord in the parables of the Workers in the Vineyard and of the Pharisee and the Publican, and as made central in Paul's preaching, was being replaced by a moralistic interpretation of salvation. We no longer hear of the futility of man's humanistic pretensions. There is no longer scorn of his imagined self-sufficiency. Rather we find an assumption that man can fit himself for salvation, and even do more than is strictly necessary on his own account. Hermas, for instance, writes: 'If thou doest any good over and above the commandment of God, thou shalt obtain greater glory for thyself.' This is strange doctrine for a follower of One who said: 'When ye shall have done all the things that are commanded you, say: "We are unprofitable servants."' And it is opposite to what Paul had declared when he said that God's methods were such 'that no flesh should glory before God' (1 Cor. i. 29).

The Didache too writes: 'Of whatsoever thou hast gained by thy hands, thou shalt give a ransom for thy sins.' This is sadly different from the ransom which Jesus Himself offered. Ignatius alone among the sub-apostolic writers is an honourable exception to this tendency back towards legalism, a tendency which has not failed to exert its influence even within the New Testament canon. The vast majority of the New Testament writers, however, are splendidly true to the Gospel and its emphasis on Grace, but who can say in what large degree they were enlightened by the published letters of Paul? But the first to be so decisively influenced and to become the medium through which Paul, though dead, could still speak his revivifying message to others was the man who wrote this inspired and inspiring restatement of the Pauline interpretation of the Gospel. If we read his utterances merely against the background of Paul's letters, there may be little of special note in them; but if we read them against the background of the spirit of that age, we catch a glimpse of the crucial part which this epistle played at a time when the Christian Church was apparently wavering indecisively between the unbelievable and dangerous splendour of the Gospel, and the more credible and safer mediocrity of 1 Clement and Hermas and the Didache.

Anderson Scott writes of this period: 'The need for reformation which began before the end of the first century was in the first instance a need . . . for the elimination of specifically Jewish principles which had perverted the truth of the Gospel, for the restoration to its due place of the Pauline doctrine of salvation by grace through faith' (RG, p. 38). It was the deliberate purpose of the author of Ephesians to supply that need. He had a clear insight into the deeper meaning of the Gospel, and an alarmed awareness of the general unfaithfulness to its message which was infecting the Church. His own emphatic restatement of Pauline doctrine was a mighty blow for the truth. In his epistle we find that 'grace' and 'faith' are made central and become the sole condition of salvation. Indeed his particular declaration of this aspect of the truth has been accepted by the Christian Church as the authentic note of the Gospel, even in preference to the actual words of Paul (Eph. ii. 1–10, especially 8–10). Under what a heavy weight of misunderstanding might not the true message of the Gospel have been hidden had not this spiritually minded man stood forward to champion the truth in the particular way he did, and at the particular time he did!

If Ephesians is interpreted in this way, we see it as a great bulwark for the truth in an age when error was gaining ground, a bulwark behind which the forces of truth were able to rally before moving out into effective counter-attack. Such a view of the epistle may awaken within us an even deeper appreciation of its value than when it held a somewhat insecure place among the genuinely Pauline writings.

The abandonment of a Pauline origin for Ephesians is not therefore all loss. There are considerable compensating gains, which may even be claimed to enhance its value. These gains may, in conclusion, be briefly summarized as follows:

1. It has value for New Testament Theology. Not only does it raise in a crucial form the question of the basis of the authority of the Bible, but it also enables scholars to determine more pre-

cisely the exact scope and content of Paul's thought and doctrine.

2. It has value for New Testament History, since it throws a ray of light on an obscure period. The story of the Christian Church between A.D. 70 and 100 is shrouded in darkness. In Ephesians, however, we can in some measure sense the atmosphere of that time. It enables us to gauge the issues with which the Church was then confronted, and presents us with one decisive contribution to the victory of truth over falsehood, made at a time when error seemed to be in the ascendant.
3. It has value for the devotional life of individual Christians and for the Church as a whole. For its removal from the Pauline Corpus gives us a more clear-cut understanding of Paul's message, without detracting in the slightest degree from the greatness of Paul. His authority remains undiminished, and at the same time we find ourselves in possession of an additional witness to the truth of which Paul had been a vigorous and clear-minded champion. In the author of Ephesians there stands before us one further witness to what he himself so aptly calls 'the truth as it is in Jesus'. His magnificent affirmation of that truth brings further confirmation to our faith. For 'at the mouth of two witnesses or three shall every word be established'. And he is a most persuasive witness and advocate of that 'faith which was once for all delivered to the saints'.

APPENDIX I

THE TEXT OF EPHESIANS

(IN COLUMN 3)

with parallel passages from

(*a*) COLOSSIANS (IN COLUMN 4)
(*b*) THE 'OTHER EIGHT' PAULINE EPISTLES (IN COLUMN 2)
(*c*) I PETER (IN COLUMN I)

THE parallels between Ephesians and Colossians are indicated by thick lines. Where the correspondence is so close as to represent a verbatim similarity, the corresponding words are undermarked with a very thick line (▬▬▬); where the correspondence is less exact, but still recognizable, the words are undermarked with a less thick line (———). Other words, where the similarity is less distinct, are marked by a thick dotted line (··········). Occasionally, also, similarities in idea are recorded, but without any underlining. For calculation purposes, however, this last group and the words undermarked with a dotted line are ignored, and only those undermarked with continuous lines are counted.

Similarly the parallels between Ephesians and the 'other eight' Pauline epistles are also marked, but in this case with thin double (═══), thin single (———), or dotted (·········) lines; and those between Ephesians and 1 Peter are indicated by wavy (〰〰) lines for close correspondence, and oblique broken lines (\\\\\\\\\\\\) for a slighter degree of similarity.

1 Peter.	
	1 Cor. i. 1–2. Παῦλος κλητὸς ἀπόστολος Χριστοῦ Ἰησοῦ διὰ θελήματος θεοῦ καὶ Σωσθένης ὁ ἀδελφὸς τῇ ἐκκλησίᾳ τοῦ θεοῦ τῇ οὔσῃ ἐν Κορίνθῳ, ἡγιασμένοις ἐν Χριστῷ Ἰησοῦ, κλητοῖς ἁγίοις. 2 Cor. i. 1–2. Παῦλος πἀόστολος Χριστοῦ Ἰησοῦ διὰ θελήματος θεοῦ καὶ Τιμόθεος ὁ ἀδελφὸς τῇ ἐκκλησίᾳ τοῦ θεοῦ τῇ οὔσῃ ἐν Κορίνθῳ σὺν τοῖς ἁγίοις πᾶσιν τοῖς οὖσιν ἐν ὅλῃ τῇ Ἀχαΐᾳ.
i. 3. εὐλογητὸς ὁ θεὸς καὶ πατὴρ τοῦ κυρίου ἡμῶν Ἰησοῦ Χριστοῦ, ὁ κατὰ τὸ πολὺ αὐτοῦ ἔλεος ἀναγεννήσας ἡμᾶς εἰς ἐλπίδα . . .	Rom. i. 7. 1 Cor. i. 3. 2 Cor. i. 2. 2 Thess. i. 2. } χάρις ὑμῖν καὶ εἰρήνη ἀπὸ θεοῦ πατρὸς ἡμῶν καὶ κυρίου Ἰησοῦ Χριστοῦ. 2 Cor. i. 3. εὐλογητὸς ὁ θεὸς καὶ πατὴρ τοῦ κυρίου ἡμῶν Ἰησοῦ Χριστοῦ . . . ὁ παρακαλῶν . . . Rom. viii. 29. οὓς προέγνω, καὶ προώρισεν συμμόρφους τῆς εἰκόνος τοῦ υἱοῦ εἰς τὸ εἶναι αὐτὸν πρωτότοκον ἐν πολλοῖς ἀδελφοῖς. Rom. viii. 15. ἐλάβετε πνεῦμα υἱοθεσίας.
i. 20. Χριστοῦ, προεγνωσμένου μὲν πρὸ καταβολῆς κόσμου.	Rom. viii. 23. υἱοθεσίαν ἀπεκδεχόμενοι, τὴν ἀπολύτρωσιν τοῦ σώματος ἡμῶν. Rom. iii. 24–6. δικαιούμενοι δωρεὰν τῇ αὐτοῦ χάριτι διὰ τῆς ἀπολυτρώσεως τῆς ἐν Χριστῷ Ἰησοῦ· ὃν προέθετο ὁ θεὸς ἱλαστήριον διὰ πίστεως ἐν τῷ αὐτοῦ αἵματι, εἰς ἔνδειξιν τῆς δικαιοσύνης αὐτοῦ διὰ τὴν πάρεσιν τῶν προγεγονότων ἁμαρτημάτων ἐν τῇ ἀνοχῇ τοῦ θεοῦ. Phil. i. 11. εἰς δόξαν καὶ ἔπαινον θεοῦ. Rom. v. 9. δικαιωθέντες νῦν ἐν τῷ αἵματι αὐτοῦ. Rom. ii. 4. ἢ τοῦ πλούτου τῆς χρηστότητος αὐτοῦ . . . καταφρονεῖς;

Ephesians i. 1–8.	Colossians.
i. 1 Παῦλος ἀπόστολος Χριστοῦ Ἰησοῦ διὰ θελήματος θεοῦ τοῖς ἁγίοις τοῖς οὖσιν [ἐν Ἐφέσῳ] καὶ 2 πιστοῖς ἐν Χριστῷ Ἰησοῦ· χάρις ὑμῖν καὶ εἰρήνη ἀπὸ θεοῦ πατρὸς ἡμῶν καὶ κυρίου Ἰησοῦ Χριστοῦ.	i. 1–2. Παῦλος ἀπόστολος Χριστοῦ Ἰησοῦ διὰ θελήματος θεοῦ καὶ Τιμόθεος ὁ ἀδελφὸς τοῖς ἐν Κολοσ- σαῖς ἁγίοις καὶ πιστοῖς ἀδελφοῖς ἐν Χριστῷ· χάρις ὑμῖν καὶ εἰρήνη ἀπὸ θεοῦ πατρὸς ἡμῶν.
3 εὐλογητὸς ὁ θεὸς καὶ πατὴρ τοῦ κυρίου ἡμῶν Ἰησοῦ Χριστοῦ, ὁ εὐλογήσας ἡμᾶς ἐν πάσῃ εὐλογίᾳ πνευματικῇ ἐν τοῖς ἐπουρανίοις ἐν	i. 4. ἐν Χριστῷ Ἰησοῦ. iii. 12. ὡς ἐκλεκτοὶ τοῦ θεοῦ ἅγιοι καὶ ἠγαπημένοι.
4 Χριστῷ, καθὼς ἐξελέξατο ἡμᾶς ἐν αὐτῷ πρὸ καταβολῆς κόσμου, εἶναι ἡμᾶς ἁγίους καὶ ἀμώμους 5 κατενώπιον αὐτοῦ, ἐν ἀγάπῃ προ-	i. 22. παραστῆσαι ὑμᾶς ἁγίους καὶ ἀμώμους καὶ ἀνεγκλήτους κατενώ- πιον αὐτοῦ.
ορίσας ἡμᾶς εἰς υἱοθεσίαν διὰ Ἰησοῦ Χριστοῦ εἰς αὐτόν, κατὰ τὴν εὐδοκίαν τοῦ θελήματος αὐ- 6 τοῦ, εἰς ἔπαινον δόξης τῆς χάριτος αὐτοῦ ἧς ἐχαρίτωσεν ἡμᾶς ἐν τῷ 7 ἠγαπημένῳ, ἐν ᾧ ἔχομεν τὴν ἀπολύτρωσιν διὰ τοῦ αἵματος	i. 13. μετέστησεν εἰς τὴν βασιλείαν τοῦ υἱοῦ τῆς ἀγάπης αὐτοῦ, ἐν ᾧ ἔχομεν τὴν ἀπολύτρωσιν, τὴν ἄφ- εσιν τῶν ἁμαρτιῶν. i. 20. εἰρηνοποιήσας διὰ τοῦ αἵματος τοῦ σταυροῦ αὐτοῦ.
αὐτοῦ, τὴν ἄφεσιν τῶν παρα- πτωμάτων, κατὰ τὸ πλοῦτος τῆς 8 χάριτος αὐτοῦ, ἧς ἐπερίσσευσεν	i. 27. τί τὸ πλοῦτος τῆς δόξης τοῦ μυστηρίου τούτου.

1 Peter.	
	Rom. v. 15. ἡ χάρις τοῦ θεοῦ . . . εἰς τοὺς πολλοὺς ἐπερίσσευσεν.
	Rom. xvi. 25. κατὰ ἀποκάλυψιν μυστηρίου χρόνοις αἰωνίοις σεσιγημένου, φανερωθέντος δὲ νῦν . . . εἰς πάντα τὰ ἔθνη γνωρισθέντος.
	Gal. iv. 4. ὅτε δὲ ἦλθεν τὸ πλήρωμα τοῦ χρόνου.
	Rom. viii. 28. τοῖς κατὰ πρόθεσιν κλητοῖς οὖσιν . . . προώρισεν.
	1 Cor. xii. 6. ὁ δὲ αὐτὸς θεὸς ὁ ἐνεργῶν τὰ πάντα ἐν πᾶσιν.
	Phil. i. 11. εἰς δόξαν καὶ ἔπαινον θεοῦ.
i. 22–5. τὰς ψυχὰς ὑμῶν ἡγνικότες ἐν τῇ ὑπακοῇ τῆς ἀληθείας εἰς φιλαδελφίαν ἀνυπόκριτον . . . ἀναγεγεννημένοι οὐκ ἐκ σπορᾶς φθαρτῆς ἀλλὰ ἀφθάρτου διὰ λόγου ζῶντος θεοῦ καὶ μένοντος διότι . . . τὸ δὲ ῥῆμα κυρίου μένει εἰς τὸν αἰῶνα. τοῦτο δέ ἐστιν τὸ ῥῆμα τὸ εὐαγγελισθὲν εἰς ὑμᾶς.	2 Cor. vi. 7. ἐν λόγῳ ἀληθείας.
	Rom. i. 16. τὸ εὐαγγέλιον· δύναμις γὰρ θεοῦ ἐστὶν εἰς σωτηρίαν παντὶ τῷ πιστεύοντι.
	Gal. iii. 2. τὸ πνεῦμα ἐλάβετε . . . ἐξ ἀκοῆς πίστεως.
	2 Cor. i. 22. ὁ . . . θεός, ὁ καὶ σφραγισάμενος ἡμᾶς καὶ δοὺς τὸν ἀρραβῶνα τοῦ πνεύματος ταῖς καρδίαις ἡμῶν.
	2 Cor. v. 5. ὁ . . . θεὸς ὁ δοὺς ἡμῖν τὸν ἀρραβῶνα ἐν τοῦ πνεύματος.
	Gal. iii. 14. ἵνα τὴν ἐπαγγελίαν τοῦ πνεύματος λάβωμεν διὰ τῆς πίστεως.
ii. 9. λαὸς εἰς περιποίησιν ὅπως τὰς ἀρετὰς ἐξαγγείλητε . . .	Rom. viii. 16. αὐτὸ τὸ πνεῦμα συνμαρτυρεῖ τῷ πνεύματι ἡμῶν ὅτι ἐσμὲν τέκνα θεοῦ· εἰ δὲ τέκνα, καὶ κληρονόμοι.
	Philem. 4–6. εὐχαριστῶ τῷ θεῷ μου πάντοτε μνείαν σου ποιούμενος ἐπὶ τῶν προσευχῶν μου, ἀκούων σου τὴν ἀγάπην καὶ τὴν πίστιν ἣν ἔχεις πρὸς τὸν κύριον Ἰησοῦν καὶ εἰς πάντας τοὺς ἁγίους, ὅπως ἡ κοινωνία τῆς πίστεώς σου ἐνεργὴς γένηται ἐν ἐπιγνώσει παντὸς ἀγαθοῦ.

Ephesians i. 8–16.	Colossians.
εἰς ἡμᾶς ἐν πάσῃ σοφίᾳ καὶ 9 φρονήσει γνωρίσας ἡμῖν τὸ μυ- στήριον τοῦ θελήματος αὐτοῦ,	iii. 16 ἐν ὑμῖν πλουσίως, ἐν πάσῃ σοφίᾳ. i. 9. ἐν πάσῃ σοφίᾳ καὶ συνέσει πνευματικῇ.
κατὰ τὴν εὐδοκίαν αὐτοῦ, ἣν 10 προέθετο ἐν αὐτῷ εἰς οἰκονομίαν τοῦ πληρώματος τῶν καιρῶν,	i. 27. ἠθέλησεν ὁ θεὸς γνωρίσαι τί τὸ πλοῦτος τῆς δόξης τοῦ μυστηρίου. i. 25. κατὰ τὴν οἰκονομίαν τοῦ θεοῦ . . . πληρῶσαι τὸν λόγον τοῦ θεοῦ.
ἀνακεφαλαιώσασθαι τὰ πάντα ἐν τῷ Χριστῷ, τὰ ἐπὶ τοῖς οὐρανοῖς 11 καὶ τὰ ἐπὶ τῆς γῆς· ἐν αὐτῷ, ἐν ᾧ	i. 16. ἐκτίσθη τὰ πάντα ἐν τοῖς οὐρανοῖς καὶ ἐπὶ τῆς γῆς. i. 20. καὶ δι' αὐτοῦ ἀποκαταλλάξαι τὰ πάντα εἰς αὐτὸν . . . εἴτε τὰ ἐπὶ τῆς γῆς εἴτε τὰ ἐν τοῖς οὐρανοῖς.
καὶ ἐκληρώθημεν προορισθέντες κατὰ πρόθεσιν τοῦ τὰ πάντα ἐνεργοῦντος κατὰ τὴν βουλὴν τοῦ 12 θελήματος αὐτοῦ, εἰς τὸ εἶναι ἡμᾶς εἰς ἔπαινον δόξης αὐτοῦ τοὺς προηλπικότας ἐν τῷ Χριστῷ·	i. 12. τὴν μερίδα τοῦ κλήρου τῶν ἁγίων. i. 5. προηκούσατε ἐν τῷ λόγῳ τῆς ἀληθείας τοῦ εὐαγγελίου.
13 ἐν ᾧ καὶ ὑμεῖς, ἀκούσαντες τὸν λόγον τῆς ἀληθείας, τὸ εὐαγγέλιον τῆς σωτηρίας ὑμῶν, ἐν ᾧ καὶ πιστεύσαντες ἐσφραγίσθητε τῷ πνεύματι τῆς ἐπαγγελίας τῷ 14 ἁγίῳ, ὅς ἐστιν ἀρραβὼν τῆς κληρονομίας ἡμῶν εἰς ἀπολύτρω- σιν τῆς περιποιήσεως, εἰς ἔπαινον τῆς δόξης αὐτοῦ.	i. 4. ἀκούσαντες τὴν πίστιν ὑμῶν ἐν Χριστῷ Ἰησοῦ καὶ τὴν ἀγάπην ἣν ἔχετε εἰς πάντας τοὺς ἁγίους.
15 διὰ τοῦτο κἀγώ, ἀκούσας τὴν καθ' ὑμᾶς πίστιν ἐν τῷ κυρίῳ Ἰησοῦ καὶ τὴν ἀγάπην τὴν εἰς 16 πάντας τοὺς ἁγίους, οὐ παύομαι	i. 9. διὰ τοῦτο καὶ ἡμεῖς, ἀφ' ἧς ἡμέρας ἠκούσαμεν, οὐ παυόμεθα ὑπὲρ ὑμῶν προσευχόμενοι καὶ αἰτούμενοι ἵνα πληρωθῆτε τὴν

1 Peter.	
	Rom. i. 8–10. πρῶτον μὲν εὐχαριστῶ τῷ θεῷ μου διὰ Ἰησοῦ Χριστοῦ περὶ πάντων ὑμῶν, ὅτι ἡ πίστις ὑμῶν καταγγέλλεται ἐν ὅλῳ τῷ κόσμῳ . . . μνείαν ὑμῶν ποιοῦμαι πάντοτε ἐπὶ τῶν προσευχῶν μου, δεόμενος . . .
	1 Thess. i. 2. εὐχαριστοῦμεν τῷ θεῷ πάντοτε περὶ πάντων ὑμῶν μνείαν ποιούμενοι ἐπὶ τῶν προσευχῶν ἡμῶν.
	2 Cor. xi. 31. ὁ θεὸς καὶ πατὴρ τοῦ κυρίου Ἰησοῦ οἶδεν.
i. 3–5. . . . εἰς ἐλπίδα ζῶσαν (Eph. i. 20) δι' ἀναστάσεως Ἰησοῦ Χριστοῦ ἐκ νεκρῶν, εἰς κληρονομίαν ἄφθαρτον καὶ ἀμίαντον καὶ ἀμάραντον, τετηρημένην ἐν οὐρανοῖς εἰς ὑμᾶς τοὺς ἐν (Eph. i. 19) δυνάμει θεοῦ φρουρουμένους διὰ πίστεως εἰς σωτηρίαν . . .	Rom. i. 21. καὶ ἐσκοτίσθη ἡ ἀσύνετος αὐτῶν καρδία. Rom. ix. 23. ἵνα γνωρίσῃ τὸν πλοῦτον τῆς δόξης αὐτοῦ. Rom. iii. 22. . . . εἰς πάντας τοὺς πιστεύοντας (cf. also 1 Cor. i. 21, 1 Thess. i. 7). Phil. iii. 21. κατὰ τὴν ἐνέργειαν (cf. 2 Thess. ii. 9). 2 Cor. xiii. 4. . . . ζήσομεν σὺν αὐτῷ ἐκ δυνάμεως θεοῦ εἰς ὑμᾶς.
iii. 21–2. . . . δι' ἀναστάσεως Ἰησοῦ Χριστοῦ, ὅς ἐστιν ἐν δεξιᾷ θεοῦ, πορευθεὶς εἰς οὐρανόν, ὑποταγέντων αὐτῷ ἀγγέλων καὶ ἐξουσιῶν καὶ δυνάμεων.	Rom. viii. 34. Χριστὸς Ἰησοῦς ὁ ἀποθανών, μᾶλλον δὲ ἐγερθείς, ὅς ἐστιν ἐν δεξιᾷ τοῦ θεοῦ. Rom. viii. 11. τὸ πνεῦμα τοῦ ἐγείραντος τὸν Ἰησοῦν ἐκ νεκρῶν. Phil. ii. 9–10. διὸ καὶ ὁ θεὸς αὐτὸν ὑπερύψωσεν καὶ ἐχαρίσατο αὐτῷ τὸ ὄνομα τὸ ὑπὲρ πᾶν ὄνομα, ἵνα ἐν τῷ ὀνόματι Ἰησοῦ πᾶν γόνυ κάμψῃ ἐπουρανίων καὶ ἐπιγείων καὶ καταχθονίων. Rom. viii. 38. οὔτε ἄγγελοι οὔτε ἀρχαὶ οὔτε ἐνεστῶτα οὔτε μέλλοντα οὔτε δυνάμεις. 1 Cor. xv. 24. ὅταν καταργήσῃ πᾶσαν ἀρχὴν καὶ πᾶσαν ἐξουσίαν καὶ δύναμιν.

Ephesians i. 16–22.

εὐχαριστῶν ὑπὲρ ὑμῶν μνείαν
ποιούμενος ἐπὶ τῶν προσευχῶν
17 μου, ἵνα ὁ θεὸς τοῦ κυρίου ἡμῶν
Ἰησοῦ Χριστοῦ, ὁ πατὴρ τῆς
δόξης, δῴη ὑμῖν πνεῦμα σοφίας
καὶ ἀποκαλύψεως ἐν ἐπιγνώσει
18 αὐτοῦ, πεφωτισμένους τοὺς ὀφθαλ-
μοὺς τῆς καρδίας ὑμῶν, εἰς τὸ
εἰδέναι ὑμᾶς τίς ἐστιν ἡ ἐλπὶς τῆς
κλήσεως αὐτοῦ, τίς ὁ πλοῦτος τῆς
δόξης τῆς κληρονομίας αὐτοῦ ἐν
19 τοῖς ἁγίοις, καὶ τί τὸ ὑπερβάλλον
μέγεθος τῆς δυνάμεως αὐτοῦ εἰς
ἡμᾶς τοὺς πιστεύοντας κατὰ τὴν
ἐνέργειαν τοῦ κράτους τῆς ἰσχύος
20 αὐτοῦ, ἣν ἐνήργηκεν ἐν τῷ Χριστῷ
ἐγείρας αὐτὸν ἐκ νεκρῶν καὶ
καθίσας ἐν δεξιᾷ αὐτοῦ ἐν τοῖς
21 ἐπουρανίοις ὑπεράνω πάσης ἀρ-
χῆς καὶ ἐξουσίας καὶ δυνάμεως
καὶ κυριότητος καὶ παντὸς ὀνό-
ματος ὀνομαζομένου οὐ μόνον ἐν
τῷ αἰῶνι τούτῳ ἀλλὰ καὶ ἐν τῷ
22 μέλλοντι· καὶ πάντα ὑπέταξεν
ὑπὸ τοὺς πόδας αὐτοῦ, καὶ αὐτὸν
ἔδωκεν κεφαλὴν ὑπὲρ πάντα τῇ

Colossians.

Eph. i. 17
ἐπίγνωσιν τοῦ θελήματος αὐτοῦ ἐν

Eph. i. 17
πάσῃ σοφίᾳ καὶ συνέσει πνευματικῇ.

i. 3. εὐχαριστοῦμεν τῷ θεῷ πατρὶ τοῦ κυρίου ἡμῶν Ἰησοῦ Χριστοῦ πάντοτε περὶ ὑμῶν προσευχόμενοι.

i. 10. αὐξανόμενοι τῇ ἐπιγνώσει τοῦ θεοῦ.

i. 27. οἷς ἠθέλησεν ὁ θεὸς γνωρίσαι τί τὸ πλοῦτος τῆς δόξης τοῦ μυστηρίου τούτου ἐν τοῖς ἔθνεσιν ὅς ἐστιν Χριστὸς ἐν ὑμῖν, ἡ ἐλπὶς τῆς δόξης.

i. 12. τὴν μερίδα τοῦ κλήρου τῶν ἁγίων ἐν τῷ φωτί.

i. 11. ἐν πάσῃ δυνάμει δυναμούμενοι κατὰ τὸ κράτος τῆς δόξης αὐτοῦ.

ii. 12. συνηγέρθητε διὰ τῆς πίστεως τῆς ἐνεργείας τοῦ θεοῦ τοῦ ἐγείραντος αὐτὸν ἐκ νεκρῶν.

i. 29. κατὰ τὴν ἐνέργειαν αὐτοῦ τὴν ἐνεργουμένην ἐν ἐμοὶ ἐν δυνάμει.

i. 18. πρωτότοκος ἐκ τῶν νεκρῶν.

iii. 1. τὰ ἄνω ζητεῖτε, οὗ ὁ Χριστός ἐστιν ἐν δεξιᾷ τοῦ θεοῦ καθήμενος.

i. 16. εἴτε κυριότητες εἴτε ἀρχαὶ εἴτε ἐξουσίαι.

i. 17–19. καὶ αὐτός ἐστιν πρὸ πάντων καὶ τὰ πάντα ἐν αὐτῷ συνέστηκεν, καὶ αὐτός ἐστιν ἡ κεφαλὴ τοῦ σώματος, τῆς ἐκκλησίας· ὅς ἐστιν

1 Peter.	
	1 Cor. xv. 27. πάντα γὰρ ὑπέταξεν ὑπὸ τοὺς πόδας αὐτοῦ. Phil. iii. 21. καὶ ὑποτάξαι αὐτῷ τὰ πάντα. 1 Cor. xii. 27 (cf. Rom. xii. 5). ὑμεῖς δέ ἐστε σῶμα Χριστοῦ. 1 Cor. xii. 6. θεὸς ὁ ἐνεργῶν τὰ πάντα ἐν πᾶσιν. 1 Cor. xv. 28. ἵνα ᾖ ὁ θεὸς πάντα ἐν πᾶσιν. Rom. xi. 36. ὅτι ἐξ αὐτοῦ καὶ δι' αὐτοῦ καὶ εἰς αὐτὸν τὰ πάντα. Rom. vi. 11. νεκροὺς μὲν τῇ ἁμαρτίᾳ.
i. 14. ὡς τέκνα ὑπακοῆς, μὴ συσχηματιζόμενοι ταῖς πρότερον ἐν τῇ ἀγνοίᾳ ὑμῶν ἐπιθυμίαις, ἀλλὰ κατὰ τὸν καλέσαντα ὑμᾶς ἅγιον καὶ αὐτοὶ ἅγιοι ἐν πάσῃ ἀναστροφῇ γενήθητε . . .	Rom. viii. 10. τὸ μὲν σῶμα νεκρὸν διὰ ἁμαρτίαν. 2 Thess. ii. 3–4. ὁ ἄνθρωπος τῆς ἀνομίας, ὁ υἱὸς τῆς ἀπωλείας, ὁ ἀντικείμενος. 2 Thess. ii. 7. τὸ γὰρ μυστήριον ἤδη ἐνεργεῖται τῆς ἀνομίας. 2 Cor. i. 12. ἀνεστράφημεν ἐν τῷ κόσμῳ.
ii. 11. ἀπέχεσθαι τῶν σαρκικῶν ἐπιθυμιῶν.	Rom. xiii. 14. καὶ τῆς σαρκὸς πρόνοιαν μὴ ποιεῖσθε εἰς ἐπιθυμίας. Rom. viii. 7. διότι τὸ φρόνημα τῆς σαρκὸς ἔχθρα εἰς θεόν . . . 1 Thess. iv. 13. καθὼς καὶ οἱ λοιποί.
i. 3. ὁ θεὸς . . . ὁ κατὰ τὸ πολὺ αὐτοῦ ἔλεος ἀναγεννήσας ἡμᾶς εἰς ἐλπίδα ζῶσαν δι' ἀναστάσεως Ἰησοῦ Χριστοῦ ἐκ νεκρῶν.	Gal. iv. 28. ἐπαγγελίας τέκνα ἐσμέν. Rom. xi. 32–3. ἵνα τοὺς πάντας ἐλεήσῃ· ὦ βάθος πλούτου καὶ σοφίας καὶ γνώσεως θεοῦ. Rom. ix. 22. σκεύη ὀργῆς κατηρτισμένα εἰς ἀπώλειαν, καὶ ἵνα γνωρίσῃ τὸν πλοῦτον τῆς δόξης αὐτοῦ ἐπὶ σκεύη ἐλέους (cf. Rom. i. 18; 2 Thess. ii. 16). Rom. iii. 24. δικαιούμενοι δωρεὰν τῇ αὐτοῦ χάριτι. Phil. iii. 20. ἡμῶν γὰρ τὸ πολίτευμα ἐν οὐρανοῖς ὑπάρχει. Rom. ix. 23. ἵνα γνωρίσῃ τὸν πλοῦτον τῆς δόξης αὐτοῦ ἐπὶ σκεύη ἐλέους.

Ephesians i. 22–ii. 7.

23 ἐκκλησίᾳ, ἥτις ἐστὶν τὸ σῶμα
αὐτοῦ, τὸ πλήρωμα τοῦ τὰ
πάντα ἐν πᾶσιν πληρουμένου.
ii. 1 καὶ ὑμᾶς ὄντας νεκροὺς τοῖς
παραπτώμασιν καὶ ταῖς ἁμαρ-
2 τίαις ὑμῶν, ἐν αἷς ποτὲ περιεπα-
τήσατε κατὰ τὸν αἰῶνα τοῦ
κόσμου τούτου, κατὰ τὸν ἄρχοντα
τῆς ἐξουσίας τοῦ ἀέρος, τοῦ
πνεύματος τοῦ νῦν ἐνεργοῦντος ἐν
3 τοῖς υἱοῖς τῆς ἀπειθείας· ἐν οἷς
καὶ ἡμεῖς πάντες ἀνεστράφημέν
ποτε ἐν ταῖς ἐπιθυμίαις τῆς
σαρκὸς ἡμῶν, ποιοῦντες τὰ θελή-
ματα τῆς σαρκὸς καὶ τῶν δια-
νοιῶν, καὶ ἤμεθα τέκνα φύσει
4 ὀργῆς, ὡς καὶ οἱ λοιποί. ὁ δὲ θεὸς
πλούσιος ὢν ἐν ἐλέει, διὰ τὴν
πολλὴν ἀγάπην αὐτοῦ ἣν ἠγάπη-
5 σεν ἡμᾶς, καὶ ὄντας ἡμᾶς νεκροὺς
τοῖς παραπτώμασιν συνεζωο-
ποίησεν τῷ Χριστῷ—χάριτί ἐστε
6 σεσωσμένοι—καὶ συνήγειρεν καὶ
συνεκάθισεν ἐν τοῖς ἐπουρανίοις
7 ἐν Χριστῷ Ἰησοῦ, ἵνα ἐνδείξηται
ἐν τοῖς αἰῶσιν τοῖς ἐπερχομένοις
τὸ ὑπερβάλλον πλοῦτος τῆς

Colossians.

ἀρχή, πρωτότοκος ἐκ τῶν νεκρῶν
ἵνα γένηται ἐν πᾶσιν αὐτὸς πρω-
τεύων, ὅτι ἐν αὐτῷ εὐδόκησεν πᾶν
τὸ πλήρωμα κατοικῆσαι.

i. 24. ὑπὲρ τοῦ σώματος αὐτοῦ, ὅ
ἐστιν ἡ ἐκκλησία.

ii. 9–10. ἐν αὐτῷ κατοικεῖ πᾶν τὸ
πλήρωμα τῆς θεότητος σωματι-
κῶς, καὶ ἐστὲ ἐν αὐτῷ πεπληρω-
μένοι, ὅς ἐστιν ἡ κεφαλὴ πάσης
ἀρχῆς καὶ ἐξουσίας (Eph. i. 21).

iii. 11. πάντα καὶ ἐν πᾶσιν Χριστός.

ii. 13. ὑμᾶς νεκροὺς ὄντας τοῖς παρα-
πτώμασιν.

iii. 7. ἐν οἷς καὶ ὑμεῖς περιεπατήσατέ
ποτε, ὅτε ἐζῆτε ἐν τούτοις.

iii. 6. δι' ἃ ἔρχεται ἡ ὀργὴ τοῦ θεοῦ.

ii. 13. καὶ ὑμᾶς νεκροὺς ὄντας τοῖς
παραπτώμασιν καὶ τῇ ἀκροβυστίᾳ
τῆς σαρκὸς ὑμῶν, συνεζωοποίησεν
ὑμᾶς σὺν αὐτῷ, χαρισάμενος ἡμῖν
πάντα τὰ παραπτώματα.

iii. 1. εἰ οὖν συνηγέρθητε τῷ Χριστῷ,
τὰ ἄνω ζητεῖτε, οὗ ὁ Χριστός ἐστιν
ἐν δεξιᾷ τοῦ θεοῦ καθήμενος.

iii. 3. ἀπεθάνετε γάρ, καὶ ἡ ζωὴ
ὑμῶν κέκρυπται σὺν τῷ Χριστῷ ἐν
τῷ θεῷ.

1 Peter.

Rom. v. 15. ἡ δωρεὰ ἐν χάριτι τῇ τοῦ ἑνὸς ἀνθρώπου, Ἰησοῦ Χριστοῦ εἰς τοὺς πολλοὺς ἐπερίσσευεν.

Rom. ii. 4. ἢ τοῦ πλούτου τῆς χρηστότητος αὐτοῦ . . . καταφρονεῖς;

Rom. iii. 24. δικαιούμενοι δωρεὰν τῇ αὐτοῦ χάριτι διὰ τῆς ἀπολυτρώσεως τῆς ἐν Χριστῷ Ἰησοῦ.

Gal. ii. 16. οὐ δικαιοῦται ἄνθρωπος ἐξ ἔργων νόμου ἐὰν μὴ διὰ πίστεως Χριστοῦ Ἰησοῦ.

Rom. iv. 16. εἶναι βεβαίαν τὴν ἐπαγγελίαν παντὶ τῷ σπέρματι οὐ τῷ ἐκ τοῦ νόμου μόνον ἀλλὰ καὶ τῷ ἐκ πίστεως.

Rom. xiii. 11. καὶ τοῦτο.

Rom. iv. 2. εἰ γὰρ Ἀβραὰμ ἐξ ἔργων ἐδικαιώθη, ἔχει καύχημα.

Rom. iii. 20. διότι ἐξ ἔργων νόμου οὐ δικαιωθήσεται πᾶσα σὰρξ ἐνώπιον αὐτοῦ.

Rom. xi. 6. εἰ δὲ χάριτι, οὐκέτι ἐξ ἔργων.

Rom. iii. 27. ποῦ οὖν ἡ καύχησις; ἐξεκλείσθη.

1 Cor. i. 28–9. ἐξελέξατο ὁ θεὸς τὰ μὴ ὄντα ἵνα τὰ ὄντα καταργήσῃ, ὅπως μὴ καυχήσηται πᾶσα σάρξ.

2 Cor. v. 17. ὥστε εἴ τις ἐν Χριστῷ, καινὴ κτίσις.

Gal. vi. 15. οὔτε γὰρ περιτομή τι ἔστιν οὔτε ἀκροβυστία ἀλλὰ καινὴ κτίσις.

1 Cor. xii. 2. οἴδατε ὅτι ὅτε ἔθνη ἦτε . . .

Rom. ix. 4. Ἰσραηλεῖται, ὧν ἡ υἱοθεσία καὶ ἡ δόξα καὶ αἱ διαθῆκαι καὶ ἡ νομοθεσία καὶ ἡ λατρεία καὶ αἱ ἐπαγγελίαι.

1 Thess. iv. 13. ἵνα μὴ λυπῆσθε καθὼς καὶ οἱ λοιποὶ οἱ μὴ ἔχοντες ἐλπίδα.

Gal. v. 4. κατηργήθητε ἀπὸ Χριστοῦ.

1 Thess. iv. 5. τὰ ἔθνη τὰ μὴ εἰδότα τὸν θεόν (Jer. x. 25; Ps. lxxix. 6).

Gal. iv. 8. τότε μὲν οὐκ εἰδότες θεόν.

Gal. iii. 28. οὐκ ἔνι Ἰουδαῖος οὐδὲ Ἕλλην, οὐκ ἔνι δοῦλος οὐδὲ ἐλεύθερος, οὐκ ἔνι ἄρσεν καὶ θῆλυ· πάντες γὰρ ὑμεῖς εἷς ἐστὲ ἐν Χριστῷ Ἰησοῦ.

2 Cor. v. 17. ὥστε εἴ τις ἐν Χριστῷ, καινὴ κτίσις. τὰ ἀρχαῖα παρῆλθεν, ἰδοὺ γέγονεν καινά.

Ephesians ii. 7–15.	Colossians.
χάριτος αὐτοῦ ἐν χρηστότητι ἐφ'	
8 ἡμᾶς ἐν Χριστῷ Ἰησοῦ· τῇ γὰρ	
χάριτί ἐστε σεσωσμένοι διὰ πί-	
στεως· καὶ τοῦτο οὐκ ἐξ ὑμῶν,	
9 θεοῦ τὸ δῶρον· οὐκ ἐξ ἔργων, ἵνα	
10 μή τις καυχήσηται. αὐτοῦ γάρ	i. 10. περιπατῆσαι ἀξίως τοῦ κυρίου
ἐσμεν ποίημα, κτισθέντες ἐν	εἰς πᾶσαν ἀρεσκίαν, ἐν παντὶ ἔργῳ
Χριστῷ Ἰησοῦ ἐπὶ ἔργοις ἀγα-	ἀγαθῷ.
θοῖς, οἷς προητοίμασεν ὁ θεὸς ἵνα	
ἐν αὐτοῖς περιπατήσωμεν.	
11 διὸ μνημονεύετε ὅτι ποτὲ ὑμεῖς	
τὰ ἔθνη ἐν σαρκί, οἱ λεγόμενοι	
ἀκροβυστία ὑπὸ τῆς λεγομένης	ii. 11. ἐν ᾧ καὶ περιετμήθητε περι-
περιτομῆς ἐν σαρκὶ χειροποιήτου,	τομῇ ἀχειροποιήτῳ ἐν τῇ ἀπεκ-
12 ὅτι ἦτε τῷ καιρῷ ἐκείνῳ χωρὶς	δύσει τοῦ σώματος τῆς σαρκός, ἐν
Χριστοῦ, ἀπηλλοτριωμένοι τῆς	τῇ περιτομῇ τοῦ Χριστοῦ.
πολιτείας τοῦ Ἰσραὴλ καὶ ξένοι	
τῶν διαθηκῶν τῆς ἐπαγγελίας,	i. 21. καὶ ὑμᾶς ποτε ὄντας ἀπηλλο-
ἐλπίδα μὴ ἔχοντες καὶ ἄθεοι ἐν	τριωμένους.
13 τῷ κόσμῳ. νυνὶ δὲ ἐν Χριστῷ	i. 22. νυνὶ δέ.
Ἰησοῦ ὑμεῖς οἵ ποτε ὄντες	i. 20. δι' αὐτοῦ ἀποκαταλλάξαι τὰ
μακρὰν ἐγενήθητε ἐγγὺς ἐν τῷ	πάντα εἰς αὐτόν, εἰρηνοποιήσας διὰ
14 αἵματι τοῦ Χριστοῦ. αὐτὸς γάρ	τοῦ αἵματος τοῦ σταυροῦ αὐτοῦ.
ἐστιν ἡ εἰρήνη ἡμῶν, ὁ ποιήσας	iii. 15. ἡ εἰρήνη τοῦ Χριστοῦ.
τὰ ἀμφότερα ἓν καὶ μεσότοιχον	ii. 14. τὸ καθ' ἡμῶν χειρόγραφον . . . ἦρκεν ἐκ τοῦ μέσου.
τοῦ φραγμοῦ λύσας, τὴν ἔχθραν,	i. 22. ἐν τῷ σώματι τῆς σαρκός.
15 ἐν τῇ σαρκὶ αὐτοῦ τὸν νόμον τῶν	ii. 14. ἐξαλείψας τὸ καθ' ἡμῶν
ἐντολῶν ἐν δόγμασιν καταργήσας,	χειρόγραφον τοῖς δόγμασιν ὃ ἦν
ἵνα τοὺς δύο κτίσῃ ἐν αὐτῷ εἰς	ὑπεναντίον ἡμῖν.

1 Peter.	
i. 3. εὐλογητὸς ὁ θεὸς καὶ πατὴρ τοῦ κυρίου ἡμῶν Ἰησοῦ Χριστοῦ, ὁ κατὰ τὸ πολὺ αὐτοῦ ἔλεος ἀναγεννήσας ἡμᾶς.	Rom. v. 1–2. εἰρήνην ἔχωμεν πρὸς τὸν θεὸν διὰ τοῦ κυρίου ἡμῶν Ἰησοῦ Χριστοῦ, δι' οὗ καὶ τὴν προσαγωγὴν ἐσχήκαμεν.
i. 23. ἀναγεγεννημένοι.	1 Cor. xii. 13. καὶ γὰρ ἐν ἑνὶ πνεύματι ἡμεῖς πάντες εἰς ἓν σῶμα ἐβαπτίσθημεν, εἴτε Ἰουδαῖοι εἴτε Ἕλληνες, εἴτε δοῦλοι εἴτε ἐλεύθεροι.
iii. 18. ὅτι καὶ Χριστὸς ἅπαξ περὶ ἁμαρτιῶν ἀπέθανεν δίκαιος ὑπὲρ ἀδικῶν, ἵνα ὑμᾶς προσαγάγῃ τῷ θεῷ θανατωθεὶς μὲν σαρκί, ζωοποιηθεὶς δὲ πνεύματι.	Phil. i. 27. πολιτεύεσθε, ἵνα . . . ἀκούω . . . ὅτι στήκετε ἐν ἑνὶ πνεύματι. Phil. iii. 20. ἡμῶν γὰρ τὸ πολίτευμα ἐν οὐρανοῖς ὑπάρχει.
ii. 4. πρὸς ὃν προσερχόμενοι.	Gal. vi. 10. μάλιστα δὲ πρὸς τοὺς οἰκείους τῆς πίστεως.
ii. 11. ἀγαπητοί, παρακαλῶ, ὡς παροίκους καὶ παρεπιδήμους ἀπέχεσθαι τῶν σαρκικῶν ἐπιθυμιῶν, αἵτινες στρατεύονται κατὰ τῆς ψυχῆς.	1 Cor. xii. 28. ἔθετο ὁ θεὸς ἐν τῇ ἐκκλησίᾳ πρῶτον ἀποστόλους, δεύτερον προφήτας. 1 Cor. iii. 6. ὁ θεὸς ηὔξανεν . . . ὁ αὐξάνων θεός.
ii. 2. ἵνα ἐν αὐτῷ αὐξηθῆτε εἰς σωτηρίαν, [3] εἰ ἐγεύσασθε ὅτι χρηστὸς ὁ κύριος πρὸς ὃν προσερχόμενοι, [4] λίθον ζῶντα, . . . [5] καὶ αὐτοὶ ὡς λίθοι ζῶντες οἰκοδομεῖσθε οἶκος πνευματικὸς εἰς ἱεράτευμα ἅγιον . . . [6] . . . λίθον ἐκλεκτὸν ἀκρογωνιαῖον ἔντιμον.	1 Cor. iii. 9–12. θεοῦ γεώργιον, θεοῦ οἰκοδομή ἐστε. κατὰ τὴν χάριν τοῦ θεοῦ τὴν δοθεῖσάν μοι ὡς σοφὸς ἀρχιτέκτων, θεμέλιον ἔθηκα, ἄλλος δὲ ἐποικοδομεῖ . . . θεμέλιον γὰρ ἄλλον οὐδεὶς δύναται θεῖναι παρὰ τὸν κείμενον, ὅς ἐστιν Ἰησοῦς Χριστός. εἰ δέ τις ἐποικοδομεῖ ἐπὶ τὸν θεμέλιον. 1 Cor. iii. 16. οὐκ οἴδατε ὅτι ναὸς θεοῦ ἐστε καὶ τὸ πνεῦμα τοῦ θεοῦ ἐν ὑμῖν οἰκεῖ; . . . ὁ γὰρ ναὸς τοῦ θεοῦ ἅγιός ἐστιν, οἵτινές ἐστε ὑμεῖς. 2 Cor. vi. 16. ἡμεῖς γὰρ ναὸς θεοῦ ἐσμεν ζῶντος.
	2 Cor. x. 1. } Gal. v. 2. } ἐγὼ Παῦλος. Philem. 1. Παῦλος δέσμιος Χριστοῦ Ἰησοῦ. Rom. xi. 13. ὑμῖν δὲ λέγω τοῖς ἔθνεσιν. Gal. i. 16. ἵνα εὐαγγελίζωμαι αὐτὸν ἐν τοῖς ἔθνεσιν.

Ephesians ii. 15–iii. 2.

ἕνα καινὸν ἄνθρωπον ποιῶν εἰρή-
16 νην, καὶ ἀποκαταλλάξῃ τοὺς ἀμ-
φοτέρους ἐν ἑνὶ σώματι τῷ θεῷ
διὰ τοῦ σταυροῦ, ἀποκτείνας τὴν
17 ἔχθραν ἐν αὐτῷ· καὶ ἐλθὼν εὐηγ-
γελίσατο εἰρήνην ὑμῖν τοῖς μα-
18 κρὰν καὶ εἰρήνην τοῖς ἐγγύς· ὅτι
δι' αὐτοῦ ἔχομεν τὴν προσαγωγὴν
οἱ ἀμφότεροι ἐν ἑνὶ πνεύματι πρὸς
19 τὸν πατέρα. ἄρα οὖν οὐκέτι ἐστὲ
ξένοι καὶ πάροικοι, ἀλλὰ ἐστὲ
συνπολῖται τῶν ἁγίων καὶ οἰκεῖοι
20 τοῦ θεοῦ, ἐποικοδομηθέντες ἐπὶ
τῷ θεμελίῳ τῶν ἀποστόλων καὶ
21 προφητῶν, ὄντος ἀκρογωνιαίου
αὐτοῦ Χριστοῦ Ἰησοῦ, ἐν ᾧ πᾶσα
οἰκοδομὴ συναρμολογουμένη αὔ-
22 ξει εἰς ναὸν ἅγιον ἐν κυρίῳ, ἐν ᾧ
καὶ ὑμεῖς συνοικοδομεῖσθε εἰς
κατοικητήριον τοῦ θεοῦ ἐν πνεύ-
ματι.

iii. 1 τούτου χάριν ἐγὼ Παῦλος ὁ
δέσμιος τοῦ Χριστοῦ Ἰησοῦ ὑπὲρ
2 ὑμῶν τῶν ἐθνῶν—εἴ γε ἠκούσατε
τὴν οἰκονομίαν τῆς χάριτος τοῦ
θεοῦ τῆς δοθείσης μοι εἰς ὑμᾶς,

Colossians.

iii. 10. καὶ ἐνδυσάμενοι τὸν νέον (ἄν-
θρωπον) τὸν ἀνακαινούμενον.

i. 20–2. καὶ δι' αὐτοῦ ἀποκαταλλάξαι
τὰ πάντα εἰς αὐτόν, εἰρηνοποιήσας
διὰ τοῦ αἵματος τοῦ σταυροῦ . . .
καὶ ὑμᾶς . . . ἐχθροὺς τῇ διανοίᾳ
. . . νυνὶ δὲ ἀποκατήλλαξεν ἐν
τῷ σώματι τῆς σαρκὸς αὐτοῦ διὰ
τοῦ θανάτου.

iii. 11. ὅπου οὐκ ἔνι Ἕλλην καὶ
Ἰουδαῖος . . βάρβαρος, Σκύθης.

ii. 7. ἐρριζωμένοι καὶ ἐποικοδομού-
μενοι ἐν αὐτῷ καὶ βεβαιούμενοι.

ii. 19. ἐξ οὗ πᾶν τὸ σῶμα διὰ τῶν
ἁφῶν καὶ συνδέσμων ἐπιχορηγού-
μενον καὶ συνβιβαζόμενον αὔξει
τὴν αὔξησιν τοῦ θεοῦ.

i. 23. ἐγὼ Παῦλος διάκονος.

i. 24–7. νῦν χαίρω ἐν τοῖς παθήμασιν
ὑπὲρ ὑμῶν . . . [25] ἡ ἐκκλησία, ἧς
ἐγενόμην ἐγὼ διάκονος κατὰ τὴν
Eph. iii. 7.
οἰκονομίαν τοῦ θεοῦ τὴν δοθεῖσάν
μοι εἰς ὑμᾶς πληρῶσαι τὸν λόγον
τοῦ θεοῦ, [26] τὸ μυστήριον τὸ ἀπο-
Eph. iii. 9.
κεκρυμμένον ἀπὸ τῶν αἰώνων καὶ
ἀπὸ τῶν γενεῶν—νῦν δὲ ἐφανερώθη

1 Peter.	
i. 10–12. περὶ ἧς σωτηρίας ἐξεζήτησαν καὶ ἐξηραύνησαν προφῆται οἱ περὶ τῆς εἰς ὑμᾶς χάριτος προφητεύσαντες, [11] ἐραυνῶντες εἰς τίνα ἢ ποῖον καιρὸν ἐδήλου τὸ ἐν αὐτοῖς πνεῦμα Χριστοῦ προμαρτυρόμενον τὰ εἰς Χριστὸν παθήματα καὶ τὰς μετὰ ταῦτα δόξας, [12] οἷς ἀπεκαλύφθη ὅτι οὐχ ἑαυτοῖς ὑμῖν δὲ διηκόνουν αὐτά, ἃ νῦν ἀνηγγέλη ὑμῖν διὰ τῶν εὐαγγελισαμένων ὑμᾶς ἐν πνεύματι ἁγίῳ	Gal. ii. 9. τὴν χάριν τὴν δοθεῖσάν μοι (cf. Rom. xii. 3 and 1 Cor. iii. 10 above). 1 Cor. ix. 17. οἰκονομίαν πεπίστευμαι. 1 Cor. iv. 1. ἡμᾶς λογιζέσθω ἄνθρωπος ὡς . . . οἰκονόμους μυστηρίων θεοῦ. 1 Cor. v. 9. ἔγραψα ὑμῖν ἐν τῇ ἐπιστολῇ. 2 Cor. xi. 6. ἰδιώτης τῷ λόγῳ, ἀλλ' οὐ τῇ γνώσει. Rom. xvi. 25–6. κατὰ ἀποκάλυψιν μυστηρίου χρόνοις αἰωνίοις σεσιγημένου, φανερωθέντος δὲ νῦν διά τε γραφῶν προφητικῶν . . . εἰς πάντα τὰ ἔθνη γνωρισθέντος. Cf. also 1 Cor. ii. 7–8 (quoted at Eph. iii. 9). Rom. viii. 17. κληρονόμοι μὲν θεοῦ, συγκληρονόμοι δὲ Χριστοῦ. Gal. iii. 29. εἰ δὲ ὑμεῖς Χριστοῦ, ἄρα τοῦ Ἀβραὰμ σπέρμα ἐστέ, κατ' ἐπαγγελίαν κληρονόμοι. Rom. xii. 5. οὕτως οἱ πολλοὶ ἓν σῶμά ἐσμεν ἐν Χριστῷ. 2 Thess. ii. 14. διὰ τοῦ εὐαγγελίου ἡμῶν. Rom. xii. 3. διὰ τῆς χάριτος τῆς δοθείσης μοι. 1 Cor. iii. 10. κατὰ τὴν χάριν τοῦ θεοῦ τὴν δοθεῖσάν μοι. Rom. v. 15. ἡ χάρις τοῦ θεοῦ καὶ ἡ δωρεὰ ἐν χάριτι. Rom. iii. 24. δικαιούμενοι δωρεὰν τῇ αὐτοῦ χάριτι. 1 Cor. xv. 9–10. ἐγὼ γάρ εἰμι ὁ ἐλάχιστος τῶν ἀποστόλων . . . χάριτι δὲ θεοῦ εἰμι ὅ εἰμι, καὶ ἡ χάρις αὐτοῦ ἡ εἰς ἐμὲ οὐ κενὴ ἐγενήθη.
Cf. i. 12.	Gal. i. 15–16. εὐδόκησεν ὁ . . . καλέσας διὰ τῆς χάριτος αὐτοῦ ἀποκαλύψαι τὸν υἱὸν

Ephesians iii. 3–9.

3 ὅτι κατὰ ἀποκάλυψιν ἐγνωρίσθη
μοι τὸ μυστήριον, καθὼς προ-
4 έγραψα ἐν ὀλίγῳ, πρὸς ὃ δύνασθε
ἀναγινώσκοντες νοῆσαι τὴν σύνε-
σίν μου ἐν τῷ μυστηρίῳ τοῦ
5 Χριστοῦ, ὃ ἑτέραις γενεαῖς οὐκ
ἐγνωρίσθη τοῖς υἱοῖς τῶν ἀνθρώ-
πων ὡς νῦν ἀπεκαλύφθη τοῖς
ἁγίοις ἀποστόλοις αὐτοῦ καὶ προ-
Col. i. 27
6 φήταις ἐν πνεύματι, εἶναι τὰ ἔθνη
συγκληρονόμα καὶ σύνσωμα καὶ
συνμέτοχα τῆς ἐπαγγελίας ἐν
Χριστῷ Ἰησοῦ διὰ τοῦ εὐαγ-
7 γελίου, οὗ ἐγενήθην διάκονος
κατὰ τὴν δωρεὰν τῆς χάριτος τοῦ
θεοῦ τῆς δοθείσης μοι κατὰ τὴν
ἐνέργειαν τῆς δυνάμεως αὐτοῦ.
8 ἐμοὶ τῷ ἐλαχιστοτέρῳ πάντων
ἁγίων ἐδόθη ἡ χάρις αὕτη, τοῖς
ἔθνεσιν εὐαγγελίσασθαι τὸ ἀνεξ-
ιχνίαστον πλοῦτος τοῦ Χριστοῦ,
9 καὶ φωτίσαι τίς ἡ οἰκονομία τοῦ
μυστηρίου τοῦ ἀποκεκρυμμένου
ἀπὸ τῶν αἰώνων ἐν τῷ θεῷ τῷ τὰ

Colossians.

τοῖς ἁγίοις αὐτοῦ, 27 οἷς ἠθέλησεν ὁ θεὸς γνωρίσαι τί τὸ πλοῦτος τῆς δόξης τοῦ μυστηρίου τούτου ἐν

Eph. iii. 6, 8.

τοῖς ἔθνεσιν, ὅς ἐστιν Χριστὸς ἐν ὑμῖν, ἡ ἐλπὶς τῆς δόξης.

iv. 16. ὅταν ἀναγνωσθῇ παρ' ὑμῖν ἡ ἐπιστολή.

iv. 3. τὸ μυστήριον τοῦ Χριστοῦ.

ii. 2. εἰς πᾶν πλοῦτος τῆς πληροφορίας τῆς συνέσεως, εἰς ἐπίγνωσιν τοῦ μυστηρίου τοῦ θεοῦ, Χριστοῦ.

i. 8. ὁ καὶ δηλώσας ἡμῖν τὴν ὑμῶν ἀγάπην ἐν πνεύματι.

i. 23. τοῦ εὐαγγελίου . . . οὗ ἐγενόμην ἐγὼ Παῦλος διάκονος.

i. 25. ἐκκλησία ἧς ἐγενόμην ἐγὼ διάκονος κατὰ τὴν οἰκονομίαν τοῦ θεοῦ τὴν δοθεῖσάν μοι.

i. 29. κατὰ τὴν ἐνέργειαν αὐτοῦ τὴν ἐνεργουμένην ἐν ἐμοὶ ἐν δυνάμει.

i. 27. γνωρίσαι τί τὸ πλοῦτος τῆς δόξης τοῦ μυστηρίου τούτου ἐν τοῖς ἔθνεσιν.

i. 26. τὸ μυστήριον τὸ ἀποκεκρυμμένον ἀπὸ τῶν αἰώνων καὶ ἀπὸ τῶν

1 Peter.	αὐτοῦ ἐν ἐμοί, ἵνα εὐαγγελίζωμαι αὐτὸν ἐν τοῖς ἔθνεσιν . . . .
	Gal. ii. 7. πεπίστευμαι τὸ εὐαγγέλιον τῆς ἀκροβυστίας.
	Rom. xi. 33. ὦ βάθος πλούτου καὶ σοφίας καὶ γνώσεως θεοῦ· ὡς ἀνεξεραύνητα τὰ κρίματα αὐτοῦ καὶ ἀνεξιχνίαστοι αἱ ὁδοὶ αὐτοῦ.
iv. 10. διακονοῦντες ὡς καλοὶ οἰκονόμοι ποικίλης χάριτος θεοῦ.	1 Cor. iv. 1. οἰκονόμους μυστηρίων θεοῦ.
	Rom. xvi. 25 (quoted at Eph. iii. 5).
	1 Cor. ii. 7–8. λαλοῦμεν θεοῦ σοφίαν ἐν μυστηρίῳ τὴν ἀποκεκρυμμένην . . . ἣν οὐδεὶς τῶν ἀρχόντων τοῦ αἰῶνος τούτου ἔγνωκεν.
iii. 18. ἵνα ὑμᾶς προσαγάγῃ τῷ θεῷ.	Rom. v. 1–2. διὰ τοῦ κυρίου ἡμῶν Ἰησοῦ Χριστοῦ δι' οὗ καὶ τὴν προσαγωγὴν ἐσχήκαμεν τῇ πίστει.
	2 Cor. iii. 4. πεποίθησιν δὲ τοιαύτην ἔχομεν διὰ τοῦ Χριστοῦ πρὸς τὸν θεόν.
	1 Cor. viii. 5. εἴτε ἐν οὐρανῷ εἴτε ἐπὶ γῆς.
	Rom. ix. 23. ἵνα γνωρίσῃ τὸν πλοῦτον τῆς δόξης αὐτοῦ.
	Rom. xv. 13, 19. ἐν δυνάμει πνεύματος ἁγίου.
	Rom. vii. 22. συνήδομαι γὰρ τῷ νόμῳ τοῦ θεοῦ κατὰ τὸν ἔσω ἄνθρωπον.
iii. 4. . . . ὁ κρυπτὸς τῆς καρδίας ἄνθρωπος ἐν τῷ ἀφθάρτῳ τοῦ πραέος καὶ ἡσυχίου πνεύματος.	2 Cor. iv. 16. εἰ καὶ ὁ ἔξω ἡμῶν ἄνθρωπος διαφθείρεται, ἀλλ' ὁ ἔσω ἡμῶν ἀνακαινοῦται.
	Rom. viii. 9–10. ὑμεῖς δὲ οὐκ ἐστὲ ἐν σαρκὶ ἀλλὰ ἐν πνεύματι, εἴπερ πνεῦμα θεοῦ οἰκεῖ ἐν ὑμῖν . . . εἰ δὲ Χριστὸς ἐν ὑμῖν . . . .
	1 Cor. iii. 16. τὸ πνεῦμα τοῦ θεοῦ ἐν ὑμῖν οἰκεῖ;
iii. 15. κύριον δὲ τὸν Χριστὸν ἁγιάσατε ἐν ταῖς καρδίαις ὑμῶν.	2 Cor. xiii. 5. ὅτι Ἰησοῦς Χριστὸς ἐν ὑμῖν . . . .
	2 Cor. i. 22. ὁ . . . δοὺς τὸν ἀρραβῶνα τοῦ πνεύματος ἐν ταῖς καρδίαις ἡμῶν.
	2 Cor. vi. 16. ἡμεῖς γὰρ ναὸς θεοῦ ἐσμεν ζῶντος· καθὼς εἶπεν ὁ θεὸς ὅτι ἐνοικήσω ἐν αὐτοῖς καὶ ἐνπεριπατήσω.

Ephesians iii. 9–18.	Colossians.
10 πάντα κτίσαντι, ἵνα γνωρισθῇ νῦν ταῖς ἀρχαῖς καὶ ταῖς ἐξουσίαις ἐν τοῖς ἐπουρανίοις διὰ τῆς ἐκκλη- σίας ἡ πολυποίκιλος σοφία τοῦ 11 θεοῦ, κατὰ πρόθεσιν τῶν αἰώνων ἣν ἐποίησεν ἐν τῷ Χριστῷ Ἰησοῦ 12 τῷ κυρίῳ ἡμῶν ἐν ᾧ ἔχομεν τὴν παρρησίαν καὶ προσαγωγὴν ἐν πεποιθήσει διὰ τῆς πίστεως αὐ-	γενεῶν· νῦν δὲ ἐφανερώθη τοῖς ἁγίοις αὐτοῦ. i. 16. ἐν αὐτῷ ἐκτίσθη τὰ πάντα ἐν τοῖς οὐρανοῖς . . . εἴτε ἀρχαὶ εἴτε ἐξουσίαι.
13 τοῦ. διὸ αἰτοῦμαι μὴ ἐνκακεῖν ἐν ταῖς θλίψεσίν μου ὑπὲρ ὑμῶν, ἥτις ἐστὶν δόξα ὑμῶν.	i. 24. νῦν χαίρω ἐν τοῖς παθήμασιν ὑπὲρ ὑμῶν, καὶ ἀνταναπληρῶ τὰ ὑστερήματα τῶν θλίψεων τοῦ Χριστοῦ.
14 τούτου χάριν κάμπτω τὰ γόνατά 15 μου πρὸς τὸν πατέρα, ἐξ οὗ πᾶσα πατριὰ ἐν οὐρανοῖς καὶ ἐπὶ γῆς	i. 16. τὰ πάντα ἐν τοῖς οὐρανοῖς καὶ ἐπὶ τῆς γῆς. i. 20. εἴτε τὰ ἐπὶ τῆς γῆς εἴτε τὰ ἐν τοῖς οὐρανοῖς.
16 ὀνομάζεται, ἵνα δῷ ὑμῖν κατὰ τὸ πλοῦτος τῆς δόξης αὐτοῦ δυνάμει κραταιωθῆναι διὰ τοῦ πνεύματος αὐτοῦ εἰς τὸν ἔσω ἄνθρωπον, 17 κατοικῆσαι τὸν Χριστὸν διὰ τῆς πίστεως ἐν ταῖς καρδίαις ὑμῶν, ἐν ἀγάπῃ ἐρριζωμένοι καὶ τεθε- 18 μελιωμένοι, ἵνα ἐξισχύσητε κατα- λαβέσθαι σὺν πᾶσιν τοῖς ἁγίοις τί	i. 11. ἐν πάσῃ δυνάμει δυναμούμενοι κατὰ τὸ κράτος τῆς δόξης αὐτοῦ. i. 27. τὸ πλοῦτος τῆς δόξης τοῦ μυστηρίου τούτου ἐν τοῖς ἔθνεσιν, ὅς ἐστιν Χριστὸς ἐν ὑμῖν. i. 29. κατὰ τὴν ἐνέργειαν αὐτοῦ τὴν ἐνεργουμένην ἐν ἐμοὶ ἐν δυνάμει. ii. 7. ἐρριζωμένοι καὶ ἐποικοδομούμενοι. i. 23. ἐπιμένετε τῇ πίστει τεθεμελιωμένοι καὶ ἑδραῖοι.

1 Peter.

Rom. viii. 38. οὔτε δυνάμεις οὔτε ὕψωμα οὔτε βάθος.

Rom. xi. 33. ὦ βάθος πλούτου καὶ σοφίας καὶ γνώσεως θεοῦ.

Rom. viii. 35. τίς ἡμᾶς χωρίσει ἀπὸ τῆς ἀγάπης τοῦ Χριστοῦ;

2 Cor. v. 14. ἡ γὰρ ἀγάπη τοῦ Χριστοῦ συνέχει ἡμᾶς.

Rom. xvi. 25. τῷ δὲ δυναμένῳ ὑμᾶς στηρίξαι κατὰ τὸ εὐαγγέλιόν μου . . . κατὰ ἀποκάλυψιν μυστηρίου . . . μόνῳ σοφῷ θεῷ, διὰ Ἰησοῦ Χριστοῦ, ᾧ ἡ δόξα εἰς τοὺς αἰῶνας τῶν αἰώνων· ἀμήν.

Rom. xi. 36. αὐτῷ ἡ δόξα εἰς τοὺς αἰῶνας· ἀμήν.

Gal. i. 5. ᾧ ἡ δόξα εἰς τοὺς αἰῶνας τῶν αἰώνων· ἀμήν.

Gal. iii. 5. ὁ . . . ἐνεργῶν δυνάμεις ἐν ὑμῖν·

Rom. xii. 1. παρακαλῶ οὖν ὑμᾶς.

2 Cor. x. 1. αὐτὸς δὲ ἐγὼ Παῦλος παρακαλῶ ὑμᾶς.

1 Thess. ii. 12. παρακαλοῦντες ὑμᾶς . . . εἰς τὸ περιπατεῖν ὑμᾶς ἀξίως τοῦ θεοῦ τοῦ καλοῦντος ὑμᾶς.

2 Thess. i. 11. ἵνα ὑμᾶς ἀξιώσῃ τῆς κλήσεως ὁ θεός.

Phil. i. 27. ἀξίως τοῦ εὐαγγελίου τοῦ Χριστοῦ πολιτεύεσθε . . . στήκετε ἐν ἑνὶ πνεύματι, μιᾷ ψυχῇ συναθλοῦντες.

1 Cor. vii. 20. ἕκαστος ἐν τῇ κλήσει ᾗ ἐκλήθη . . . μενέτω.

1 Cor. x. 17. ἓν σῶμα οἱ πολλοί ἐσμεν.

1 Cor. xii. 12–13. καθάπερ γὰρ τὸ σῶμα ἕν ἐστιν, καὶ μέλη πολλὰ ἔχει, πάντα δὲ τὰ μέλη τοῦ σώματος πολλὰ ὄντα, ἕν ἐστιν

Ephesians iii. 18–iv. 5.	Colossians.
τὸ πλάτος καὶ μῆκος καὶ ὕψος καὶ	ii. 9. ἐν αὐτῷ κατοικεῖ πᾶν τὸ πλή-
19 βάθος, γνῶναί τε τὴν ὑπερβάλ-	ρωμα τῆς θεότητος σωματικῶς,
λουσαν τῆς γνώσεως ἀγάπην τοῦ	καὶ ἐστὲ ἐν αὐτῷ πεπληρωμένοι.
Χριστοῦ, ἵνα πληρωθῆτε εἰς πᾶν	i. 19. ἐν αὐτῷ εὐδόκησεν πᾶν τὸ
τὸ πλήρωμα τοῦ θεοῦ.	πλήρωμα κατοικῆσαι.
20 τῷ δὲ δυναμένῳ ὑπὲρ πάντα	i. 9. ἵνα πληρωθῆτε τὴν ἐπίγνωσιν
ποιῆσαι ὑπερεκπερισσοῦ ὧν αἰτού-	τοῦ θελήματος αὐτοῦ.
μεθα ἢ νοοῦμεν κατὰ τὴν δύναμιν	i. 29. κατὰ τὴν ἐνέργειαν αὐτοῦ τὴν
21 τὴν ἐνεργουμένην ἐν ἡμῖν, αὐτῷ	ἐνεργουμένην ἐν ἐμοὶ ἐν δυνάμει.
ἡ δόξα ἐν τῇ ἐκκλησίᾳ καὶ ἐν	
Χριστῷ Ἰησοῦ εἰς πάσας τὰς	
γενεὰς τοῦ αἰῶνος τῶν αἰώνων·	i. 26. ἀπὸ τῶν αἰώνων καὶ ἀπὸ τῶν
ἀμήν.	γενεῶν.
iv. 1 παρακαλῶ οὖν ὑμᾶς ἐγὼ ὁ	
δέσμιος ἐν κυρίῳ ἀξίως περιπα-	i. 10. περιπατῆσαι ἀξίως τοῦ κυρίου.
τῆσαι τῆς κλήσεως ἧς ἐκλήθητε,	
2 μετὰ πάσης ταπεινοφροσύνης καὶ	iii. 12. ἐνδύσασθε . . . ταπεινοφροσύ-
πραΰτητος, μετὰ μακροθυμίας,	νην, πραΰτητα, μακροθυμίαν, ἀν-
ἀνεχόμενοι ἀλλήλων ἐν ἀγάπῃ,	εχόμενοι ἀλλήλων.
3 σπουδάζοντες τηρεῖν τὴν ἑνότητα	
τοῦ πνεύματος ἐν τῷ συνδέσμῳ	iii. 14. ἐπὶ πᾶσιν δὲ τούτοις τὴν ἀγάπην, ὅ ἐστιν σύνδεσμος τῆς
4 τῆς εἰρήνης ἓν σῶμα καὶ ἓν πνεῦμα,	τελειότητος. καὶ ἡ εἰρήνη τοῦ
καθὼς καὶ ἐκλήθητε ἐν μιᾷ ἐλπίδι	Χριστοῦ βραβευέτω ἐν ταῖς καρ- δίαις ὑμῶν, εἰς ἣν καὶ ἐκλήθητε ἐν
5 τῆς κλήσεως ὑμῶν· εἷς κύριος, μία	ἑνὶ σώματι.

1 Peter.	
iv. 10. ἕκαστος καθὼς ἔλαβεν χάρισμα, εἰς ἑαυτοὺς αὐτὸ διακονοῦντες ὡς καλοὶ οἰκονόμοι ποικίλης χάριτος θεοῦ.	σῶμα, οὕτως καὶ ὁ Χριστός· καὶ γὰρ ἐν ἑνὶ πνεύματι ἡμεῖς πάντες εἰς ἓν σῶμα ἐβαπτίσθημεν . . . καὶ πάντες ἓν πνεῦμα ἐποτίσθημεν. Rom. xii. 5–6. οἱ πολλοὶ ἓν σῶμά ἐσμεν ἐν Χριστῷ . . . ἔχοντες δὲ χαρίσματα κατὰ τὴν χάριν τὴν δοθεῖσαν ἡμῖν. 1 Cor. xii. 4–6. . . . τὸ δὲ αὐτὸ πνεῦμα . . . καὶ ὁ αὐτὸς κύριος . . . ὁ δὲ αὐτὸς θεός, ὁ ἐνεργῶν τὰ πάντα ἐν πᾶσιν.
iii. 18. Χριστὸς . . . θανατωθεὶς μὲν σαρκὶ ζωοποιηθεὶς δὲ πνεύματι· ἐν ᾧ καὶ τοῖς ἐν φυλακῇ πνεύμασιν πορευθεὶς ἐκήρυξεν. iv. 6. εἰς τοῦτο γὰρ καὶ νεκροῖς εὐηγγελίσθη, ἵνα κριθῶσι μὲν κατὰ ἀνθρώπους σαρκί, ζῶσι δὲ κατὰ θεὸν πνεύματι. (The above two passages appear to deal with the same belief as Eph. iv. 9.)	1 Cor. viii. 6. εἷς θεὸς ὁ πατήρ, ἐξ οὗ τὰ πάντα, καὶ ἡμεῖς εἰς αὐτόν, καὶ εἷς κύριος Ἰησοῦς Χριστὸς δι' οὗ τὰ πάντα. Rom. ix. 5. ὁ ὢν ἐπὶ πάντων, θεός. Rom. xi. 36. ὅτι ἐξ αὐτοῦ καὶ δι' αὐτοῦ καὶ εἰς αὐτὸν τὰ πάντα. 1 Cor. xiii. 7. ἡ ἀγάπη . . . πάντα πιστεύει, πάντα ἐλπίζει. 1 Cor. xiii. 13. πίστις, ἐλπίς, ἀγάπη. Rom. xii. 3. λέγω γὰρ διὰ τῆς χάριτος τῆς δοθείσης μοι . . . ἑκάστῳ ὡς ὁ θεὸς ἐμέρισεν μέτρον πίστεως.
v. 2. ποιμάνατε τὸ ἐν ὑμῖν ποίμνιον τοῦ θεοῦ.	Rom. x. 6–7. τίς ἀναβήσεται εἰς τὸν οὐρανόν; . . . τίς καταβήσεται εἰς τὴν ἄβυσσον;
	1 Cor. xii. 28. ἔθετο ὁ θεὸς . . . ἀποστόλους . . . προφήτας . . . διδασκάλους. 1 Cor. xiv. 12, 26. πρὸς (τὴν) οἰκοδομήν.
ii. 5. οἰκοδομεῖσθε οἶκος πνευματικὸς εἰς ἱεράτευμα ἅγιον ἀνενέγκαι πνευματικὰς θυσίας εὐπροσδέκτους θεῷ διὰ Ἰησοῦ Χριστοῦ. iv. 10–11. διακονοῦντες . . . εἴ τις διακονεῖ.	2 Cor. x. 8, xiii. 10. εἰς οἰκοδομήν (cf. 1 Cor. xiv. 5). 1 Cor. xii. 27. ὑμεῖς δέ ἐστε σῶμα Χριστοῦ. Phil. iii. 11. εἴ πως καταντήσω εἰς τὴν ἐξανάστασιν τὴν ἐκ νεκρῶν. Philem. 6. ὅπως ἡ κοινωνία τῆς πίστεώς σου ἐνεργὴς γένηται ἐν ἐπιγνώσει παντὸς ἀγαθοῦ [τοῦ] ἐν ἡμῖν εἰς Χριστόν.

Ephesians iv. 5–14.

6 πίστις, ἓν βάπτισμα· εἷς θεὸς καὶ
πατὴρ πάντων, ὁ ἐπὶ πάντων καὶ
7 διὰ πάντων καὶ ἐν πᾶσιν. ἑνὶ δὲ
ἑκάστῳ ἡμῶν ἐδόθη ἡ χάρις κατὰ
τὸ μέτρον τῆς δωρεᾶς τοῦ Χρι-
8 στοῦ. διὸ λέγει· ἀναβὰς εἰς ὕψος
ᾐχμαλώτευσεν αἰχμαλωσίαν, ἔδω-
9 κεν δόματα τοῖς ἀνθρώποις. τὸ δὲ
ἀνέβη τί ἐστιν εἰ μὴ ὅτι καὶ
κατέβη εἰς τὰ κατώτερα μέρη τῆς
10 γῆς; ὁ καταβὰς αὐτός ἐστιν καὶ
ὁ ἀναβὰς ὑπεράνω πάντων τῶν
οὐρανῶν, ἵνα πληρώσῃ τὰ πάντα.
11 καὶ αὐτὸς ἔδωκεν τοὺς μὲν ἀπο-
στόλους, τοὺς δὲ προφήτας, τοὺς
δὲ εὐαγγελιστάς, τοὺς δὲ ποι-
12 μένας καὶ διδασκάλους, πρὸς τὸν
καταρτισμὸν τῶν ἁγίων εἰς ἔργον
διακονίας, εἰς οἰκοδομὴν τοῦ σώ-
13 ματος τοῦ Χριστοῦ, μέχρι καταν-
τήσωμεν οἱ πάντες εἰς τὴν ἑνότητα
τῆς πίστεως καὶ τῆς ἐπιγνώσεως
τοῦ υἱοῦ τοῦ θεοῦ, εἰς ἄνδρα
τέλειον, εἰς μέτρον ἡλικίας τοῦ
14 πληρώματος τοῦ Χριστοῦ, ἵνα

Colossians.

i. 18–19. ἵνα γένηται ἐν πᾶσιν αὐτὸς πρωτεύων, ὅτι ἐν αὐτῷ εὐδόκησεν πᾶν τὸ πλήρωμα κατοικῆσαι.

i. 28. διδάσκοντες πάντα ἄνθρωπον ἐν πάσῃ σοφίᾳ ἵνα παραστήσωμεν πάντα ἄνθρωπον τέλειον ἐν Χριστῷ.

ii. 9. ἐν αὐτῷ κατοικεῖ πᾶν τὸ πλήρωμα τῆς θεότητος.

1 Peter.	1 Cor. xiv. 20. μὴ παιδία γίνεσθε ταῖς φρεσίν, ἀλλὰ τῇ κακίᾳ νηπιάζετε, ταῖς δὲ φρεσὶν τέλειοι.
	1 Cor. iii. 1. ὡς νηπίοις ἐν Χριστῷ.
	1 Cor. xi. 3. παντὸς ἀνδρὸς ἡ κεφαλὴ ὁ Χριστός ἐστιν.
	2 Cor. x. 8, xiii. 10. εἰς οἰκοδομήν.
	1 Cor. xiv. 12. πρὸς τὴν οἰκοδομὴν τῆς ἐκκλησίας.
i. 18. ἐλυτρώθητε ἐκ τῆς ματαίας ὑμῶν ἀναστροφῆς πατροπαραδότου.	
i. 14. . . . ταῖς πρότερον ἐν τῇ ἀγνοίᾳ ὑμῶν ἐπιθυμίαις.	Rom. i. 21. γνόντες τὸν θεὸν οὐχ ὡς θεὸν ἐδόξασαν ἢ ηὐχαρίστησαν, ἀλλὰ ἐματαιώθησαν ἐν τοῖς διαλογισμοῖς αὐτῶν, καὶ ἐσκοτίσθη ἡ ἀσύνετος αὐτῶν καρδία.
ii. 2–3. ἵνα ἐν αὐτῷ αὐξηθῆτε εἰς σωτηρίαν, εἰ ἐγεύσασθε ὅτι χρηστὸς ὁ κύριος.	Rom. i. 24. διὸ παρέδωκεν αὐτοὺς ὁ θεὸς ἐν ταῖς ἐπιθυμίαις τῶν καρδιῶν αὐτῶν εἰς ἀκαθαρσίαν.
	2 Cor. xii. 21. ἐπὶ τῇ ἀκαθαρσίᾳ καὶ πορνείᾳ καὶ ἀσελγείᾳ ᾗ ἔπραξαν.
	Gal. v. 19. τὰ ἔργα τῆς σαρκὸς . . . πορνεία, ἀκαθαρσία, ἀσέλγεια.
	Rom. ix. 1. ἀλήθειαν λέγω ἐν Χριστῷ.
	Rom. vi. 6. τοῦτο γινώσκοντες ὅτι ὁ παλαιὸς ἡμῶν ἄνθρωπος συνεσταυρώθη.

Ephesians iv. 14–22.	Colossians.
μηκέτι ὦμεν νήπιοι, κλυδωνιζό-	
μενοι καὶ περιφερόμενοι παντὶ	ii. 22. κατὰ τὰ ἐντάλματα καὶ διδα-
ἀνέμῳ τῆς διδασκαλίας ἐν τῇ	σκαλίας τῶν ἀνθρώπων.
κυβίᾳ τῶν ἀνθρώπων, ἐν πανουρ-	
γίᾳ πρὸς τὴν μεθοδίαν τῆς πλάνης,	
15 ἀληθεύοντες δὲ ἐν ἀγάπῃ αὐξήσω-	i. 18. αὐτός ἐστιν ἡ κεφαλὴ τοῦ
μεν εἰς αὐτὸν τὰ πάντα, ὅς ἐστιν	σώματος.
16 ἡ κεφαλή, Χριστός, ἐξ οὗ πᾶν τὸ	ii. 19. τὴν κεφαλήν, ἐξ οὗ πᾶν τὸ
σῶμα συναρμολογούμενον καὶ	σῶμα διὰ τῶν ἁφῶν καὶ συνδέσμων
συνβιβαζόμενον διὰ πάσης ἁφῆς	ἐπιχορηγούμενον καὶ συνβιβαζό-
τῆς ἐπιχορηγίας κατ᾽ ἐνέργειαν	μενον αὔξει τὴν αὔξησιν τοῦ θεοῦ.
ἐν μέτρῳ ἑνὸς ἑκάστου μέρους τὴν	ii. 2. συνβιβασθέντες ἐν ἀγάπῃ.
αὔξησιν τοῦ σώματος ποιεῖται εἰς	i. 29. κατὰ τὴν ἐνέργειαν.
οἰκοδομὴν ἑαυτοῦ ἐν ἀγάπῃ.	
17 τοῦτο οὖν λέγω καὶ μαρτύρομαι	ii. 4. τοῦτο λέγω.
ἐν κυρίῳ, μηκέτι ὑμᾶς περιπατεῖν	
καθὼς καὶ τὰ ἔθνη περιπατεῖ ἐν	
18 ματαιότητι τοῦ νοὸς αὐτῶν, ἐσκο-	
τωμένοι τῇ διανοίᾳ ὄντες ἀπηλ-	i. 21. καὶ ὑμᾶς ποτε ὄντας ἀπηλλο-
λοτριωμένοι τῆς ζωῆς τοῦ θεοῦ,	τριωμένους καὶ ἐχθροὺς τῇ διανοίᾳ.
διὰ τὴν ἄγνοιαν τὴν οὖσαν ἐν	
αὐτοῖς, διὰ τὴν πώρωσιν τῆς	
19 καρδίας αὐτῶν, οἵτινες ἀπηλγη-	
κότες ἑαυτοὺς παρέδωκαν τῇ	
ἀσελγείᾳ εἰς ἐργασίαν ἀκαθαρσίας	iii. 5. ἀκαθαρσίαν . . . πλεονεξίαν.
20 πάσης ἐν πλεονεξίᾳ. ὑμεῖς δὲ οὐχ	ii. 6–7. ὡς οὖν παρελάβετε τὸν
21 οὕτως ἐμάθετε τὸν Χριστόν, εἴ γε	Χριστὸν Ἰησοῦν τὸν κύριον, ἐν
αὐτὸν ἠκούσατε καὶ ἐν αὐτῷ	αὐτῷ περιπατεῖτε . . . καθὼς ἐδιδά-
ἐδιδάχθητε καθώς ἐστιν ἀλήθεια	χθητε.
22 ἐν τῷ Ἰησοῦ, ἀποθέσθαι ὑμᾶς	i. 23. εἴ γε . . . .
κατὰ τὴν προτέραν ἀναστροφὴν	
τὸν παλαιὸν ἄνθρωπον τὸν φθειρό-	iii. 8–10. ἀπόθεσθε καὶ ὑμεῖς τὰ πάντα
μενον κατὰ τὰς ἐπιθυμίας τῆς	. . . ἀπεκδυσάμενοι τὸν παλαιὸν

1 Peter.	
	Rom. xii. 2. μεταμορφοῦσθε τῇ ἀνακαινώσει τοῦ νοός. Gal. iii. 27. Χριστὸν ἐνεδύσασθε. Rom. xiii. 12. ἀποθώμεθα . . . ἐνδυσώμεθα . . . 14 ἐνδύσασθε τὸν κύριον Ἰησοῦν Χριστόν.
iv. 1. καὶ ὑμεῖς τὴν αὐτὴν ἔννοιαν ὁπλίσασθε.	2 Cor. v. 17. τὰ ἀρχαῖα παρῆλθεν, ἰδοὺ γέγονεν καινά. Rom. xii. 5. οἱ πολλοὶ ἓν σῶμά ἐσμεν ἐν Χριστῷ τὸ δὲ καθ' εἷς ἀλλήλων μέλη.
iv. 6. ἵνα . . . ζῶσι δὲ κατὰ θεὸν πνεύματι.	1 Cor. xv. 34. ἐκνήψατε δικαίως καὶ μὴ ἁμαρτάνετε. Rom. xii. 19. ἀλλὰ δότε τόπον τῇ ὀργῇ.
ii. 1. ἀποθέμενοι οὖν πᾶσαν κακίαν καὶ πάντα δόλον.	Rom. ii. 21. ὁ κηρύσσων μὴ κλέπτειν, κλέπτεις; 1 Thess. iv. 11. ἐργάζεσθαι ταῖς χερσὶν ὑμῶν . . . ἵνα . . . μηδενὸς χρείαν ἔχητε. 1 Cor. iv. 12. καὶ κοπιῶμεν ἐργαζόμενοι ταῖς ἰδίαις χερσίν. Rom. ii. 10. παντὶ τῷ ἐργαζομένῳ τὸ ἀγαθόν. Gal. vi. 10. ἐργαζώμεθα τὸ ἀγαθὸν πρὸς πάντας. 1 Thess. v. 19. τὸ πνεῦμα μὴ σβέννυτε. Rom. viii. 23. τὴν ἀπαρχὴν τοῦ πνεύματος ἔχοντες . . . υἱοθεσίαν ἀπεκδεχόμενοι τὴν ἀπολύτρωσιν τοῦ σώματος ἡμῶν. 2 Cor. i. 22. ὁ θεός, ὁ καὶ σφραγισάμενος ἡμᾶς καὶ δοὺς τὸν ἀρραβῶνα τοῦ πνεύματος.
ii. 1. ἀποθέμενοι οὖν πᾶσαν κακίαν.	1 Cor. xi. 1. μιμηταί μου γίνεσθε, καθὼς κἀγὼ Χριστοῦ. 1 Cor. iv. 16. μιμηταί μου γίνεσθε. Phil. iii. 17. συνμιμηταί μου γίνεσθε.
iii. 8. εὔσπλαγχνοι.	1 Thess. i. 6. καὶ ὑμεῖς μιμηταὶ ἡμῶν ἐγενήθητε καὶ τοῦ κυρίου. 1 Cor. iv. 14. ὡς τέκνα μου ἀγαπητὰ νουθετῶν.

Ephesians iv. 22–v. 1.	Colossians.
23 ἀπάτης, ἀνανεοῦσθαι δὲ τῷ πνεύ-	ἄνθρωπον σὺν ταῖς πράξεσιν αὐτοῦ,
24 ματι τοῦ νοὸς ὑμῶν καὶ ἐνδύσα-	καὶ ἐνδυσάμενοι τὸν νέον τὸν
σθαι τὸν καινὸν ἄνθρωπον τὸν	ἀνακαινούμενον εἰς ἐπίγνωσιν κατ'
κατὰ θεὸν κτισθέντα ἐν δικαιοσύνῃ	εἰκόνα τοῦ κτίσαντος αὐτόν.
καὶ ὁσιότητι τῆς ἀληθείας.	
25 διὸ ἀποθέμενοι τὸ ψεῦδος λαλεῖτε	
ἀλήθειαν ἕκαστος μετὰ τοῦ πλη-	
σίον αὐτοῦ, ὅτι ἐσμὲν ἀλλήλων	iii. 8. ἀπόθεσθε καὶ ὑμεῖς τὰ πάντα,
26 μέλη. ὀργίζεσθε καὶ μὴ ἁμαρτά-	ὀργήν, θυμόν, . . . μὴ ψεύδεσθε εἰς
νετε· ὁ ἥλιος μὴ ἐπιδυέτω ἐπὶ	ἀλλήλους.
27 παροργισμῷ ὑμῶν, μηδὲ δίδοτε	
28 τόπον τῷ διαβόλῳ. ὁ κλέπτων	
μηκέτι κλεπτέτω, μᾶλλον δὲ	
κοπιάτω ἐργαζόμενος ταῖς ἰδίαις	
χερσὶν τὸ ἀγαθόν, ἵνα ἔχῃ μετα-	
29 διδόναι τῷ χρείαν ἔχοντι. πᾶς	iii. 8. αἰσχρολογίαν ἐκ τοῦ στόματος
λόγος σαπρὸς ἐκ τοῦ στόματος	ὑμῶν.
ὑμῶν μὴ ἐκπορευέσθω, ἀλλὰ εἴ	iv. 6. ὁ λόγος ὑμῶν πάντοτε ἐν
τις ἀγαθὸς πρὸς οἰκοδομὴν τῆς	χάριτι.
χρείας, ἵνα δῷ χάριν τοῖς ἀκούου-	
30 σιν. καὶ μὴ λυπεῖτε τὸ πνεῦμα τὸ	
ἅγιον τοῦ θεοῦ, ἐν ᾧ ἐσφραγίσθητε	
31 εἰς ἡμέραν ἀπολυτρώσεως. πᾶσα	iii. 19. μὴ πικραίνεσθε πρὸς αὐτάς.
πικρία καὶ θυμὸς καὶ ὀργὴ καὶ	iii. 8. ἀπόθεσθε . . . ὀργήν, θυμόν,
κραυγὴ καὶ βλασφημία ἀρθήτω	κακίαν, βλασφημίαν, αἰσχρολογίαν
32 ἀφ' ὑμῶν σὺν πάσῃ κακίᾳ. γίνεσθε	ἐκ τοῦ στόματος ὑμῶν.
δὲ εἰς ἀλλήλους χρηστοί, εὔσπλαγ-	iii. 12. ἐνδύσασθε . . . σπλάγχνα
χνοι, χαριζόμενοι ἑαυτοῖς καθὼς	οἰκτιρμοῦ, χρηστότητα . . . χαριζό-
καὶ ὁ θεὸς ἐν Χριστῷ ἐχαρίσατο	μενοι ἑαυτοῖς . . . καθὼς καὶ ὁ
ὑμῖν.	κύριος ἐχαρίσατο ὑμῖν.
v. 1 γίνεσθε οὖν μιμηταὶ τοῦ θεοῦ,	

1 Peter.	
ii. 5. ἀνενέγκαι πνευματικὰς θυσίας εὐπροσδέκτους θεῷ διὰ Ἰησοῦ Χριστοῦ.	Gal. ii. 20. . . . τοῦ υἱοῦ τοῦ θεοῦ τοῦ ἀγαπήσαντός με καὶ παραδόντος ἑαυτὸν ὑπὲρ ἐμοῦ.
	Phil. iv. 18. . . . δεξάμενος παρὰ Ἐπαφροδίτου τὰ παρ' ὑμῶν, ὀσμὴν εὐωδίας, θυσίαν δεκτήν, εὐάρεστον τῷ θεῷ.
	Cf. also 2 Cor. ii. 14–16.
	Rom. i. 28. τὰ μὴ καθήκοντα.
	1 Cor. v. 11. ἐάν τις ἀδελφὸς ὀνομαζόμενος ᾖ πόρνος ἢ πλεονέκτης ἢ εἰδωλολάτρης.
	Gal. v. 19–21. πορνεία, ἀκαθαρσία, ἀσέλγεια, εἰδωλολατρεία, . . . προεῖπον ὅτι οἱ τὰ τοιαῦτα πράσσοντες βασιλείαν θεοῦ οὐ κληρονομήσουσιν.
	1 Cor. vi. 9. ἢ οὐκ οἴδατε ὅτι ἄδικοι θεοῦ βασιλείαν οὐ κληρονομήσουσιν; . . . οὔτε πόρνοι οὔτε εἰδωλολάτραι . . . οὔτε πλεονέκται . . . βασιλείαν θεοῦ κληρονομήσουσιν.
	Rom. i. 18. ἀποκαλύπτεται γὰρ ὀργὴ θεοῦ ἀπ' οὐρανοῦ ἐπὶ πᾶσαν ἀσέβειαν.
	2 Cor. vi. 14. μὴ γίνεσθε ἑτεροζυγοῦντες ἀπίστοις· τίς γὰρ μετοχὴ δικαιοσύνῃ καὶ ἀνομίᾳ, ἢ τίς κοινωνία φωτὶ πρὸς σκότος;
ii. 9. . . . τοῦ ἐκ σκότους ὑμᾶς καλέσαντος εἰς τὸ θαυμαστὸν αὐτοῦ φῶς.	1 Thess. v. 5. πάντες γὰρ ὑμεῖς υἱοὶ φωτός ἐστε καὶ υἱοὶ ἡμέρας.
	Gal. v. 22. ὁ δὲ καρπὸς τοῦ πνεύματός ἐστιν . . . .
	Phil. i. 11. πεπληρωμένοι καρπὸν δικαιοσύνης.
	Rom. xii. 2. . . . εἰς τὸ δοκιμάζειν ὑμᾶς τί τὸ θέλημα τοῦ θεοῦ, τὸ ἀγαθὸν καὶ εὐάρεστον καὶ τέλειον.
	Phil. iv. 18. εὐάρεστον τῷ θεῷ.
	Rom. xiii. 12. ἀποθώμεθα οὖν τὰ ἔργα τοῦ σκότους, ἐνδυσώμεθα δὲ τὰ ὅπλα τοῦ φωτός.
	1 Cor. xiv. 24–5. ἐλέγχεται ὑπὸ πάντων . . . τὰ κρυπτὰ τῆς καρδίας αὐτοῦ φανερὰ γίνεται.

Ephesians v. 1–13.	Colossians.
2 ὡς τέκνα ἀγαπητά, καὶ περι-	iii. 12. ἅγιοι καὶ ἠγαπημένοι.
Col. iii. 12.	
πατεῖτε ἐν ἀγάπῃ καθὼς καὶ	
ὁ Χριστὸς ἠγάπησεν ὑμᾶς καὶ	
παρέδωκεν ἑαυτὸν ὑπὲρ ἡμῶν	
προσφορὰν καὶ θυσίαν τῷ θεῷ εἰς	
3 ὀσμὴν εὐωδίας. πορνεία δὲ καὶ	iii. 5. νεκρώσατε . . . πορνείαν, ἀκα-
ἀκαθαρσία πᾶσα ἢ πλεονεξία	θαρσίαν . . . τὴν πλεονεξίαν.
μηδὲ ὀνομαζέσθω ἐν ὑμῖν, καθὼς	iii. 8. αἰσχρολογίαν.
4 πρέπει ἁγίοις, καὶ αἰσχρότης καὶ	
μωρολογία ἢ εὐτραπελία, ἃ οὐκ	
ἀνῆκεν, ἀλλὰ μᾶλλον εὐχαριστία.	ii. 7. περισσεύοντες ἐν εὐχαριστίᾳ.
5 τοῦτο γὰρ ἴστε γινώσκοντες, ὅτι	
πᾶς πόρνος ἢ ἀκάθαρτος ἢ πλεον-	iii. 5. πορνείαν, ἀκαθαρσίαν, . . . πλεον-
έκτης, ὅ ἐστιν εἰδωλολάτρης, οὐκ	εξίαν, ἥτις ἐστὶν εἰδωλολατρεία.
ἔχει κληρονομίαν ἐν τῇ βασιλείᾳ	
6 τοῦ Χριστοῦ καὶ θεοῦ. μηδεὶς	ii. 4. ἵνα μηδεὶς ὑμᾶς παραλογίζηται
ὑμᾶς ἀπατάτω κενοῖς λόγοις· διὰ	ἐν πιθανολογίᾳ.
ταῦτα γὰρ ἔρχεται ἡ ὀργὴ τοῦ	ii. 8. διὰ . . . κενῆς ἀπάτης.
θεοῦ ἐπὶ τοὺς υἱοὺς τῆς ἀπειθείας.	iii. 6. δι' ἃ ἔρχεται ἡ ὀργὴ τοῦ θεοῦ.
7 μὴ οὖν γίνεσθε συνμέτοχοι αὐτῶν.	
8 ἦτε γάρ ποτε σκότος, νῦν δὲ φῶς	
ἐν κυρίῳ· ὡς τέκνα φωτὸς περι-	
9 πατεῖτε,—ὁ γὰρ καρπὸς τοῦ φωτὸς	
ἐν πάσῃ ἀγαθωσύνῃ καὶ δικαιο-	
10 σύνῃ καὶ ἀληθείᾳ—δοκιμάζοντες	
11 τί ἐστιν εὐάρεστον τῷ κυρίῳ, καὶ	iii. 20. τοῦτο γὰρ εὐάρεστόν ἐστιν ἐν
μὴ συνκοινωνεῖτε τοῖς ἔργοις τοῖς	κυρίῳ.
ἀκάρποις τοῦ σκότους, μᾶλλον δὲ	
12 καὶ ἐλέγχετε, τὰ γὰρ κρυφῇ γινό-	
μενα ὑπ' αὐτῶν αἰσχρόν ἐστιν καὶ	iii. 8. αἰσχρολογίαν.
13 λέγειν· τὰ δὲ πάντα ἐλεγχόμενα	

1 Peter.	
	Rom. xiii. 11. καὶ τοῦτο εἰδότες τὸν καιρόν, ὅτι ὥρα ἤδη ὑμᾶς ἐξ ὕπνου ἐγερθῆναι . . . ἡ νὺξ προέκοψεν, ἡ δὲ ἡμέρα ἤγγικεν.
	1 Cor. iii. 10. ἕκαστος δὲ βλεπέτω πῶς οἰκοδομεῖ. Gal. i. 4. ἐκ τοῦ αἰῶνος τοῦ ἐνεστῶτος πονηροῦ. Rom. xii. 2. εἰς τὸ δοκιμάζειν ὑμᾶς τί τὸ θέλημα τοῦ θεοῦ.
	1 Cor. xiv. 15. ψαλῶ τῷ πνεύματι, ψαλῶ δὲ καὶ τῷ νοΐ. Phil. i. 3–4. εὐχαριστῶ τῷ θεῷ μου . . . πάντοτε . . . ὑπὲρ πάντων ὑμῶν. 1 Thess. v. 18. ἐν παντὶ εὐχαριστεῖτε.
v. 5. νεώτεροι, ὑποτάγητε πρεσβυτέροις· πάντες δὲ ἀλλήλοις τὴν ταπεινοφροσύνην ἐγκομβώσασθε.	Gal. v. 13. διὰ τῆς ἀγάπης δουλεύετε ἀλλήλοις.
iii. 1. ὁμοίως γυναῖκες ὑποτασσόμεναι τοῖς ἰδίοις ἀνδράσιν.	1 Cor. xi. 3. παντὸς ἀνδρὸς ἡ κεφαλὴ ὁ Χριστός ἐστιν, κεφαλὴ δὲ γυναικὸς ὁ ἀνήρ.
iii. 7. οἱ ἄνδρες ὁμοίως συνοικοῦντες κατὰ γνῶσιν.	Gal. ii. 20. τοῦ υἱοῦ τοῦ θεοῦ τοῦ ἀγαπήσαντός με καὶ παραδόντος ἑαυτὸν ὑπὲρ ἐμοῦ.
	1 Cor. vi. 11. ἀλλὰ ἀπελούσασθε, ἀλλὰ ἡγιάσθητε.
i. 25. τοῦτο δέ ἐστιν τὸ ῥῆμα τὸ εὐαγγελισθὲν εἰς ὑμᾶς.	Rom. x. 9. ὅτι ἐὰν ὁμολογήσῃς τὸ ῥῆμα ἐν τῷ στόματί σου, ὅτι κύριος Ἰησοῦς.

Ephesians v. 13–25.	Colossians.
ὑπὸ τοῦ φωτὸς φανεροῦται· πᾶν	
γὰρ τὸ φανερούμενον φῶς ἐστιν.	
14 διὸ λέγει·	
ἔγειρε, ὁ καθεύδων,	
καὶ ἀνάστα ἐκ τῶν νεκρῶν,	
καὶ ἐπιφαύσει σοι ὁ Χριστός.	
15 βλέπετε οὖν ἀκριβῶς πῶς περι-	
πατεῖτε, μὴ ὡς ἄσοφοι ἀλλ' ὡς	iv. 5. ἐν σοφίᾳ περιπατεῖτε πρὸς τοὺς
16 σοφοί, ἐξαγοραζόμενοι τὸν και-	ἔξω, τὸν καιρὸν ἐξαγοραζόμενοι.
ρόν, ὅτι αἱ ἡμέραι πονηραί εἰσιν.	
17 διὰ τοῦτο μὴ γίνεσθε ἄφρονες,	
ἀλλὰ συνίετε τί τὸ θέλημα τοῦ	
18 κυρίου. καὶ μὴ μεθύσκεσθε οἴνῳ,	
ἐν ᾧ ἐστιν ἀσωτία, ἀλλὰ πλη-	
19 ροῦσθε ἐν πνεύματι, λαλοῦντες	iii. 16. διδάσκοντες καὶ νουθετοῦντες
ἑαυτοῖς ψαλμοῖς καὶ ὕμνοις καὶ	ἑαυτούς, ψαλμοῖς, ὕμνοις, ᾠδαῖς
ᾠδαῖς πνευματικαῖς, ᾄδοντες καὶ	πνευματικαῖς ἐν τῇ χάριτι ᾄδοντες
ψάλλοντες τῇ καρδίᾳ ὑμῶν τῷ	ἐν ταῖς καρδίαις ὑμῶν τῷ θεῷ·
20 κυρίῳ, εὐχαριστοῦντες πάντοτε	καὶ πᾶν ὅ τι ἐὰν ποιῆτε ἐν λόγῳ
ὑπὲρ πάντων ἐν ὀνόματι τοῦ	ἢ ἐν ἔργῳ, πάντα ἐν ὀνόματι κυρίου
κυρίου ἡμῶν Ἰησοῦ Χριστοῦ τῷ	Ἰησοῦ, εὐχαριστοῦντες τῷ θεῷ
21 θεῷ καὶ πατρί, ὑποτασσόμενοι	πατρὶ δι' αὐτοῦ.
ἀλλήλοις ἐν φόβῳ Χριστοῦ.	iii. 22. ὑπακούετε . . . φοβούμενοι
	τὸν κύριον.
22 αἱ γυναῖκες τοῖς ἰδίοις ἀνδράσιν	iii. 18. αἱ γυναῖκες, ὑποτάσσεσθε
23 ὡς τῷ κυρίῳ, ὅτι ἀνήρ ἐστιν	τοῖς ἀνδράσιν, ὡς ἀνῆκεν ἐν κυρίῳ.
κεφαλὴ τῆς γυναικὸς ὡς καὶ	
ὁ Χριστὸς κεφαλὴ τῆς ἐκκλησίας,	i. 18. καὶ αὐτός ἐστιν ἡ κεφαλὴ τοῦ
24 αὐτὸς σωτὴρ τοῦ σώματος. ἀλλὰ	σώματος, τῆς ἐκκλησίας.
ὡς ἡ ἐκκλησία ὑποτάσσεται τῷ	
Χριστῷ, οὕτως καὶ αἱ γυναῖκες	
25 τοῖς ἀνδράσιν ἐν παντί. οἱ ἄνδρες,	iii. 19. οἱ ἄνδρες, ἀγαπᾶτε τὰς
ἀγαπᾶτε τὰς γυναῖκας, καθὼς	γυναῖκας.
καὶ ὁ Χριστὸς ἠγάπησεν τὴν ἐκ-	
κλησίαν καὶ ἑαυτὸν παρέδωκεν	

I Peter.	
iii. 20. διεσώθησαν δι' ὕδατος. ὃ καὶ ὑμᾶς ἀντίτυπον νῦν σώζει βάπτισμα	2 Cor. xi. 2. παρθένον ἁγνὴν παραστῆσαι τῷ Χριστῷ. I Cor. vii. 3–4. τῇ γυναικὶ ὁ ἀνὴρ τὴν ὀφειλὴν ἀποδιδότω, ὁμοίως δὲ καὶ ἡ γυνὴ τῷ ἀνδρί. ἡ γυνὴ τοῦ ἰδίου σώματος οὐκ ἐξουσιάζει ἀλλὰ ὁ ἀνήρ· ὁμοίως δὲ καὶ ὁ ἀνὴρ τοῦ ἰδίου σώματος οὐκ ἐξουσιάζει ἀλλὰ ἡ γυνή.
	Rom. xii. 5. οἱ πολλοὶ ἓν σῶμά ἐσμεν ἐν Χριστῷ, τὸ δὲ καθ' εἷς ἀλλήλων μέλη. I Cor. xii. 12. καθάπερ γὰρ τὸ σῶμα ἕν ἐστιν καὶ μέλη πολλὰ ἔχει, πάντα δὲ τὰ μέλη τοῦ σώματος πολλὰ ὄντα ἕν ἐστιν σῶμα, οὕτως καὶ ὁ Χριστός. I Cor. xii. 27. ὑμεῖς δέ ἐστε σῶμα Χριστοῦ καὶ μέλη ἐκ μέρους.
	I Cor. vi. 15–16. οὐκ οἴδατε ὅτι τὰ σώματα ὑμῶν μέλη Χριστοῦ ἐστιν; . . . ἔσονται γάρ, φησίν, οἱ δύο εἰς σάρκα μίαν.
	I Cor. vii. 2. ἕκαστος τὴν ἑαυτοῦ γυναῖκα ἐχέτω.

Ephesians v. 25–vi. 4.	Colossians
26 ὑπὲρ αὐτῆς, ἵνα αὐτὴν ἁγιάσῃ	
καθαρίσας τῷ λουτρῷ τοῦ ὕδατος	
27 ἐν ῥήματι, ἵνα παραστήσῃ αὐτὸς	i. 28. ἵνα παραστήσωμεν πάντα ἄν-
ἑαυτῷ ἔνδοξον τὴν ἐκκλησίαν, μὴ	θρωπον τέλειον ἐν Χριστῷ.
ἔχουσαν σπίλον ἢ ῥυτίδα ἤ τι τῶν	i. 22. παραστῆσαι ὑμᾶς ἁγίους καὶ
τοιούτων, ἀλλ' ἵνα ᾖ ἁγία καὶ	ἀμώμους καὶ ἀνεγκλήτους κατενώ-
28 ἄμωμος. οὕτως ὀφείλουσιν [καὶ]	πιον αὐτοῦ.
οἱ ἄνδρες ἀγαπᾶν τὰς ἑαυτῶν	iii. 19. οἱ ἄνδρες, ἀγαπᾶτε τὰς
γυναῖκας ὡς τὰ ἑαυτῶν σώματα.	γυναῖκας.
ὁ ἀγαπῶν τὴν ἑαυτοῦ γυναῖκα	
29 ἑαυτὸν ἀγαπᾷ. οὐδεὶς γάρ ποτε	
τὴν ἑαυτοῦ σάρκα ἐμίσησεν, ἀλλὰ	
ἐκτρέφει καὶ θάλπει αὐτήν, καθὼς	
30 καὶ ὁ Χριστὸς τὴν ἐκκλησίαν, ὅτι	
μέλη ἐσμὲν τοῦ σώματος αὐτοῦ.	
31 ἀντὶ τούτου καταλείψει ἄνθρωπος	
[τὸν] πατέρα καὶ [τὴν] μητέρα καὶ	
προσκολληθήσεται πρὸς τὴν γυ-	
ναῖκα αὐτοῦ, καὶ ἔσονται οἱ δύο	
32 εἰς σάρκα μίαν. τὸ μυστήριον	
τοῦτο μέγα ἐστίν, ἐγὼ δὲ λέγω	
εἰς Χριστὸν καὶ εἰς τὴν ἐκκλησίαν.	
33 πλὴν καὶ ὑμεῖς οἱ καθ' ἕνα	
ἕκαστος τὴν ἑαυτοῦ γυναῖκα	
οὕτως ἀγαπάτω ὡς ἑαυτόν, ἡ δὲ	
γυνὴ ἵνα φοβῆται τὸν ἄνδρα.	
vi. 1 τὰ τέκνα, ὑπακούετε τοῖς	iii. 20. τὰ τέκνα, ὑπακούετε τοῖς
γονεῦσιν ὑμῶν ἐν κυρίῳ· τοῦτο	γονεῦσιν κατὰ πάντα, τοῦτο γὰρ
2 γάρ ἐστιν δίκαιον. τίμα τὸν	εὐάρεστόν ἐστιν ἐν κυρίῳ.
πατέρα σου καὶ τὴν μητέρα, ἥτις	iv. 1. τὸ δίκαιον . . . παρέχεσθε.
ἐστὶν ἐντολὴ πρώτη ἐν ἐπαγγελίᾳ,	
3 ἵνα εὖ σοι γένηται καὶ ἔσῃ μακρο-	
4 χρόνιος ἐπὶ τῆς γῆς. καὶ οἱ	
πατέρες, μὴ παροργίζετε τὰ	iii. 21. οἱ πατέρες, μὴ ἐρεθίζετε τὰ
τέκνα ὑμῶν, ἀλλὰ ἐκτρέφετε αὐτὰ	τέκνα ὑμῶν ἵνα μὴ ἀθυμῶσιν.
ἐν παιδείᾳ καὶ νουθεσίᾳ κυρίου.	

1 Peter.	
ii. 18. οἱ οἰκέται, ὑποτασσόμενοι ἐν παντὶ φόβῳ τοῖς δεσπόταις . . . τοῦτο γὰρ χάρις εἰ διὰ συνείδησιν θεοῦ ὑποφέρει τις λύπας.	Rom. vi. 16. δοῦλοί ἐστε ᾧ ὑπακούετε. Phil. ii. 12. πάντοτε ὑπηκούσατε . . . μετὰ φόβου καὶ τρόμου. 2 Cor. vii. 15. μετὰ φόβου καὶ τρόμου ἐδέξασθε αὐτόν. Gal. i. 10. ἢ ζητῶ ἀνθρώποις ἀρέσκειν; εἰ ἔτι ἀνθρώποις ἤρεσκον, Χριστοῦ δοῦλος οὐκ ἂν ἤμην. 1 Cor. vii. 22. ὁ ἐλεύθερος κληθεὶς δοῦλός ἐστιν Χριστοῦ. Phil. i. 1. δοῦλοι Χριστοῦ Ἰησοῦ. 2 Cor. v. 10. ἵνα κομίσηται ἕκαστος τὰ διὰ τοῦ σώματος πρὸς ἃ ἔπραξεν, εἴτε ἀγαθὸν εἴτε φαῦλον. 1 Cor. xii. 13. εἴτε δοῦλοι εἴτε ἐλεύθεροι. Gal. iii. 28. οὐκ ἔνι δοῦλος οὐδὲ ἐλεύθερος. Rom. ii. 11. οὐ γάρ ἐστιν προσωπολημψία παρὰ τῷ θεῷ.
i. 17. . . . τὸν ἀπροσωπολήμπτως κρίνοντα.	Gal. vi. 17. τοῦ λοιποῦ. Phil. iii. 1. τὸ λοιπόν. Rom. xiii. 12. ἐνδυσώμεθα δὲ τὰ ὅπλα τοῦ φωτός.
v. 8. ὁ ἀντίδικος ὑμῶν διάβολος.	1 Cor. xvi. 13. γρηγορεῖτε, στήκετε ἐν τῇ πίστει, ἀνδρίζεσθε, κραταιοῦσθε. 2 Cor. ii. 11. ἵνα μὴ πλεονεκτηθῶμεν ὑπὸ τοῦ Σατανᾶ, οὐ γὰρ αὐτοῦ τὰ νοήματα ἀγνοοῦμεν.
iv. 1. ὁπλίσασθε. v. 8. ὁ ἀντίδικος ὑμῶν διάβολος . . . περιπατεῖ ζητῶν τίνα καταπιεῖν· ᾧ ἀντίστητε στερεοὶ τῇ πίστει.	2 Cor. x. 3–4. ἐν σαρκὶ γὰρ περιπατοῦντες οὐ κατὰ σάρκα στρατευόμεθα—τὰ γὰρ ὅπλα τῆς στρατείας ἡμῶν οὐ σαρκικὰ ἀλλὰ δυνατὰ τῷ θεῷ πρὸς καθαίρεσιν ὀχυρωμάτων.

Ephesians vi. 5–13.

5 οἱ δοῦλοι, ὑπακούετε τοῖς κατὰ
σάρκα κυρίοις μετὰ φόβου καὶ
τρόμου ἐν ἁπλότητι τῆς καρδίας
6 ὑμῶν ὡς τῷ Χριστῷ, μὴ κατ᾽
ὀφθαλμοδουλίαν ὡς ἀνθρωπάρε-
σκοι, ἀλλ᾽ ὡς δοῦλοι Χριστοῦ
ποιοῦντες τὸ θέλημα τοῦ θεοῦ ἐκ
7 ψυχῆς, μετ᾽ εὐνοίας δουλεύοντες
ὡς τῷ κυρίῳ καὶ οὐκ ἀνθρώποις,
8 εἰδότες ὅτι ἕκαστος ἐάν τι ποιήσῃ
ἀγαθόν, τοῦτο κομίσεται παρὰ
κυρίου, εἴτε δοῦλος εἴτε ἐλεύ-
9 θερος. καὶ οἱ κύριοι, τὰ αὐτὰ
ποιεῖτε πρὸς αὐτούς, ἀνιέντες τὴν
ἀπειλήν, εἰδότες ὅτι καὶ αὐτῶν καὶ
ὑμῶν ὁ κύριός ἐστιν ἐν οὐρανοῖς,
καὶ προσωποληψία οὐκ ἔστιν
10 παρ᾽ αὐτῷ. τοῦ λοιποῦ, ἐνδυνα-
μοῦσθε ἐν κυρίῳ καὶ ἐν τῷ
11 κράτει τῆς ἰσχύος αὐτοῦ. ἐνδύ-
σασθε τὴν πανοπλίαν τοῦ θεοῦ
πρὸς τὸ δύνασθαι ὑμᾶς στῆναι
πρὸς τὰς μεθοδίας τοῦ διαβόλου.
12 ὅτι οὐκ ἔστιν ἡμῖν ἡ πάλη πρὸς
αἷμα καὶ σάρκα, ἀλλὰ πρὸς τὰς
ἀρχάς, πρὸς τὰς ἐξουσίας, πρὸς
τοὺς κοσμοκράτορας τοῦ σκότους
τούτου, πρὸς τὰ πνευματικὰ τῆς
13 πονηρίας ἐν τοῖς ἐπουρανίοις. διὰ
τοῦτο ἀναλάβετε τὴν πανοπλίαν
τοῦ θεοῦ, ἵνα δυνηθῆτε ἀντιστῆναι
ἐν τῇ ἡμέρᾳ τῇ πονηρᾷ καὶ
ἅπαντα κατεργασάμενοι στῆναι.

Colossians.

iii. 22. οἱ δοῦλοι, ὑπακούετε κατὰ
πάντα τοῖς κατὰ σάρκα κυρίοις, μὴ
ἐν ὀφθαλμοδουλίαις ὡς ἀνθρωπάρε-
σκοι, ἀλλ᾽ ἐν ἁπλότητι καρδίας
φοβούμενοι τὸν κύριον. 23 ὃ ἐὰν
ποιῆτε, ἐκ ψυχῆς ἐργάζεσθε ὡς
τῷ κυρίῳ καὶ οὐκ ἀνθρώποις,
24 εἰδότες ὅτι ἀπὸ κυρίου ἀπολήμ-
ψεσθε τὴν ἀνταπόδοσιν τῆς κλη-
ρονομίας. τῷ κυρίῳ Χριστῷ δου-
λεύετε. 25 ὁ γὰρ ἀδικῶν κομίσεται
ὃ ἠδίκησεν καὶ οὐκ ἔστιν προσωπο-
λημψία. iv. 1 οἱ κύριοι, τὸ δίκαιον
καὶ τὴν ἰσότητα τοῖς δούλοις
παρέχεσθε, εἰδότες ὅτι καὶ ὑμεῖς
ἔχετε κύριον ἐν οὐρανῷ.

i. 11. ἐν πάσῃ δυνάμει δυναμούμενοι
κατὰ τὸ κράτος τῆς δόξης αὐτοῦ.

i. 16. εἴτε ἀρχαὶ εἴτε ἐξουσίαι.

1 Peter.	
i. 13. διὸ ἀναζωσάμενοι τὰς ὀσφύας τῆς διανοίας ὑμῶν.	1 Thess. v. 8. ἐνδυσάμενοι θώρακα πίστεως καὶ ἀγάπης καὶ περικεφαλαίαν ἐλπίδα σωτηρίας.
v. 12. χάριν τοῦ θεοῦ, εἰς ἣν στῆτε.	
	2 Thess. iii. 3. καὶ φυλάξει ἀπὸ τοῦ πονηροῦ.
	Phil. iv. 6. ἐν παντὶ τῇ προσευχῇ καὶ τῇ δεήσει.
	1 Thess. v. 17. ἀδιαλείπτως προσεύχεσθε, ἐν παντὶ εὐχαριστεῖτε.
	1 Cor. xiv. 15. προσεύξομαι τῷ πνεύματι.
	Rom. xv. 30. . . . ἐν ταῖς προσευχαῖς ὑπὲρ ἐμοῦ πρὸς τὸν θεὸν ἵνα ῥυσθῶ . . . .
	2 Cor. i. 11. . . . συνυπουργούντων καὶ ὑμῶν ὑπὲρ ἡμῶν τῇ δεήσει ἵνα . . . .
	2 Thess. iii. 1. τὸ λοιπὸν προσεύχεσθε, ἀδελφοί, περὶ ἡμῶν ἵνα ὁ λόγος τοῦ κυρίου τρέχῃ.
	Philem. 9. τοιοῦτος ὢν ὡς Παῦλος πρεσβύτης, νυνὶ δὲ καὶ δέσμιος Χριστοῦ Ἰησοῦ.
	2 Cor. v. 20. ὑπὲρ Χριστοῦ οὖν πρεσβεύομεν.
	1 Thess. ii. 2. ἐπαρρησιασάμεθα ἐν τῷ θεῷ ἡμῶν λαλῆσαι πρὸς ὑμᾶς τὸ εὐαγγέλιον τοῦ θεοῦ.
	Phil. i. 12. τὰ κατ' ἐμέ.

Ephesians vi. 14–23.	Colossians.
14 στῆτε οὖν περιζωσάμενοι τὴν ὀσφὺν ὑμῶν ἐν ἀληθείᾳ, καὶ ἐν- δυσάμενοι τὸν θώρακα τῆς δι- 15 καιοσύνης, καὶ ὑποδησάμενοι τοὺς πόδας ἐν ἑτοιμασίᾳ τοῦ εὐαγ- 16 γελίου τῆς εἰρήνης, ἐν πᾶσιν ἀναλαβόντες τὸν θυρεὸν τῆς πί- στεως, ἐν ᾧ δυνήσεσθε πάντα τὰ βέλη τοῦ πονηροῦ τὰ πεπυρωμένα 17 σβέσαι· καὶ τὴν περικεφαλαίαν τοῦ σωτηρίου δέξασθε, καὶ τὴν μάχαιραν τοῦ πνεύματος, ὅ ἐστιν	iv. 12. ἵνα σταθῆτε τέλειοι.
18 ῥῆμα θεοῦ, διὰ πάσης προσευχῆς	i. 8. ἐν πνεύματι.
καὶ δεήσεως, προσευχόμενοι ἐν παντὶ καιρῷ ἐν πνεύματι, καὶ εἰς αὐτὸ ἀγρυπνοῦντες ἐν πάσῃ προσ- καρτερήσει καὶ δεήσει περὶ πάν- 19 των τῶν ἁγίων, καὶ ὑπὲρ ἐμοῦ, ἵνα μοι δοθῇ λόγος ἐν ἀνοίξει τοῦ στόματός μου, ἐν παρρησίᾳ γνωρί- σαι τὸ μυστήριον τοῦ εὐαγγελίου,	iv. 2–4. τῇ προσευχῇ προσκαρτερεῖτε, γρηγοροῦντες ἐν αὐτῇ ἐν εὐχαρι- στίᾳ προσευχόμενοι ἅμα καὶ περὶ ἡμῶν, ἵνα ὁ θεὸς ἀνοίξῃ ἡμῖν θύραν τοῦ λόγου, λαλῆσαι τὸ μυστήριον τοῦ Χριστοῦ, δι' ὃ καὶ δέδεμαι, ἵνα φανερώσω αὐτὸ ὡς δεῖ με λαλῆσαι.
20 ὑπὲρ οὗ πρεσβεύω ἐν ἁλύσει, ἵνα ἐν αὐτῷ παρρησιάσωμαι ὡς δεῖ με λαλῆσαι.	i. 4. εἰς πάντας τοὺς ἁγίους.
21 ἵνα δὲ εἰδῆτε καὶ ὑμεῖς τὰ κατ' ἐμέ, τί πράσσω, πάντα γνωρίσει ὑμῖν Τύχικος ὁ ἀγαπητὸς ἀδελφὸς καὶ πιστὸς διάκονος ἐν κυρίῳ, 22 ὃν ἔπεμψα πρὸς ὑμᾶς εἰς αὐτὸ τοῦτο, ἵνα γνῶτε τὰ περὶ ἡμῶν καὶ παρακαλέσῃ τὰς καρδίας ὑμῶν.	iv. 7. τὰ κατ' ἐμὲ πάντα γνωρίσει ὑμῖν Τύχικος ὁ ἀγαπητὸς ἀδελφὸς καὶ πιστὸς διάκονος καὶ σύνδουλος ἐν κυρίῳ, ὃν ἔπεμψα πρὸς ὑμᾶς εἰς αὐτὸ τοῦτο, ἵνα γνῶτε τὰ περὶ ἡμῶν καὶ παρακαλέσῃ τὰς καρδίας ὑμῶν.

1 Peter.	
i. 8. ὃν οὐκ ἰδόντες ἀγαπᾶτε.	Rom. i. 7. 1 Cor. i. 3. 2 Cor. i. 2. 2 Thess. i. 2. } χάρις ὑμῖν καὶ εἰρήνη ἀπὸ θεοῦ πατρὸς . . . καὶ κυρίου Ἰησοῦ Χριστοῦ.
iii. 4. ὁ κρυπτὸς τῆς καρδίας ἄνθρωπος ἐν τῷ ἀφθάρτῳ τοῦ πραέος καὶ ἡσυχίου πνεύματος.	

Ephesians vi. 23–4.	Colossians.
23 εἰρήνη τοῖς ἀδελφοῖς καὶ	
ἀγάπη μετὰ πίστεως ἀπὸ θεοῦ	
πατρὸς καὶ κυρίου Ἰησοῦ Χρι-	
24 στοῦ. ἡ χάρις μετὰ πάντων τῶν	iv. 18. ἡ χάρις μεθ' ὑμῶν.
ἀγαπώντων τὸν κύριον ἡμῶν	
Ἰησοῦν Χριστὸν ἐν ἀφθαρσίᾳ.	

APPENDIX II

PARALLELS TO COLOSSIANS IN EPHESIANS

In this Appendix the verses in Colossians are listed in order individually, and the verses in Ephesians which seem in some measure to reflect them are entered opposite. The similarity is sometimes very close and sometimes only slight. Its extent may be ascertained by cross-reference to Appendix I.

Colossians	*Ephesians*
i. 1–2	i. 1–2
3	i. 16
4	i. 1; i. 15; i. 16–17; vi. 18
5	i. 13
6	
7	
8	iii. 5; vi. 18
9	i. 15; i. 16; iii. 19; i. 8; i. 17
10	ii. 10; iv. 1; i. 17
11	i. 19; vi. 10; iii. 16
12	i. 11
13	i. 7
14	i. 7
15	
16	iii. 9; i. 10; iii. 10; iii. 15
17	v. 1
18	i. 22; iv. 16; v. 23
19	iii. 19; i. 23
20	ii. 13; i. 7; ii. 15–16; i. 10; iii. 15
21	ii. 12; ii. 16; iv. 18
22	ii. 13; ii. 16; v. 27; i. 4
23	iii. 2; iii. 17; iii. 6; iii. 1; iii. 7
24	iii. 1; iii. 13; i. 23
25	iii. 7; iii. 2
26	iii. 9; iii. 21; iii. 5
27	i. 9; i. 18; iii. 8; iii. 16
28	v. 27
29	iii. 7; iii. 16; iii. 20; iv. 16
ii. 1	
2	iv. 16
3	
4	iv. 17; v. 6

Colossians	*Ephesians*
ii. 5	
6	iv. 21
7	iii. 17; ii. 20
8	v. 6
9	iii. 19; iv. 13; i. 23
10	i. 21
11	ii. 11
12	i. 20
13	ii. 1; ii. 5
14	ii. 15
15	
16	
17	
18	
19	iv. 16; ii. 21
20	
21	
22	iv. 14
23	
iii. 1	ii. 6; i. 20
2	
3	
4	
5	v. 3; iv. 19; v. 5
6	v. 6
7	ii. 3
8	iv. 22; iv. 29; iv. 31; v. 12
9	iv. 25; iv. 22
10	ii. 15; iv. 24
11	
12	iv. 32; v. 2; iv. 2
13	iv. 2; iv. 32; v. 2
14	iv. 3
15	ii. 14; iv. 4
16	i. 8; v. 19
17	v. 20
18	v. 21–2
19	v. 28
20	vi. 1; v. 11
21	vi. 4
22	vi. 5; v. 21
23	vi. 7; vi. 5
24	vi. 8; vi. 6
25	vi. 8–9

Colossians	*Ephesians*
iv. 1	vi. 9
2	vi. 18
3	vi. 19; iii. 4
4	vi. 20
5	v. 15; v. 16
6	iv. 29
7	vi. 21
8	vi. 22
9	
10	
11	
12	
13	
14	
15	
16	iii. 4
17	
18	vi. 24

APPENDIX III

PARALLELS TO EPHESIANS IN COLOSSIANS

In this Appendix the verses in Ephesians which have parallels in Colossians are indicated in tabulated form, in such a way as to show the verse-sequences in Ephesians which roughly correspond to verse-sequences in Colossians.

COLUMN A gives the verses in Ephesians which have parallels in Colossians.

COLUMNS B, C, and D give the parallel verses in Colossians, with brackets to indicate where a sequence of verses in Ephesians is related to a sequence of verses in Colossians.

COLUMN E gives the verses in Colossians which are reflected in Ephesians but which lie outside the verse-sequence which is predominantly influencing the author of Ephesians in that particular passage.

Two things should be specially noted because they are important factors in assessing the relationship of the author of Ephesians to Colossians:

(i) The large number of entries in column E.

(ii) The fact that in the verse-sequences indicated in Columns B, C, and D the individual verses are reproduced in Ephesians in a totally different order from that in which they occur in Colossians.

This appendix is commented on in pages 63–6.

	Ephesians	Colossians			
	A	B	C	D	E
(a) Eph. i. 1–23 = Col. i. 1–27	i. 1–2	i. 1–2			
		i. 4			
	4	i. 22			
	7	i. 14			
		i. 20			
	8	i. 9			iii. 16(?)
	9	i. 27			
	10	i. 16?			
		i. 20			
	11	i. 12			
	13	i. 5			
	15–17	i. 3–4			
		i. 9–10			
	18	i. 12			
		i. 27			
(b) Eph. i. 20–ii. 22 = Col. ii. 7–14	20		ii. 12		iii. 1
	21	i. 16	ii. 10		
	22–3	i. 18–19			
		i. 24			
	23		ii. 9–10		
Eph. ii. 12–16 = Col. i. 20–2	ii. 1		ii. 13		
	2				iii. 7
	3				iii. 6
	5		ii. 13		
	6				iii. 1
	10				i. 10
	11		ii. 11		
(c)	12	i. 21			
	13	i. 20			
		i. 22			
	15	i. 20	ii. 14		
	16	i. 20–2			
	20		ii. 7		
	21		ii. 19?		
	22		ii. 7		
(d) Eph. iii. 1–21 = Col. i. 23–9	iii. 1–5	i. 24–7			
	4				iv. 3
					iv. 16
	6	i. 23			
	7	i. 25			
		i. 29			
	8	i. 27			
	9	i. 26			
	10				i. 16?
	13	i. 24			
	15				i. 16
					i. 20
	16	i. 27			i. 11
		i. 29			
	17	i. 23			ii. 7
	19				ii. 9
					i. 9
					i. 19
	20	i. 29			
	21	i. 26?			

	Ephesians	Colossians			
	A	B	C	D	E
	iv. 1				i. 10
Eph. iv. 2–4 = Col. iii. 12–15 (e)	2			iii. 12	
	3			iii. 14	
	4			iii. 15	
	13				ii. 9–10
	14				ii. 22
	16				i. 18 / i. 29? / ii. 2 / ii. 19
	17				ii. 4
	18				i. 21
	19				iii. 5
	20–1				ii. 6–7
Eph. iv. 22–v. 6 = Col. iii. 5–13 (f)	22–4			iii. 8–10	
	25			iii. 8	
	29			iii. 8	iv. 6
	31			iii. 8	
	32			iii. 12	
	v. 1			iii. 12	
	2			iii. 13	
	3			iii. 5	
	4			iii. 8?	
	5			iii. 5	
	6			iii. 6	ii. 4 / ii. 8
	11				iii. 20
	12				iii. 8?
	15–16				iv. 5
Eph. v. 19–vi. 9 = Col. iii. 16–iv. 1 (g)	19–20			iii. 16–17	
	21			iii. 22	
	22			iii. 18	
	23				i. 18
	24			iii. 18	
	25			iii. 19	
	27				i. 22 / i. 28
	28			iii. 19	
	vi. 1			iii. 20	
	4			iii. 21	
	5–8			iii. 22–5	
	9			iii. 25 / iv. 1	
	10				i. 11
	12				i. 16
Eph. vi. 18–22 = Col. iv. 2–8 (h)	18–20			iv. 2–4	i. 4? / i. 8?
	21–2			iv. 7–8	
	24				iv. 18

APPENDIX IV

PARALLELS BETWEEN PHILIPPIANS AND THE OTHER PAULINE EPISTLES

Exact parallels are undermarked with double lines (═══); close, but not exact parallels, with a single line (———); and slighter parallels with a thin dotted line (··········). Where the passage in Philippians has more than one parallel in the other epistles, the words are underlined also with a broken line (- - - - -). Passages where there is similarity of thought but no close similarity of expression are entered, but without any underlining.

In comparing this appendix with Appendix I it should be noted that here the verses which have no parallels in the other epistles are entirely omitted, whereas in the text of Ephesians in Appendix I they were included. Unless this is borne in mind, a superficial comparison of the two appendixes will be misleading.

This appendix is commented on in pages 108–10.

Philippians.	
i. 1. . . . πᾶσιν τοῖς ἁγίοις ἐν Χριστῷ Ἰησοῦ τοῖς οὖσιν ἐν Φιλίπποις σὺν ἐπισκόποις καὶ διακόνοις ² χάρις ὑμῖν καὶ εἰρήνη ἀπὸ θεοῦ πατρὸς ἡμῶν καὶ κυρίου Ἰησοῦ Χριστοῦ. ³ εὐχαριστῶ τῷ θεῷ μου ἐπὶ πάσῃ τῇ μνείᾳ ὑμῶν.	1 Cor. i. 2. ἡγιασμένοις ἐν Χριστῷ Ἰησοῦ, κλητοῖς ἁγίοις, σὺν πᾶσιν τοῖς ἐπικαλουμένοις . . . . Rom. i. 7. 1 Cor. i. 3. 2 Cor. i. 2. Gal. i. 3. Eph. i. 2. 2 Thess. i. 2. } χάρις ὑμῖν καὶ εἰρήνη ἀπὸ θεοῦ πατρὸς ἡμῶν καὶ κυρίου Ἰησοῦ Χριστοῦ. Rom. i. 8. πρῶτον μὲν εὐχαριστῶ τῷ θεῷ μου διὰ Ἰησοῦ Χριστοῦ περὶ πάντων . . . . Philem. 4. εὐχαριστῶ τῷ θεῷ μου πάντοτε μνείαν σου ποιούμενος . . .
i. 5. (εὐχαριστῶ) ἐπὶ τῇ κοινωνίᾳ ὑμῶν εἰς τὸ εὐαγγέλιον . . .	1 Cor. ix. 23. πάντα δὲ ποιῶ διὰ τὸ εὐαγγέλιον, ἵνα συνκοινωνὸς αὐτοῦ γένωμαι. 1 Cor. i. 8. . . . ὃς καὶ βεβαιώσει ὑμᾶς ἕως τέλους ἀνεγκλήτους ἐν τῇ ἡμέρᾳ τοῦ κυρίου ἡμῶν Ἰησοῦ Χριστοῦ.

Philippians.	
6 πεποιθὼς αὐτὸ τοῦτο ὅτι ὁ ἐναρξάμενος ἐν ὑμῖν ἔργον ἀγαθὸν ἐπιτελέσει ἄχρι ἡμέρας Χριστοῦ Ἰησοῦ· 7 καθώς ἐστιν δίκαιον ἐμοὶ τοῦτο φρονεῖν ὑπὲρ πάντων ὑμῶν, διὰ τὸ ἔχειν με ἐν τῇ καρδίᾳ ὑμᾶς, ἔν τε τοῖς δεσμοῖς μου, καὶ ἐν τῇ ἀπολογίᾳ καὶ βεβαιώσει τοῦ εὐαγγελίου συνκοινωνούς μου τῆς χάριτος πάντας ὑμᾶς ὄντας.	1 Thess. v. 23. ὁλόκληρον ὑμῶν τὸ πνεῦμα . . . ἀμέμπτως ἐν τῇ παρουσίᾳ τοῦ κυρίου ἡμῶν Ἰησοῦ Χριστοῦ τηρηθείη. Philem. 13. ἐν τοῖς δεσμοῖς τοῦ εὐαγγελίου. Col. iv. 18. μνημονεύετέ μου τῶν δεσμῶν. Eph. iii. 1. ἐγὼ Παῦλος ὁ δέσμιος τοῦ Χριστοῦ. Eph. iv. 1. ἐγὼ ὁ δέσμιος ἐν κυρίῳ. Philem. 1. Παῦλος δέσμιος Χριστοῦ Ἰησοῦ.
i. 8. μάρτυς γάρ μου ὁ θεός.	Rom. i. 9. μάρτυς γάρ μού ἐστιν ὁ θεός. 2 Cor. i. 23. ἐγὼ δὲ μάρτυρα τὸν θεὸν ἐπικαλοῦμαι. 1 Thess. ii. 5. . . . θεὸς μάρτυς.
i. 9. καὶ τοῦτο προσεύχομαι, ἵνα ἡ ἀγάπη ὑμῶν ἔτι μᾶλλον καὶ μᾶλλον περισσεύῃ ἐν ἐπιγνώσει καὶ πάσῃ αἰσθήσει	Col. i. 9. προσευχόμενοι καὶ αἰτούμενοι ἵνα πληρωθῆτε τὴν ἐπίγνωσιν τοῦ θελήματος. Philem. 4–6. προσευχῶν μου, ἀκούων σου τὴν ἀγάπην καὶ τὴν πίστιν . . . ὅπως ἡ κοινωνία τῆς πίστεώς σου ἐνεργὴς γένηται ἐν ἐπιγνώσει παντὸς ἀγαθοῦ.
i. 10. εἰς τὸ δοκιμάζειν ὑμᾶς τὰ διαφέροντα.	Rom. ii. 18. δοκιμάζεις τὰ διαφέροντα. Rom. xii. 2. εἰς τὸ δοκιμάζειν ὑμᾶς.
i. 11. πεπληρωμένοι καρπὸν δικαιοσύνης τὸν διὰ Ἰησοῦ Χριστοῦ, εἰς δόξαν καὶ ἔπαινον θεοῦ.	Eph. v. 9. ὁ γὰρ καρπὸς τοῦ φωτὸς ἐν πάσῃ ἀγαθωσύνῃ καὶ δικαιοσύνῃ. Eph. i. 6, 12, 14. εἰς ἔπαινον τῆς δόξης αὐτοῦ . . . .
i. 12. τὰ κατ' ἐμέ.	Col. iv. 7. τὰ κατ' ἐμέ. Eph. vi. 21. τὰ κατ' ἐμέ.

Philippians.	
i. 17. οἱ δὲ ἐξ ἐριθείας.	Rom. ii. 8. τοῖς δὲ ἐξ ἐριθείας.
i. 19. τοῦτό μοι ἀποβήσεται εἰς σωτηρίαν διὰ τῆς ὑμῶν δεήσεως.	2 Cor. i. 11. συνυπουργούντων καὶ ὑμῶν ὑπὲρ ἡμῶν τῇ δεήσει.
i. 20. κατὰ τὴν ἀποκαραδοκίαν . . . μου.	Rom. viii. 19. ἡ . . . ἀποκαραδοκία τῆς κτίσεως.
i. 20. μεγαλυνθήσεται Χριστὸς ἐν τῷ σώματί μου.	1 Cor. vi. 20. δοξάσατε δὴ τὸν θεὸν ἐν τῷ σώματι ὑμῶν.
i. 21. ἐμοὶ γὰρ τὸ ζῆν Χριστός.	Gal. ii. 20. ζῇ δὲ ἐν ἐμοὶ Χριστός. Rom. viii. 10. εἰ δὲ Χριστὸς ἐν ὑμῖν . . . . Col. iii. 4. ὁ Χριστὸς . . . ἡ ζωὴ ἡμῶν.
i. 23. συνέχομαι δὲ ἐκ τῶν δύο, τὴν ἐπιθυμίαν ἔχων εἰς τὸ ἀναλῦσαι καὶ σὺν Χριστῷ εἶναι, πολλῷ γὰρ μᾶλλον κρεῖσσον· τὸ δὲ ἐπιμένειν τῇ σαρκὶ ἀναγκαιότερον δι' ὑμᾶς.	2 Cor. v. 8. θαρροῦμεν δὲ καὶ εὐδοκοῦμεν μᾶλλον ἐκδημῆσαι ἐκ τοῦ σώματος καὶ ἐνδημῆσαι πρὸς τὸν κύριον.
i. 27. ἀξίως τοῦ εὐαγγελίου τοῦ Χριστοῦ πολιτεύεσθε.	1 Thess. ii. 12. περιπατεῖν ὑμᾶς ἀξίως τοῦ θεοῦ τοῦ καλοῦντος ὑμᾶς. Col. i. 10. περιπατῆσαι ἀξίως τοῦ κυρίου. Eph. iv. 1. ἀξίως περιπατῆσαι τῆς κλήσεως. Eph. ii. 19. συνπολῖται τῶν ἁγίων.
i. 27. στήκετε ἐν ἑνὶ πνεύματι, μιᾷ ψυχῇ συναθλοῦντες.	Eph. iv. 4. ἓν σῶμα καὶ ἓν πνεῦμα. Eph. ii. 18. ἐν ἑνὶ πνεύματι. 1 Cor. xii. 13. ἐν ἑνὶ πνεύματι . . . ἐβαπτίσθημεν.
i. 29. τὸ ὑπὲρ αὐτοῦ πάσχειν.	2 Thess. i. 5. . . . βασιλείας τοῦ θεοῦ, ὑπὲρ ἧς καὶ πάσχετε . . . .
ii. 1. σπλάγχνα καὶ οἰκτιρμοί.	Col. iii. 12. σπλάγχνα οἰκτιρμοῦ.

Philippians.	
ii. 2. ἵνα τὸ αὐτὸ φρονῆτε.	2 Cor. xiii. 11. τὸ αὐτὸ φρονεῖτε. Rom. xv. 5. τὸ αὐτὸ φρονεῖν ἐν ἀλλήλοις.
ii. 3. ἀλλήλους ἡγούμενοι ὑπερέχοντας ἑαυτῶν.	Rom. xii. 10. τῇ τιμῇ ἀλλήλους προηγούμενοι.
ii. 4. μὴ τὰ ἑαυτῶν ἕκαστοι σκοποῦντες, ἀλλὰ τὰ ἑτέρων ἕκαστοι.	1 Cor. x. 24. μηδεὶς τὸ ἑαυτοῦ ζητείτω ἀλλὰ τὸ τοῦ ἑτέρου. 1 Cor. x. 33. . . . μὴ ζητῶν τὸ ἐμαυτοῦ σύμφορον ἀλλὰ τὸ τῶν πολλῶν . . . . 1 Cor. xiii. 5 (ἡ ἀγάπη) οὐ ζητεῖ τὰ ἑαυτῆς.
ii. 7. . . . ἑαυτὸν ἐκένωσεν μορφὴν δούλου λαβών	2 Cor. viii. 9. . . . δι' ὑμᾶς ἐπτώχευσεν πλούσιος ὤν . . . .
ii. 9–11. διὸ καὶ ὁ θεὸς αὐτὸν ὑπερύψωσεν καὶ ἐχαρίσατο αὐτῷ τὸ ὄνομα τὸ ὑπὲρ πᾶν ὄνομα, [10] ἵνα ἐν τῷ ὀνόματι Ἰησοῦ πᾶν γόνυ κάμψῃ ἐπουρανίων καὶ ἐπιγείων καὶ καταχθονίων, [11] καὶ πᾶσα γλῶσσα ἐξομολογήσηται ὅτι κύριος Ἰησοῦς Χριστὸς εἰς δόξαν θεοῦ πατρός.	Eph. i. 20. καθίσας ἐν δεξιᾷ αὐτοῦ ἐν τοῖς ἐπουρανίοις [21] ὑπεράνω πάσης ἀρχῆς καὶ ἐξουσίας καὶ δυνάμεως καὶ κυριότητος καὶ παντὸς ὀνόματος ὀνομαζομένου οὐ μόνον ἐν τῷ αἰῶνι τούτῳ ἀλλὰ καὶ ἐν τῷ μέλλοντι· [22] καὶ πάντα ὑπέταξεν ὑπὸ τοὺς πόδας αὐτοῦ καὶ αὐτὸν ἔδωκεν κεφαλὴν ὑπὲρ πάντα . . . . Rom. xiv. 11. πᾶσα γλῶσσα ἐξομολογήσεται τῷ θεῷ. Rom. x. 9. ἐὰν ὁμολογήσῃς ἐν τῷ στόματί σου κύριον Ἰησοῦν, καὶ πιστεύσῃς ἐν τῇ καρδίᾳ σου . . . σωθήσῃ. See also 1 Cor. xii. 3.
ii. 12. μετὰ φόβου καὶ τρόμου.	2 Cor. vii. 15. Eph. vi. 5. } μετὰ φόβου καὶ τρόμου.
ii. 13. θεὸς γάρ ἐστιν ὁ ἐνεργῶν ἐν ὑμῖν καὶ τὸ θέλειν καὶ τὸ ἐνεργεῖν.	1 Cor. xii. 6. ὁ δὲ αὐτὸς θεὸς ὁ ἐνεργῶν τὰ πάντα ἐν πᾶσιν.

Philippians.	
	I Thess. ii. 13. . . . θεοῦ, ὃς καὶ ἐνεργεῖται ἐν ὑμῖν τοῖς πιστεύουσιν. Rom. vii. 18. τὸ γὰρ θέλειν παράκειταί μοι, τὸ δὲ κατεργάζεσθαι τὸ καλὸν οὔ. 2 Cor. iii. 5. ἡ ἱκανότης ἡμῶν ἐκ τοῦ θεοῦ, ὃς καὶ ἱκάνωσεν ἡμᾶς διακόνους.
ii. 16. φαίνεσθε . . . εἰς καύχημα ἐμοὶ εἰς ἡμέραν Χριστοῦ, ὅτι οὐκ εἰς κενὸν ἔδραμον οὐδὲ εἰς κενὸν ἐκοπίασα.	2 Cor. i. 14. καύχημα ὑμῶν ἐσμεν καθάπερ καὶ ὑμεῖς ἡμῶν ἐν τῇ ἡμέρᾳ τοῦ κυρίου ἡμῶν Ἰησοῦ. I Thess. ii. 19. τίς γὰρ ἡμῶν ἐλπὶς ἢ χαρὰ ἢ στέφανος καυχήσεως—ἢ οὐχὶ καὶ ὑμεῖς—ἔμπροσθεν τοῦ κυρίου ἡμῶν Ἰησοῦ ἐν τῇ αὐτοῦ παρουσίᾳ; I Thess. iii. 5. μὴ . . . εἰς κενὸν γένηται ὁ κόπος ἡμῶν.
ii. 17. ἀλλὰ εἰ καὶ σπένδομαι ἐπὶ τῇ θυσίᾳ καὶ λειτουργίᾳ τῆς πίστεως ὑμῶν, χαίρω.	Rom. xv. 16. εἰς τὸ εἶναί με λειτουργὸν Χριστοῦ Ἰησοῦ εἰς τὰ ἔθνη, ἱερουργοῦντα τὸ εὐαγγέλιον τοῦ θεοῦ, ἵνα γένηται ἡ προσφορὰ τῶν ἐθνῶν εὐπρόσδεκτος.
iii. 1. χαίρετε.	2 Cor. xiii. 11. } I Thess. v. 16. } χαίρετε.
iii. 3. ἡμεῖς γάρ ἐσμεν ἡ περιτομή, οἱ πνεύματι θεοῦ λατρεύοντες καὶ καυχώμενοι ἐν Χριστῷ Ἰησοῦ καὶ οὐκ ἐν σαρκὶ πεποιθότες.	Rom. ii. 28. οὐ γὰρ ὁ ἐν τῷ φανερῷ Ἰουδαῖός ἐστιν, οὐδὲ ἡ ἐν τῷ φανερῷ ἐν σαρκὶ περιτομή· ἀλλ' ὁ ἐν τῷ κρυπτῷ Ἰουδαῖος, καὶ περιτομὴ καρδίας ἐν πνεύματι οὐ γράμματι . . . . Rom. i. 9. θεός, ᾧ λατρεύω ἐν τῷ πνεύματί μου ἐν τῷ εὐαγγελίῳ τοῦ υἱοῦ αὐτοῦ. 2 Cor. xi. 18. ἐπεὶ πολλοὶ καυχῶνται κατὰ τὴν σάρκα, κἀγὼ καυχήσομαι . . . [22] Ἑβραῖοί εἰσιν; κἀγώ.

Philippians.	
iii. 4. εἴ τις δοκεῖ ἄλλος πεποιθέναι ἐν σαρκί, ἐγὼ μᾶλλον . . . ἐκ γένους Ἰσραήλ, φυλῆς Βενιαμείν, Ἑβραῖος ἐξ Ἑβραίων . . .	Ἰσραηλεῖταί εἰσιν; κἀγώ. σπέρμα Ἀβραάμ εἰσιν; κἀγώ. Rom. xi. 1. καὶ γὰρ ἐγὼ Ἰσραηλείτης εἰμί, ἐκ σπέρματος Ἀβραάμ, φυλῆς Βενιαμείν.
iii. 9. μὴ ἔχων ἐμὴν δικαιοσύνην τὴν ἐκ νόμου, ἀλλὰ τὴν διὰ πίστεως Χριστοῦ, τὴν ἐκ θεοῦ δικαιοσύνην ἐπὶ τῇ πίστει.	Rom. iii. 21. νυνὶ δὲ χωρὶς νόμου δικαιοσύνη θεοῦ πεφανέρωται, μαρτυρουμένη ὑπὸ τοῦ νόμου καὶ τῶν προφητῶν, δικαιοσύνη δὲ θεοῦ διὰ πίστεως Ἰησοῦ Χριστοῦ εἰς πάντας τοὺς πιστεύοντας. (Cf. also Rom. i. 17 and x. 3.)
iii. 10. τοῦ γνῶναι αὐτὸν καὶ τὴν δύναμιν τῆς ἀναστάσεως αὐτοῦ καὶ κοινωνίαν παθημάτων αὐτοῦ, συμμορφιζόμενος τῷ θανάτῳ αὐτοῦ, εἴ πως καταντήσω εἰς τὴν ἐξανάστασιν τὴν ἐκ νεκρῶν.	Eph. i. 19. καὶ τί τὸ ὑπερβάλλον μέγεθος τῆς δυνάμεως αὐτοῦ εἰς ἡμᾶς τοὺς πιστεύοντας κατὰ τὴν ἐνέργειαν τοῦ κράτους τῆς ἰσχύος αὐτοῦ, ἣν ἐνήργηκεν ἐν τῷ Χριστῷ ἐγείρας αὐτὸν ἐκ νεκρῶν. Rom. vi. 4. συνετάφημεν οὖν αὐτῷ διὰ τοῦ βαπτίσματος εἰς τὸν θάνατον, ἵνα ὥσπερ ἠγέρθη Χριστὸς ἐκ νεκρῶν διὰ τῆς δόξης τοῦ πατρός, οὕτως καὶ ἡμεῖς ἐν καινότητι ζωῆς περιπατήσωμεν. εἰ γὰρ σύμφυτοι γεγόναμεν τῷ ὁμοιώματι τοῦ θανάτου αὐτοῦ, ἀλλὰ καὶ τῆς ἀναστάσεως ἐσόμεθα. (Cf. also Rom. viii. 17, Col. ii. 12, 2 Cor. iv. 10–11, and Gal. v. 24.)
iii. 12. διώκω δὲ εἰ καὶ καταλάβω . . . . iii. 14. κατὰ σκοπὸν διώκω εἰς τὸ βραβεῖον.	1 Cor. ix. 24. εἷς δὲ λαμβάνει τὸ βραβεῖον; οὕτως τρέχετε ἵνα καταλάβητε.
iii. 16. εἰς ὃ ἐφθάσαμεν, τῷ αὐτῷ στοιχεῖν.	Gal. vi. 16. ὅσοι τῷ κανόνι τούτῳ στοιχήσουσιν . . . . Gal. v. 25. εἰ ζῶμεν πνεύματι, πνεύματι καὶ στοιχῶμεν. Rom. iv. 12. . . . τοῖς στοιχοῦσιν τοῖς ἴχνεσιν . . . .

Philippians.	
	1 Cor. iv. 16. 1 Cor. xi. 1. } μιμηταί μου γίνεσθε. 1 Thess. i. 7. ὥστε γενέσθαι ὑμᾶς τύπον πᾶσιν.
iii. 17. συμμιμηταί μου γίνεσθε, ἀδελφοί, καὶ σκοπεῖτε τοὺς οὕτω περιπατοῦντας καθὼς ἔχετε τύπον ἡμᾶς.	2 Thess. iii. 9. . . . ἵνα ἑαυτοὺς τύπον δῶμεν ὑμῖν εἰς τὸ μιμεῖσθαι ἡμᾶς.
iii. 19. ὧν ὁ θεὸς ἡ κοιλία . . . οἱ τὰ ἐπίγεια φρονοῦντες.	Rom. xvi. 18. οἱ γὰρ τοιοῦτοι τῷ κυρίῳ ἡμῶν Χριστῷ οὐ δουλεύουσιν ἀλλὰ τῇ ἑαυτῶν κοιλίᾳ. Col. iii. 2. τὰ ἄνω φρονεῖτε, μὴ τὰ ἐπὶ τῆς γῆς. Rom. xii. 16. . . . μὴ τὰ ὑψηλὰ φρονοῦντες . . . .
iii. 20. ἡμῶν γὰρ τὸ πολίτευμα ἐν οὐρανοῖς ὑπάρχει, ἐξ οὗ καὶ σωτῆρα ἀπεκδεχόμεθα κύριον Ἰησοῦν Χριστόν.	Eph. ii. 19. συνπολῖται τῶν ἁγίων καὶ οἰκεῖοι τοῦ θεοῦ. Eph. ii. 6. συνεκάθισεν (ἡμᾶς) ἐν τοῖς ἐπουρανίοις ἐν Χριστῷ Ἰησοῦ. Eph. i. 20. (Χριστὸν) καθίσας ἐν δεξιᾷ αὐτοῦ ἐν τοῖς ἐπουρανίοις. 1 Cor. i. 7. . . . ἀπεκδεχομένους τὴν ἀποκάλυψιν τοῦ κυρίου ἡμῶν Ἰησοῦ Χριστοῦ. Rom. viii. 19. τὴν ἀποκάλυψιν τῶν υἱῶν τοῦ θεοῦ ἀπεκδέχεται.
iii. 21. ὃς μετασχηματίσει τὸ σῶμα τῆς ταπεινώσεως ἡμῶν σύμμορφον τῷ σώματι τῆς δόξης αὐτοῦ, κατὰ τὴν ἐνέργειαν	1 Cor. xv. 43. σπείρεται ἐν ἀτιμίᾳ, ἐγείρεται ἐν δόξῃ. Rom. viii. 29. προώρισεν συμμόρφους τῆς εἰκόνος τοῦ υἱοῦ αὐτοῦ. Eph. i. 19. Col. i. 29. } κατὰ τὴν ἐνέργειαν.
iv. 1. ἀδελφοί μου ἀγαπητοὶ καὶ ἐπιπόθητοι, χαρὰ καὶ στέφανός μου.	1 Thess. ii. 19. τίς γὰρ ἡμῶν ἐλπὶς ἢ χαρὰ ἢ στέφανος καυχήσεως— ἢ οὐχὶ καὶ ὑμεῖς—; . . . ὑμεῖς γάρ ἐστε ἡ δόξα ἡμῶν καὶ ἡ χαρά.

Philippians.	
iv. 2. παρακαλῶ . . . τὸ αὐτὸ φρονεῖν ἐν κυρίῳ.	Rom. xv. 5. τὸ αὐτὸ φρονεῖν ἐν ἀλλήλοις κατὰ Χριστὸν Ἰησοῦν. 2 Cor. xiii. 11. τὸ αὐτὸ φρονεῖτε.
iv. 6. ἐν παντὶ τῇ προσευχῇ καὶ τῇ δεήσει.	Eph. vi. 18. διὰ πάσης προσευχῆς καὶ δεήσεως.
iv. 7. ἡ εἰρήνη τοῦ θεοῦ ἡ ὑπερέχουσα πάντα νοῦν φρουρήσει τὰς καρδίας ὑμῶν.	Col. iii. 15. ἡ εἰρήνη τοῦ Χριστοῦ βραβευέτω ἐν ταῖς καρδίαις ὑμῶν.
iv. 9. καὶ ὁ θεὸς τῆς εἰρήνης ἔσται μεθ' ὑμῶν.	Rom. xv. 33. ὁ δὲ θεὸς τῆς εἰρήνης μετὰ πάντων ὑμῶν. 2 Cor. xiii. 11. καὶ ὁ θεὸς τῆς ἀγάπης καὶ τῆς εἰρήνης ἔσται μεθ' ὑμῶν.
iv. 18. δεξάμενος . . . τὰ παρ' ὑμῶν, ὀσμὴν εὐωδίας, θυσίαν δεκτήν.	Eph. v. 2. Χριστὸς . . . παρέδωκεν ἑαυτὸν ὑπὲρ ἡμῶν προσφορὰν καὶ θυσίαν τῷ θεῷ εἰς ὀσμὴν εὐωδίας.
iv. 19. ὁ δὲ θεός μου πληρώσει πᾶσαν χρείαν ὑμῶν κατὰ τὸ πλοῦτος αὐτοῦ ἐν δόξῃ ἐν Χριστῷ Ἰησοῦ.	Rom. ix. 23. . . . ἵνα γνωρίσῃ τὸν πλοῦτον τῆς δόξης αὐτοῦ ἐπὶ σκεύη ἐλέους. Eph. iii. 16. ἵνα δῷ ὑμῖν κατὰ τὸ πλοῦτος τῆς δόξης αὐτοῦ δυνάμει κραταιωθῆναι. Eph. i. 18. } Col. i. 27. } ὁ πλοῦτος τῆς δόξης.
iv. 23. ἡ χάρις τοῦ κυρίου Ἰησοῦ Χριστοῦ μετὰ τοῦ πνεύματος ὑμῶν.	Gal. vi. 18. ἡ χάρις τοῦ κυρίου ἡμῶν Ἰησοῦ Χριστοῦ μετὰ τοῦ πνεύματος ὑμῶν. Rom. xvi. 20. ἡ χάρις τοῦ κυρίου ἡμῶν Ἰησοῦ μεθ' ὑμῶν. 1 Cor. xvi. 23. ἡ χάρις τοῦ κυρίου Ἰησοῦ μεθ' ὑμῶν. (Cf. also 1 Thess. v. 28 and 2 Thess. iii. 18.)

APPENDIX V

PARALLELS TO PHILIPPIANS IN THE OTHER PAULINE EPISTLES

In the preceding Appendix (IV) the passages in Philippians which are echoed in the other Pauline epistles were listed and quoted, along with the parallel passages to which they correspond. In this appendix these parallel passages from the other Pauline epistles are listed again, but in the order in which they occur in their own epistle.

If more than one parallel to the verse in Philippians occurs in the other Pauline epistles, the other parallels are noted in column 3. Since these double and triple parallels are discounted in our treatment of Ephesians, they should, for the sake of fairness in comparison, also be discounted in our calculations based on Philippians.

Column 4 contains the list of parallels which remain when the double (or triple) parallels have been omitted. Occasionally, however, a parallel is noted in column 4 in spite of the presence of other parallels in column 3. This is done only when it corresponds more closely than the others to the relevant words in Philippians.

It will be seen that, with only slight exceptions, there are no recurring or sustained parallels with outstanding passages in other epistles. Such groupings as might appear to reflect acquaintance with prolonged sequences of verses in other letters are marked by brackets, and are discussed on pages 114–16.

Philippians	*Romans*	*Other Epistles*	*Romans*
i. 2	i. 7	1 Cor. i. 3; Gal. i. 3, &c.	..
i. 3	i. 8	Philem. 4	..
i. 8	i. 9	2 Cor. i. 23; 1 Thess. ii. 5	i. 9
i. 17	ii. 8	..	ii. 8
i. 10	ii. 18	..	ii. 18
iii. 9	iii. 21	..	iii. 21
iii. 16	iv. 12	Gal. v. 25, vi. 16	iv. 12
iii. 10	vi. 4	..	vi. 4
ii. 13	vii. 18	..	vii. 18
i. 20	viii. 19	..	viii. 19
iii. 21	viii. 29	..	viii. 29
iv. 19	ix. 23	Eph. i. 18, iii. 16; Col. i. 27	..
ii. 11	x. 9	..	x. 9
iii. 4	xi. 1	..	xi. 1
i. 10	xii. 2	..	xii. 2
ii. 3	xii. 10	..	xii. 10
ii. 11	xiv. 11	..	xiv. 11
ii. 2, iv. 2	xv. 5	2 Cor. xiii. 11	..
iv. 9	xv. 33	2 Cor. xiii. 11	..
iii. 19.	xvi. 18	..	xvi. 18

Philippians	*1 Corinthians*	*Other Epistles*	*1 Corinthians*
i. 1	i. 2	..	i. 2
iii. 20	i. 7	..	i. 7
i. 19	i. 11	..	i. 11
iii. 17	iv. 16	1 Cor. xi. 1	..
i. 20	vi. 20	..	vi. 20
i. 5, 7	ix. 23	..	ix. 23
iii. 12, 14	ix. 24	..	ix. 24
ii. 4	x. 24	..	x. 24
ii. 13	xii. 6	1 Thess. ii. 13	..
i. 27	xii. 13	Eph. ii. 18	..

Philippians	*2 Corinthians*	*Other Epistles*	*2 Corinthians*
ii. 16	i. 14	1 Thess. ii. 19	i. 14
i. 8	i. 23	Rom. i. 9	..
ii. 12	vii. 15	Eph. vi. 5	..
iii. 4	xi. 18	..	xi. 18
ii. 2, iv. 2	xiii. 11	Rom. xv. 5	..
iii. 1	xiii. 11	1 Thess. v. 16	..
iv. 9	xiii. 11	Rom. xv. 33	..

Philippians	*Galatians*	*Other Epistles*	*Galatians*
i. 21	ii. 20	..	ii. 20
iii. 16	v. 25	Gal. vi. 16; Rom. iv. 12	..
iii. 16	vi. 16	Gal. v. 25; Rom. iv. 12	vi. 16
iv. 23	vi. 18	Rom. xvi. 20	vi. 18

Philippians	*Ephesians*	*Other Epistles*	*Ephesians*
i. 11	i. 6, 12, 14	..	i. 6, 12, 14
iii. 10	i. 19	..	i. 19
iii. 21	i. 19	Col. i. 29	..
iii. 20	i. 20	Eph. ii. 6	i. 20
ii. 9–10	i. 20–1	..	i. 20–1
iii. 20	ii. 6	Eph. i. 20	..
i. 27	ii. 18	..	ii. 18
i. 27, iii. 20	ii. 19	..	ii. 19
iv. 19	iii. 16	Eph. i. 18; Rom. ix. 23	iii. 16
iv. 18	v. 2	..	v. 2
i. 11	v. 9	..	v. 9
ii. 12	vi. 5	2 Cor. vii. 15	..
iv. 6	vi. 18	..	vi. 18
i. 12	vi. 21	Col. iv. 7	..

Philippians	*Colossians*	*Other Epistles*	*Colossians*
i. 9	i. 9	Philem. 6	..
iii. 19	iii. 2	..	iii. 2
ii. 1	iii. 12	..	iii. 12
iv. 7	iii. 15	..	iii. 15
i. 12	iv. 7	Eph. vi. 21	..
i. 5	iv. 8	Philem. 13	..

Philippians	*1 Thess.*	*Other Epistles*	*1 Thess.*
iii. 17	i. 7	2 Thess. iii. 9	..
i. 8	ii. 5	Rom. i. 9	..
ii. 13	ii. 13	1 Cor. xii. 6	..

Philippians	*1 Thess.*	*Other Epistles*	*1 Thess.*
ii. 16	ii. 19	2 Cor. i. 4	..
iv. 1	ii. 19	..	ii. 19
ii. 16	iii. 5	..	iii. 5
iii. 1	v. 6	2 Cor. xiii. 11	..

Philippians	*2 Thess.*	*Other Epistles*	*2 Thess.*
iii. 17	iii. 9	1 Thess. i. 7	iii. 9

Philippians	*Philemon*	*Other Epistles*	*Philemon*
i. 9	6	Col. i. 9	6
i. 7	13	Col. iv. 18	13

APPENDIX VI

PARALLELS TO EPHESIANS IN THE OTHER PAULINE EPISTLES

The verses in the 'other eight' Pauline epistles, which in Appendix I are quoted as having parallels in Ephesians, are here listed in the order in which they appear in their own epistle. The parallels in Ephesians are also noted, along with those in the other Pauline epistles.

This method of tabulating the parallels gives some indication of the extent to which each individual epistle appears to be echoed in Ephesians, and also it enables the reader to distinguish those groups of verses which provide several parallels.

The brackets in column D indicate these groups of verses. In view of the complete lack in Philippians of such recurrent borrowing from certain sequences of verses in the other letters, the presence of this phenomenon in Ephesians is instanced in Chapter XIII, pages 118–37, as evidence of literary dependence between Ephesians and the 'other eight' Pauline epistles. Parallels between isolated phrases as in Philippians can be sufficiently explained by identity of authorship. This 'sustained' parallelism does not equally lend itself to the same explanation.

The significance of these bracketed passages in column D is examined in pages 118 ff.

Explanation

In this Appendix the five columns are constituted as follows:

1. COLUMN X: The passages in Ephesians which are parallel to those noted in column A.

2. COLUMN A: The verses in the 'other eight' Pauline epistles which appear to have echoes in Ephesians.

3. COLUMN B: If the passage from Ephesians already noted in column X is also paralleled in Colossians, the context in Colossians is entered here; and there is an initial probability that any borrowing that may have taken place will be from the Colossian context.

4. COLUMN C: If the passage in Ephesians is paralleled in more than one of the 'other eight' Pauline epistles, the other contexts are noted here. There is an initial probability that these are explicable as stock phrases in Paul's vocabulary rather than as evidence of an imitator at work.

5. COLUMN D: The verses noted in this column are those from column A for which there is no second parallel noted in either column B or C. It is these which constitute the material for the investigation in Chapter XIII.

X	A	B	C	D
Ephesians	*Romans*	*Colossians*	*Other Epistles*	*Romans*
i. 2	i. 7	i. 2 (part)	1 Cor. i. 3; 2 Thess. i. 2	..
i. 16	i. 8–9	..	1 Thess. i. 2; Philem. 4	..
i. 13	i. 16	..	..	i. 16
v. 6	i. 18	iii. 5	..	..
iv. 17–18	i. 21	..	..	i. 21 }
iv. 18–19	i. 24	..	..	i. 24 }
v. 4	i. 28	..	..	i. 28
ii. 7	ii. 4	..	..	ii. 4
iv. 28	ii. 10	..	Gal. vi. 10	..
vi. 9	ii. 11	iii. 25 (part)	..	ii. 11?
ii. 9	iii. 20	..	Rom. xi. 6	iii. 20? }
i. 19	iii. 22	..	1 Cor. i. 21; 1 Thess. i. 7	..
ii. 5	iii. 24	..	..	iii. 24
ii. 8	iii. 24	..	..	iii. 24
i. 7	iii. 24–5	i. 14	..	..
ii. 9	iii. 27	..	..	iii. 27
ii. 9	iv. 2	..	..	iv. 2 }
iii. 11–12	v. 1–2	..	..	v. 1–2 }
ii. 18	v. 2	..	..	v. 2 }
iii. 7	v. 15	..	..	v. 15
ii. 8	v. 15	..	..	v. 15
iv. 22	vi. 6	iii. 9	..	..
ii. 1	vi. 11	ii. 13	..	..
iii. 17	vii. 22	..	2 Cor. iv. 16	..
iii. 16–17	viii. 9–10	..	..	viii. 9–10 }
ii. 5	viii. 10	ii. 13	..	..
i. 5	viii. 15	..	..	viii. 15
i. 14	viii. 16–17	..	..	viii. 16–17
iii. 6	viii. 17	..	..	viii. 17
i. 5	viii. 23	..	..	viii. 23
i. 11	viii. 28	..	..	viii. 28
i. 4–5	viii. 29	..	..	viii. 29
i. 20	viii. 34	..	..	viii. 34
iii. 19	viii. 35	..	2 Cor. v. 14	..
i. 21	viii. 38	..	..	viii. 38
iii. 18	viii. 38	..	..	viii. 38 }
iv. 21	ix. 1	..	..	ix. 1
ii. 12	ix. 4	..	..	ix. 4
i. 18	ix. 23	i. 27	..	..
ii. 7	ix. 23	i. 27	..	..
iii. 16	ix. 23	i. 27	..	..
iv. 9	x. 5, 8	..	..	x. 5, 8
v. 27	x. 9	..	..	x. 9
ii. 9	xi. 6	..	..	xi. 6
iii. 1	xi. 13	..	..	xi. 13

X	A	B	C	D
Ephesians	*Romans*	*Colossians*	*Other Epistles*	*Romans*
ii. 4	xi. 32–3	..	..	xi. 32–3
iii. 8	xi. 32–3	..	..	xi. 32–3
iii. 10	xi. 32–3	..	..	xi. 32–3
iv. 6	xi. 36	..	..	xi. 36
iii. 21	xi. 36	..	..	xi. 36
iv. 1	xii. 1	..	2 Cor. x. 1	xii. 1?
iv. 23	xii. 2	..	..	xii. 2
v. 10	xii. 2	..	..	xii. 2
v. 17	xii. 2	..	..	xii. 2
iii. 2	xii. 3	..	1 Cor. iii. 10; Gal. ii. 9	..
iii. 7	xii. 3	..	1 Cor. iii. 10; Gal. ii. 9	..
iv. 7	xii. 3	..	..	xii. 3
i. 23	xii. 5	i. 24	..	xii. 5?
iv. 4	xii. 5	iii. 15	..	xii. 5?
iv. 25	xii. 5	..	..	xii. 5
iv. 7	xii. 6	..	1 Cor. iii. 10; Gal. ii. 9	..
iv. 24	xiii. 12	iii. 8, 10	..	..
v. 8, 11	xiii. 12	..	..	xiii. 12
vi. 10	xiii. 12	..	..	xiii. 12
ii. 3	xiii. 14	..	..	xiii. 14
iv. 24	xiii. 14	iii. 10	..	..
iii. 9	xvi. 25–6	i. 26	1 Cor. ii. 7–8	xvi. 25–6?
iii. 3	xvi. 25	i. 26	..	xvi. 25?
iii. 20–1	xvi. 25–7	..	Cf. Gal. i. 5	xvi. 25–7 (part)

Ephesians	*1 Cor.*	*Colossians*	*Other Epistles*	*1 Cor.*
i. 1	i. 1–2	i. 1–2	2 Cor. i. 1–3	i. 1–2?
i. 2	i. 3	..	Rom. i. 7; 2 Thess. i. 2	..
ii. 9	i. 29–30	..	Rom. iii. 27; Rom. iv. 2	i. 29–30?
iii. 4–5	ii. 7–8	i. 26	..	..
iii. 9	ii. 7–8	i. 26	..	..
ii. 21	iii. 6	ii. 29?	..	iii. 6?
ii. 21	iii. 9	..	..	iii. 9
iii. 2	iii. 10	..	Rom. xii. 3, &c.	..
iii. 7	iii. 10	..	Rom. xii. 3, &c.	..
ii. 20	iii. 12	..	..	iii. 12
ii. 21	iii. 16	..	Cf. 2 Cor. vi. 16	iii. 16
iii. 2–3	iv. 1	i. 25–6	..	..
iii. 9	iv. 1	i. 25–6?	..	iv. 1?
iv. 28	iv. 12	..	..	iv. 12
v. 1	iv. 14	..	..	iv. 14
v. 1	iv. 16	..	..	iv. 16
v. 3	v. 11	iii. 5	..	..
v. 5	vi. 9	..	Gal. v. 21	..
v. 26	vi. 11	..	..	vi. 11
v. 31	vi. 15–16	..	..	vi. 15–16
iv. 1	vii. 20	..	..	vii. 20
vi. 6	vii. 22	..	Gal. i. 10	..
iii. 15	viii. 5	Cf. i. 20	..	viii. 5?
iv. 6	viii. 5–6	..	..	viii. 5–6
iii. 2	ix. 17	..	..	ix. 17

X	A	B	C	D
Ephesians	*1 Cor.*	*Colossians*	*Other Epistles*	*1 Cor.*
v. 1	xi. 1	..	Phil. iii. 17; cf. 1 Cor. iv. 16	xi. 1?
iv. 16	xi. 3	i. 18	..	xi. 3?
v. 23	xi. 3	..	..	xi. 3
ii. 11	xii. 2	..	..	xii. 2
iv. 4–6	xii. 4–6	..	..	xii. 4–6
i. 11	xii. 6	..	..	xii. 6
i. 23	xii. 6	..	1 Cor. xv. 28	xii. 6
iv. 4	xii. 12	iii. 15	Rom. xii. 5	xii. 12
v. 30	xii. 12	..	..	xii. 12
ii. 16	xii. 13	i. 22	..	xii. 13?
ii. 18	xii. 13	..	Phil. i. 27	xii. 13?
iv. 4–6	xii. 27	..	..	xii. 27
iv. 12	xii. 27	..	..	xii. 27
ii. 20	xii. 28	..	..	xii. 28
iv. 11	xii. 28	..	..	xii. 28
iv. 12	xiv. 5	..	2 Cor. x. 8, xiii. 10	xiv. 5
iv. 16	xiv. 12	..	2 Cor. x. 8, xiii. 10	xiv. 12
iv. 14	xiv. 20	..	..	xiv. 20
v. 13	xiv. 24–5	..	..	xiv. 24–5
iv. 12	xiv. 26	..	Rom. xv. 2	..
iii. 8	xv. 9–10	..	..	xv. 9–10
i. 21	xv. 24	..	..	xv. 24
i. 22	xv. 27	..	..	xv. 27
i. 23	xv. 28	..	..	xv. 28

Ephesians	*2 Cor.*	*Colossians*	*Other Epistles*	*2 Cor.*
i. 1–2	i. 1–2	i. 1–2	1 Cor. i. 3, &c.	i. 1–2?
i. 3	i. 3	..	..	i. 3
ii. 3	i. 12	..	..	i. 12
i. 13	i. 22	..	..	i. 22
iv. 30	i. 22	..	..	i. 22
iii. 10	iii. 4	..	..	iii. 4
iii. 17	iv. 16	..	Rom. vii. 22	..
i. 14	v. 5	..	2 Cor. i. 22	..
iii. 19	v. 14	..	Rom. viii. 35	..
ii. 10	v. 17	..	..	v. 17
ii. 15	v. 17	..	Gal. vi. 15	v. 17?
vi. 20	v. 20	..	..	v. 20
i. 13	vi. 7	i. 5	..	..
v. 8	vi. 14	..	..	vi. 14
vi. 5	vii. 15	..	Phil. ii. 12	..
iv. 16	x. 8	..	Cf. 1 Cor. xiv. 12	x. 8?
iii. 4	xi. 6	..	..	xi. 6
i. 17	xi. 31	i. 3	..	..
iv. 19	xii. 21	..	Gal. v. 19	..
i. 19	xiii. 4	..	..	xiii. 4
iii. 17	xiii. 5	i. 27	..	..
iv. 16	xiii. 10	..	Cf. 1 Cor. xiv. 12	xiii. 10?

Ephesians	*Galatians*	*Colossians*	*Other Epistles*	*Galatians*
vi. 6	i. 10	..	1 Cor. vii. 22	i. 10
iii. 1	i. 16	..	Rom. xi. 3	..
iii. 8	i. 16	..	..	i. 16

X	A	B	C	D
Ephesians	*Galatians*	*Colossians*	*Other Epistles*	*Galatians*
iii. 2	ii. 9	..	1 Cor. iii. 10; Rom. xii. 3	ii. 9
ii. 9	ii. 16	..	..	ii. 16
v. 2	ii. 20	..	..	ii. 20
v. 25	ii. 20	..	..	ii. 20
i. 13	iii. 2	..	..	iii. 2
iii. 20	iii. 5	..	..	iii. 5
i. 13	iii. 14	..	..	iii. 14
iv. 24	iii. 27	iii. 10	Rom. xiii. 14	..
ii. 13–14	iii. 28	..	..	iii. 28
iii. 6	iii. 29	..	..	iii. 29
i. 10	iv. 4	..	..	iv. 4
iv. 19	v. 19	..	2 Cor. xii. 21	..
v. 5	v. 21	..	1 Cor. vi. 9	..
ii. 19	vi. 10	..	..	vi. 10
iv. 28	vi. 10	..	Rom. ii. 10	..
ii. 11	vi. 15	..	..	vi. 15
ii. 15	vi. 15	..	2 Cor. v. 17	vi. 15?
vi. 10	vi. 17	..	..	vi. 17

Ephesians	*Philippians*	*Colossians*	*Other Epistles*	*Philippians*
vi. 6	i. 1	..	Gal. i. 10	..
v. 20	i. 3–4	..	..	i. 3–4
v. 9	i. 11	..	..	i. 11
i. 6, 12, 14	i. 11	..	..	i. 11
vi. 21	i. 12	iv. 7	..	..
ii. 18	i. 27	..	1 Cor. xii. 13	i. 27?
ii. 19	i. 27	..	..	i. 27
iv. 1–3	i. 27	..	Cf. 1 Cor. xii. 13	i. 27
i. 21	ii. 9–10	..	..	ii. 9–10
vi. 5	ii. 12	..	2 Cor. vii. 15	..
ii. 19	iii. 20	..	..	iii. 20
i. 19	iii. 21	i. 29	2 Thess. ii. 9	..
i. 22	iii. 31	..	1 Cor. xv. 27	..
vi. 18	iv. 6	..	..	iv. 6
v. 2	iv. 18	..	..	iv. 18
v. 10	iv. 18	..	..	iv. 18

Ephesians	*1 Thess.*	*Colossians*	*Other Epistles*	*1 Thess.*
i. 16	i. 2	..	Philem. 4	..
vi. 20	ii. 2	..	..	ii. 2
iv. 1	ii. 12	i. 12	Rom. xii. 1	ii. 12?
ii. 12	iv. 5	..	..	iv. 5
iv. 28	iv. 11	..	1 Cor. iv. 12	..
ii. 3	iv. 13	..	..	iv. 13
ii. 12	iv. 13	..	..	iv. 13
vi. 14–16	v. 8	..	..	v. 8
iv. 30	v. 19	..	..	v. 19

Ephesians	*2 Thess.*	*Colossians*	*Other Epistles*	*2 Thess.*
vi. 23	i. 2	..	Rom. i. 7; 1 Cor. i. 3	..

X	A	B	C	D
Ephesians	*Philemon*	*Colossians*	*Other Epistles*	*Philemon*
iii. 1	1	..	..	1
i. 16	4–5	i. 4, 9 (part)	..	4–5
iv. 13	6	..	..	6
vi. 20	9	..	..	9

INDEX I. NAMES AND SUBJECTS

INDEX II. GREEK WORDS

INDEX III. SCRIPTURE REFERENCES

OLD TESTAMENT

NEW TESTAMENT